Date	Period/Regime	Historical Events	Biblical Events
1000 BC	IRON AGE II	A Temple, arguably from this period, is built on the Temple Mount in Jerusalem, also a series of strategically-located forts. There is evidence that what is today the island of Jezirat Faraun on the Red Sea was used as a maritime base. c.925 Pharaoh **Sheshonq** records at Karnak his highly-successful invasion of Canaan, confirmed also from archaeological findings at sites such as Megiddo in present-day Israel.	David's son and successor **Solomon** builds Temple at Jerusalem, also a string of forts to protect his borders. In alliance with the Canaanitic Hiram, he founds on the Red Sea a maritime base for joint, far-flung trading expeditions (1 Kings 3-11). Shortly after the succession of Solomon's son **Rehoboam**, internal differences cause the kingdom to split in two, as Israel (under **Jeroboam**) and Judah. This weakness is quickly exploited by Egypt's Pharaoh **Shishak** who invades (1 Kings 14).
900 BC		Archaeologically, evidence of intelligent refortification of Israel, also of an ivory-decorated palace at Samaria. c.853 Assyrian records attest to a King **Ahab** of Israel at this time, who deployed 2000 chariots against the Assyrians. A stele depicts King **Jehu** making deep obeisance to Assyria's **Shalmaneser III**.	Although 1 Kings 16-22 has little good to say about King **Ahab**, his building projects, also the ivory house at Samaria, are glancingly mentioned. 1 Kings 22 records Ahab's death. c.841-814 By assassination and murder, **Jehu** usurps the Israel throne (2 Kings 8).
800 BC		721 Assyrian **Sargon** reports successful conquest of Israel, many of whose inhabitants are deported. c.701 Assyrian **Sennacherib**, despite a successful campaign elsewhere in Judah, mysteriously fails to capture **Hezekiah**'s Jerusalem.	Books of Amos, Hosea, Micah and Isaiah 1-39 are written. 716 In Judah, accession of **Hezekiah** and religious reforms. Energetic preparations to defend Jerusalem from Assyrians. **Sennacherib**'s siege is seemingly miraculously repulsed (2 Kings 18).
700 BC		Apparent disappearance of the Ark of the Covenant. Jewish mercenaries build Temple at Elephantine in Upper Egypt.	687 Following Hezekiah's death, accession of Canaanitic **Manasseh** (2 Kings 21). 640 Accession of **Josiah**. 622 Apparent discovery of Deuteronomistic Torah (2 Kings 22). Josiah orders religious reforms, suppressing Canaanitic practices, and granting the Jerusalem Temple the sole right to perform animal sacrifices (2 Kings 23).
600 BC		586 Capture and destruction of Jerusalem by Babylonian **Nebuchadnezzar**. 539 Persian **Cyrus** defeats Babylonians, and allows deported peoples to return.	Capture and destruction of Jerusalem, followed by the leading Judahites' deportation to Babylon, and period of Babylonian exile (2 Kings 25). Completion of Kings chronicles and writing of Jeremiah, Ezekiel and Lamentations. Judahites returning to Jerusalem erect Second Temple. Writing of Malachi, Job, Proverbs, Song of Songs and many of the Psalms.
500 BC	Persian rule	404 Accession of Persian King **Artaxerxes II**. Destruction of Yahwist Temple at Elephantine. Jewish colony ceases shortly after.	Expatriates **Nehemiah** and **Ezra** travel to Judah, with **Artaxerxes** (II?)'s support, to revitalise a still 'third world' Jerusalem, and to canonise chosen religious works as what can now be called the Jewish Bible. Books of Nehemiah and Ezra written, also Isaiah 40 onwards. Annals are edited to become 1 and 2 Chronicles.
400 BC	Macedonian rule	332 Macedonian **Alexander the Great** defeats Persian King **Darius III**. On Alexander's untimely death, his general **Ptolemy** takes over Egypt, and Judah with it.	
300 BC	Ptolemaic rule	Judahite Jews are encouraged to colonise and proliferate in Alexandria in order to make it the Mediterranean's leading entrepot.	At Alexandria, translation into Greek of the Jewish Bible, already comprising most of the present-day Hebrew Bible, as the Septuagint.
200 BC	Syrian rule Independence, under high priests	167 Persecution by **Antiochus IV Epiphanes** successfully overthrown, bringing in rule by high priests. 134-104 **John Hyrcanus** rules as high priest. 104 Successor **Aristobulus** adopts title of king as well as high priest, a policy continued by **Alexander Jannaeus**, who succeeds the next year.	c.190 Book of Ecclesiasticus written by Ben Sira. c.164 Book of Daniel written as allegory. Priest **Mattathias** of the Hasmon family revolts against imposition of Hellenic life style, a struggle continued by his sons after his death (1 and 2 Maccabees).
100-1 BC	Jewish priest 'kings' Roman rule	Emergence of Pharisees as opponents of high priestly/Sadducee royal aspirations. 76 Death of Jannaeus, followed by Sadducee-Pharisee conflict. Some Dead Sea Scrolls written. 63 Roman **Pompey** takes Jerusalem. c.37 **Herod the Great**, as Roman puppet, takes charge of Judaea. Implements massive enlargement of Temple Mount. 4 Death of Herod.	Christian gospel of Matthew records birth of Galilean **Jesus** during Herod's reign.
1-100 AD	Roman rule Revolt	27-36 Roman **Pontius Pilate** is governor of Judaea. c.64 Roman authors attest to spread to Rome of belief that Galilean Jesus was the Messiah, or Christ. 67-70 Jewish revolt, followed by Roman razing of Temple of Jerusalem, and thereby cessation of high priests and animal sacrifices as features of Jewish religion.	Galilean-born Jesus crucified during time of **Pontius Pilate**. Writing of Matthew, Mark, Luke and John gospels, also book of Acts and Letters of Paul to Thessalonians, Philippians, Corinthians, Romans, Colossians and Ephesians.
101-300 AD	Roman rule	c.125 Earliest-surviving fragment of Christian gospel (John) dates from this time. Disinclined to recognise Jesus as the Messiah, Pharisee rabbis shape the Jewish religion's future.	Despite sporadic suppressions, cheaply-produced Christian gospels, including apocryphal versions, proliferate across the Roman Empire, attesting to Jesus as Messiah.
301-400 AD		Under **Constantine the Great**, official toleration of Christianity as a religion of the Roman Empire.	Creation of expensive bound codices such as Sinaiticus and Vaticanus as earliest-known Christian Bibles.

THE BIBLE IS HISTORY

THE BIBLE AS HISTORY

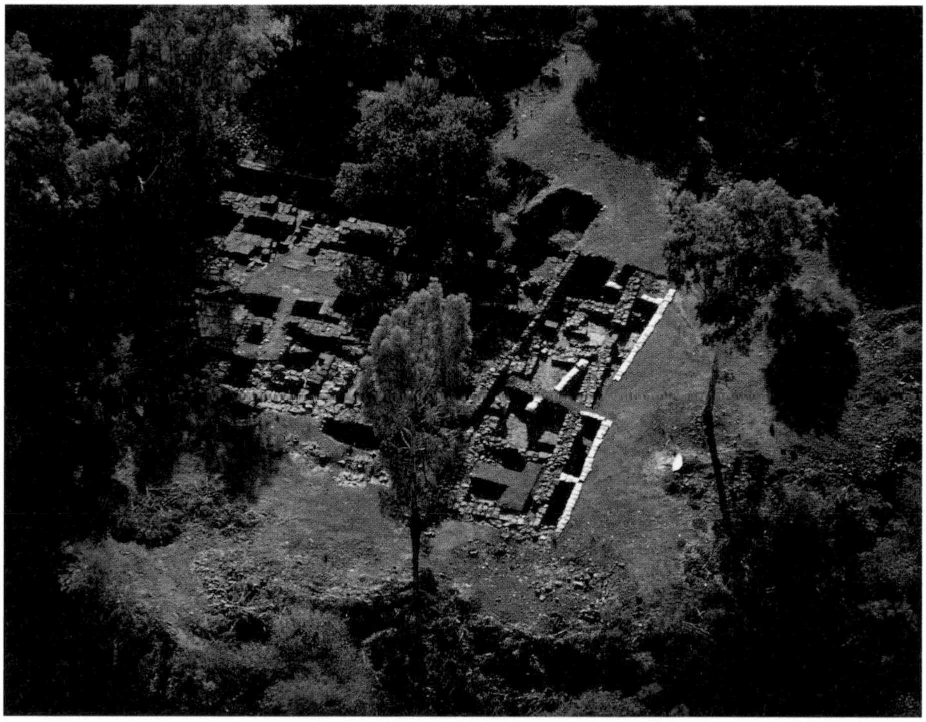

IAN WILSON

WEIDENFELD & NICOLSON
LONDON

First published in the United Kingdom in 1999
by Weidenfeld & Nicolson

This 2007 edition published by Barnes & Noble, Inc.,
by arrangement with Weidenfeld & Nicolson.

ISBN-13: 978-0-7607-9349-7
ISBN-10: 0-7607-9349-2

Printed and bound in Italy

10 9 8 7 6 5 4 3 2 1

CONTENTS

THE BIBLICAL WORLD

The region in which most of the events described in the Bible took place. The Biblical and Biblically-associated place-names are shown within the context of the present-day political boundaries. As can be noted from the inset (bottom left), the tiny Israel-Palestine region straddles a friction-point of three of the great plates forming the Earth's crust. This may well offer 'natural' explanations for some of the more 'miraculous' Biblical events, such as the collapse of the walls of Jericho in the time of Joshua.

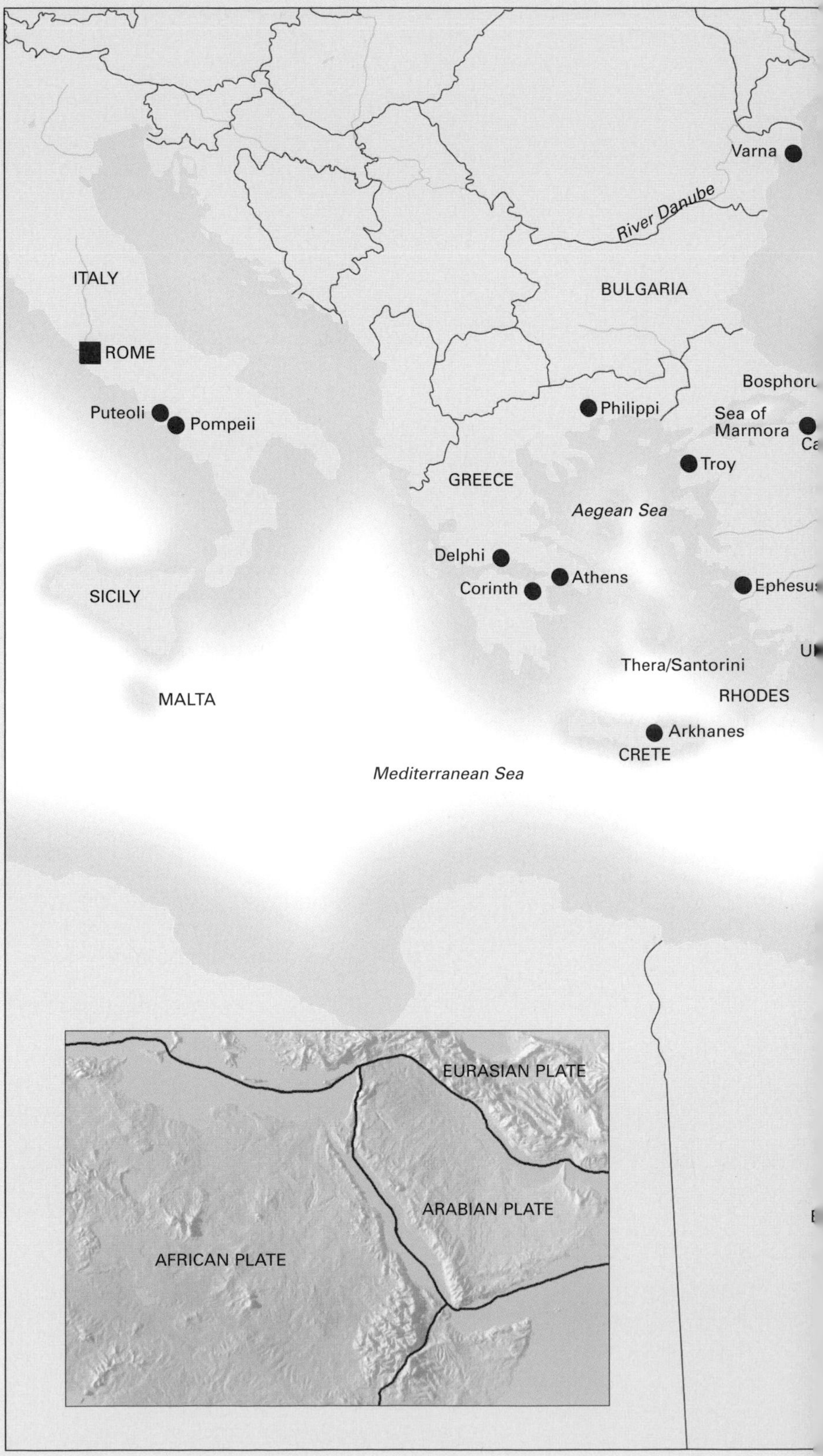

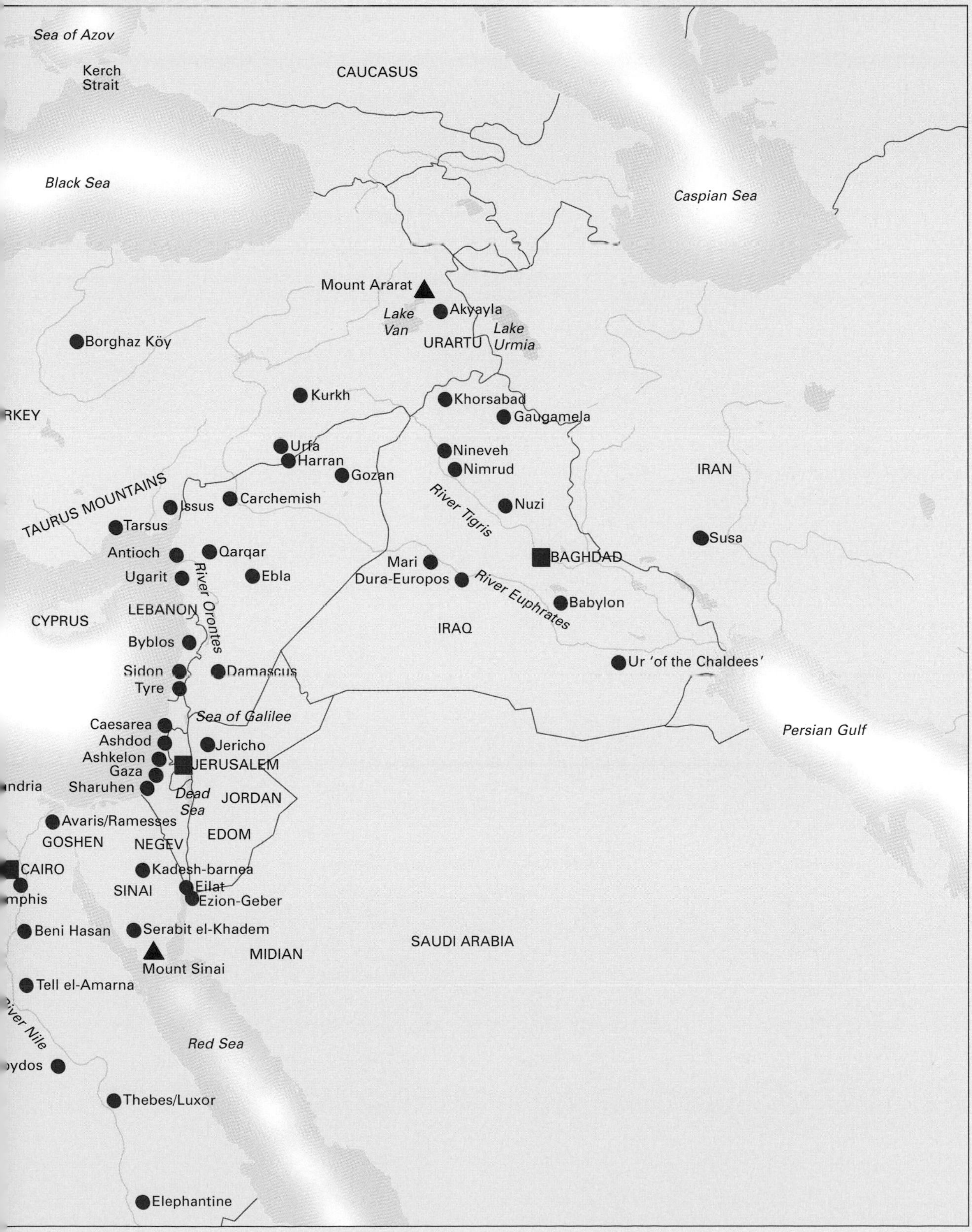

Sea of Azov
Kerch Strait
CAUCASUS
Black Sea
Caspian Sea
Mount Ararat
Lake Van
Akyayla
URARTU
Lake Urmia
Borghaz Köy
Kurkh
Khorsabad
Gaugamela
RKEY
Urfa
Harran
Nineveh
Nimrud
Gozan
IRAN
TAURUS MOUNTAINS
Issus
Carchemish
River Tigris
Nuzi
Tarsus
Susa
Antioch
Qarqar
BAGHDAD
Mari
Ugarit
Ebla
Dura-Europos
River Euphrates
River Orontes
Babylon
CYPRUS
LEBANON
IRAQ
Byblos
Ur 'of the Chaldees'
Sidon
Damascus
Tyre
Sea of Galilee
Persian Gulf
Caesarea
Ashdod
Jericho
Ashkelon
JERUSALEM
Gaza
ndria
Sharuhen
Dead Sea
JORDAN
Avaris/Ramesses
GOSHEN
NEGEV
EDOM
CAIRO
Kadesh-barnea
SINAI
Eilat
mphis
Ezion-Geber
Beni Hasan
Serabit el-Khadem
SAUDI ARABIA
MIDIAN
Mount Sinai
Tell el-Amarna
iver Nile
Red Sea
ydos
Thebes/Luxor
Elephantine

THE LAND OF THE BIBLE
Mount Hermon
Sidon
Tyre
Laish/Dan
LEBANON MOUNTAINS
Hazor
ARAM
Mediterranean Sea
Acre
Aphek
Capernaum
Gamla
Migdal
Sea of Galilee
Tel Hadar Geshur
GALILEE
Sepphoris
River Kishon
Mount Carmel
Mount Tabor
Nazareth
Qishon
Dor
Jezreel Valley
Endor
Yano'am
Megiddo
Jezreel
Ramoth Gilead
Caesarea
Taanach
Beth-shan
Mount Gilboa
Pella
AMMON
PLAIN OF SHARON
River Jordan
Samaria
Mount Ebal
Shechem
River Jabbok
Mount Gerizim
Tell Deir Alla
Tel Qasile
Adam
Aphek
Joppa
Shiloh
Ebenezer
Bethel
Ai
Gibeah
Jericho
Gezer
Emmaus
Nob
River Sorek
Zorah
JERUSALEM
Ashdod
Timnah
Beth-Shemesh
Qumran
SHEPHELAH
Kedron Valley
Ekron
Mount Nebo
Ashkelon
Gath
Bethlehem
Mareshah
Tekoa
Dead Sea
Lachish
WILDERNESS OF JUDAEA
Eglon
Hebron
Dibon
Gaza
Sharuhen
Debir
Ein Gedi
River Amon
MOAB
Masada
Bab edh-Dhra
Beer-sheba
Arad
Tell es-Seba (Ziklag?)
Hormah
Sodom?
Kerak (Kir-haraseth)
Zoar
Tamar
NEGEV
Arabah Valley
Bozrah
Kadesh-barnea

PREFACE

IN AN AGE of irreligion and over-specialisation, to write at a popular level on the history behind the Bible is no easy task – and to do so accurately and objectively is even harder. The last seriously successful attempt, Dr Werner Keller's *The Bible as History*, was more than forty years ago, since which time archaeological findings in Israel and elsewhere have advanced spectacularly. This book is an attempt to be *The Bible as History* for the 'turn of the 3rd millennium' generation, and the wealth and complexity of the material is such that it will no doubt have its flaws and failings, despite my every concern to avoid these.

For difficult choices abound at every turn, as for instance in respect of choice of translation into English. Although in the interests of ecumenism I have used the New Jerusalem Publication Society *Tanakh* for most Hebrew Bible/Old Testament passages, and the Jerusalem Bible for the New Testament, some adjustments have been needed to suit this book's styling, necessitating that these fine translations be used more as guides than shackles.

Another difficulty has involved nomenclature or labels, which Biblically can so often be misleading. Since 'Israelites', 'Canaanites' and 'Phoenicians' had different meanings at different times, I have sometimes used ostensibly clumsy expressions such as 'Jacob's descendants' and 'Moses' followers' in the interests of greater clarity. In certain instances I have preferred to use a Hebrew word untranslated, such as *nabi* rather than the commonly-used but misleading 'prophet', but have provided a glossary to demystify such terms.

It is near impossible to list all the individuals, archaeologists, geologists, botanists, palaeographers, theologians, photographers, illustrators, etc., whose labours have contributed to this book, but for me a particularly useful 'Bible' has been the American journal *Biblical Archaeology Review*, to which I have subscribed for the last fifteen years. Thanks to the vision and tenacity of its editor Hershel Shanks, numerous world-class archaeologists have made their findings accessible to a wider public than just their fellow specialists, and my first knowledge of these, together with the fine photographs commissioned to accompany them, has often come from *Biblical Archaeology Review*'s pages.

My thanks go to Claire and Tony Evans, Professor Euan Nisbet, Professor Ian Plimer, Leen Ritmeyer, Dr Ted Rose, Professor William Ryan and Professor Peter Warren for their assistance on various points. Also to Fr Neil Byrne, my local parish priest, for his always insightful and often most timely homilies. Also to Anthony Cheetham, Michael Dover, Judith Flanders and Caroline Knight for commissioning this book, and to the admirable Toucan Books, in the persons of Robert Sackville West, Christine Vincent and Andrew Kerr-Jarrett for their dedication and professionalism bringing a complex combination of text and illustrations into being within a desperately tight schedule.

Nor could I ever forget one absolutely crucial form of support, in the person of my wife Judith, who was by my side during my research trips to Israel and Egypt; who read, checked and advised on every manuscript chapter; who prepared many of the illustrations, and who shared with me all the trials and tribulations of seeing this book through to publication.

Ian Wilson
Bellbowrie, Queensland, Australia,
July 1999

Left: It was within this comparatively small territory that much of the events of the book we know now as the Bible took place.

INTRODUCTION: A ROCKY ROAD

WRITE A BOOK on the Bible, and you must expect people to throw rocks at you.

For my wife Judith and me, that happened quite literally in 1994 while we were on that most Biblical of roads, the one from Jericho to Jerusalem. Driving through a strangely empty suburban Bethany, all seemed peaceful enough. The two young men leaning on a lamppost appeared relaxed and unthreatening. But one thing we had not realised: our chosen route was through a Palestinian district, and as our dusty Nissan drew close, a chunk of rock was hurtling towards our windscreen. To our assailants, our rental car's yellow numberplates[1] branded us as hated Jews. We were therefore worthy targets in their age-old feud over the very soil we were travelling across.

For us the incident was over in a moment, the Nissan's windscreen wiper, bent at a crazy angle, receiving the worst of the impact. Altogether more long-term and serious are the huge divisions that beset almost everything to do with the Bible and the Jewish people, scars so deep-seated that no one seriously writing about the subject can avoid disturbing the wounds afresh, however hard he or she may try do otherwise.

For aside from the many busy 20th-century minds who automatically reject anything and everything to do with the Bible, even among those who count themselves as its adherents, difficulties abound. Not least is the difficulty that there is no agreement about what the Bible actually is.

Thus, to cite but the broadest examples, practising Jews have the so-called Hebrew Bible, a collection of thirty-nine books originally written in Hebrew, which took its present-day text, names and order only in the 8th century AD. Protestant Christians revere this same collection, arranged in a different order, as their Old Testament. For them, however, an additional twenty-seven so-called New Testament books are most crucial. These were originally written in Greek. Jews refuse to recognise these latter books, while Roman Catholic Christians, although sharing the Protestants' regard for the New Testament, add to their Bibles certain older Jewish books, such as Judith, 1 and 2 Maccabees and Ecclesiasticus.

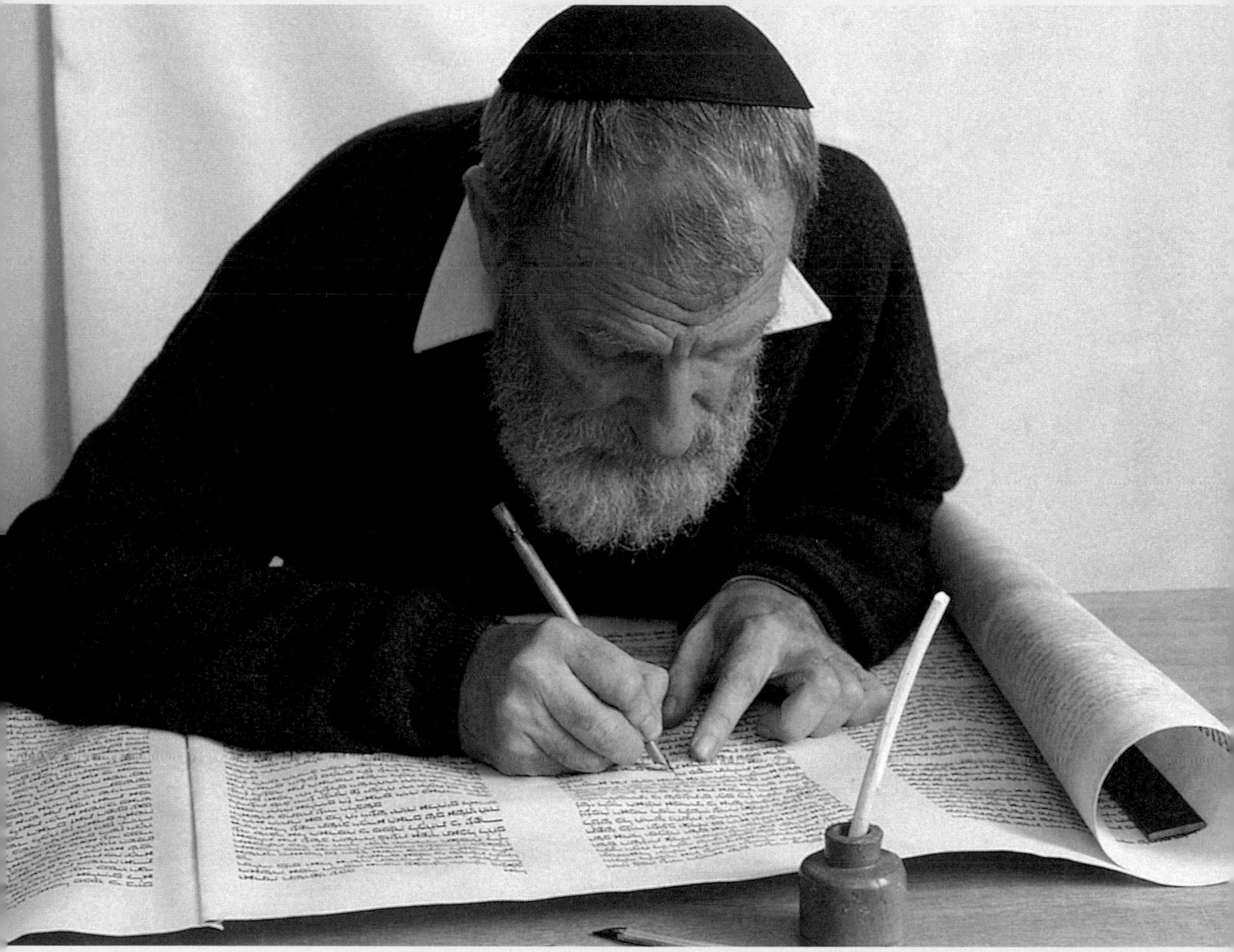

Book of History ... and contention. A rabbi corrects a handwritten scroll of the Hebrew Bible, following a tradition of his ancestors that is well over two thousand years old.

Protestants and Jews alike reject these as 'apocrypha'. No less provocative is the issue of which Biblical text and translation should be followed. Samaritan Jews and 'orthodox' Jews have long been at odds over the ways that their 'Five Books of Moses' differ textually from one another. Roman Catholic Christians have only comparatively recently dropped reliance on their traditional but flawed Latin Vulgate. There are still English-speaking Protestants who fail to grasp that the Bible did not actually originate with the 17th-century 'thee' and 'thou' archaisms of their beloved 'King James' version.

Even among the latest, modernised, English-language translations of the Bible, there are major differences of interpretation, and no single version is neutral enough for Jews, Protestants, Catholics and rationalist agnostics to accept in common. As but one example, few Christians feel comfortable in regarding the fire-and-brimstone deity of the earlier books of the Old Testament as being one and the same as the all-loving God of their later gospels. Yet if the Hebrew name Yahweh is used for this Old Testament deity, as in the Catholic Jerusalem Bible, this can be of offence to Jews, who firmly opt for the title 'the Lord' in their *Tanakh*[2] translation of their scriptures into English.

Even the name you give the 'land of the Bible' can raise intense animosities. Refer to it as 'the Holy Land', and every rationalist will dismiss you as a hopelessly biased 'true believer'. Call it Palestine and you will alienate the many fine Jews whose archaeology features prominently in the pages of this book. This name is, in any case, historically correct only for the five centuries from the time of the Roman Emperor Hadrian to the arrival of the Arab Moslems, and for the British mandate between 1919 to 1948. Refer to the land as Israel and you run into a historical difficulty. In the 1st millennium BC, a major part of it was called Judah. Israel was applicable to it for only a tiny fraction of its long history. Certainly, it will offend those fine Arab people, some of them staunch Christians, who are so fiercely proud to call themselves Palestinians.

Even if concentrating on matters of theoretically factual history, irrespective of religion or politics, there still surfaces the religious problem of how dates should be quoted. Using the politically-correct[3], religiously-neutral and increasingly-favoured BCE (Before the Common Era) and CE (Common Era) will satisfy Jews and agnostics, but mystify the uninformed and irritate most Christian readers. Using the long-established but clearly Christian-biased BC (Before Christ) and AD (Anno Domini) has clarity, tradition and Christians on your side[4], but risks alienating many agnostics and Jews.

Nor does the dilemma end there. For today we are heirs to more than 150 years of Biblical archaeology. Beginning in the early 19th century with enthusiasts such as American geographer Edward Robinson, who tramped uncharted ruins marrying their Arab names with their Biblical ones, this became more and more a scientific discipline with every decade of the 20th century. The 1950s sprouted a galaxy of archaeological 'greats' such as Britain's Dame Kathleen Kenyon and Israel's Yigael Yadin. Each year throughout Israel there are dozens of government-controlled and professionally-directed digs, the staffing of which is supplemented by volunteers of all ages and nationalities, who work unpaid, helping to shed fresh light on the pages of the Bible.

But this has not built up a bastion of pure, uncontested facts of Biblical history. Even the best archaeologists have little consensus among them, and often fiercely disagree even over their basic methodologies. Thus, Dame Kathleen Kenyon's methods, once regarded as state-of-the-art, are now widely execrated among the present generation of Israeli archaeologists. These even adjudge as wrong some of their own mentor Yadin's most acclaimed conclusions. Archaeological journals reverberate with arguments between archaeologists about whether a particular find may be, say, an altar or a watch-tower, a 'cultic installation' or an olive press, stables or storehouses. The long-established method of dating by pottery styles (Middle Bronze Age II, Iron Age I, etc), which varies from one archaeologist to another[5], can be far more hit-and-miss than is popularly realised. This is made worse by the failure of even some of the most famed archaeologists to produce a formal, published report of their findings. In these cases, it would have been rather better had they left their finds in the ground.

Even when archaeologists do publish their results, authoritatively quoting some impressively precise early dates, all too often they fail to make clear that any datings before 664 BC almost invariably depend upon which chronology for Egypt's pharaohs they happen to follow. Egyptologists are deeply divided into 'high' and 'low' chronology camps. This division has arisen because the assumptions behind their so-called Sothic dates – dates once supposed firmly to determine the reigns of Egypt's pharaohs – are now regarded as seriously flawed.[6]

If the world of Biblical archaeology is riven with such problems, that of Biblical textual studies is no less contentious. The modern approach to textual studies was pioneered by 19th-century German theologian Julius Wellhausen, who more than a century ago cast serious doubts upon the historicity of the earlier Biblical books. Today, such studies are almost formally divided into two diametrically-opposed schools of thought, the 'maximalists' on the one hand, and the 'minimalists' on the other. For the 'maximalists', whose ranks include most mainstream, modern-minded churchmen and Jewish scholars, the Bible text is recognised as including some myths, some mistakes and anachronisms caused by later editors, yet nonetheless enshrining a large substratum of fact. 'Minimalists', on the other hand, who include Thomas Thompson and Denmark's Niels Peter Lemche, insist on rejecting the historicity even of the Biblical kings David and Solomon. And because the theoretically 'early' Old Testament books show unmistakable signs of later editing – editing dated by them to as late as the 4th and even 2nd centuries BC – they dismiss these, virtually *in toto*, as of no historical value whatsoever.

The activities of a variety of Biblical extremists, some of them recognised but maverick scholars, others outright charlatans, have added further confusion. Pandering to those who want to believe the Bible's literal, historical truth in every word, an Australian group, Amazing Truth Publications, led by 'noted explorer [and] archaeologist' Jonathan Gray and 'Biblical archaeologist'[7] Ron Wyatt, have claimed 'amazing discoveries'. These include finding the ark of Noah, the site of Sodom and Gomorrah, the site of the crossing of the Red Sea and the Ark of the Covenant. Any

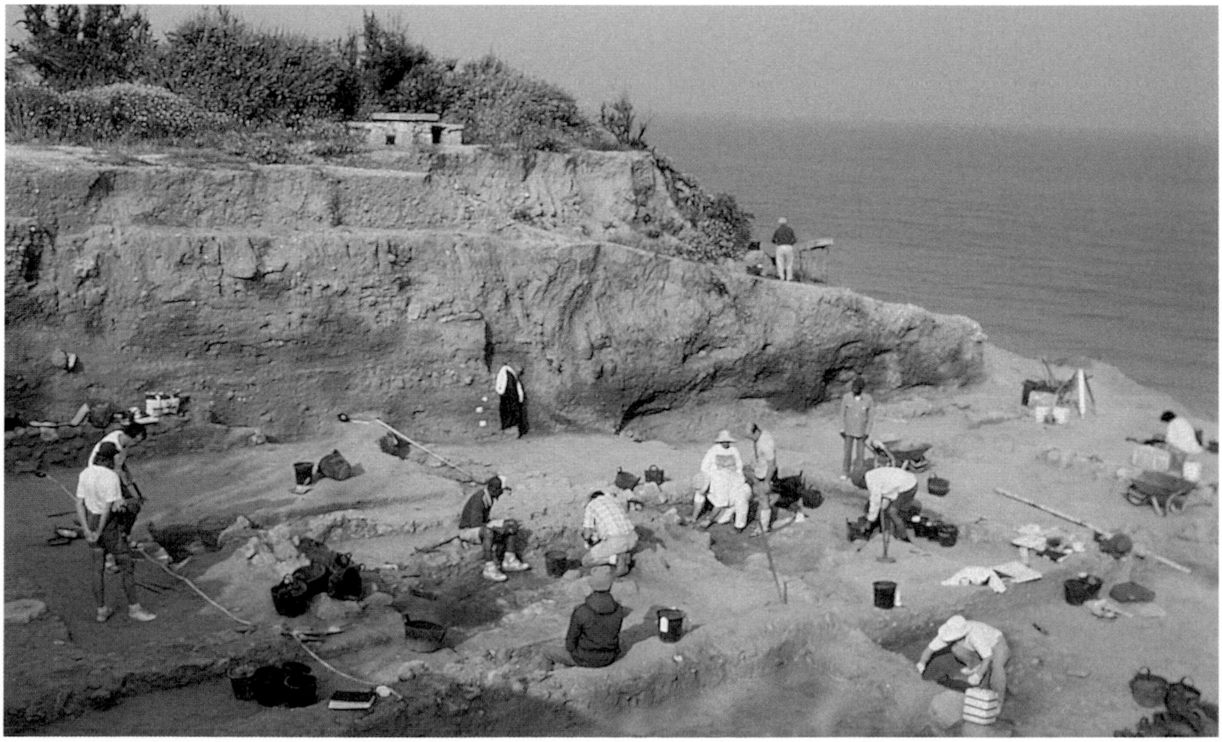

Archaeological volunteers excavate the site of Biblical Ashkelon, on the Mediterranean coast of present-day Israel.

one such discovery would have brought this group instant overnight fame, had it been backed by serious evidence. But this is something their fuzzy videos and literature conspicuously lack. Swelling such ranks has been American journalist Michael Drosnin with his best-selling *Bible Code*, claiming that the Bible's text is a series of mathematically-coded prophecies, some of these pertaining to events as recent as the Kennedy assassinations and the Oklahoma bombings.

Another similarly extremist approach was pioneered by Russian-born American Immanuel Velikovsky and carried over to the present day by others such as Britain's David Rohl and Egyptian Ahmed Osman. They have argued that a massive chronological mistake occurred in the conventional marrying of ancient Egypt's history with the Biblical record. In the 1950s, Velikovsky caused a stir by lowering the dates of the theoretically 15th-century BC woman Pharaoh Hatshepsut to the time of 10th-century BC King Solomon, enabling Hatshepsut to be identified as the Queen of Sheba. Rohl assigns the theoretically 14th-century BC Pharaoh Akhenaten to the Biblical King David's 11th century BC, enabling David to be identified with a known troublemaker of Akhenaten's time.[8]

Such theories can sound plausible. But one of the most absolute dates we have from antiquity is for a ship wrecked off Uluburun, Turkey.[9] The tree rings from its firewood cargo enabled the time of its wreck to be dated almost exactly to the year 1316 BC.[10] On the ship was found a scarab of Pharaoh Akhenaten's wife Nefertiti, who according to the Velikovsky/Rohl calculations would not be born for another three hundred years. So there is very good reason for remaining at least broadly within the conventional chronologies.

This carefully-reasoned, middle-of-the-road approach is essentially the one we will try to follow throughout this book. As a liberal-minded convert to Roman Catholicism, I cannot deny that my leanings may be somewhat more towards those of the maximalists rather than the minimalists. Yet being by training a historian, I have no inclination or sympathy for the worthless 'Bible was right' fixes of the Gray/Wyatt variety, nor for the chronological violations of the Velikovkys and the Rohls, however much these might *seem* to be on my side.

Instead, my overriding concern will be to look at the latest findings by the mainstream of serious, properly recognised Biblical archaeologists and scholars, many of them Israelis. My concern will be to weigh these up as dispassionately as possible to see how they may support or conflict with the Bible text. It has been said with considerable justice that most of the Bible is impossible to 'prove' historically. Proof will most certainly not be our aim. Rather, it will be to use the latest findings to gain a greater insight into the peoples and happenings that lay behind the Bible's pages and how its individual books came to be written and by whom. Thereby, we shall hopefully gain a better appreciation of the Bible as recording real history and being of real and lasting value to and beyond our own time.

I am under no illusions that the road will be anything other than difficult and rocky at times. And some of the choices I have necessarily made, such as retaining BC and AD and referring to the Old Testament God as Yahweh, may well not be favoured by all readers, even though any offence caused will be as unintended as that aroused by our Jericho-to-Jerusalem rental car's Israeli numberplates.

However, if the end result is that the uncommitted reader feels a greater respect for the Bible than previously, then all the effort – and we are about to review a chronological period spanning over three millennia – will have been more than worthwhile.

Underwater clues support conventional Biblical datings. This scarab of the 14th-century BC Egyptian Queen Nefertiti (above) was found in an ancient shipwreck off Turkey, datable from its firewood cargo to *c.*1316 BC. It has helped confound sensationalists who argue for a radical shifting of conventional ancient chronology.

1

DID THE BIBLE BEGIN IN TURKEY?

AS THE Biblical archaeologist William Dever has remarked, with much sound sense, 'No archaeologist in his right mind would go searching for the Garden of Eden.'[1] We will therefore not dream of arguing that the Biblical Adam and Eve were actual historical figures. But the whole Biblical Creation story, in the way it was put together, can help us understand how the Bible's first book, Genesis, came into being. As was recognised by textual scholars working independently of each other as far back as the 18th century, the Creation story with which the Genesis book begins shows unmistakable signs of having originally existed in at least two different versions, which someone at a later stage combined to form the text that has come down to us.

Thus, if we read from Genesis chapter 1 to chapter 2, verse 3, we find the Creator described as first bringing into being the heavens and the earth, then the plants and animals, and finally man and woman (together), all in that very specific order. If we then read on, from Genesis 2:4 through to 2:25, we find the story repeated, except that this time man is created first, then plants, then animals, and finally woman, the last, to feminists' undying indignation, being mentioned almost as an afterthought. Underlining these indications that our present text is derived from at least two different earlier versions, is the fact that the first version's Hebrew word for the Creator is consistently Elohim, meaning 'gods', while the second version's is YHWH, later vocalised[2] as Yahweh, broadly meaning 'I AM WHO AM'.

This strange doubling up does not occur solely with regard to Genesis's Creation story, for other Genesis stories also betray the same curiosity, as do the Bible's next three books: Exodus, Leviticus and Numbers. As is now generally accepted by all but extreme fundamentalists, the easily-definable textual strands that now appear so integrated in the first Biblical books must once have existed as independent written documents, slightly differing from one another in their facts, but closely related. Then, at one or more points in time, an editor or editors wove them together so that their joins now seem invisible. According to the most widely accepted deductions by textual scholars, no fewer than four independent original sources were combined to make up the present Bible's first five books:

Mount Ararat in eastern Turkey. Why does the Bible describe its people's supreme ancestor, Noah, as beginning humankind's repopulation in a remote part of what is today Turkey?

'E', a source in which the deity is called El, or (in its plural form) Elohim;
'J', a source that calls the deity Yahweh (spelt by Germans with a 'J');
'P' a source preoccupied with priestly matters but also incorporating some earlier material, including the 'heaven/earth/plants/animals, then man and woman' version of the Creation story;
'D', written by someone principally but not entirely responsible for the book of Deuteronomy.

With due deference to the minimalists, there are signs, even in the first Biblical book, traditionally attributed to Moses, that some of its editing occurred as late as the 5th century BC, when the entire Jewish world was under Persian rule. For example, the concept of the first two humans living in a garden smacks of its

Unmistakeably evoking the Bible story of Noah's flood, a cuneiform tablet of the Gilgamesh epic. When first deciphered in 1872, this was recognised to be a version of the Biblical Flood story featuring 'Utnapishtim' in place of Noah. Other versions of the same story have since come to light, some dating back to the early 2nd millennium BC.

originating in Persia, where gardens were fashionable, rather than with a people whose early life style involved moving from place to place in tents. Likewise, the concept of the 'spirit of God' 'sweeping over the waters', which appears in Genesis's second verse, occurs nowhere else in the rest of the Hebrew-language Bible, yet it was a common idea in Persian writings.

Particularly noteworthy of the 'J' version is that its Yahweh often does things of a very anthropomorphic or 'human-bodied' kind, quite different from the physically less limited way that 'he' is represented in almost all other parts of the Bible. Thus, in the elements of 'J' found in Genesis 3, Yahweh is described as 'walking' in the Garden of Eden (verse 9), and as making animal-skin clothes for Adam and Eve to help them hide their nakedness (verse 21). Overall, the impression is of a source still embodying traces of older, rather primitive traditions. These would date back to the time before the main body of the Bible developed its distinctive concepts of a disembodied deity.

How old, of course, is the moot, and at this stage unanswerable, question. By its very nature, the Creation story offers nothing intrinsic to which serious dating criteria can be applied. The 4004 BC calculation promulgated by editions of the King James Bible from 1701 onwards, and now rejected by all but the most extreme fundamentalists, has long been superseded by the findings of geological science.

Nonetheless, what about Genesis's next major element: the story of Noah and the Flood? As told in chapters 7 through 9, the Creator God, displeased with the wickedness that had spread throughout his Creation, decided to destroy it with a massive flood, but took pity on one man, Noah. He ordered Noah to build a large boat, or 'ark', and into this Noah was instructed to load a representative selection of all living creatures, together with himself and his family. As torrential rains flooded the entire earth to a great height, only Noah and those with him in the ark were able to escape drowning. When, eventually, the ark grounded upon a high mountain, and the waters subsided, these survivors stepped out and became the new parents from whom everyone and everything alive today is supposedly descended.

Thanks to the story's Sunday school familiarity, it is very easy to dismiss it as just another tale that is too tall to have any historical value. For there is no archaeological or geological evidence that the entire world has ever been inundated with a flood of the magnitude described in Genesis, certainly within the million or so years of something resembling humankind. Yet an undeniable fact about the Biblical Flood story is that it is genuinely very ancient in its origins, as is evident from texts independent of the Biblical record.

In 1872, a young British banknote-engraver called George Smith, whose 'leisure' activity was deciphering a collection of Babylonian cuneiform tablets unearthed two decades earlier by the British explorer Sir Henry Layard, discovered on tablet XI an unmistakable parallel with the Biblical story of Noah:

Genesis 8:6-10
At the end of forty days Noah opened the porthole he had made in the ark and sent out the raven. This went off and flew back and forth. Then he sent out the dove to see whether the waters were receding. The dove, finding nowhere to perch, returned to him in the ark, for there was water over the whole surface of the earth. After waiting seven more days he again sent out the dove. In the evening the dove came back to him and there was a new olive branch in its beak. So Noah realised that the waters were receding.

Cuneiform Tablet
When the seventh day dawned I loosed a dove and let her go. She flew away, but finding no resting place she returned. Then I loosed a swallow, and she flew away but finding no resting place she returned. I loosed a raven, she saw that the waters had retreated, she ate, she flew around, she cawed and she did not come back.

When Smith realised that a crucial part of this narrative must be on another portion of tablet that was nowhere among Layard's collection, with typical Victorian derring-do he travelled all the way to Nineveh to try to find it. And despite the Nineveh site's vast sprawl, he succeeded in doing so only five days after his arrival. Overall, what he had found was the so-called 'Gilgamesh Epic'[3], set out on twelve cuneiform tablets. In this the hero Utnapishtim, an unmistakable Babylonian counterpart of Noah, was divinely warned of the coming of a universal flood. He was urged to 'build a boat' and to take up into it 'the seed of all living creatures'.

Just like the Biblical Noah, Utnapishtim made his boat, coated it with bitumen to make it watertight and used it to save himself, his family and a collection of animals from the flood. When the waters started to recede, he sent out birds to check on their progress. Later, he grounded on a high mountain in order to regenerate all living things. He offered a sacrifice and received a divine assurance that such an event would never happen again. There could be no doubt of some link, filial or otherwise, between this and the Genesis story.

Before the 'Flood' of 5600 BC. According to marine scientists Ryan and Pitman, prior to 5600 BC the Mediterranean had not broken through the Bosporus Strait. What is now the Black Sea was a freshwater lake, sustaining a diversity of aquatic life appropriate to a freshwater environment, and arguably with many populous human settlements along its shores.

Today, we know that the tablets Smith found were not especially old, dating merely from the 7th century BC. But other substantially older Gilgamesh copies have been found, including a fragment from Megiddo in the north of present-day Israel, as well as further variants such as the Sumerian tale of Ziusudra and the Babylonian 'Atrahasis Epic', both of which date as far back as the 19th century BC. Some versions of a 19th-century BC list of the ancient Sumerian kings also refer to some very early (and purportedly very long-lived) kings, who are described as having reigned 'before the Flood', as if this was a real one-time, albeit long-past, historical event.

Few legends, particularly ones as widespread as the Flood story, spring out of nothing. So could the ancient Jewish, Sumerian and Babylonian traditions have their common origin in some genuinely-historical happening? In the 1920s, excavating the ancient Sumerian city of Ur in what is today Iraq, British archaeologist Sir Leonard Woolley[4] found an 11-foot-thick layer of silt, with occupational remains above and below it, which he claimed as evidence of the Biblical Flood. However, as is now generally recognised, Woolley's flood cannot have been related to the Sumerian King List, let alone to the Genesis story. Seemingly, it was a purely localised catastrophe[5] of a kind that happened from time to time elsewhere in Mesopotamia, due to the low-lying terrain.

Altogether more interesting have been recent discoveries by American marine geologists William Ryan and Walter Pitman of Columbia University's Lamont-Doherty Earth Observatory.[6] In 1993, on board a Russian research vessel, the *Aquanaut*, to which they brought American equipment for profiling and sampling the sea-bed, Ryan and Pitman made a careful survey of the bed of the Black Sea. Today, southern Russia's River Don flows into a huge northern part of the Black Sea, called the Sea of Azov. But they found that the Sea of Azov was once dry land with the Don zigzagging over it. The river then flowed due south across a broad floodplain, through what is now the Kerch Strait, and into what was then a much smaller Black Sea lake.

Ryan and Pitman took core samples from the Black Sea's bed, which were analysed by their research assistant Candace Major. These showed that while the sea-bed's topmost, and therefore most recent, layer of sediment contained molluscs such as *Mytilus galloprovincialis* that live only in seawater, immediately underlying this was an older layer rich in *Dreissena rostriformis* molluscs and other organisms that live only in freshwater. So, what is today the Black Sea must once have been a freshwater lake. The region just south of the Kerch Strait must have been the River Don's one-time delta. Furthermore, the sea's change to saltwater can only have been comparatively recent, since even the very oldest of the molluscs in the silt of the upper, seawater layer have been consistently

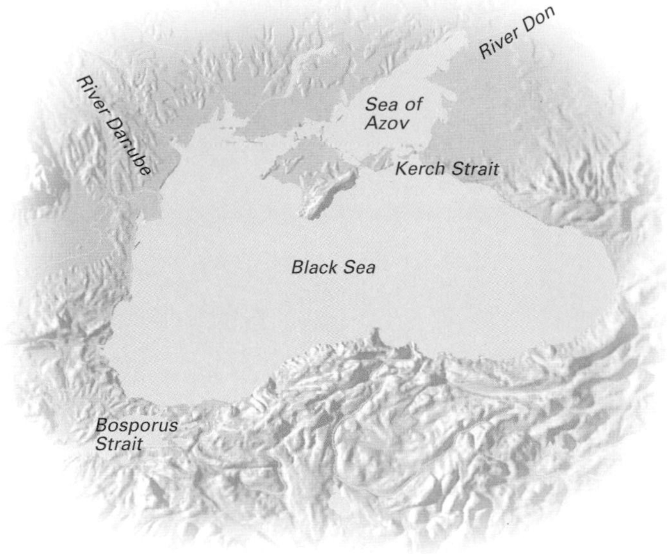

After the Flood of 5600 BC. The Mediterranean has broken through the Bosporus Strait, introducing salt water to the former lake, and inundating a huge area, particulary low-lying land to the region's north.

radiocarbon-dated to no earlier than c.5600 BC.

From these and similar findings Ryan and Pitman have deduced that following the last ice age the saltwater Mediterranean was considerably lower than its present level. At that time, the Bosporus, dividing the Mediterranean from the Black Sea, was not a strait as it is today, but dry land. What we now know as the Black Sea consisted of an ice age freshwater lake, fed by meltwater and rivers, lying some 350 feet below the then sea-level. This lake would have been a considerably smaller body of water than the present-day sea. Even so, it would have attracted surrounding human settlement.

As the post-ice age melting continued, along with some exceptionally-wet climatic conditions[7], there was a general rise in world sea-levels. Sometime around 5600 BC, the salty Mediterranean suddenly began spilling over the Bosporus and into the lake, killing all the lake's freshwater shellfish, and arguably much else besides. As envisaged by Ryan and Pitman: 'Ten cubic miles of water poured through each day, two hundred times what flows over Niagara Falls, enough to cover Manhattan Island each day to a depth of over half a mile.' According to their calculations, some 60,000 square miles of what would have been prime dry land around the old lake's shores was engulfed beneath up to 500 feet of water. It was a massive catastrophe for all human and animal life in the vicinity.

So far, Ryan and Pitman's findings have been based almost entirely on sea bed profiling and analysis of the organic remains found in sediment cores. It remains to be seen if future underwater archaeology will discover actual pre-Flood human settlements beneath the Black Sea's shallower areas. Meanwhile, their theory certainly accounts for a surprising number of ancient technological firsts from around the Black Sea. Among these are the world's oldest-known textile, dating to 7000 BC, found at Çayönü in eastern Turkey. Another is the world's oldest-known wine-making, dating to c.5000 BC, at Hajji Firuz Tepe, near Lake Urmia just across the border in Iran (suggesting that it may be no myth when Genesis 9:20 accredits Noah with being 'the first to plant the vine').[8] Also, there was a highly sophisticated metallurgy industry that flourished c.6000 BC at what is now Varna on the Black Sea's Bulgarian shores[9], only mysteriously to disappear very likely at the same time as Ryan and Pitman's 'flood'. Their theory further readily explains why so many peoples within the Black Sea's widest environs, from the Aryans of India with their *Rig Veda*, to the Greeks with their Deucalion legend, to the Jews with their Genesis book, have some kind of Flood story as part of their most ancient folklore.

Walter Pitman (left) and William Ryan (right) photographed while pursuing their Black Sea researches.

Another element, particular to the Genesis version of the Flood story, neatly accords with the Black Sea flood hypothesis. It also argues for the

Abraham's true Ur? Urfa in south-eastern Turkey, with nearby Serug and Harran – both family names associated with the Biblical Abraham.

story's origins lying deep in the Jewish people's own roots, rather than having been cribbed from the Babylonians as the minimalists would claim. According to Genesis 8:4, Noah's ark came to rest on the first properly identifiable geographical feature mentioned in the Bible: 17,000-foot-high Mount Ararat – none other than the most notable high point to the south-east of the Black Sea, in what is today north-eastern Turkey. This inevitably raises the question: why should a people, who for millennia have been besotted with their right to the land today called Israel, have located the very first post-Flood soil to be trodden by their ultimate ancestor in Turkey?

Here, any support has to be dispelled for the various theories that remains of Noah's ark might survive on Mount Ararat. In 1955 the French adventurer Fernand Navarra enthusiastically brought down from the mountain some chunks of wood which he claimed to be from the ark embedded in ice high above the snow line. In fact, these were carbon-dated to the 7th or 8th centuries AD, consistent with an Armenian tradition that Byzantine monks built a remote retreat house on Ararat. More recently, 'Amazing Truth' Australians Ron Wyatt and Jonathan Gray made claims for a fossilised Noah's ark at Akyayla, 12 miles south-east of Ararat. This has been authoritatively explained away as a metamorphic rock formation typically found at points of friction between the earth's tectonic plates.[10]

There is another, more important argument. If we look to the various ancient Flood stories, it is the Hurrian one to which the Biblical Genesis story is most akin. The little-known Hurrians are again associated with Turkey, and specifically with the Urartu region of north-eastern Turkey, just south of the Black Sea. The Hurrians' name for Noah was Nahmizuli, linguistically closest to the Biblical Noah's (*Nhm* in the original vowel-less Hebrew). Just like Noah's ark, Nahmizuli's came to rest on Mount Ararat. This may not be wholly conclusive that a vessel of some such Nhm had ever washed up on Ararat after a Black Sea Flood, the mountain being some 200 miles from the Black Sea at its nearest point. But it does at least push us into seriously considering whether the Jewish people's origins (which even they have never claimed to be in Israel) may have been somewhere in eastern Turkey.

For another myth of the Bible, both ancient and modern, needs to be laid to rest. This concerns the place of origin of that famous descendant of Noah to whom all Jews look as their common ancestor: the herdsman Abraham.[11] In what sounds like a definitive statement of Abraham's roots, Genesis's eleventh chapter mentions his 'native land' as having been 'Ur of the Chaldeans' (Genesis 11:28), a statement which seems at face value unmistakably to identify this Ur as the famous one in present-day Iraq. For the Chaldeans certainly took over this Ur's lower Mesopotamian region during the 1st millennium BC. And equally this Ur certainly was where, in the 1920s, British archaeologist Sir Leonard Woolley found fascinating remains of the much earlier Sumerian civilisation. Woolley himself surmised that the Biblical Abraham hailed from this city.[12]

Careful study of the Biblical text, however, suggests that both Woolley and the 1st millennium BC Biblical editor who may have added the words 'of the Chaldeans' were very, very wrong. For however boring the Bible's genealogies may seem to us – all those interminable lists of who-'begat'-whom of the King James translation – Genesis 11's specific listing of Abraham's descent from Noah turns out to be more interesting than at first meets the eye.

Thus, in verse 20, we find that Abraham's great-grandfather was called Serug, in verse 22 that his grandfather and brother were called Nahor, in verse 24 that his father was called Terah, and in verse 26 that he had a second brother called Harran. All of these personal names correspond to ancient placenames located neither in what is today Israel, nor anywhere near Chaldean Ur in present-day Iraq, but instead once again in Turkey.

As noted decades ago by Dead Sea Scrolls scholar Roland de Vaux, and also by British oriental studies specialist J.B. Segal[13], Serug, referred to in Neo-Assyrian texts as Sarugi, is today's Sürüç in south-eastern Turkey. What was once Terah, referred to in 18th-century BC cuneiform tablets from Mari, is today's Tell Turahi in the same region. Nahor, as yet unidentified on present-day maps, is known from cuneiform records, particularly those of ancient Mari, as well as from Genesis 24:10, to have been in the same locality. Ruin-dotted Harran, Biblically specified as the place where Abraham's father took his family to settle (Genesis 11:31), and likewise referred to in the 18th-century BC Mari tablets, still exists a few miles to Sürüç's east. Above all, dominating this entire region, and anciently known as Orhay or Urhay, is south-eastern Turkey's regional capital Urfa, which not only has a local folklore most stridently proclaiming it as the place where Abraham grew up[14], but also possesses a name surely too similar to Ur for coincidence.

Nor is this all. For there can be little doubt that the plain of Aram, on which today's Urfa/Ur stands, is the Paddan-Aram repeatedly referred to as the place where Abraham's wife's parents came from, as in Genesis 28, and where Abraham's son and grandson would seek out their wives in Genesis 24:10 and 28:2. And given that this region's later Aramaean inhabitants became the sworn enemies of the Israelites of the 1st millennium BC, the tradition that Abraham and his kin hailed from this locality was hardly likely to have been invented by the Bible's compilers.

In the light of all this, we seem at least to have some interesting signs that the people from whom the Bible sprang could well have had their origins in today's Turkey. Had their ancestor Abraham stayed there, who knows how different all history might have been?

But as we learn from Genesis 13, when Abraham was no less than seventy-five years old, he was divinely guided to journey with his wife Sarah, his nephew Lot and his flocks all the way southwards to what would turn out to be Canaan. And it is with the outcome of that momentous journey that the Bible story really begins.

The Bible's Turkish roots? The Pool of Abraham in present-day Urfa is in the very region in which Abraham's father Terah settled, according to Genesis 11:31.

2

'THE CANAANITES WERE THEN IN THE LAND'

ACCORDING TO Genesis's chapter 12, Abraham set out from Turkish Harran with his wife, nephew, servants and flocks, and headed 'for the land of Canaan'. This land was apparently part of an empire which stretched 'from Sidon all the way to Gerar near Gaza, and all the way to Sodom, Gomorrah, Admah and Zeboiim near Lesha' (Genesis 10:19). We know from elsewhere in Genesis that the latter locations were in the environs of the Dead Sea.

In the case of Abraham, we are obliged to agree with the minimalists that he is a figure we cannot consider historical in any meaningful way. We cannot be sure, even to the nearest century, when he may have lived, the best guesses being either the later part of the 3rd millennium BC or the earlier part of the 2nd millennium BC. But there is no doubt that the land of Canaan, Biblically named as Abraham's destination, was real enough. It was broadly today's southern Lebanon, Israel and western Jordan, a region remarkable for its extraordinary diversity. Fringed by the snow-peaked Anti-Lebanon mountains and watered by their runoff, its northern part is verdant with fine agricultural land and graced by the freshwater Sea of Galilee, 689 feet below sea level. It would seem to have been much the same in antiquity, for an ancient Egyptian tale of the early 2nd millennium BC, that of Sinuhe[1], tells us that it was:

> a good land . . . Figs were in it, as well as vines. More abundant was its wine than water. Its honey was plentiful, its olives profuse. Every fruit was on its trees. Barley was there along with emmer wheat. There was no limit to all its cattle.[2]

Further south, however, with the exception of the Mediterranean coastal plain, the terrain becomes steadily more arid with every mile travelled southwards. The north-south spine of hills that borders the plain imperceptibly merges into the rugged and parched, though spectacular, Negev Desert. Further east, the winding Jordan river empties, ultimately uselessly, into the 41-mile-long Dead Sea, 1337 feet below sea-level, the saltiest and most mineral-laden body of water in the world. In few countries anywhere are there such great geographical contrasts within distances a mere half-day's car journey from each other.

On Abraham's arrival in this Canaan, reportedly his first actions were to build

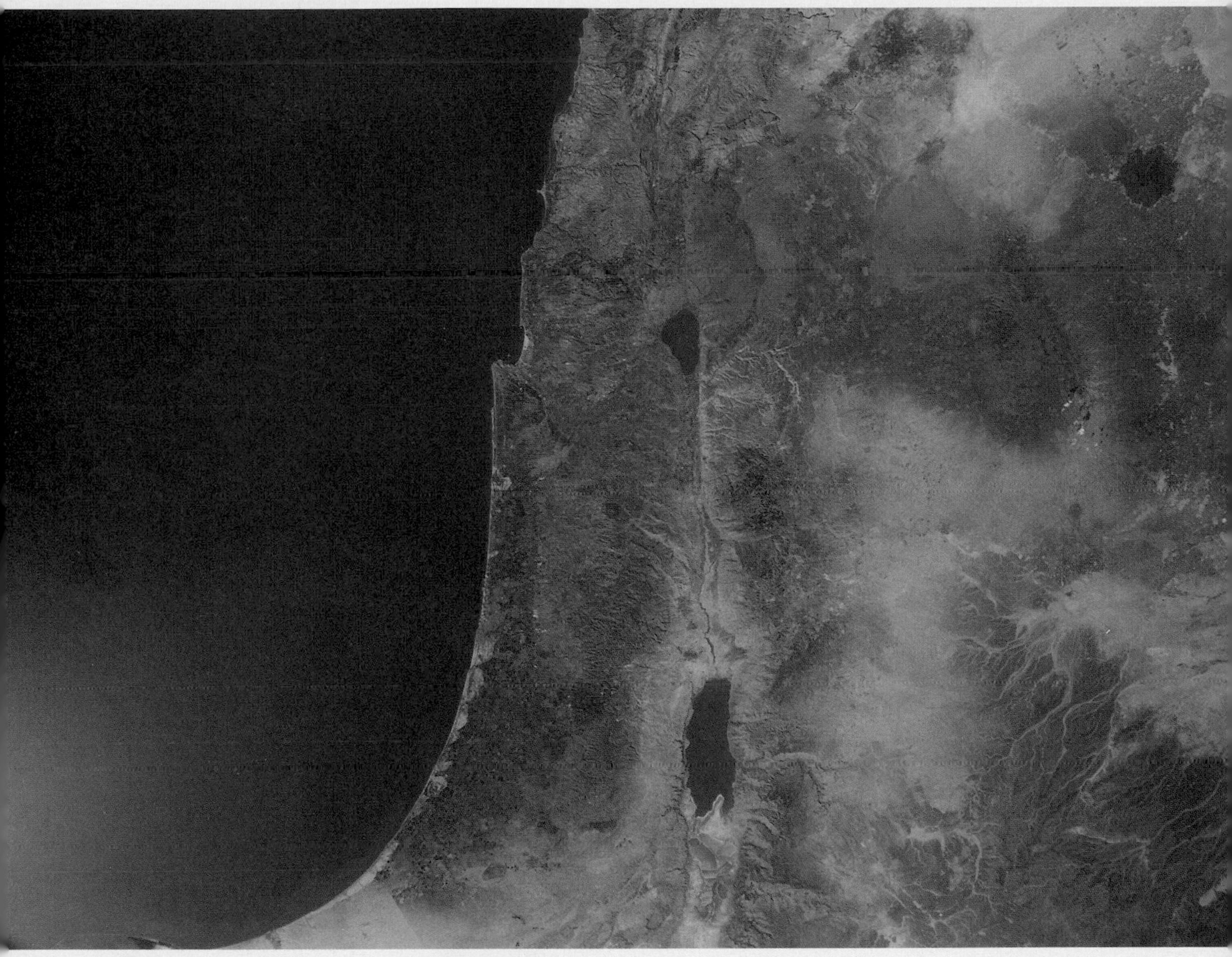

God's eye view. A photograph from space of the 'land of the Bible' shows the diversity of terrain. This was the stage for most of the events described in the Bible.

two altars: one at 'the site of Shechem', today fiercely Palestinian Nablus between mounts Ebal and Gerizim; the other in 'mountainous' terrain 'with Bethel to the west and Ai to the east' (Genesis 12:8). Thus, his chosen first base was the central hill country immediately adjoining the Mediterranean coastal plain. He was clearly avoiding getting too close to the mainly plain-based fortified cities of 'the Canaanites', the people who, we are specifically told, were 'in the land at the time' (Genesis 12:6), together with their apparently close affiliates 'the Kenites, Kenisites, Kadmonites, Hittites, Perizzites, Rephaim, Amorites, Girgashites and Jebusites' (Genesis 15:19-21).

Of the general credibility of this information there can be no doubt. The earliest extra-Biblical references to Canaanites occur among some 25,000 cuneiform tablets from *c.*1800 BC, discovered sixty years ago at Mari on the

middle Euphrates, but modern-day archaeological excavations in Israel indicate that broadly these same peoples occupied the country from much earlier. Contemporary Egyptian sources suggest that they were divided into a number of independent city-states, often at war with each other. Independently, archaeological findings show that they gave their cities increasingly elaborate fortification systems, doubtless as much to protect themselves from each other as from more foreign aggressors. Compared with their Mesopotamian and Egyptian neighbours, the Canaanites have remained relatively obscure, largely due to a dearth of surviving written records. Nevertheless, pictorial and other evidence of their life style shows that they lived to a high level of luxury and sophistication.

Our chief interest, however, concerns their religion. To all appearances, it was akin to that of the other ancient peoples of their time, with animal sacrifice as one of their most important rites. Major Canaanite towns as far back as the early 3rd millennium BC featured a stone altar-platform, called a *bamah*, or high place, typically some 5 feet high and 26 feet across[3], on which such sacrifices were performed.

Information about the deities to whom sacrifice was made is confused by the interchangeability of gods amongst the different peoples. Fragmentary 12th-century BC mythology texts[4] found at Ras Shamra, ancient Ugarit, suggest that there was a chief male god, or father of the gods, El (God), often called 'Bull El' in Ugaritic texts. Independent or interchangeable was also Baal (The Lord). He took localised names such as Baal Saphon (the 'Baal Zephon' of Exodus 14:1). His main motif seems to have been a young bull, reminiscent of ancient Crete's bull cult, as enshrined in the Minotaur legend. It is as a young bull that Baal (or El) appears in the topmost register of a Canaanitic cult stand of the 10th century BC, found at Taanach in northern Israel.

There was also a cow-horned female deity, Anat, apparently prone, after beautifying herself with scent and make-up, to committing acts of terrible slaughter. Also extremely powerful, and partly sharing Anat's attributes, was El's consort Astarte, alternatively known as Ashtoreth, Asherah, Athirat, Ishtar and Artemis. She was the ancient and near-universal Mother Goddess, intimately connected with fertility. Surviving Canaanitic depictions of her, from the 2nd and 1st millennium BC, exhibit much the same motifs as those associated with her counterparts in Sumer, Egypt and Minoan Crete. Almost invariably depicted frontally, and commonly naked, she could be portrayed atop a lion holding up lotus leaves and snakes. Or beween two lions. Or non-corporally as a stylised sacred tree. Or as a pillar between two goats – in which mode she was called an Asherah. Or just as the pubic triangle of the female genitalia. Priests shown attending her ancient Sumerian counterpart Ishtar are depicted doing so stark naked[5], and in Egyptian portrayals one god accompanying her does so with penis erect. There is also much to suggest that she played a crucial part in selecting and sanctioning Near Eastern kings. To mark this, an act of sexual intercourse, in

Above: A 10th-century BC cult stand from Taanach seems to show the Canaanitic pantheon of gods. Below: The deity El or Baal in the guise of a young bull.

The Canaanitic fertility goddess Astarte/Ashtoreth as portrayed on a 14th-century BC gold pendant found at Ras Shamra, the ancient Ugarit.

the form of a sacred marriage, seems to have taken place between her high priestess and the incumbent monarch. Such rites may well lie behind the temple prostitution heard more of later in the Bible.

According to the Biblical account, it was on the fringes of the milieu practising these rites – a very urban milieu, and no doubt one regarding itself as cultured and civilised – that the wealthy but childless hillbilly Abraham arrived with his wife, nephew and flocks, much like a Crocodile Dundee in Manhattan. As evident from the 'J' sections of Genesis, Abraham's god was the very bellicose male Yahweh. As is also evident, whereas 'towny' or settled-farmer gods such as El and Ashtoreth invariably had their permanent city-centre sacrifice places, adjoined by palace-like temples where their images were housed, for Abraham's Yahweh an impromptu altar on a hillside sufficed. The sacrifice itself was more important than its accoutrements.

And Abraham's sacrificial efforts seem to have pleased his Yahweh. For in messages that Abraham purportedly 'heard' from him, in much the same way that many kings of the 3rd and 2nd millennia BC reported hearing commands from their respective gods[6], Abraham was promised that he would at long last – aged seventy-five! – sire children. Furthermore, their descendants would multiply so prolifically that the whole land of Canaan would become theirs, and in due time they would become as numberless as the stars (Genesis 15:5). As a first sign of this promise, and apparently with his barren wife Sarah's[7] specific approval, Abraham successfully fathered a son by an Egyptian servant girl. This was followed by Sarah herself producing a son, Isaac, who grew up to be a fine young man.

All might, therefore, have seemed perfect until Abraham received a fresh divine message: that Isaac must be sacrificed as a 'burnt offering'. Clearly knowing exactly what procedures were expected of him, Abraham went to a high place (Genesis 22:2), built an altar, piled firewood on this (Genesis 22:9), bound Isaac, placed him on the pyre and then took out a knife (Genesis 22:10).

No matter when this section of Genesis was written, the intention behind this knife cannot be mistaken. It would be used to kill Isaac, by making him bleed to death, so that his body could then be roasted and offered up to Yahweh. Reportedly, however, Abraham's hand was stayed at the last moment by a fresh divine message to the effect that he was merely being tested. A ram caught in a nearby bush was substituted. The crisis was over and Isaac's life was spared.

For those who have received some kind of religious instruction, the very familiarity of the Abraham and Isaac story means that one question is all too rarely asked: what on earth possessed Abraham to be minded to perform such a grisly rite? If we look to the surrounding cultures of the first three millennia BC, the answer is apparent enough. For among a number of these peoples, and especially the Canaanites, the sacrifice of a young son or daughter in special circumstances was still a very real and necessary part of their religious and communal life.

Archaeologically, the most graphic evidence of this derives from the Minoans of Crete, whose religion, as we have noted, had close affinities with that of the Canaanites. In 1979, while excavating a hillside temple of *c.*1700 BC at Arkhanes in northern Crete, Greek archaeologists Yannis and Efi Sakellarakis discovered the remains of four individuals apparently killed in the midst of performing such a sacrifice.[8] In the westernmost room of the temple they found three skeletons. The first was of a woman in her late twenties, who had fallen face downwards. The second was a 6-foot-tall man in his late thirties, on his back, his arms in a position suggesting that he had been trying to protect himself from something collapsing overhead. The third was a youth lying on a small stone platform, arms and legs in an awkward foetal position, as if he had been bound, exactly as described of Isaac in Genesis 22:10. There was a cultic bronze knife across his body. Outside in a passageway lay a fourth skeleton. This individual had apparently been struck down while carrying a bull-decorated jar, probably containing blood, into the temple's central room. Life-size 'feet of clay' and burnt wood found in this same room indicated that it housed a god (or goddess) statue.

As inferred by the Sakellarakises, the 6-foot man (an individual of some substance judging by his ring and seal), together with the woman found with him, had just finished sacrificing the young man, when their temple was struck by a devastating earthquake, instantly killing them and the jar-carrier. The whole building and its contents were then

Above: Artist's reconstruction of the 2nd-millennium BC 'human sacrifice' as discovered on Crete, with (below) the site as it looks today.

The 'sacrifice of Iphigenia', an episode from Homer's *Iliad*, as depicted in a 1st-century AD fresco in the House of the Tragic Poet at Pompeii. Note Artemis/Astarte on her pillar at left.

swiftly consumed by fire. Very reminiscent of the Sakellarakises' findings, Homer's *Iliad* describes the Greek commander Agamemnon sacrificing his daughter Iphigenia to the goddess Artemis (Canaanite Astarte's Greek counterpart), in order to get the right winds for sailing to Troy. A lively depiction of this found at Pompeii features Artemis standing on a pillar, flanked by goats, and holding out lotus flowers, in the exact manner of much earlier Canaanitic examples. Abraham's former home town of Harran is similarly known to have had a tradition of human sacrifice.[9] That such a rite, and specifically burnt offering human sacrifice, was practised among the Canaanites is also apparent from horrified mentions in later Biblical books. These refer to royal children, both sons and daughters, being consigned 'to the fire of Molech' (e.g. 2 Kings 23:10). The Canaanites' direct descendants, the Carthaginians, were certainly still practising the same kind of human sacrifice as late as the 2nd century BC. Evidence for this comes from children's bodies in jars excavated in Carthage's special Tophet area where they were buried.

After Isaac's life was spared, Abraham seems to have turned to male circumcision as a substitute for human sacrifice. The rite was apparently not practised by the Canaanites, but it was certainly not new or exclusive to Abraham – various ancient peoples, including the Egyptians, practised it. It is described as a mark of the special 'covenant' between Yahweh and Abraham and his descendants. And of course it has been perpetuated to this day.

Bearing in mind that we are talking about the very birth of the Jewish religion, it would be helpful to have a real guide to when Abraham lived. Here, the Liverpool University Egyptologist Professor Kenneth Kitchen[10], who would certainly count himself a maximalist rather than a minimalist, has noted that 'covenants' also feature in ancient literature outside the Bible, and tended to take different forms at different periods. The Abrahamic pattern seems to be most closely comparable with examples from among the cuneiform tablets of c.1800 BC found at Mari in northern Mesopotamia. Similarly indicative may be the fact that Abraham fathered his first son Ishmail by his wife Sarah's servant girl, surrogacy-style with Sarah's consent.[11] As evident from cuneiform tablets from Mari's neighbour Nuzi, dating from the same c.1800 BC period, if a man's wife was barren, it was her positive duty to find another woman to bear her husband's children. The resultant offspring thereupon became hers as if she had borne them herself. The same Nuzi tablets also explain the otherwise baffling instances in Genesis 12, 20 and 26, in which both Abraham and his son Isaac apparently introduced their wives as their sisters to friendly monarchs they visited. The Nuzi tablets make clear that when a man married he could impart particular sanctity to this state if he adopted his wife as his sister. All such elements, therefore, strongly indicate that whatever the degree of editing early Biblical books such as Genesis may have received at a later date, at least something of their content harked back to sometime around the very early 2nd millennium BC.

The Dead Sea, seen from space. The shallower southern section, seen in vivid blue below the Lisan Peninsula, is where any submerged remains of a Sodom and Gomorrah are likely to be found.

A great deal of the uncertainty concerning Abraham's dates could be resolved if an inscription turned up, referring to one or more of the nine kings listed, as warring against each other in Genesis 14:1-2. Frustratingly, nothing of this kind has come to light. All that can be said is that if there ever was such a war between two coalitions, the most likely period is again between 2000 and 1800 BC, when greater Mesopotamia swarmed with 'major and minor city-states, combining and re-combining in ever-changing alliances'.[12] According to the Genesis text, one of these two coalitions comprised the kings of Sodom, Gomorrah, Admar, Zeboiim and Zoar, so there was understandable excitement in 1976 when Italian epigrapher Giovanni Pettinato claimed to have found these names, in the very same order, on cuneiform tablets of 2300 BC that his colleague Paolo Matthiae had excavated at Ebla, a neighbouring city to Mari and Nuzi in northern Mesopotamia. So far, however, Pettinato has mysteriously failed to substantiate this discovery.

Nonetheless, the crucial question remains: might the cities of Sodom and Gomorrah have once existed, with the Biblical story of their destruction by 'fire and brimstone' (Genesis 19:24), recording, however imperfectly, a once real event? Here, a particularly fascinating element is the way in which the book of Genesis remarks pointedly of the time before the cities' destruction: 'how well watered was the whole

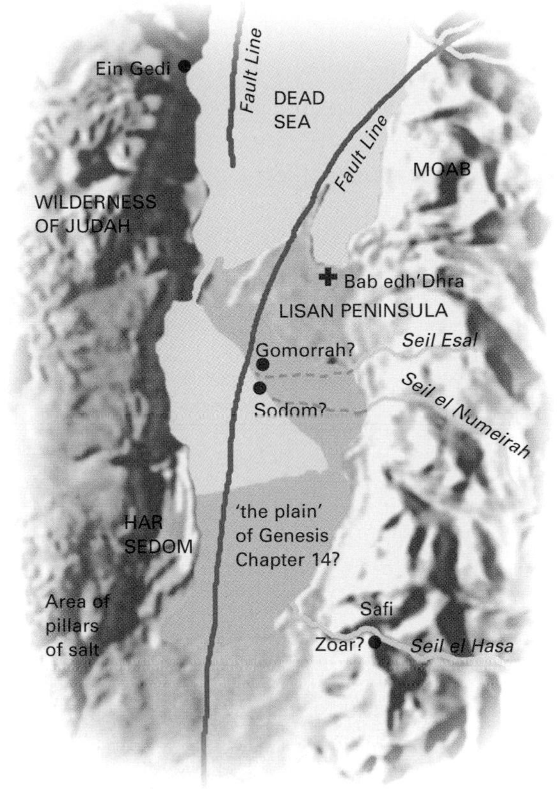

KEY

Area of original 'plain'?

Former river course?

✚ Populous cemetery here, abandoned *c.*2100 BC

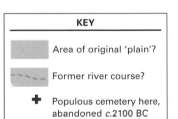

The southern Dead Sea, showing how the likely sites of Biblical Sodom and Gomorrah lay on one of the world's most unstable fault lines. The region remains one fraught with topographical changes.

plain of the Jordan, all of it, all the way to Zoar [a neighbour of Sodom and Gomorrah]' (Genesis 13:10). Purportedly, it was this good irrigation that inspired Abraham's nephew Lot to 'pitch his tents' in this locality.

Today, such conditions are completely unthinkable in the Dead Sea region, characterised as it is by lifeless saltwater, crags of salt and an all-pervading stench of sulphur. Yet is it possible that the Genesis story embodies a genuine memory of a time before some seismological event caused the region to assume this character?

Certainly, the Dead Sea region is seriously unstable geologically, since it is part of a major fault line in the earth's crust that stretches from Turkey's Taurus Mountains all the way south to Lake Victoria in Central Africa. Equally undeniable, this time from archaeology, is the fact that the region was much more populous for a period up to some time in the late 3rd millennium BC. During the 1960s the tragically short-lived American archaeologist Paul Lapp[13], while working at Bab edh'Dhra (gate of the arm), on the Dead Sea's now desolate Lisan Peninsula, uncovered part of a large Early Bronze Age city. Nearby was a vast cemetery containing so many bodies that it seems also to have served other nearby cities – arguably Sodom and Gomorrah among them – so far unlocated. As Lapp and his successors further discovered, this flourishing populace suddenly ceased their occupancy around 2100 BC and in very fiery circumstances.[14]

Exactly what happened is not yet fully understood. As envisaged by British geologists Graham M. Harris and A.P. Beardow[15], however, the Dead Sea was at that time much shallower than it is now. The local inhabitants' main occupation seems to have been harvesting the region's abundant bitumen. A major seismic catastrophe then occurred that dramatically changed the face of the whole region. And just as the Minoan 'human sacrifice' temple caught fire during the Cretan earthquake, so arguably the bitumen heaps that were the livelihood of the citizens of Sodom and Gomorrah ignited in an uncontrollable inferno. For any onlooker this may have looked like the sulphurous 'brimstone' raining from the sky, as Biblically described. The inhabitants would have been overwhelmed in moments. Much that had been dry land would have flooded, and the whole formerly flourishing area been turned into the desolate wasteland it has been ever since. That the book of Genesis should remember the region in its pre-2100 BC state is testimony in itself that the Biblical story has its basis in real historical happenings.

None of this, of course, goes anywhere even close to establishing Abraham as a true historical character. Nonetheless, according to Genesis 23, he purchased a so-called Cave of Machpelah as a burial place for himself, his wife Sarah and their immediate descendants. At today's strife-torn Hebron, just a few miles south of Jerusalem, is what is said to be this very cave, marked by the fortress-like Haram el Khalil.

Biblically, a great deal of importance seems to have been attached to this site, for Abraham and his retinue are said to have moved from place to place without ever

owning the land on which their flocks grazed. So this particular patch would have represented his and his descendants' first proper legal foothold in what became Israel. Whatever historical credibility we may attach to it, the Genesis text emphasises that a proper transaction took place with the land's previous owner, apparently a Hittite. As a further measure of the cave's importance, when Abraham's grandson Jacob died in Egypt, considerable efforts were seemingly made to bring him back to this cave, obviously to rest with his great forebear.

Furthermore, although the Machpelah cave story is found only in the Bible's less ancient 'P' strand, there is undeniably a cave below present-day Hebron's Haram el Khalil mosque. This stands within 23-foot-high walls erected as long ago as the 1st century BC by King Herod the Great to honour the site of Abraham's burial place. When in the early 12th century this was taken over by Christian monks, one of these, Arnoul, is said to have lowered himself down a shaft in the floor to find himself in a dirt-filled corridor. This was cleared and found to lead to a basilica-like

The fortress-like Haram el Khalil, now occupied by a mosque. It was built by Herod the Great in the 1st century BC to mark what was even then believed to be the burial place of Abraham and his family.

room, then to a grotto with bones buried in the floor, finally to another grotto where Arnoul and his fellows came across more bones, which they identified as those of Abraham and Isaac.

By 1163, while the site was still in Christian hands, it had already become something of a tourist attraction, with proper steps leading down into it. When the Moslems defeated the Christians and created the mosque, access into the cave was sealed with a stone slab firmly held down by four iron pegs. A cupola was built over a narrow shaft that seemed to provide an alternative entrance.

However, following the Israelis' victory in the Six-Day War of 1967, when they won Hebron from Jordan, the then-Minister of Defence, the archaeologically-inclined Moshe Dayan, arranged a hasty, impromptu investigation. The way they chose of getting into the cave, in order to avoid too great disruption of the mosque, was via the shaft covered by the cupola. This was found to be so narrow that the task of squeezing down into it was eventually given to a security officer's pencil-slim, twelve-year-old daughter, Michal.

With her elders waiting anxiously overhead, Michal gamely lowered herself down some 12 feet by rope to find herself in what appears to have been the same basilica-like room that Arnoul had reported seven hundred years before. She also located and photographed the steps by which the 12th-century pilgrims had made their access, noting above these the stone slab that the Moslems had secured with iron pegs.

But as for any tombs, she found only three 2-foot-wide stone slabs, the middle one of which, about 6 feet high, bore a partially-preserved Arab inscription, which Moshe Dayan identified as a verse from the Koran. With the limited resources available to her, Michal was unable to determine whether these were actual tombstones or simply blocked access to other parts of the complex, and in deference to Moslem sensibilities, as well as those of Jewish ultra-orthodox extremists, no further investigation has been attempted since.[16]

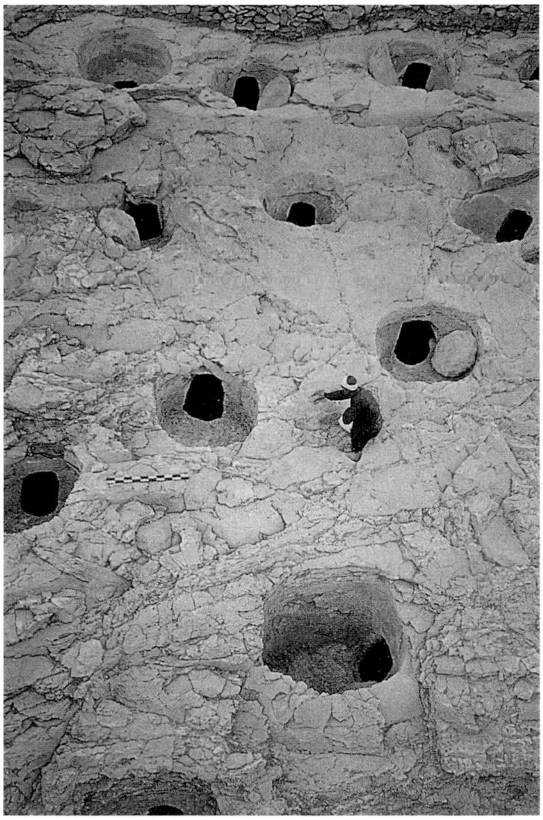

A typical Middle Bronze Age 1 cemetery near Hebron (right), showing how the Abraham tombs may originally have looked. Note the 'rolling' stones, next to several entrances, that acted like doors.

It is therefore impossible for anyone to know whether Hebron's Machpelah cave houses or housed the bones of Abraham and his immediate kindred. Even so, Israeli archaeologist Rivka Gonen has argued for a strong likelihood that it is a genuine burial complex dating at least as far back as the *c.*2000 BC period. It probably consisted of a number of small, unconnected burial caves, each entered through a vertical shaft. And certainly, cave tombs of this kind have been excavated elsewhere in the vicinity[17], the Genesis text corroborating that Abraham's belonged to just such a complex (Genesis 23:11).

3

WITH 'JACOB'S BROOD' IN EGYPT

ACCORDING TO the book of Genesis, Abraham was promised by his deity Yahweh that he would found a whole people, and within two generations the fulfilment of that promise seems to have been well under way.

Reportedly, his son Isaac fathered two sons: Jacob and Esau. Esau's lineage became the Edomite people who would go on to take over what is now part of Jordan. Jacob, who likewise continued in the family tradition of semi-nomadic sheep-herding, was instructed by his El god that from henceforth he would be known as Isra-el (ruling with El), and that the land of Canaan would one day belong to his descendants. By two different wives and their respective slave-girls Jacob duly sired twelve sons: Reuben, Simeon, Levi, Judah, Issachar, Zebulun, Joseph, Benjamin, Gad, Asher, Dan and Napthtali, all of whom were apparently born in the Paddan-Aram (Genesis 35:26), or Urfa-Harran region of Abraham's roots. From each of these sprang one of the 'twelve tribes of Israel' from which every present-day Jew is theoretically descended. But as Jacob came to be divinely advised, he and his brood's more immediate destiny lay in Egypt, in the Nile Delta region, where they would multiply to become 'a great nation' (Genesis 46:3).

That there was an Asiatic chieftain called Jacob, who established himself in Canaan during the first half of the 2nd millennium BC, and who went on to rule over the northern part of Egypt, is supported by independent historical and archaeological evidence. Throughout Egypt and the Sudan numerous scarabs, or beetle-like seals, have been found, inscribed in Egyptian hieroglyphs: Y'kob-HR. This name is now accepted as an Egyptianisation of the West Semitic Yaqub-Haddu, or 'Jacob', while other hieroglyphs unmistakably indicate that this Jacob was some kind of ruler. Evidence that Jacob originated specifically in Canaan emerged in 1969 when a near-identical Jacob scarab was found in Israel during excavations at Shiqmona on the outskirts of present-day

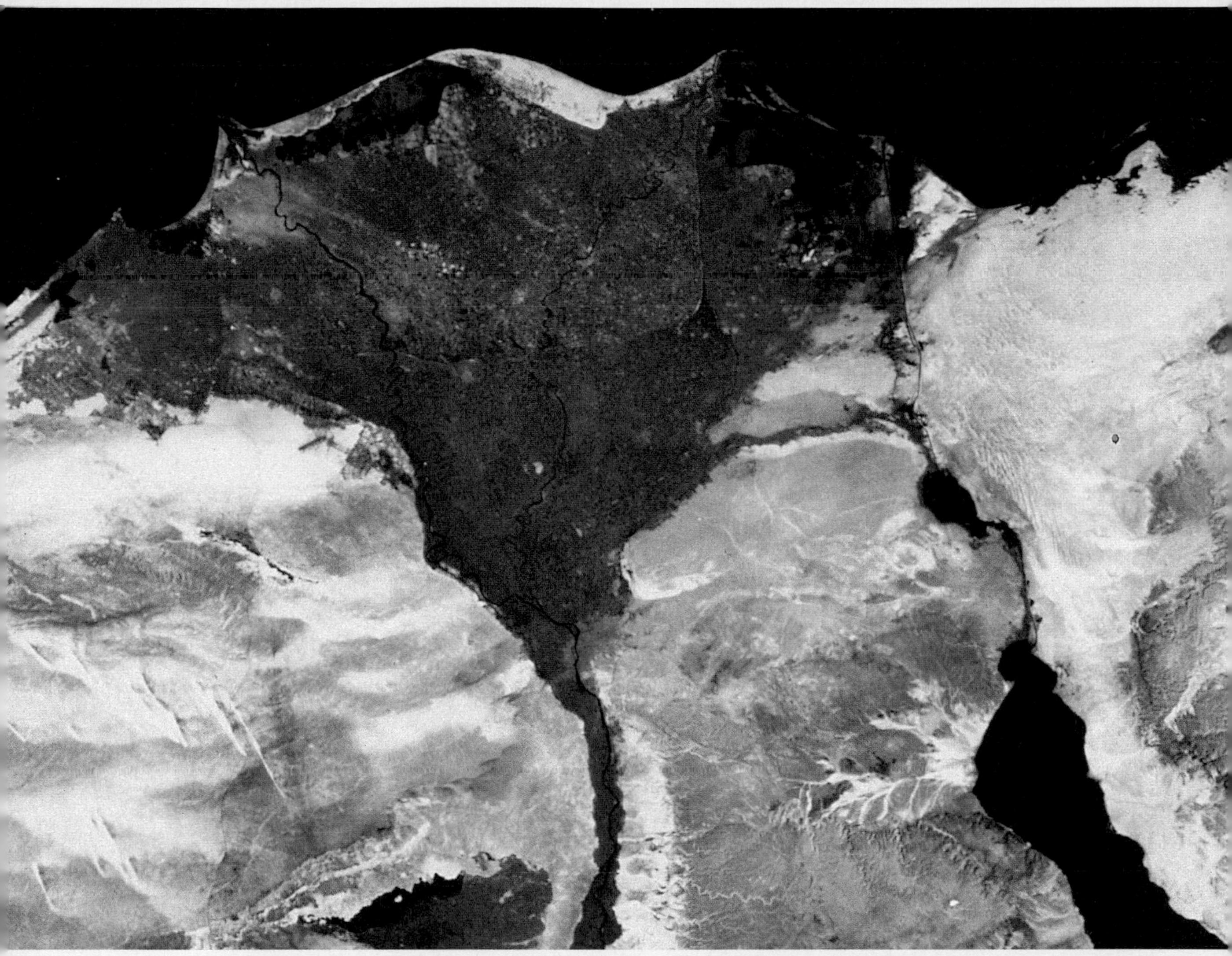

Above: Viewed from space, the triangular-shaped Nile Delta region to which the tribes of Jacob would have travelled from Canaan. The scarab found at Haifa, inscribed Y'qb-HR, or Jacob.

Haifa.[1] And since this Canaan scarab dates contextually to around 1750 BC, whereas its equivalents found in Egypt seem to be from around a century later, the strong inference is that Jacob started a dynasty that continued into Egypt.

But even if there was an Asiatic chieftain called Jacob, whether or not the Biblical one, who can be accepted as a genuinely historical personage, how did he and his brood come to establish themselves in a country as developed as Egypt? The book of Genesis' version is essentially the well-known tale of Jacob's favourite son Joseph. According to this, Joseph's jealous brothers sold him to traders who took him to Egypt, where after early misadventures he became appointed the country's chancellor. This was a result of his convincingly interpreting a dream that had been troubling the reigning pharaoh. In the role of chancellor Joseph successfully steered Egypt through the successive periods of plenty and famine that the

dream had forecast. This culminated in his brothers' coming to him, in complete ignorance of his identity, to seek his permission to bring their flocks from Canaan into Egypt for emergency pasturage. After Joseph had identified himself and become reconciled with them, he arranged, reputedly with his pharaoh's full aproval, for two things: for his father Jacob to be brought to Egypt (where according to Genesis 47:28 he lived for a further seventeen years), and for his whole family to be allowed to settle in the Nile Delta, where they became very populous.

As the Canadian Egyptologist Professor Donald Redford has pointed out[2], there are many features in this part of Genesis suggesting that it was written later than the events described, and that it is thereby of doubtful historicity. For instance, it lacks the primitive 'covenant' elements. The later Old Testament books do not allude back to it in the way they do to the stories of Abraham. The traders who took Joseph to Egypt are described as doing so on camels, generally understood not to have been domesticated until the next millennium. The names in the story, although Egyptian, have forms peculiar to the 1st rather than the 2nd millennium BC. The very title 'pharaoh' did not become adopted by Egyptian monarchs until the 14th century BC. Furthermore, the pharaoh whom Joseph is supposed to have served is never named Biblically, nor is there evidence from any Egyptian reign that an Asiatic called Joseph ever became chancellor.

If Joseph stockpiled grain in the years of plenty, he would have done so in a granary like that in the model from a 19th-century BC tomb (above).

A harvesting scene (detail) from a tomb at Thebes. Harvests depended on the level of each Nile flood, carefully recorded by the ancient Egyptians on still-extant Nilometers.

Even so, the background circumstances of the Joseph story were several years of abundant harvests, during which Joseph reportedly stockpiled the surpluses in granaries, followed by an equivalently lengthy famine. Given that, ancient Egypt's 'Nilometers' are not to be overlooked. Because the height of the Nile's annual flooding was always directly proportional to the abundance or otherwise of that year's harvest, the Egyptians used Nilometers to record each year's flood levels. These show that there actually was a phase of particularly dramatic fluctuations around the reigns of the 19th- or early 18th-century BC monarchs Senwosret III and Amenemhet III.[3] Furthermore, it was precisely in Senwosret III's time, uniquely in all Egyptian history, that the great estates formerly owned by Egypt's nobles passed to the monarchy. They did so in circumstances that are far from clear, unless the Biblical Joseph story might just happen to hold the key:

> So Joseph gained possession of all the farmland in Egypt for Pharaoh, every Egyptian having sold his field because the famine was too much for them; thus the land passed over to Pharaoh. (Genesis 47:20)

So could Senwosret III or Amenemhet III, or both, have had an Asiatic chancellor called Joseph, who manipulated the circumstances of a prolonged national famine to centralise power in the monarchy's favour? Certainly, the records of their time are sparse enough for this to be possible.[4] One little-documented chancellor of the period, Ankhu, rather neatly matches British Egyptologist Professor Kenneth Kitchen's deduction that Joseph's Biblically-quoted Egyptian name Zaphenath-paneah (Genesis 41:45) was originally Zat-en-aph Pa'aneah, or 'he-who-is-called Ankh'. This reconstruction is strengthened by the fact that 'he-who-is-called' prefixes are common among Asiatic slaves listed in a mid-18th-century BC papyrus of the Egyptian monarch Sebekhotpe III.[5]

Also, only quite recently, and undoubtedly dating from around this same period, the remains of an enormous statue of an unidentified non-royal dignitary have been found in the Nile Delta. From the sheer size of his statue and its accompanying tomb, he clearly achieved a position of very considerable power and importance under the Egyptian monarchy, yet his yellow-ochre skin colour and page-boy bob mode of hairstyling show that he was Asiatic. So could he have been the Biblical Joseph/'he-who-is-called-Ankhu'? The possibility is undeniably there.[6]

Incontrovertible archaeological evidence has come to light that Asiatics from the Canaan region infiltrated into the Nile Delta between the 18th and 16th centuries BC. They dislodged the native Egyptians, took over political power throughout northern Egypt and forced the native Egyptian monarchy to retreat far to the south. That something of this kind occurred has long been glimpsed from the surviving writings of the 3rd-century BC chronicler Manetho, the first known Egyptian to compile a history of his country in Greek.[7] According to Manetho, in the reign of a king 'Tutimaeus' (probably Dedumose, an obscure monarch of the 18th century BC):

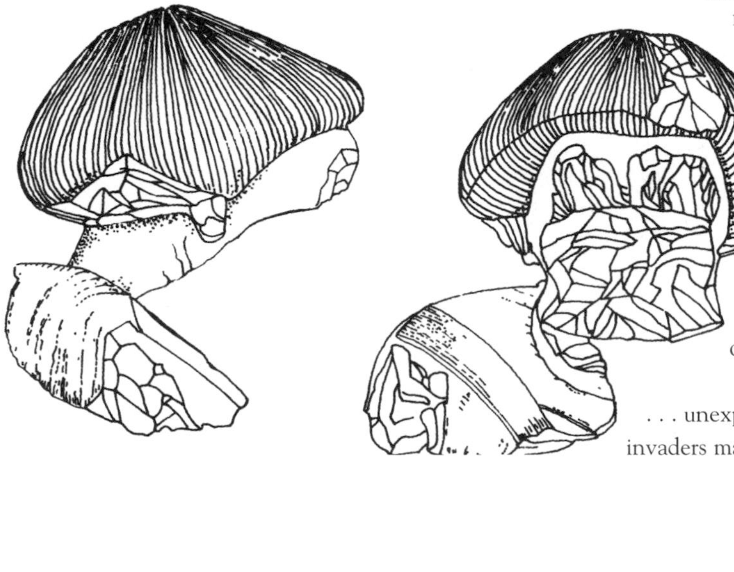

Chancellor 'Ankhu', alias the Biblical Joseph? Some historians have suggested that this head, from the seated statue of an Asiatic dignitary, found in a very fragmentary state in the eastern Nile Delta, might depict the Biblical Joseph.

> . . . unexpectedly, from the regions of the East, foreign invaders marched in . . . By main force they easily

overpowered the rulers of the land. They then burned out cities ruthlessly, razed to the ground the temples of the gods, and treated all the natives with cruel hostility, massacring some and leading into slavery the wives and children of others . . . Their race bore the generic name of Hyksos, which means king-shepherds.[8]

As some indication of the seeming permanence of this 'Hyksos' invasion, Manetho, without indicating that his list was necessarily comprehensive or in correct sequence, named no fewer than six of the dynasty of occupying Hyksos kings: Salitis, Bnon, Apachnan, Apop/Apopis, Iannas and Assis. As for his term Hyksos, this has long caused scholarly head-scratching. Although as an Egyptian writing in Greek Manetho ought to have known the meaning of the ancient Egyptian word *hk3 h3s.t*, the general consensus is that the word's truer meaning, rather than 'king-shepherds', was simply 'foreigners'.

Greater light than Manetho's began to be shed from 1966 when a methodical young Austrian Egyptologist, Manfred Bietak, arrived in the eastern part of Egypt's Nile Delta. He was intent upon excavating a mound called Tell el-Dab'a on which earlier archaeological surveys had reported occasional 2nd-millennium BC artefacts. Unlike the more southerly parts of Egypt, where ancient structures are mostly surrounded by clean, dry, easy-to-brush-away sand, the Nile Delta is in general very unpromising-looking terrain for excavation. It is predominantly flat, muddy and waterlogged, with most of its building remains of mud-brick. So Bietak had taken upon himself a less than enviable task.

Nonetheless, he and his assistants painstakingly began digging down to reveal the Tell el-Dab'a mound's successive layers of occupation, and as they did so a hitherto largely unknown picture began to emerge. There was evidence that native Egyptians had first founded a township on the site sometime around 2000 BC, but a change in the type of graves showed that it soon became occupied by increasing numbers of Asiatic peoples. Although some of these infiltrators were fierce-looking individuals buried with axes of a distinctive duck-bill shape, it was also clear that not all were mere destruction-bent marauders. Geophysical studies showed that before the site became silted up (as it is today), it stood on a major eastern branch of the Nile that flowed out into the Mediterranean 25 miles to the north. From huge quantities of broken imported ceramics, far more than it would have been practical to transport overland, it was obvious that the occupying Asiatics had operated it as a major trading port. Later strata revealed evidence of an impressive palace, the remains of which showed that those who used it were worshippers of the Canaanitic god Baal. Graves from the same period included many male warriors physically akin to the ancient north Canaanitic inhabitants of what is today the Lebanon.

Clearly, then, many of these Asiatic peoples who settled in the Nile Delta were urban warrior and mercantile Canaanites of the kind the sheep-herders Abraham and Jacob had warily but symbiotically moved among while in

Tell el-Dab'a, a major site of Asiatic settlement during the 2nd millennium BC. The flat alluvial terrain is typical of that in which the Austrian archaeologist Dr Manfred Bietak has conducted his excavations.

Canaan. For us, Bietak's excavations provided a fascinating additional finding. In the same site's environs, he found evidence of occupation by other Asiatic peoples whom he specifically termed 'nomads', that is, tent-dwellers owning flocks of grazing animals.

A very positive indication of these people's presence was the abundance of joints of lamb and mutton found in the Hyksos/Canaanite graves. The town-dwellers used these meats to feed their dead, but lamb and mutton must also have comprised an important part of their day-to-day diet. By all logic, therefore, close to where the urban population lived there roamed large flocks of sheep, inevitably necessitating the proximity also of appropriate herdspeople to look after them. This readily corresponded to the book of Genesis' description of the livelihood of Joseph's brothers:

> The men are shepherds; they have always been breeders of livestock, and they have brought with them their flocks and herds and all that is theirs. (Genesis 46:32)

Supplementing these findings, ancient Egyptian records likewise leave no doubt that such semi-nomadic herdspeople constantly hovered on the Nile Delta's eastern fringes. Thus, the ancient Egyptian 'story of Sinuhe', from the early 2nd millennium BC, tells how an aristocratic Egyptian fugitive Sinuhe, close to dying of thirst, managed to get just across Egypt's north-eastern border (little more than 20 miles from Tell el-Dab'a). There, he was almost immediately rescued by a very Biblical-sounding tribe of animal-herders. In Sinuhe's words:

> I heard the sound of the lowing of cattle, and caught sight of some pastoralists. The leader among them, *who had been in Egypt* [italics mine] recognised me. Then he gave me water, and after I had gone with him to his tribe he boiled milk for me.[9]

The Prophecy of Neferty, from the same period, indicates that although these nomadic peoples were far from always welcome in Egypt, they were wont to venture into the country with their flocks:

> The Asiatics shall not be allowed to come down to Egypt, that they might ask for water beggar-fashion to water their flocks.[10]

As pictorial evidence of how such peoples could and did make tolerated infiltrations, an 8-foot-long tomb painting from this period, found at Beni Hasan, south of Cairo, depicts the arrival at Egypt's eastern frontier of eight Asiatic men, four women, three children, two donkeys, an ibex and a gazelle. They were apparently part of a group of thirty-seven Hyksos coming to trade in eye make-up. The men's hair-styles are strongly reminiscent of that of the mysterious Ankhu statue. One of the weapons they are carrying is unmistakably a Canaanitic duck-bill-shaped axe of the kind that Bietak found in the Tell el-Dab'a graves. Long a matter of note has been the multi-coloured garments they are wearing. They are reminiscent of the Biblical Joseph's *ketonet passim*, or 'coat of many colours' (Genesis 37:3), as this is famously translated in the King James Authorised Version of the Bible. Unfortunately, since modern-day Bible translators prefer to render this as: 'long robe with full sleeves'[11], 'coat with long sleeves'[12], 'ornamented tunic'[13] or 'decorated tunic'[14] – any such parallel has been more than a little undermined.

A further fact complicates the identification of any one of these semi-nomadic, animal-herding peoples with the Biblical 'sons of Jacob'. Although Near Eastern texts from Egypt and Mesopotamia refer repeatedly throughout the 2nd millennium BC to itinerant Habiru, or Hapiru, all of whom it is highly tempting to equate with the Biblical 'Ibri, or Hebrews, many of the very same texts make clear that these were not any specific ethnic group but instead trouble-making mercenaries of mixed origin. It is true that early

Hyksos arrive in Egypt. Detail from a 19th-century BC Egyptian wall-painting, found at Beni Hasan. It depicts a long procession of Asiatics, specifically labelled 'Hyksos', arriving at the Egyptian frontier. One man (not shown here) carries a duck-billed axe like those found in graves around Tell el-Dab'a.

2nd-millennium BC texts found at Mari indicate that among these same marauding Habiru were 'Benjaminites', who matched the Biblical tribe purportedly descended from Jacob's son Benjamin. But the best that can be said is that while some 'sons of Jacob' may very likely have been active Habiru mercenaries, by no means all of those designated Habiru were ethnically Hebrew or in any other way necessarily descended from the Biblical Jacob.

Despite these semantic complexities, another fact is more than evident from Manfred Bietak's continuing Tell el-Dab'a excavations. Asiatics from Canaan – some warriors, others merchants and others semi-nomadic pastoralists – did settle in large numbers in the eastern part of the Nile Delta between the 18th and 16th century BC. From what we know of the pastoralists, these very readily matched the Biblical account of the 'sons of Jacob', settling and 'increasing greatly' in this same region. Furthermore, from the Septuagint version of the Bible compiled in northern Egypt in the 3rd century BC, we know that the 'region of Goshen', in which they are said to have settled (Genesis 47:27), was near the present-day town of Faqus, only 4 miles from Bietak's Tell el-Dab'a.[15]

But what exactly was Tell el-Dab'a during the Hyksos period, that it should have become such a major focal point of all this Asiatic settlement? According to the Egyptian chronicler Manetho, after the Hyksos kings had forced the native Egyptian monarchy to retrench in the south, they built for themselves a capital city 'very favourably situated on the east of the Bubastite branch of the Nile [i.e. in the eastern Nile Delta], and called Avaris after an ancient religious tradition'. This city they 'rebuilt and fortified with massive walls' and garrisoned with 'as many as 240,000 armed men'.[16] As one contemporary Egyptian observer described its appearance during its time of Hyksos/Canaanite occupation:

> Its walls are high and crowned with harems with windows through which the women peer out like animals in their holes.[17] A crowded harbour stands to the north, and the land around is flat. While desert lies to the east, there are vineyards in the vicinity and these produce wine for the court.[18]

As now agreed by a consensus of Egyptologists, however uninspiring Bietak's Tell el-Dab'a may look in the present-day, it was none other than this harbour capital Avaris. And on the evidence of Hyksos scarabs and other artefacts found as far afield as Crete and Baghdad, this would appear to have been the hub of a very significantly-sized Hyksos/Canaanite empire. One inscription describes Apop/Apopis, who ruled from it, as having 'set all foreign countries under his feet'. Not only did the Hyksos/Canaanites make it something of a 2nd-millennium BC Alexandria, but just as in Canaan, they appear to have been fine cultivators of the very fertile land all around it. Unless provoked, they even behaved as very civilised neighbours to the native Egyptians whom they had dislodged. As one courtier at the native Egyptian court felt obliged to admit:

> The finest of their fields are ploughed for us, our cattle are pastured in the Delta. Emmer is sent for our pigs, our cattle are not taken away.[19]

But inevitably it could only be a matter of time before the native Egyptian monarchy, humiliatingly forced as it had been to make a new capital for itself down south at Thebes (present-day Luxor), tried to make a comeback, though not without suffering some very serious set-backs at first. For instance, Egypt's king Seqenenre Tao I, contemporary with Apop/Apopis, seems to have made a valiant attempt. He is the one Egyptian monarch, in all the country's long history, whose mummy bears unmistakable signs that he was killed in battle. As generally agreed by those who have examined this mummy, he died in terrible agony from having been hacked about the head by the very Hyksos, duck-billed type of axe that Bietak and his helpers found in the graves at Tell el-Dab'a, a type also carried by the seemingly peaceful traders depicted in the Beni Hasan wall-painting.

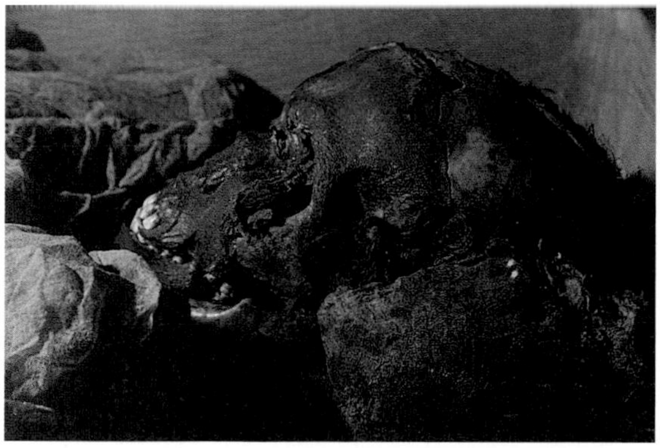

Killed by the 'Hyksos'? Pharaoh Seqenenre Tao I, the only mummy of an ancient Egyptian monarch to show obvious evidence of a violent death.

In the mid-16th century BC there was one native Egyptian pharaoh, Ahmose, who managed to overcome these Asiatic occupiers. He did so, as is historically known, in a fierce land and sea battle fought in and around the stout-walled Avaris. Directly as a result of Ahmose's victory, according to the same Egyptian chronicler Manetho, the Hyksos were forced to abandon their colonisation of the Nile Delta, departing in much the same huge numbers in which they arrived. In Manetho's words:

> No fewer than 240,000 entire households with their families left Egypt and travelled the desert to Syria.

So just as there had earlier been large infiltrations of Canaanitic Asiatics into Egypt, now its reverse occurred, a similarly-sizeable exodus. This raises the thought: what happened to those nomadic shepherds who had accompanied, if not preceded, the Canaanites into Egypt to settle on the fringes of Avaris? For if, as we can now be sure, something resembling the Biblically-described settlement of 'Jacob's brood' in Egypt really happened, might their even more famous 'Exodus' from Egypt have been a real event also?

4

Coming out with 'Signs and Wonders'

THE SONS of Jacob's descendants retained a powerful folk memory that their ancestors had departed from Egypt in some quite exceptional circumstances. Indicative of this is the fact that the later Biblical books repeatedly refer back to this event, as in the 8th-century BC book of Amos: 'Hear . . . O people of Israel . . . concerning the whole family that I brought up from the land of Egypt' (Amos 3:1).

Harking back even more powerfully to this is the world's oldest surviving commemorative ceremony: the *Seder*, or Passover. To this day, traditional Jewish families, wherever they may be in the world, gather on a particular night in spring to eat a special meal commemorating the events of their 'Exodus' from Egypt, just as they have for at least three thousand years. Their dining table will be laid out with some very strange foods: bitter herbs, unleavened bread and a single cooked bone (traditionally lamb), which should be almost completely de-fleshed. Before they eat this, the youngest person present must ask: 'Why is this night different from all other nights?' One of the older persons will answer by quoting the history of Jewish origins, as most usefully summarised in the book of Deuteronomy:

> My father was a wandering Aramaean who went down to Egypt as a small group of men and stayed there until they became a nation, great, mighty and populous. The Egyptians ill-treated us, they oppressed us and inflicted harsh slavery on us. But we called on Yahweh, God of our ancestors. Yahweh heard our voice and our misery, our toil and our oppression, and Yahweh brought us out of Egypt with mighty hand and outstretched arm, with great terror and with signs and wonders. (Deuteronomy 26:5-8)[1]

Biblically, the 'great terror' and 'signs and wonders' were, of course, the famous 'ten plagues' and the concomitant 'parting of the waters' that enabled those oppressed to make a successful escape from their tormentors. The memory of the very sudden, spontaneous nature of this event is preserved not least via the *matzot*, or unleavened bread, traditionally insisted upon throughout the week of Passover commemorations. Its unleavened state recalls the haste with which the departure had to be made.

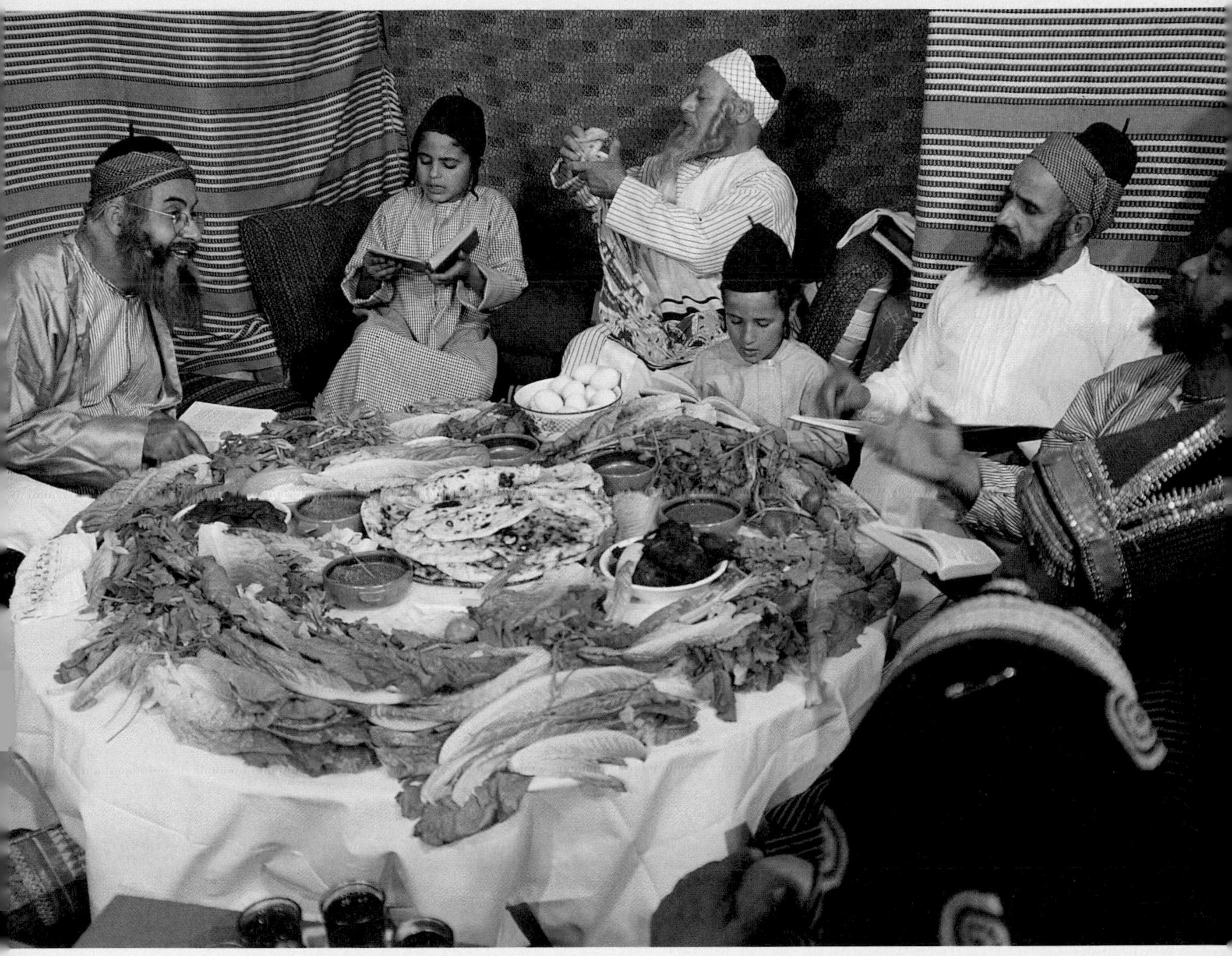

Yemenite Jews celebrate the *Seder*, or Passover, commemorating their ancestors' escape from Egypt, amidst 'signs and wonders'.

Frustratingly, however, if we try to identify in history exactly when such a set of circumstances might have happened, we encounter a minefield of scholarly controversy. Recently, American Biblical historian Edwin Yamauchi has described it as Biblical archaeology's 'greatest failure' that 'neither Egyptian nor Israelite data have been able to settle the issue of the date, route and nature of the Exodus'.[2] The highly respected German Biblical scholar Martin Noth[3] has opined that the majority of the peoples who later became the twelve tribes of Israel had probably never been in Egypt at all, a view retaining strong support.

Central to this issue of whether the Biblical Exodus occurred is the question of when it might have happened. The book of Exodus's seemingly definitive statement that the Egyptians forced Jacob's descendants, upon their enslavement, to build 'the garrison cities for pharaoh: Pithom and Ramesses' (Exodus 1:11) has arguably caused a huge amount of misunderstanding. For putting together of the words 'Ramesses' and 'building' automatically conjures up the 19th Dynasty pharaoh Ramesses II, renowned for his ambitious building projects. And if Ramesses II was the pharaoh who forced the Biblical peoples to work on building a city named after him, then logically Jacob's descendants could not have made their escape from Egypt any earlier than his time: the 13th century BC.

Between 1927 and 1955, the French Egyptologist Pierre Montet carried out excavations at the Nile Delta site known as Tanis, which seemed to reinforce such a dating. He found an unusually high proportion of monuments inscribed with the familiar cartouche of Ramesses II, also a temple with hieroglyphs referring to 'Ramesses' as a city name. There were no signs of earlier settlement, suggesting that it was Ramesses II who had founded the site. Montet assumed that Tanis must have been the city the Bible calls Ramesses, and if the Biblical 'oppression' occurred at all, it must have been during Ramesses II's reign. During the succeeding decades scholar after scholar accepted Montet's findings. They also noted that there was no historical evidence from around Ramesses' time either of any 'plagues' or of any Asiatic slaves making a dash for freedom. So they concluded that these Biblically-described events were most likely mere myths.

Only in comparatively recent times has it become recognised that Montet made a colossal error. Tanis was not the original site of Ramesses city, nor was it founded by Ramesses II, but instead two centuries later. It was so littered with Ramessid monuments because these had once genuinely belonged to the original Ramesses. But around 1000 BC, this became too silted up to function as the major harbour and crossroads city it had formerly been, and the monuments were transported to Tanis.

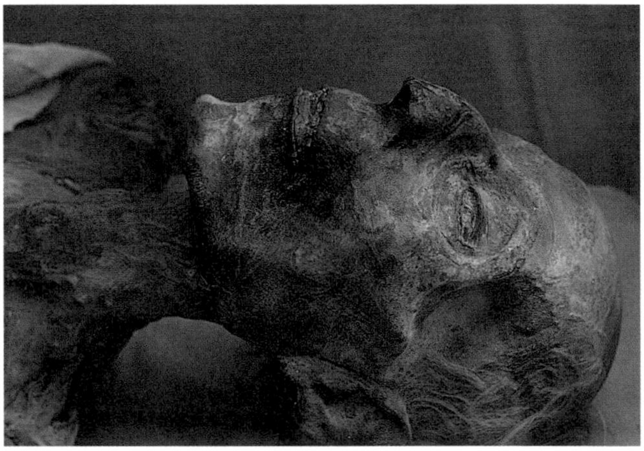

The mummy of the 19th Dynasty Pharaoh Ramesses II is in the Egyptian Museum, Cairo. Because of the Biblical reference to building 'Ramesses', he has long been thought the pharaoh who oppressed Jacob's descendants in Egypt.

So where was the true, original Ramesses? Thanks largely to the Austrian Egyptologist Dr Manfred Bietak, we now know that it was none other than the Nile Delta city described in the last chapter, under the name Avaris. After expelling the Canaanite Hyksos to the north around 1550 BC, Egypt's 18th Dynasty pharaohs went on to rule from Thebes, 350 miles to the south. Here they already had a magnificent palace, and their chief deity Amun had his vast temple. But the 19th Dynasty pharaohs Seti I and Ramesses II, recognising Avaris's strategic advantages, began a major redevelopment of the then-neglected site. They created a vast 'new town' to its north-east, in what today is Qantir, complete with a beautifully-tiled palace. The development honoured the 400th anniversary of Avaris's tutelary deity Baal under his Egyptian name Seth. As a characteristic finishing touch, Ramesses gave the city the new name 'Ramesses' after himself.

So a question now arises: must it still have been during Ramesses II's reign, in the 13th century BC, that the Biblical Jacob's descendants toiled on the rebuilding of Ramesses? Or, as the new information allows, might their 'oppression' have been much earlier, while the city was still known as Avaris? In this case, a later editor may simply have changed the name to Ramesses because that was how it was known in his time.

In ostensible favour of the first alternative is that both in the Biblical story of Joseph and his brothers settling in Egypt and in that of their descendants' later departure under Moses, the respective pharaohs seem to have been located close to the sons of Jacob's

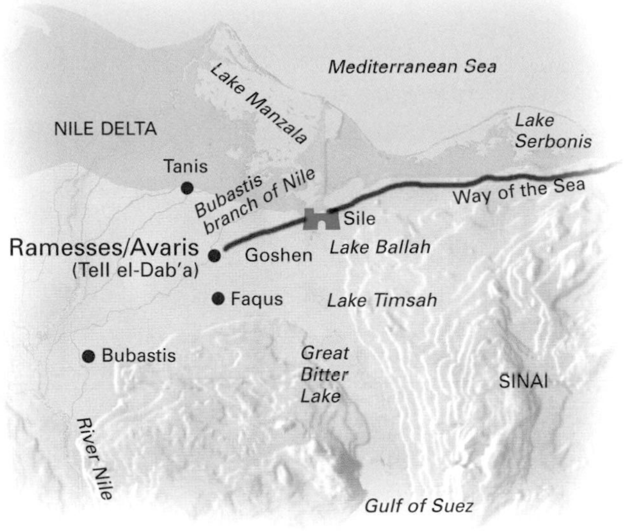

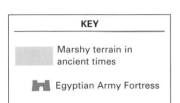

The eastern Nile Delta, showing the relative locations of Tell el-Dab'a and Tanis, also the Way of the Sea route along which the Canaanite warlords would have escaped eastwards to Sharuhen, after the fall of Avaris.

'Goshen' area. There is no suggestion that either Joseph or Moses had to travel the 350 miles south to Thebes. If, as suggested, Joseph lived some time during the 12th or 13th Dynasties, there is no historical problem, since the pharaohs of these dynasties had palaces in northern Egypt, including Avaris. They would, therefore, have been readily accessible to anyone living in Goshen. Likewise, if Moses had lived in Ramesses II's reign, he would have had no difficulty, because of Ramesses' rebuilding of former Avaris.

If, on the other hand, we try to date Moses and the oppression earlier than Ramesses' reign, we have to face a seemingly awkward fact about Ramesses' 18th Dynasty predecessors. Theoretically, from the time of their victory over the Hyksos onwards, they maintained Thebes as their capital, requiring Moses to travel 350 miles for any audience, which the Biblical text does not even begin to suggest. Does this mean that Ramesses II had to be the pharaoh of the Biblical oppression? Or can there be an alternative?

In fact, if we look to the Biblical Exodus story's two main components – a mass departure of Jacob's descendants from the Nile Delta and a series of spectacular 'act of God' cataclysms preceding this – there is not the slightest historical indication of any such events in Ramesses II's time. But something along these lines undeniably did happen shortly after Pharaoh Ahmose had captured Avaris.

For, as we learned in the last chapter, the Egyptian chronicler Manetho reported some kind of mass migration from Egypt some time shortly after the Canaanites' defeat by Ahmose. In Manetho's words:

> The Hyksos were defeated, driven out of all the rest of Egypt, and confined in a place called Avaris. . . . [Later] no fewer than 240,000 entire households with their possessions left Egypt and traversed the desert to Syria.

The surviving contemporary information about Ahmose's victory and subsequent reign is extremely sketchy. It is largely deriving from a veteran admiral[4] called Ahmose (not to be confused with his same-name pharaoh), who took part in the fight for Avaris and inscribed his memoirs on the walls of his tomb at el-Kab, 50 miles south of Thebes:

> There was fighting in the water of the canal [of Avaris] . . . Thereupon I made a capture. . . . Then Avaris was despoiled, and I brought away spoil thence: one man, three women . . . And His Majesty [i.e. pharaoh Ahmose] gave them to me for slaves. Then Sharuhen was besieged for three years. Then His Majesty despoiled it. Thereupon I carried off spoil from there: two women and a hand.[5]

Historians are generally agreed in their interpretation of admiral Ahmose's observation that Sharuhen was besieged so soon after the fall of Avaris and for such a long time. They conclude that a significant number of Avaris's Canaanite war-lords, when they saw that defeat was inevitable, escaped in their fastest chariots. They made their way eastwards along the Mediterranean coast road to take refuge in Sharuhen, the first major

Canaanite city north-east of the Egyptian border. Later mentioned as part of the Biblical tribe of Simeon's territory[6], this is generally identified as modern-day Tel el-Ajjul, 4 miles south of present-day Gaza, and ideally located at the mouth of the Wadi Ghazzeh, where it commanded its particular sector of the Way of the Sea. Archaeological excavations have revealed that it was a wealthy metropolis during the Hyksos period. It was most likely the place where Avaris's king and his accompanying war-lords halted their flight. As admiral Ahmose indicates, his pharaoh namesake pursued the warrior Canaanites all the way to its walls, then resolutely besieged them there for three years, clearly determined to ensure they would never threaten his country again.

This leaves unanswered many questions surrounding the departure from Egypt of the '240,000 entire households with their possessions' recorded by Manetho. By any standards such an evacuation would have been an exceptional movement of peoples, with heavily-laden families making their way slowly eastwards on foot rather than by chariot. Since the Egyptian chariots could easily have stopped, annihilated and plundered so vulnerable a procession, this must signify that the Egyptians at least tolerated its departure.

So when and how might this evacuation have happened? The question is particularly pressing, given admiral Ahmose's clear account of the Egyptians' initial policy. On capturing Avaris, they enslaved those unable to make a quick getaway, a group that inevitably included the pastoralists with their sheep flocks.

Germane to this issue is an event that happened within a matter of decades after Avaris's fall. It was a 'signs and wonders'-type disaster that almost certainly affected northern Egypt, and would have enabled those who had been enslaved to make their escape unexpectedly. For although far too little historical information has survived concerning the victorious Pharaoh Ahmose – not even his tomb has been found – one fact is certain. Either towards the end of his reign, or at most within fifty years of it, there occurred the greatest natural disaster to affect the eastern Mediterranean region throughout the last several thousand years.

Above: Pharaoh Ahmose's golden ceremonial axe, with royal cartouches in the upper panel, and in the centre a depiction of him killing one of the Hyksos. Left: Admiral Ahmose's account of his namesake's victory over the Hyksos, as preserved in his tomb at el-Kab.

A minor volcanic eruption on the island of Thera in 1939 sends iron oxide into the Mediterranean, poisoning fish for miles around.

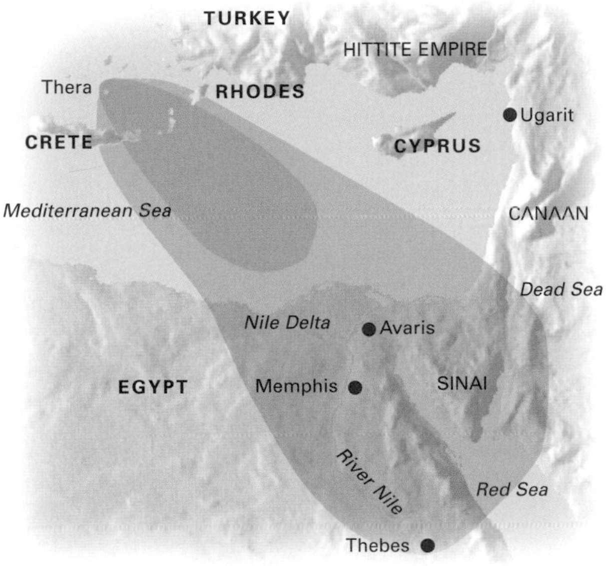

KEY

- Area of sea-bed Theran ash deposits
- Projected path of ash cloud

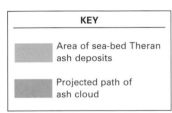

As deduced from sea-bed samples, the path of the ash cloud from the Theran eruption, south-eastwards towards northern Egypt.

It was a massive volcanic eruption of the Aegean island of Santorini, or Thera, 600 miles to the north-west of the Nile Delta. In Ahmose's time this was inhabited by a colony of Minoans originating from Crete, 60 miles to its south. The eruption has been so obscured by the passage of time that it was hardly suspected until the 1960s, when two American geologists, Dragoslav Ninkovich and Bruce Heezen[7], presented their findings from sea-bed core samples. These showed that a 200,000-square-mile area of the eastern Mediterranean sea-bed, extending in a swathe from Thera south-eastwards towards northern Egypt, is covered with a layer of volcanic ash. Since this ash has the same unique 'fingerprint' as huge mounds of ash that can still be seen heaped cliff-high above a one-time Minoan house on Thera, it must have come from the same eruption.

Geologists have calculated that the eruption was massive. Its closest parallels in modern times have been the eruptions of the Indonesian volcanoes of Tambora in 1815 and Krakatau[8] in 1883, also to a lesser extent the Caribbean's Mount Pelée in 1902 and Washington State's Mount St Helens in 1980. In the bigger eruptions, the effects were felt over several thousand square miles, each time with accompanying 'plagues' such as a vast, choking ash cloud, severe weather disturbances and disruption of animal life.

This raises two questions. Could such far-flung effects of the Minoan-period eruption have reached northern Egypt? If so, could they have been responsible for the Biblical 'plagues' which reportedly so overawed the Egyptians that they allowed those they had enslaved to leave with their 'flocks and herds' (Exodus 12:32)? Undeniably, there are some highly provocative parallels between commonly reported accompaniments of modern-day volcanic eruptions and the Biblically-reported 'plagues':

Exodus 7:20-21	*Volcanic eruption phenomena*
All the water in the Nile was turned into blood and the fish in the Nile died.	Even at times of minor activity from the Thera volcano, submarine exhalations of iron oxide can colour the sea red for several miles around, killing fish up to 20 miles away.
Exodus 10:21-23 Thick darkness descended upon the land of Egypt for three days. People could not see one another, and for three days no one could get up from where he was.	Ash clouds from major volcanic eruptions characteristically plunge the regions they pass over into prolonged daytime darkness. The island of Java, for instance, 300 miles from Tambora, experienced thirty-six hours of pitch darkness when the Tambora ash cloud passed over it in 1815.
Exodus 9:23-26 Thunder and hail rained down . . . The hail was very heavy – fire flashing in the midst of hail – such as had not fallen on the land of Egypt since it had become a nation. Throughout the land of Egypt the hail struck down all that were in the open, both man and beast; the hail also struck down all the grasses of the field[s] and shattered all the trees . . .	Thunder-like noises from the Krakatau eruption were heard at Alice Springs and even Perth in Australia, up to 3000 miles away. Heavy showers of pellety volcanic ash and actual hail commonly affect places thousands of miles away. Vermont in the USA, for instance, was just one of many places that experienced exceptionally-heavy and unseasonal hail for up to a year after the Tambora eruption.
Exodus 9:8-11 A fine dust . . . [will] cause an inflammation breaking out in boils on man and beast throughout the land of Egypt.	Ash from volcanic eruptions can cause severe skin irritations. People in the path of the Mount St Helens ash cloud covered their skin for this reason.
Exodus 9:6 All the livestock of the Egyptians died.	Grazing animals are common casualties of volcanic eruptions, both as a result of asphyxia and of ash smothering and poisoning the vegetation they feed on. In the Mount St Helens eruption, plants 250 miles away became so thickly coated with ash that all photosynthesis was halted.
Exodus 8:2; also 10:13-15 Frogs came up and covered the land . . . locusts invaded all the land of Egypt . . . in a thick mass; never before had there been so many . . . they ate up all the grasses, and all the fruit of the trees which the hail had left.	Unusual swarmings of insects and other pests have been commonly reported accompaniments of modern-day eruptions: e.g. stinging yellow ants, foot-long black centipedes and deadly tropical vipers as a preliminary to the Mount Pelée eruption of 1902.

How the 'first born' of Egypt died? (Exodus 12:29). A relief from the Temple of Amun at Karnak shows the Canaanites sacrificing their first-born from a city's walls, in order to appease the wrath of their gods. Note the small boy on the right is being held by a woman, arguably a priestess, while the girl on the left is being held by a man.

The Biblical story's final 'plague' – the death of the first-born (Exodus 12: 29-30) – is easy enough to interpret as a classic response to divine anger by the many people in the Nile Delta who still worshipped the Hyksos/Canaanite gods. For these, as we have seen, human sacrifice was the recognised way of appeasing the gods in moments of such *extremis*, as evident from a Canaanitic text found at Ugarit, prescribing such an offering to Baal:

> A first-born, Baal, we shall sacrifice
> A child we shall fulfil.[9]

Egyptian reliefs at Thebes, dating from the 13th century BC, show urban Canaanites under siege offering their children to the gods. It was an attempt to prevent their city being captured by the Egyptians. Their response during a natural disaster would have been the same. Arguably, only Jacob's descendants, the herdspeople, because of the transcending circumcision rite instituted by their ancestor Abraham, would have felt no obligation to adhere to this: hence, their famous 'passing over' in the case of this particular plague.

But is there any Egyptian documentation of such a catastrophe? Although this period is so poorly documented, in the late 1940s French archaeologists working at the Temple of Karnak, Luxor, found fragments of a stele set up by Ahmose. Despite being broken and with some of its opening section missing, the following extract offers some hints:

> (7) . . . the gods declared their
> (8) discontent. . . The gods [caused] the sky to come in a tempest of r[ain], with darkness in the western region and the sky being
> (9) unleashed, without [cessation, louder than] the cries of the masses, . . . [while the rain raged] on the mountains louder than the noise of the
> (10) cataract which is at Elephantine. Every house, every quarter that they reached . . .
> (11) . . . floating on the water like skiffs of papyrus opposite the royal residence for a period of . . . day(s)
> (12) while a torch could not be lit in the Two Lands [i.e. anywhere in Egypt][10]

The fascination of this text, as its French editor Claude Vandersleyen has pointed out[11], is that such an elaborate account of a natural disaster is unique in Egyptian records. Even the normally ultra-sceptical Donald Redford had to acknowledge: 'The striking resemblance between this catastrophic storm and some of the traditional [Biblical] "plagues" seems more than fortuitous.'[12] A feature is that the whole country, as far south as Thebes, seems to have been affected. Had this happened almost anywhere else, it might have seemed nothing untoward – but in rainless Egypt . . . ? In fact, torrential rain, either out of season or in places where it does not normally happen at all, is typical of the far-flung effects of major volcanic eruptions. In the case of the Tambora eruption of 1815, weather patterns around the world were severely affected for over a year.

Nor is this all. Recently, while excavating the remains of a royal palace on the ancient Avaris site, Manfred Bietak came across a number of lumps of pumice.[13] The context in which some were found was sufficiently sealed for him to date them positively: they must have been deposited in this location some time between Ahmose's reign and that of Pharaoh Tuthmosis II, i.e. approximately the period 1524-1479 BC. Scientific analysis confirmed that these lumps derived from the Thera eruption.[14]

But the further corollary to this finding, one that took even Bietak by surprise, was that the same royal palace in which the pumice lumps were found, together with an

Based on a reconstruction by Dr Manfred Bietak, an artist's impression of the 'enormous platform' of mud-brick which the 18th-century BC Pharaoh Ahmose built at Avaris following his victory over the Hyksos/Canaanites. Was it this one which the Biblical 'sons of Jacob' toiled with 'mortar and bricks'?

accompanying 'enormous platform'[15] and other related constructions, was not of Hyksos/Canaanite construction as he had previously supposed. Instead, there was evidence that these edifices had been built for Egyptian royal occupation just after the fall of Avaris. The palace had been constructed to quite magnificent standards, and included, most unusually, a section decorated with Minoan frescoes. Some scholars have speculated that Pharaoh Ahmose's mother, Queen Aahotpe, was a Minoan.[16]

These findings answer satisfactorily all the former objections that the Biblical Exodus could not have happened during the 18th Dynasty, because the 18th Dynasty monarchs remained based in Thebes. Undeniably, immediately after defeating the Hyksos/ Canaanites, Ahmose, the 18th Dynasty's founder, built a palace, as if for his own occupation, at Avaris. And Avaris was little more than a stone's throw from where Jacob's descendants, with their herds, would have been based at their Goshen. Equally clearly, Ahmose was minded to make his edifice as impregnable as possible from any Canaanitic attempt to recapture it. So he put in hand the building of an 'enormous platform', the original extent of which has yet to be uncovered, but which would have needed an enormous amount of unskilled manpower. Then we learn, unsurprisingly, that this fortification platform was made of mud-brick, the standard building material in the Nile Delta. It is surely impossible not to recall the book of Exodus's so-anguished words describing the forced conscription of those who had previously lived as animal herders:

> The Egyptians ruthlessly imposed upon the Israelites the various labours that they had made them perform. Ruthlessly they made life bitter for them with harsh labour at mortar and bricks and with all sorts of tasks in the field.
> (Exodus 1:13-14)

There is good reason, therefore, for believing that Ahmose rounded up all the Asiatic Nile Delta residents, including Jacob's descendants, who had been unable to make a quick escape with the Canaanitic war-lords. He forced them into the work necessary to make Avaris, the future Ramesses, an Egyptian capital and 'garrison city' (Exodus 1:11), after its fall as a Canaanite/Hyksos one. Arguably, therefore, the 18th Dynasty's Ahmose, not the 19th Dynasty's Ramesses II, was the true pharaoh of the Biblical oppression.

This leads to another question. If it had been Ahmose's policy to make Avaris a capital city, and to force the local captured Asiatics to work on rebuilding and refortifying it, what was it that subsequently caused him to change his mind on both counts: abandoning Avaris in favour of Thebes, and allowing the '240,000 entire households with their possessions' to leave the country?

As shown by the Ahmose inscription at Luxor, there was, specifically in Ahmose's reign and arguably triggered by the Thera eruption, an unprecedented storm-type natural disaster. In accord with contemporary wisdom, Ahmose would have attributed this to the 'discontent' of the gods. A major attribute of Baal/Seth, the Canaanitic god of Avaris, was his power over storms. Doubtless, Ahmose would have interpreted the daytime darkness and all the other 'plague' phenomena as signs that this god needed appeasing for the defeat of his people. In the light of this, Ahmose may have considered it prudent to base himself back at Thebes, whose god Amun had given him his victory. Confronted with petitions from the leaders of the accursed Asiatics who had multiplied so disastrously while in the Delta, he may well also have felt pushed into allowing them their freedom, on condition that they quit Egyptian territory, taking their 'flocks and herds' with them. Arguably, it was in such circumstances that the mass evacuation of 240,000 described by Manetho took place. Equally arguably, one group among these was the descendants of Jacob who, according to Exodus, had been living in Goshen in Avaris' closest environs.

'The Egyptians ruthlessly ... made life bitter for them with harsh labour at mortar and bricks.' (Exodus 1:13-14). This scene of brick-making comes from the tomb of the 18th dynasty 'prime minister' Rekhmire, on the west bank at Luxor.

As Exodus makes clear, it was all very frightening and confused as this evacuee band hastened to take the same Way of the Sea route out of Egypt that the fleeing Canaanite war-lords would have used for their dash to Sharuhen. Along the Mediterranean coast this road ran through a region referred to in Egyptian texts as the 'marshes of Twfy', noted for its rushes or reeds. A relief of the 19th Dynasty pharaoh Seti I provides a graphic near-contemporary image of this as a reed-lined body of crocodile-infested water controlled by an army frontier-post, the 'Wall of the Ruler'. Given the confused nature of the events, the Egyptians guarding this post may well not have received the royal instructions that the previously enslaved Asiatics should be allowed to depart.

Whatever the case, in the Biblical account what happened next was the so-called 'Miracle of the Sea'. Purportedly, the *Yam suph*, or 'sea of reeds', in the frontier's vicinity miraculously dried enough to allow the evacuees to cross it, then returned with a huge rush that swamped the Egyptian army chariotry (Exodus 14). At face value it is, of course, one of those 'tall stories' that the rationalist understandably tosses aside as so much moonshine, and no doubt the original facts have become distorted in the retelling.

Yet Biblical textual scholars point to the 'victory song' that accompanies the 'J', or 'Yahwist', strand of the story in Exodus 15:1-18, complete with a women's version that follows as verses 20-21:

Sing to Yahweh, for he has triumphed gloriously;
Horse and rider he has hurled into the sea.[17]

A relief of the 19th Dynasty pharaoh Seti I shows Egypt's north-eastern frontier, often referred to in Egyptian texts as the 'Wall of the Ruler', as a marshy region infested with crocodiles, and controlled by an army post.

This happens to embody Hebrew language characteristics indicating that it genuinely is one of the oldest elements in the entire Bible, older than either the 'J' or 'E' textual strands.

Furthermore, no circumstance could be more supportive of the theory that a volcano was indeed highly active somewhere in the Mediterranean. For it is a matter of hard scientific fact that tsunamis, or grossly exaggerated tidal movements, are common accompaniments of major eruptions. This happened, for example, in August 1883 at Bandora, on the west coast of India, shortly after Krakatau had erupted 3000 miles to the east:

> An extraordinary phenomenon of tides was witnessed . . . The tide came in, at its usual time, and in a proper way. After some time the reflux of the tide went to the sea in an abrupt manner and with great impetus, and the fish not having time to retire with the waves, remained scattered on the seashore and dry places. And the fishermen, young and old, had a good and very easy task to perform in capturing food-sized and palatable fish . . . being an extraordinary event never seen or heard before by the old men.[18]

As the report continues, the return of the sea later that day was no less extraordinary:

> Suddenly the flux came with a great current of water, more swift than a horse's running.

Arguably, the sight of such an extraordinary phenomenon on the Way of the Sea, particularly the unexpected tidal inrush that swamped the Egyptian chariotry, could not have been regarded by 'Jacob's brood' as anything other than a 'sign and wonder' *par excellence*. Good cause, therefore, for very quickly immortalising it in a celebratory song extolling their god Yahweh for his 'strength', for his 'warrior' qualities and his capacity to deliver his people. For us, of course, the altogether more sober deductions, that these events happened in the reign of Pharaoh Ahmose (*c.*1550-1525 BC), and were related to the island of Thera erupting 600 miles away, must remain at best tentative. Even giving a date to the Thera eruption, which according to geologists was a two-stage event, perhaps a couple of decades apart, remains far from sure[19]. All that can be said is that dating the Biblical Exodus events to the reign of the 18th Dynasty's pharaoh Ahmose, and thereby towards the end of the 16th century BC, seems more sensible than dating them to around the time of Ramesses II two centuries later, even though the latter remains the prevailing wisdom. Whenever it happened, if 'Jacob's brood' had genuinely made their escape across the Egyptian frontier, what next lay in store for them?

5

WITH MOSES IN NO MAN'S LAND

THE EGYPTIANS were apparently desperate to set free those they had hitherto enslaved. As we noted earlier, this strongly indicates that they regarded the Thera-linked 'plagues' as some exceptionally powerful magic by the god of the defeated Asiatics. Reportedly, the Egyptians not only positively encouraged those with 'flocks and herds' (Exodus 12:31) to take these with them – the animals seem to have survived rather better than the Egyptians' own cattle – they also provided 'objects of silver and gold, and clothing' (Exodus 12:35). The silver and gold were a form of currency. The clothing was an essential for slaves, who were mostly kept semi-naked, for going out into the world again. The overall impression from such largesse is that the Egyptians believed the Asiatics had put some kind of curse on their country, and were extremely anxious to be released from it. Manetho's later comment that the Egyptians had 'a horror of shepherds' quite possibly denoted a lingering folk memory of these events.

Once the Asiatic evacuees had safely crossed the Egyptian border, where should they go next? The unexpectedness of their release meant that they had no chance to make advance plans. Their large numbers and the fact that they had lived for so many centuries in the Nile Delta meant that they could hardly expect to be welcomed back anywhere. Some of the more pure-bred Canaanites might have felt sufficiently acceptable to carry on along the Way of the Sea and take the direct route back into Canaan, just as their chariot-borne overlords had done earlier. But for the Turkey-originating and Habiru-tinged 'sons of Jacob', who had never been closer to Canaanitic society than merely camping on its fringes, no such option existed. According to Exodus, their one firm decision was not to 'take the road to the land of the Philistines, although this was the nearest way' (Exodus 13:17) – incidentally, this is another clear instance of a subsequent Biblical editor anachronistically supplying a geographical name from his own time, since the Philistines did not even begin to occupy this coastal strip until much later. The districts of Canaan that were most readily approached from Egypt were already occupied by 'Amalekites . . . in the Negev region; Hittites, Jebusites and Amorites . . . [in] the hill country, and Canaanites . . . by the sea and along the Jordan'

A satellite photograph of the triangular-shaped Sinai peninsula. Although arid, parts are to this day capable of sustaining numbers of itinerant herds-people and their grazing animals.

(Numbers 13:29). These peoples were all apparently regarded as too strong to be confronted directly, at least at this very early stage.

Clearly, in such circumstances someone very inspired was needed to take the difficult decisions, and the Biblical record leaves us in no doubt about that person's name: Moses. We have to accept Moses as another Biblical character who is not mentioned in any other contemporary source. Scepticism is certainly legitimate concerning his infancy story in which an Egyptian princess is said to have found him adrift on the Nile in a 'basket of rushes'. An almost identical tale, dating back to the 3rd millennium BC, had been told of the Mesopotamian Sargon of Akkad[1].

Altogether more credible is the suggestion that Moses' upbringing was very Egyptian, despite his parents' reported descent from Jacob's son Levi, which automatically placed him in the priestly caste. The Egyptian influence is consistent

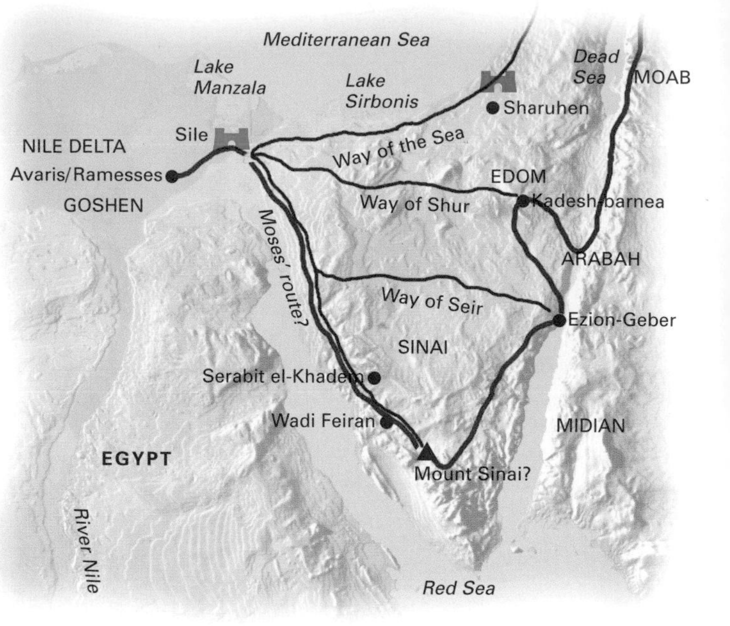

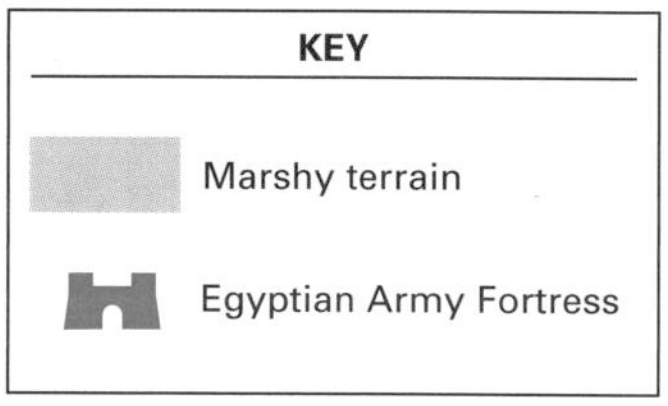

Which route across the Sinai did Moses and his followers take after fleeing Egypt? Of various proposed alternatives, including the Way of Seir, still used by Mecca-bound Moslems, the likeliest is the most southerly, skirting the Jebel Musa, traditionally believed to have been the Biblical Mount Sinai.

with what is known of the ousted former Canaanite rulers of Avaris, that they adopted some very Egyptian ways, just as the Romans would later adopt many Greek ways. It is also evident in his name, 'Moses', now common in Hebrew as 'Moshe', but actually Egyptian in origin. In the vowel-less written form of ancient Egyptian, 'ms' literally means 'born of'. As any perusal of pharaoh lists shows, it was a popular affix to Egyptian royal names during the second half of the 2nd millennium BC, hence Kamose (born of the spirit), Ramesses (born of Ra) and Tuthmosis (born of Thoth).

So what sort of individual was Moses? We might expect a stateless, refugee band of newly-freed slaves to look to some demagogic Rambo as their leader. Moses, however, despite his killing of an Egyptian overseer and being obliged to go into exile for it, was apparently rather inarticulate (Exodus 4:10) and 'the most humble of men' (Numbers 12:3). Biblically, his chief quality was his intense rapport with the god he is said to have encountered during his exile in a 'burning bush' on a desert mountain (Exodus 3). He and at least one group among those following him ascribed their escape from Egypt to this god. Indeed, on the strength of his 'bush encounter', it seems to have been Moses who determined that henceforth Isra-el's sons should know this god, not as El, but as Yahweh or 'I AM WHO AM' (Exodus 3:13-15).

Also, although Moses is usually described in English Biblical translations as a 'prophet', the term is actually misleading, since the original Hebrew word *nabi* denotes, not a fortune-teller, but someone 'flowing' or 'welling up' with the words of a deity speaking from within him. For this reason, in this book, the word will be left in its original Hebrew. As will become evident later, the Canaanites already had their own caste of such *nabiim* (the plural form), who acted as voice-pieces for their gods Baal and El. Moses was the first and greatest of those who performed the same function for Yahweh.

For the motley band of evacuees, their immediate priority was choosing the best route to avoid the peoples who already occupied southern Canaan. The Biblical text gives a long series of place-names, but these are so obscure – for the most part they were probably remote watering-holes frequented only by nomads – that trying to trace them on any present-day map of the Sinai peninsula is very difficult. One late-in-the-itinerary location that modern-day scholars are generally agreed upon is Kadesh-barnea (Numbers 20:1), thought to have been the present-day Tell Ein-el-Qudeirat in the Negev desert, well to the Sinai's north. It is the earlier tortuous, cross-Sinai itinerary that poses the challenge. Ironically, of the variety of routes suggested, it is the one that looks least likely that continues to attract the greatest reasoned support. It runs south-eastwards away from Canaan, down Sinai's eastern coastline, towards the mountainous country at Sinai's southernmost tip.

The southern Sinai route would have taken the group with all its herds and possessions hundreds of miles in the wrong direction. Even so, as the veteran Israeli archaeologist Itzhaq Beit-Arieh has pointed out[2], it is the only area in the entire peninsula with

The Wadi Feiran oasis, which some identify as the Biblical 'Elim', as it looks today. Behind is the Jebel Serbal, thought by some to have been the Biblical Mount Sinai.

sufficient water, camel-thorn bush and other resources capable of sustaining a sizeable number of itinerant herdspeople and their grazing animals. Admittedly, that number would have to be more in the order of the region's present-day 10,000 nomadic and semi-nomadic Bedouin inhabitants, rather than the Biblical 600,000 evacuee males of Numbers 26:51, or the 240,000 refugee households of the later Egyptian chronicler Manetho. Yet an exodus even of 10,000 would have been an impressive number by ancient population standards. In the case of this southern route, among a series of present-day oases that may correspond to the ones listed in the Bible, the picturesque Wadi Feiran is particularly compelling. Early Christian monks confidently identified it as Exodus 15:27's Elim with its 'twelve water springs and seventy palm trees'.

Whatever the group's exact route, it was imperative that at least one of them knew the region well enough to guide them through it. This person would also have to know that any peoples already inhabiting it were well disposed. In this regard, the second chapter of Exodus assumes fresh significance. It tells us that after Moses had killed the Egyptian overseer he fled to 'the land of Midian', a territory usually indicated rather vaguely in Bible atlases as just to the east of the Sinai. According to the ancient

Egyptians, it was inhabited by tribes they described as *Shosu*, or foot-slogging pastoralists. This is consistent with the occupation the Bible itself ascribes to the Midianites. Moreover, directly contemporary Egyptian sources[3] specifically name the god of these peoples as *Yhw*, i.e. Yahweh. Scholars increasingly accept the reference as the earliest extra-Biblical occurrence in ancient documents of this god name. Furthermore, according to Exodus 2:21, during his earlier stay with the Midianites, Moses had married a daughter of their priest Jethro. It seems scarcely coincidental that the first friendly encounter he and his followers had in the Sinai should have been with this same Jethro. Reportedly, Jethro made a special journey to their encampment, and there listened to the story of how they had escaped Egypt, sacrificed with them a burnt offering to Yahweh and advised his son-in-law on how best to set up a legal system for this multitude.

This said, it has so far proved impossible to find unequivocal archaeological evidence for this or any other tarryings in the southern Sinai by Moses' followers. If their utensils were mostly biodegradable animal skins and crude handmade pots, they may well have left little by which they could ever be positively identified. Nonetheless, at least a thousand years before Moses' time, the Egyptians were already visiting the region to exploit its copper and turquoise deposits. Using the local Midianites as workers, they established major mining settlements at sites known today as Wadi Maghara and Serabit

Below: Serabit el-Khadem, one of the Egyptians' important mining centres in southern Sinai. Right: A figurine bearing the writing directly ancestral to the Hebrew alphabet, and dating to the 15th-century BC 'Exodus' period, as discovered at Serabit el-Khadem.

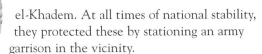

el-Khadem. At all times of national stability, they protected these by stationing an army garrison in the vicinity.

Had such a garrison been stationed in the southern Sinai at the time of the Exodus, we can be virtually certain that Moses and his followers would have chosen another route. But in this period of hiatus between the Hyksos/Canaanite and Egyptian regimes, the region was unlikely to have such a garrison, giving Moses and his group the opportunity to linger in it at least temporarily.

In this regard, just over a century ago, the pioneering British archaeologist Sir William Flinders Petrie made a fascinating discovery at Serabit el-Khadem. He found a series of inscriptions in a curious and interesting-looking pictographic-alphabetic script dating, apparently, from around 1500 BC – that is, the very time, according to our reconstruction, of the Biblical wanderings in the wilderness. The inscriptions were found on a sandstone sphinx[4] now in the British Museum, and on a number of other statues as

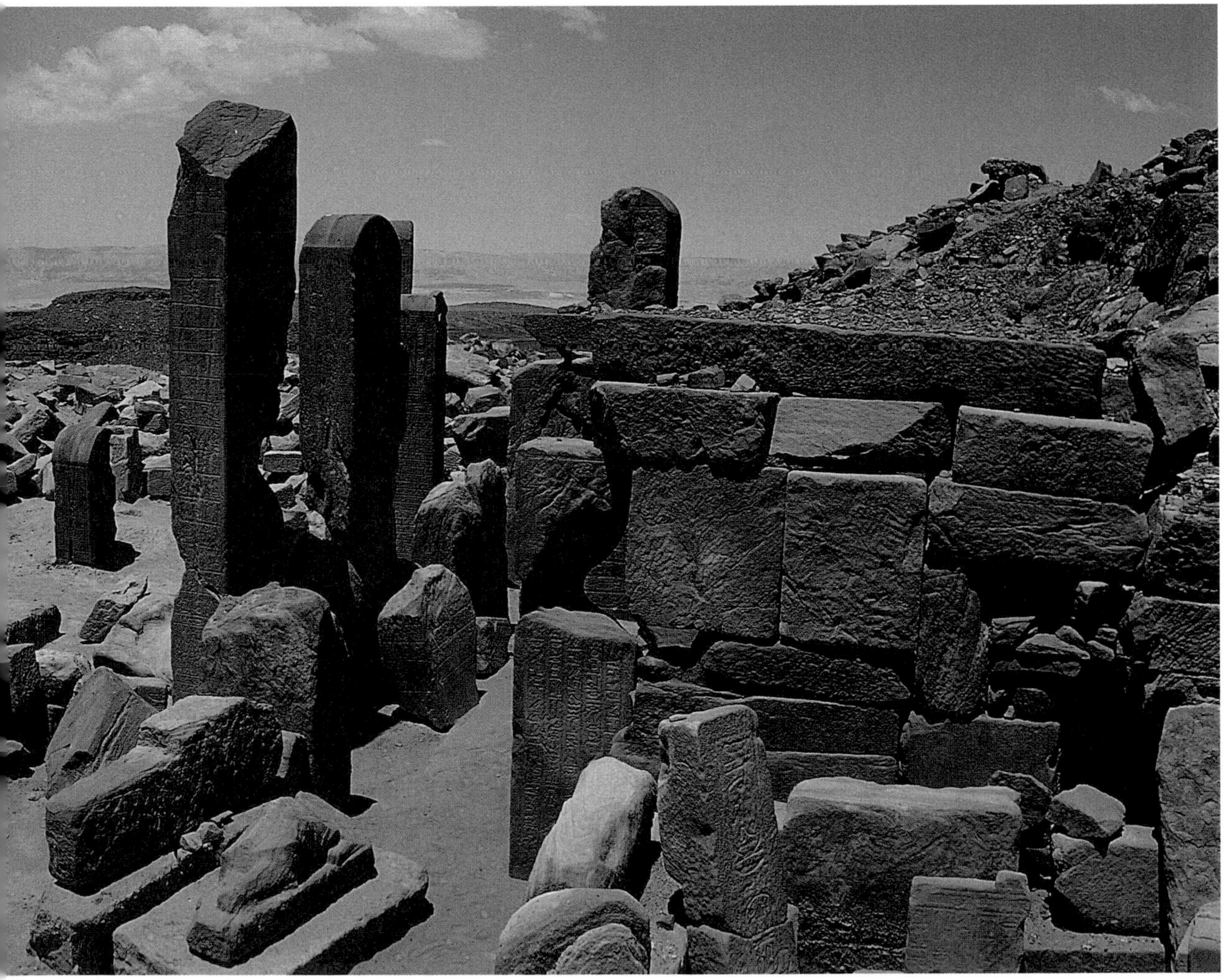

A	B	G	D	H	W	Z	H	T	Y	K	L	M	N	S	'	P	Q	R	S	T
	OX	HOUSE		FISH	E MAN AT PRAYER	TH	I	E FENCE?			PALM OF HAND	OX-GOAD	WATER	SNAKE	X	O EYE	THROW STICK		HUMAN HEAD	BOW	CROSS
PROTO-SINAITIC SCRIPT 15th c. BC																					
BYBLOS TOMB (Phoenician) 10th c. BC																					
MOABITE STONE (Moabite/Hebrew) 9th c. BC																					
ROYAL JAR HANDLES (Hebrew) 8th c. BC																					
LACHISH POTSHERD (Hebrew) 6th c. BC																					
ARAMAIC PAPYRUS (Aramaic) 5th c. BC																					
DEAD SEA SCROLL (Hebrew) 1st c. BC																					
HEBREW BIBLE 9th c. AD																					
GREEK ALPHABET	A	B	Γ	Δ	E	(F)	Z	H	Θ	I	K	Λ	M	N	Ξ	O	Π	Q	P	Σ	T

well as rock faces in the vicinity. Their most intriguing feature is that, although written in pictographs which are clearly based on Egyptian hieroglyphs, the language itself is Semitic-Canaanite, the very tongue that Moses and his followers would have spoken. Scholars generally agree that this so-called Proto-Sinaitic script was the direct ancestor of both written Hebrew and our own alphabet.

Obviously, given the still tentative dating of the Exodus to the late 16th or early 15th century BC, it would be optimistic in the extreme to claim that these inscriptions were written by Moses and his followers. Nor is there any sign of Yahwism, for some refer to *Ba'lat*, 'the Lady', denoting the Canaanite goddess Astarte/Ashtoreth. Nonetheless, one thing is undeniable. Immediately after the Jethro rendezvous, Moses is described as going up Mount Sinai to receive the Ten Commandments from Yahweh, whereupon the first-ever mention of writing in the Bible occurs. According to Exodus 32, Moses descended from Mount Sinai with tablets of stone which, at Yahweh's dictation, he had inscribed 'on the one side and on the other' (Exodus 32:15). These sound uncannily like the stelae that were fashionable in both Egypt and Mesopotamia around this time.

As intriguing as the tablets themselves is the revolution in socio-religious mentality they represented. Once they left Egypt, Moses and his followers would have become stateless. They passed outside the jurisdiction of any king, becoming, in effect, true *Habiru*. Yet Moses' adopted policy, rather than try to impose himself as some kind of king or chieftain, was apparently to act as a voice-piece expressing the will of the similarly stateless and homeless god he represented. Among the 'new' laws he 'received' was one proscribing the polygamous way of life that even Abraham and other ancestors had led. The incestuous marriage of brother and sister as practised among native Egyptian royalty was also proscribed, along with much else. When it came to interpreting how such laws should be administered, Moses made it clear that no king was needed. The key lay in god-given decisions, expressed by a collectively-recognised, god-speaking man like himself.

Another thing is clear from the book of Exodus, and supportive of its underlying truth. While Moses personally may have been against worshipping any god image in an urban temple, in the manner of the Canaanites, there were certainly some people among his followers who had been brought up in such practices and were not minded to abandon them. Illustrating this is the story of the so-called 'golden calf', the idol which infuriated

Although written in pictographs based on Egyptian hieroglyphs, the characters of the so-called Proto-Sinaitic script, found at Serabit el-Khadem, later developed into Hebrew characters and, via Greek, into our modern-day alphabet. The Serabit el-Khadem finds were among the earliest alphabetic inscriptions yet discovered. One possibility is that the script originated a century or so earlier among the generation of Canaanites who controlled Avaris before this was won back by the Egyptians.

Moses, even though his own priestly brother Aaron was involved in creating it, particularly when he found everyone dancing to it when he came down from Sinai.

As we are told in Exodus 32, this 'calf' was not something the evacuees had brought with them out of Egypt. Instead, it had to be specially crafted from the jewellery the Egyptians had given them, suggesting that they had been obliged to leave behind any or all god statues. But if that was the case, why a calf? In fact, this is another example of mistranslation by the King James Bible editors. The more accurate rendition from the Hebrew is 'young bull', which as we have already seen was one of the forms taken by the Canaanite god Baal.

As recently as 1990, archaeologists working at Ashkelon on the coast of present-day Israel found a silvered bronze statuette of just such a young bull, surrounded by the remains of a pottery-type shrine. Surprisingly tiny, just 4½ inches long by 4 inches high, it probably stood in the shrine[5] inside a sanctuary at the foot of Ashkelon's mid-2nd millennium BC ramparts. Visitors were most likely expected to make an offering to it before they ascended the ramp leading to the city's gate. It may be recalled that a similar young bull, flanked by winged sphinxes, and again identified as the god Baal/El, features in the topmost register of the Canaanitic cult stand found at Taanach. A further Canaanitic feature in the Exodus story is the description of Moses' followers 'dancing' before the statue. Much later in the Bible, priests of Baal are described as performing a distinctive 'hopping dance about the altar', in association with the sacrifice of a bull, in the time of the *nabi* Elijah (1 Kings 18:26).

A silver 'calf', or more accurately, young bull, dating to the middle of the 2nd millennium BC, discovered in 1990 during excavations at Ashkelon. Just 4 inches high, it was found amidst the broken pieces of its ceramic 'shrine', seen here re-assembled.

Arguably, therefore, the Exodus story accurately describes the kind of object any Canaanites among Moses' band were likely to worship. At the same time, it tells us that many of those who came out of Egypt with Moses clung to that culture's traditional belief system. Even from the Biblical record, then, it seems misguided to suppose that anything resembling the 'religion of Abraham, Jacob and Joseph' had become at all firmly established. Those who left Egypt may have included both 'Mosesite' followers of Yahweh, and 'Aaronite' followers of Baal/El and Astarte, with the golden calf incident as the first of many in which these two belief systems came into serious conflict.

If, therefore, we accept both the golden calf and Moses' tablets as credible one-time historical objects, what of that equally famous object: the container for the tablets

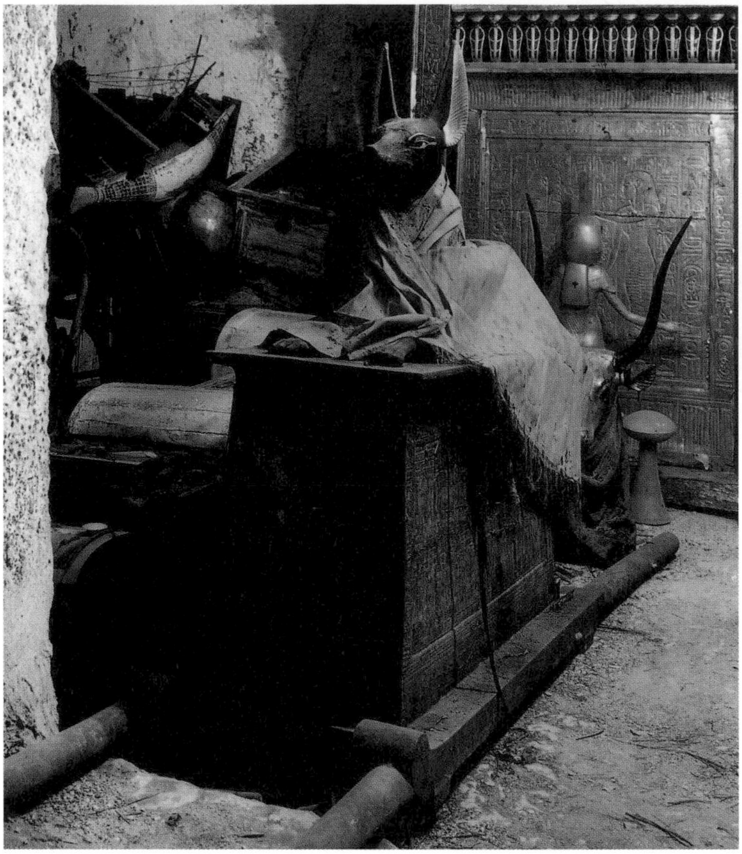

known as the Ark (from the Latin *arca*, a chest, after its Hebrew equivalent *aron*)? Apparently, just as the golden calf was constructed in the Sinai desert, so too was the Ark. Its maker, one of several metalworkers among the evacuees, was named Bezaleel ben Uri (Exodus 35:30), literally 'In the shadow of El, the son of my Light', and therefore one belonging to the El, rather than the Yahweh faction.

As in the case of the golden calf, melted-down ornaments from the Egyptians were used for the Ark's metal components. Fascinatingly, the copper workings in the southern Sinai could have provided the furnaces for such work. There is also something very Egyptian about what we are told of the Ark's construction details. By converting the Biblical cubit into its known imperial equivalent, we can deduce it to have been a rectangular chest, measuring nearly 4 feet long by just over 2 feet high and 2 feet wide. It was made from gilded 'shittim' wood, generally understood to be acacia, with two winged 'cherubim' on its lid (Exodus 25:18-22; 37:7-9). It was transported using two long wooden carrying poles (Exodus 37:4; 1 Kings 8:8).

Prototype for the Biblical Ark? This gilded wooden shrine with long carrying poles, topped with a statue of Anubis, appears as it was first found on the opening up of the tomb of Tutankhamun. The Biblical Ark would have been similar in size and materials, but topped with winged sphinxes in place of Anubis.

We can be confident of these details from supportive descriptions dating from a time when the Ark was an undoubted historical object. In addition, similar Egyptian chests from around this same period are strikingly suggestive of its construction by a people newly out of Egypt. For instance, when Egyptologist Howard Carter opened up Tutankhamun's tomb in the 1920s, he found immediately in front of the entrance to its Treasury a gilded wood shrine, measuring 3 feet 2 inches by 1 foot 9 inches, with an image of the jackal god Anubis on its lid. It was equipped with 9-foot-long carrying poles. In the Temple of Karnak at Luxor a similar long-poled Ark, or *barque*, of the god Khonsu is depicted. Shaven-headed priests are carrying it in procession during the Opet festival.

Common ornaments in such shrines were winged 'angelic' beings, variously referred to as 'sphinxes' or 'cherubim'. They were depicted fanning their wings to symbolise the way they were believed to protect the divinity housed within the shrine. Examples of these can be seen on either side of the Khonsu shrine, also on either side of the golden calf on the Canaanitic cult stand found at Taanach. They also feature on royal thrones. So is it coincidence that the Biblical Ark made by Bezaleel ben Uri was reportedly topped by two similar winged cherubim, flanking an empty space believed to be the very throne of the invisible Yahweh?

If we are honest, the lines between the old Canaanitic religion and Moses' Yahwism, as these existed during the 2nd millennium BC, are likely to have been very much more blurred than we might suppose from the Biblical text. The same would also be true of the

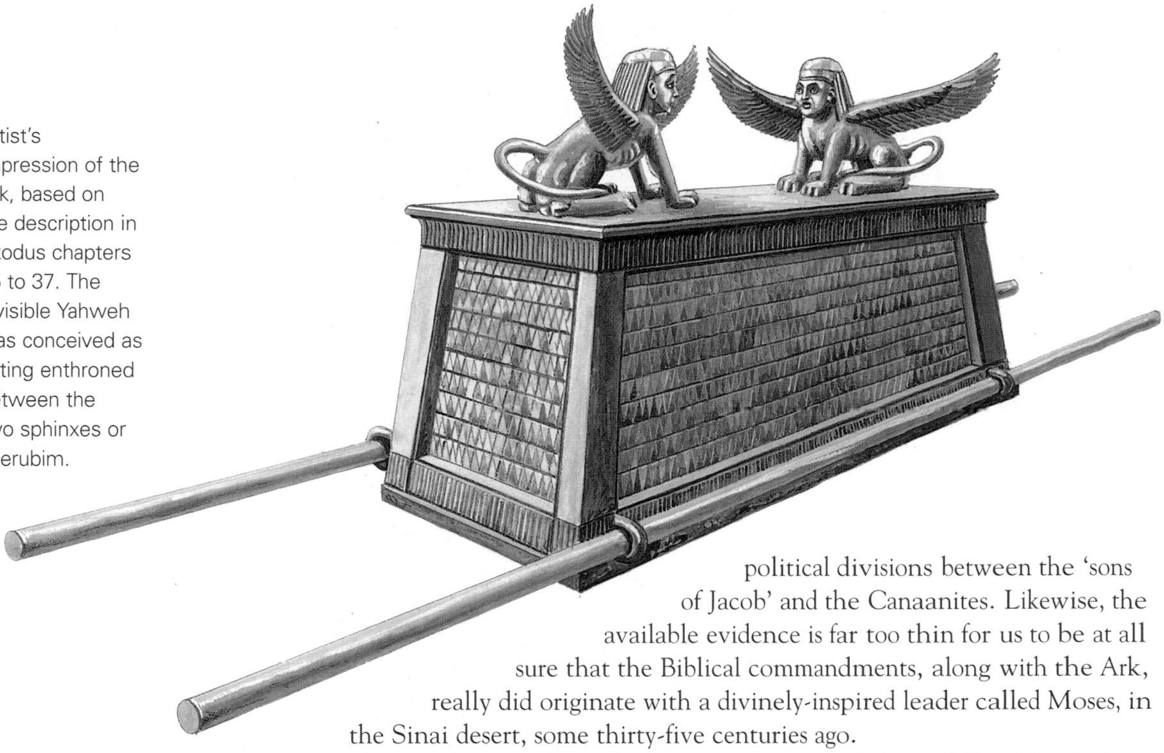

Artist's impression of the Ark, based on the description in Exodus chapters 25 to 37. The invisible Yahweh was conceived as sitting enthroned between the two sphinxes or cherubim.

political divisions between the 'sons of Jacob' and the Canaanites. Likewise, the available evidence is far too thin for us to be at all sure that the Biblical commandments, along with the Ark, really did originate with a divinely-inspired leader called Moses, in the Sinai desert, some thirty-five centuries ago.

But whatever happened out there, some time around the middle of the 2nd millennium BC, a massive exodus of Asiatics from the Nile Delta did undoubtedly take place. It is also a matter of fact that at least one group proceeded northwards, ultimately dislodging some of the Canaanitic peoples they had previously feared so much. This was the 'conquest of Canaan', another of the Bible's stirring and well-known episodes. Yet if the task of evaluating the evidence has been difficult enough so far, trying to discern the historical truth of the conquest will be even more so.

Canaanite war-lord on his throne. Detail from an ivory knife-handle of *c.*12th century BC, found at Megiddo. Note again the winged sphinxes flanking the throne.

6

CONQUEST? WHAT CONQUEST?

ACCORDING TO the Biblical record, after Moses' followers had spent some time in the Sinai wilderness, they marched northwards to linger for a while at Kadesh-barnea. As noted earlier, this has been reliably identified as the present-day Tell Ein-el-Qudeirat. From there spies set out on a reconnaissance trip, and their report, plus the experience of some harrying by the southern Canaanites, made it clear that Canaan was still impenetrable from the south. Moses' followers then skirted the similarly unfriendly territories of kindred peoples such as the Edomites and the Moabites. Moses having died along the way, they pitched camp at Abel-Shittim (the Acacias), an unidentified site on the eastern side of the River Jordan opposite Jericho. Their approach plan was to travel north through the present-day kingdom of Jordan to a point where they could cross the River Jordan and strike into Canaan from the east. Beginning with the Battle of Jericho, their general Joshua led them to a series of victories, enabling them to secure a decisive foothold in the country, though not without some help from their Yahweh.

Various arguments have been voiced against this account of a northward advance. Among them is the absence of any evidence that the Edomite and Moabite peoples, described as having confronted Moses' followers along this route, existed during the second half of the 2nd millennium BC. During the 1930s American rabbi Nelson Glueck surveyed the purported 'Edomite' territory, east of the Dead Sea and south down the Arabah valley to Aqaba. His findings seemed to show that the region was empty, population-wise, throughout the 2nd millennium BC. In the early 1970s, excavations by British archaeologist Mrs Crystal Bennett at the Edomite capital Bozrah turned up no evidence that this had been settled before the 1st millennium BC[1]. And broadly the same findings have been claimed for Moabite Dibon, mentioned on the itinerary in Numbers 33. The present-day Tell Dhiban shows no signs of occupation corresponding to any conceivable date when the conquest might have occurred.

In fact, such claims prove just one thing. As in the case of Moses' followers in the Sinai, their kindred itinerant Shosu, such as the Edomites and Moabites, who used mostly animal-skins as containers, did not leave sufficiently lasting evidence

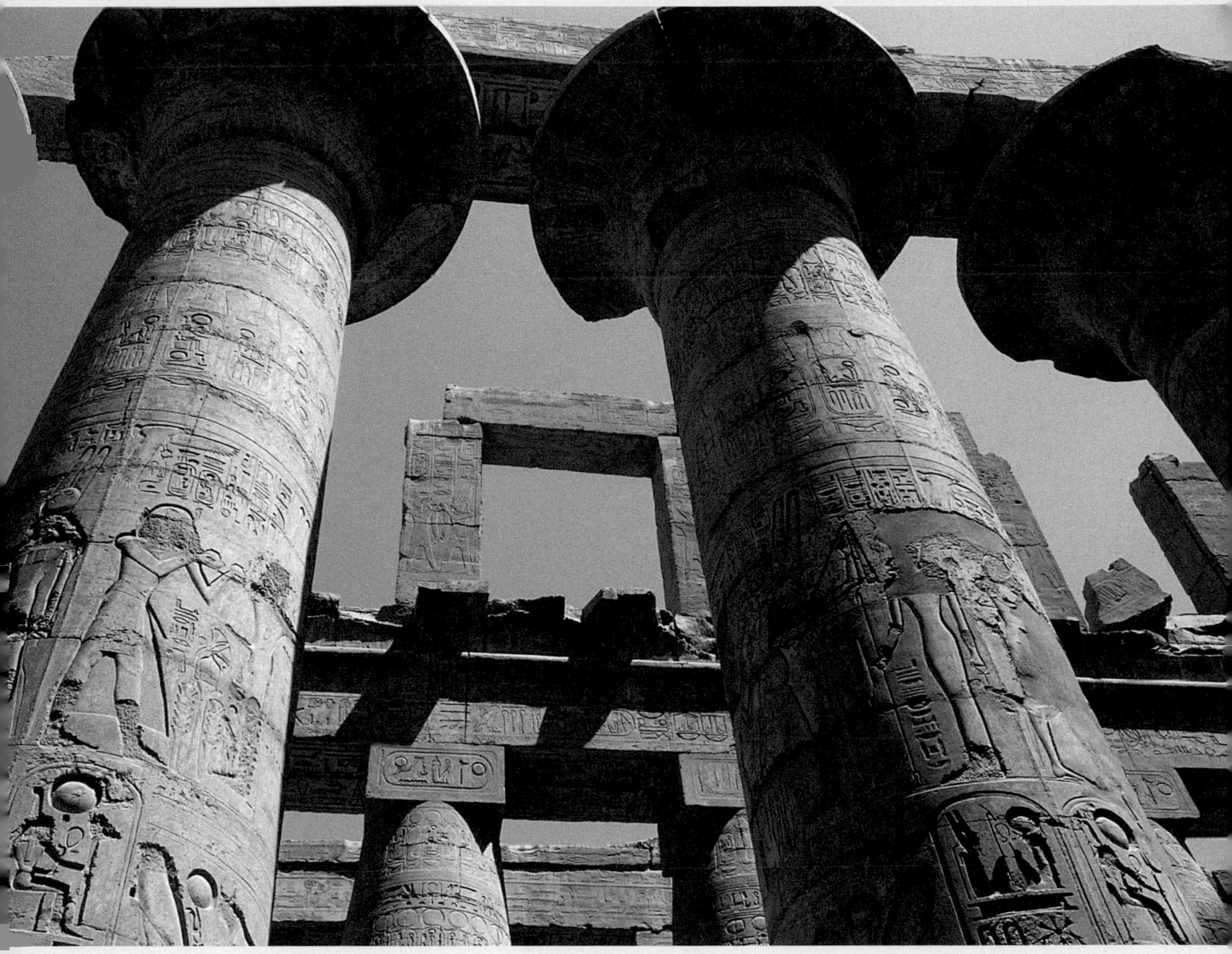

The walls of the Temple of Amun at Karnak include itineraries of ancient routes through what is now Jordan. These match the northwards route reportedly taken by Moses' followers.

of themselves for archaeologists to pick it up three millennia later. For not only are Nelson Glueck's interpretations today widely discredited archaeologically, but there is also unmistakable literary evidence that such Shosu-type animal-herders were active in Edom at least as early as the 13th century BC. This derives from an Egyptian papyrus of this period now held in the British Museum:

> The scribe Inena communicating to his lord . . . [We] have finished letting the Shosu tribes of Edom pass the fortress of [Pharaoh] Merneptah . . . to keep them alive and to keep their cattle alive . . .[2]

There is also confirmation of the northwards itinerary, 'Iyim . . . Dibon-gad . . . Abel-Shittim[3] . . . Jordan', as described in Numbers 33:45-50. Among ancient Egyptian campaign routes into Canaan inscribed on the walls of the Temple of

Karnak at Luxor is one from the time of Tuthmosis III in the 15th century BC. It lists 119 Canaanitic place-names, specifically including Iyin, Dibon, Abel and Jordan in exactly the same sequence as in the Bible, enabling American scholar Charles Krahmalkov to conclude as recently as 1994:

> The biblical story of the invasion of Transjordan that sets the stage for the conquest of all Palestine is told against a background that is historically accurate. The Israelite invasion route described in Numbers 33:50 was . . . an official, heavily trafficked Egyptian road through the Transjordan in the Late Bronze Age [i.e. *c.*1550-1200 BC]. And the city of Dibon was in fact a station on that road in the Late Bronze Age . . . To date archaeologists may not have found its ruins, but it surely existed.[4]

If the story of the progress of the refugee 'Israel' tribes has been credible thus far, what of the biblical account of the events that followed, the conquest of Canaan itself? For this, our main sources are the books of Joshua and Judges, which, together with the books of Samuel and Kings, form the so-called Deuteronomistic History. This is generally regarded as having been produced in its present form as late as the 7th century BC, but is believed to be based on earlier sources, now lost, Biblically referred to under names such as the 'Book of Jashar'[5] (Joshua 10:13; 2 Samuel 1:18) and the 'Book of the Wars of Yahweh' (Numbers 21:14). As in the case of the earlier canonical books, although later editorial anachronisms may have crept in, we should expect a firm basis of fact.

And at face value the book of Joshua does seem very factual. It relates how spies were sent out from the Abel-Shittim encampment to reconnoitre the Canaanite town of Jericho on the far side of the River Jordan, and the territory beyond it. This kind of preliminary information-gathering seems to have been a crucial feature of the insurgents' strategy. Once the spies had returned, the insurgents struck, aided by a friendly Jericho prostitute called Rahab. As in the case of the preceding Exodus events, there were some miraculous-seeming happenings, notably an interruption of the River Jordan's normal flow, enabling Joshua's men to ford it easily, along with the even more fortunate collapse of Jericho's walls. Following Jericho's capture, the narrative very matter-of-factly informs us of the steady fall of other towns, first Ai, then Hebron, Lachish and Eglon, all very credibly in the same central hill country earlier favoured by Abraham. Later, they took Hazor to the north. After each of their victories, it was apparently the custom of Joshua's fighting men to return to their wives, children and 'cattle', left behind at their new, within-Canaan base-camp, Gilgal.

This conquest is one of the best-known episodes in the Bible, but it is also one of the most seriously disputed. Thus, according to the German scholar Julius Wellhausen[6], the story of Jericho's fall sprang from a plot by later members of the large Judah tribe to rewrite their ancestral history in a way that was favourable to their own memory. According to Wellhausen's more recent compatriots Albrecht Alt and Martin Noth, supported by some distinguished Israeli archaeologists such as the late Yohanan Aharoni, there never was any conquest of Canaan. All that happened was that Joshua and his men, whoever they might have been, peacefully infiltrated areas that had previously gone unoccupied. As a further variant, Michigan University's George Mendenhall[7] has postulated the theory that some underprivileged Canaanite peasants merely revolted against their more aristocratic countrymen.

Ostensibly, there is some sound reasoning behind such views. For if an exodus dated around the Ramesses II era is accepted, the conquest of Canaan would have happened at the end of the Late Bronze Age, i.e. around 1200 BC or later. If this were the case, there can be no doubt, archaeologically, that the high-ramparted, walled cities Biblically described as confronting Joshua and his men would have presented no obstacle at all. For by then their walls had already long since gone. They had been tumbled back in the late 16th and 15th centuries BC. According to the conventional wisdom, this was the work of Egypt's 18th Dynasty pharaohs, who vigorously reduced Canaan to an Egyptian colony in order to make sure that the Canaanites would never invade them again.

It is important, therefore, to proceed carefully, avoiding assumptions and trying to set the events, if indeed they happened at all, in their historical and geographical setting.

First, we need to remind ourselves who the 'enemy' Canaanites actually were. As the Bible repeatedly informs us, those occupying Canaan in the time of Moses and his immediate successors included not only Canaanites as such, but also Hittites, Amorites, Perizzites, Hivites, Girgashites, Jebusites and 'Anakim' – in other words, a multicultural mish-mash for whom 'Canaanites' was a convenient general label. During the Middle Bronze Age period, these peoples quarrelled incessantly among themselves, and for that reason, among others, they cleverly fortified their cities with ramparted walls and daunting slopes, archaeologically known as *glacis*, plastered smooth to give attackers no foothold. Jericho's fortifications had essentially these characteristics.

While the book of Joshua gives no indication that Joshua's fighting force was equipped with anything like horses, chariots or even armour (and we may safely assume that they had none of these), the Canaanite war-lord elite had all three. Corroborating Biblical descriptions of the Canaanites as 'powerful' and equipped with 'chariots'[8], a near-contemporary Canaanite ivory knife-handle, found at Megiddo in northern Israel, depicts a helmeted, armoured Canaanite war-lord driving a chariot, bristling with arrows and bearing a massive spear. He is accompanied by similarly well-armed foot-soldiers, while abjectly lashed to his horses are two naked but still turbaned Shosu, seemingly freshly-captured in a skirmish. To the left of the scene (see page 63) this same war-lord relaxes on his sphinx-decorated throne, attended by a long-skirted woman bringing him a towel and a lotus blossom, while behind her a second woman strums a nine-string lyre, reminding us that the Canaanites, like the 'sons of Jacob', were enthusiastic music lovers.

Clearly, Canaanite war-lords lived to a very high standard. From the military viewpoint, it is also evident that their chariots were formidable fighting platforms, the equivalent of

A Canaanite war-lord returning in his chariot, with two captured Shosu lashed to his horses. Detail from an ivory knife-handle of *c.*12th century BC found at Megiddo. For the left-hand section of this same ivory, depicting the war-lord at home, see page 63.

armoured tanks in modern-day land combat. On any flat, even ground in which these could move freely and at speed, the warriors fighting from them could inflict terrible damage on less well equipped opposing infantry. It was this same weapon that is believed to have enabled the Hyksos/Canaanites to gain control so easily of Lower Egypt, until the Egyptians developed their own equivalents and turned the tables on them.

This campaign by the pharaohs of the 18th and 19th Dynasties against the Canaanites is often portrayed in reliefs from the time, and it is precisely this fact that has led many scholars to cast doubt on the conquest of Canaan by a band of semi-nomads led by a Joshua. Throughout the period in which any semi-nomadic refugees from Thera-ravaged Egypt might have fought their way into Canaan, Canaan was an Egyptian province, a factor the Biblical record does not even hint at.

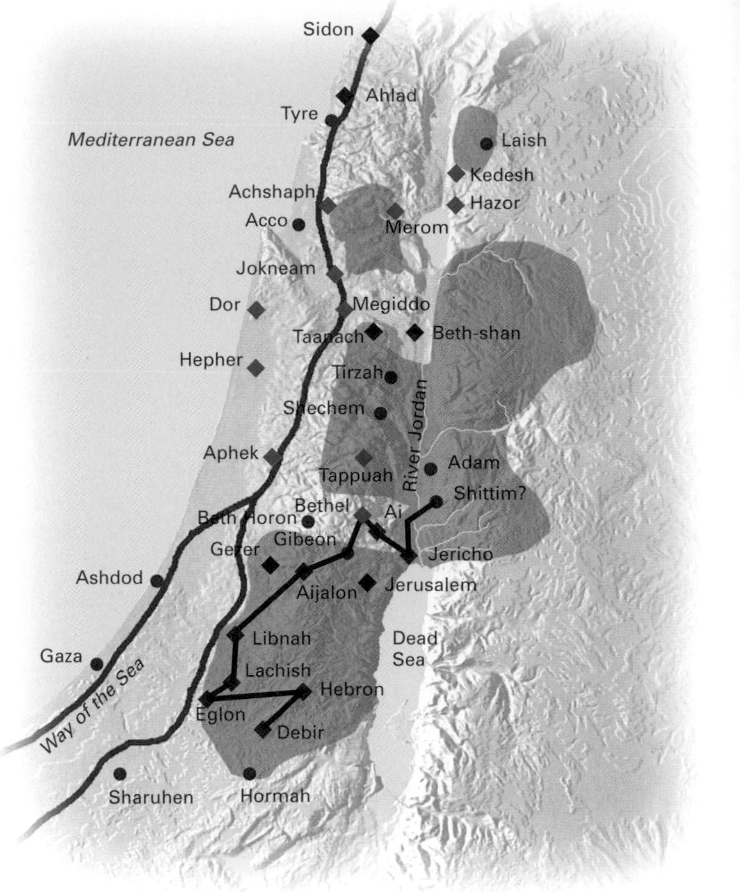

KEY

Joshua's claimed 'conquest' route

Areas of opponent tribal infiltration

Canaanitic Royal City, according to Joshua 12

City conquered by Joshua, according to Joshua 6-11

City unconquered, according to Judges 1

Some of the chief Canaanitic cities, and the route of Joshua's conquest, according to the Biblical account.

Archaeology seems to support this. Town after town in Canaan shows evidence of either destruction or a cessation of occupation at the end of the Middle Bronze Age, normally dated to around the time of Pharaoh Ahmose, i.e. the late 16th century BC. If we take an imaginary tour northwards up the Way of the Sea from Egypt, we come first to Sharuhen. As already noted, Pharaoh Ahmose, following his Avaris victory, besieged and sacked the city. Archaeological findings at the site confirm that it was, indeed, conquered and abandoned at the end of the Middle Bronze Age. Likewise, Tel Masos (Biblical Hormah) sported Canaanitic ramparts up to the end of the Middle Bronze Age, then suddenly ceased to exist and remained an empty site throughout the subsequent Late Bronze Age. It was the same at Tell Beit Mirsim, ancient Debir, also at Hebron, just to the south of Jerusalem, and Lachish, the present-day Tell ed-Duweir. A little further north, the Middle Bronze Age city of Beitin, identified as ancient Bethel, suffered destruction, and was then only minimally reoccupied. East of Jerusalem, Jericho shows evidence that its City IV suffered violent destruction. British archaeologist Kathleen Kenyon argued that this occurred at the end of the Middle Bronze Age. Further north, Hazor, as a slight variation, shows evidence of having been very violently burnt at the same period, although in this instance it was subsequently reoccupied.

Among archaeologists excavating these sites, the assumption has long been that most, if not all, these destructions were suffered at the hands of early 18th Dynasty Egyptian pharaohs. They assume this, even though, as readily acknowledged by Egyptologist Donald Redford, Egyptian and other archival sources for this period are 'maddening' for

Artist's impression of a typical Middle Bronze Age Canaanitic city, with high walls and steep, plastered slopes, archaeologically known as *glacis*. By the time conventionally ascribed to Joshua, these walls had been swept away.

not telling us so directly. While Canaanites returning from the Nile Delta following the Hyksos' defeat are sometimes considered as possible candidates, the 'sons of Jacob' under Joshua are almost never taken into account[9], because it has been believed that they remained in Egypt until around the 1200s.

Epitomising the problem is the story of Jericho. It was not until the beginning of this century that the uninspiring mound of Tell es-Sultan, 820 feet below sea-level in the Jordan Valley, was identified as the Biblical Jericho, and then only thanks to Germans Ernst Sellin and Carl Watzinger. Between 1907 and 1911, they uncovered and mapped some extensive walls, though their datings of these lacked modern methodology. In the 1930s British archaeologist John Garstang uncovered a collapsed double city wall, which he identified as having belonged to Jericho City IV. He dated it to the Late Bronze Age, c.1400 BC, and since this collapse was followed by a major destruction and the abandonment of the city, he inferred that it was the work of Joshua and his followers.

In the 1950s, however, Garstang's deductions were overturned when the then-leading British archaeologist Kathleen Kenyon, using her own more scientific excavation techniques, insisted that the true date of Jericho IV's fall must have been at the end of the Middle Bronze Age, well over a century earlier. Along with everyone else in the 1950s, Kenyon assumed that the Exodus, if it had happened at all, happened around the time of Ramesses II. As a result, any possibility that Joshua could have had anything to do with Jericho IV's destruction was out of the question.

However, although Kenyon enjoyed a considerable international reputation up to her death in 1978, her interpretations have, in their turn, been revised during the last two decades. Not only are today's generation of Israeli archaeologists deeply critical of her, but also American Biblical scholar Bryant T. Wood[10] has re-evaluated both her findings and those of Garstang. He has determined that, whatever date may be ascribed to Jericho IV's fall, the circumstances of it are too uncannily similar to those of the fall of Joshua's Jericho to be dismissed lightly.

Thus, the walls that protected Jericho IV against attack were not only intact up to the time of its fall, but impressively so, just as the book of Joshua tell us of Joshua's Jericho. In classic Canaanite style, their lower part consisted of an outer stone retaining wall, holding in place a steep plastered *glacis*. Topping this, ramparts-style, was an upper parapet wall, and immediately inside this were houses built into the walls. These precisely correspond to the Biblical description of the house of Jericho prostitute Rahab, who reportedly helped Joshua's spies escape by letting them down with a rope through her window, 'for her dwelling was at the outer side of the city wall and she lived in the actual wall' (Joshua 2:15).

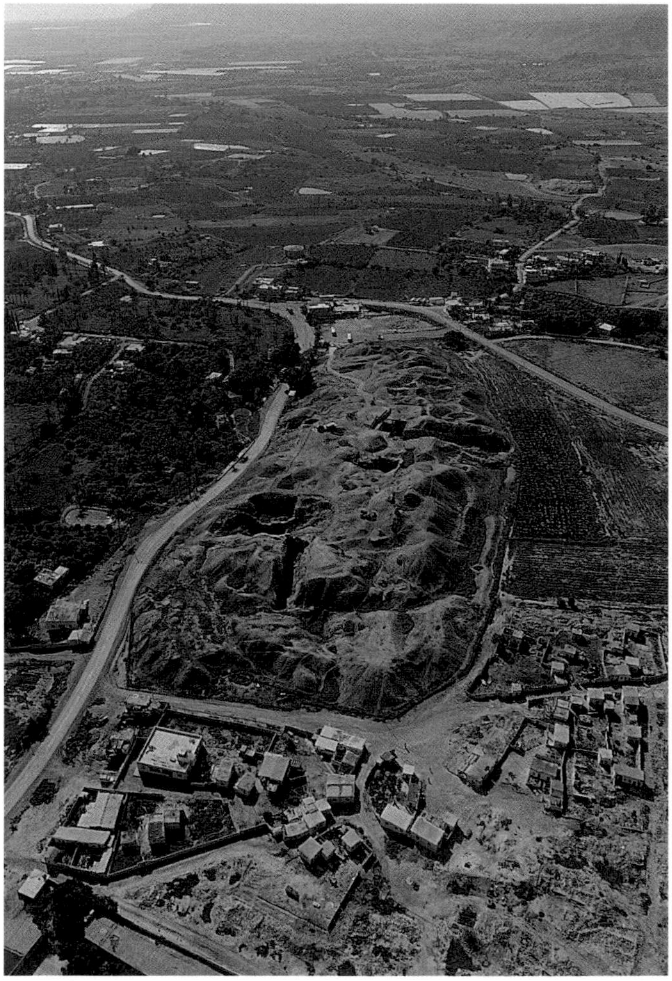

Equally pertinent was the fact that Jericho IV did not fall following a protracted siege of the kind the Egyptians normally conducted. The typical Egyptian method of capturing a city was for their army to arrive just before harvest-time. They would prevent the defenders from gaining access to this harvest and use it themselves while they waited until those inside the city were starved into submission. But nothing of this kind can have happened in the case of Jericho City IV. For, as found by both Garstang and Kenyon, even the houses of Jericho's most ordinary citizens were stocked with storage jars still brimming with grain[11].

As noted by Wood, one of the most significant pieces of archaeological information, evident even in Kenyon's excavation reports, is the major and unexplained collapse of Jericho IV's walls. In her methodical manner, Kenyon made three cuts through Jericho's walls to show how they had been built. One of them she extended beyond the outer stone retaining wall, where she came across a rubble of red mud-brick blocks which had clearly tumbled from the city's upper parapet wall[12]. Besides the collapsed walls, some of the buildings were affected, with at least one skeleton found crushed beneath fallen masonry[13].

Could the collapse have been the result of an earthquake? Since Jericho lies near a fault in the earth's crust extending southwards to the Dead Sea and ultimately to East Africa – the same seismic instability that may have been responsible for the demise of Sodom and Gomorrah – there is nothing far-fetched about this idea. It is a matter of straight historical fact that its environs are prone to such disasters. As recently as 11 July 1927, an earthquake in the region killed 500 people, caused the collapse of many hundreds of buildings, and was responsible for four serious rock-falls along the Jericho to Jerusalem road[14].

However, whatever it was that made Jericho IV's upper walls collapse, this represents only part of the story. For in what can only have been the immediate aftermath of this

The mound of Tell es-Sultan, the site of Biblical Jericho, as it looks today. It lies 800 feet below sea-level and has claimed to be the oldest and lowest city on earth.

collapse, all Jericho's buildings were, in Kenyon's words, 'violently destroyed by fire'[15]. She elaborated this statement in her published report:

> The destruction was complete. Walls and floors were blackened or reddened by fire, and every room was filled with fallen bricks, timbers and household utensils; in most rooms the fallen debris was heavily burnt, but the collapse of the walls of the eastern rooms seems to have taken place before they were affected by the fire.[16]

Noteworthy here is Kenyon's reference to the prior collapse of the walls in the eastern rooms. This indicates that Jericho suffered an earthquake just before someone invaded the city and set fire to it. But this is as nothing compared to what the events – destruction by fire, followed by an abandonment that reduced Jericho to a wall-less ghost city – tell us about the invaders.

For as Kenyon herself recognised, in the case of Jericho at least, the Egyptians may be discounted as invaders. Not only was Jericho a backwater from any Egyptian point of view, far removed from the Way of the Sea coastal plain which was their main operating territory, but also their normal policy was not to wreak any such wanton destruction. Instead, they colonised and gathered tribute.

Yet if it was not the Egyptians, Kenyon's favoured candidates – the land-hungry Hyksos/Canaanite invaders returning from their settlement in Egypt – are hardly more plausible. After all, the last thing a group of this kind would do, would be to destroy and abandon a city they had fought for in order to make it a new home. This would be particularly the case with Jericho, which has one of the best water supplies anywhere in Israel, including a natural spring pumping out water at the rate of 17¾ gallons per second. A revealing mark of Jericho IV's conquerors is that they not only scorned to take it over themselves, but they also disdained to loot the many bushels of freshly-harvested grain that lay in the citizens' houses.

This gives rise to a very necessary question: despite all the doubts, most particularly arising from dating issues, could Jericho IV's conquerors have been Joshua and his followers, after all? When this possibility is considered, the parallels between Biblical story and archaeological evidence become too striking to ignore.

Thus, according to the book of Joshua, the Canaanite Jericho that Joshua and his men confronted was strongly fortified (Joshua 2:5, 7, 15; 6:5, 20). The archaeological evidence shows that this was true also of Jericho IV, and of no subsequent phase of settlement at this site until several centuries later. According to the book of

Was Jericho IV the Biblical Jericho? A section of Jericho IV's walls shows the rubble of red bricks, as if caused by the sudden collapse of a wall. Kathleen Kenyon found evidence of similar collapse in some of the city's buildings.

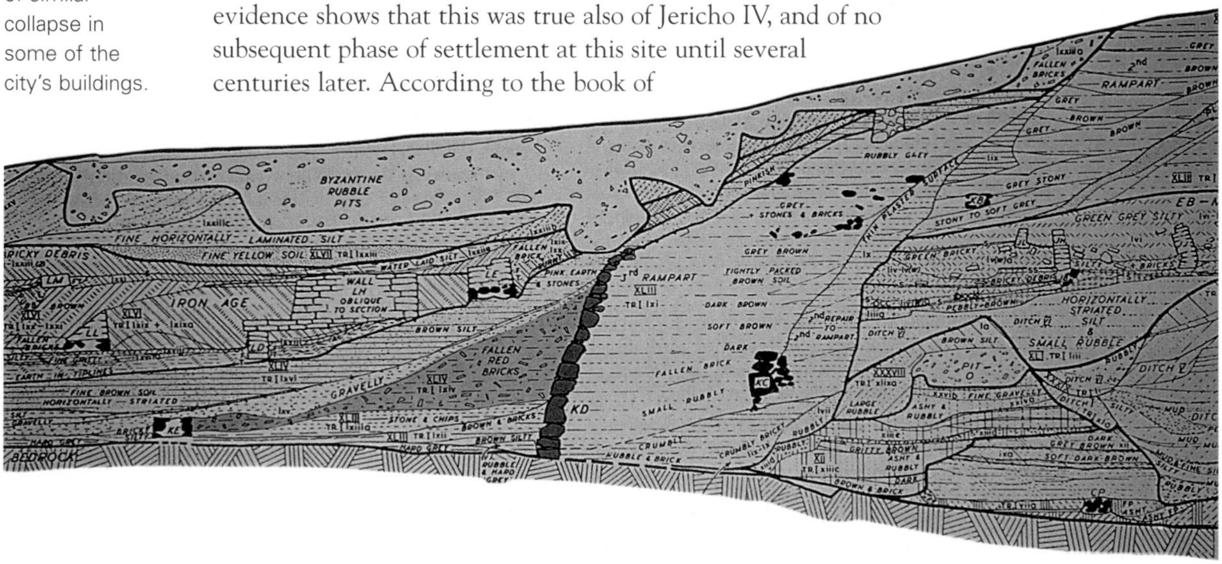

Joshua, the Joshua-led attack on Jericho occurred just after the spring harvest (Joshua 2; 3:15; 5:10; 6). As already noted, the archaeologists excavating Jericho IV's houses found them brimming with freshly-harvested grain. According to the book of Joshua, it was a divinely-orchestrated collapse of Jericho's walls that caused the city to fall to Joshua and his men (Joshua 6:20). The archaeological findings show that Jericho IV's upper city walls, and some of its houses inside those walls, collapsed, as from an earthquake. According to the book of Joshua, Joshua and his men were specifically forbidden to plunder the city (Joshua 6:17), having been enjoined instead to burn it and everything inside it (Joshua 6:24). As we have just seen, the archaeological evidence is emphatic: not even Jericho IV's grain stocks were looted. Instead, the city was thoroughly torched.

Artist's impression of how Jericho IV's walls collapsed, allowing invaders to enter and destroy the city. Were these Joshua and his men?

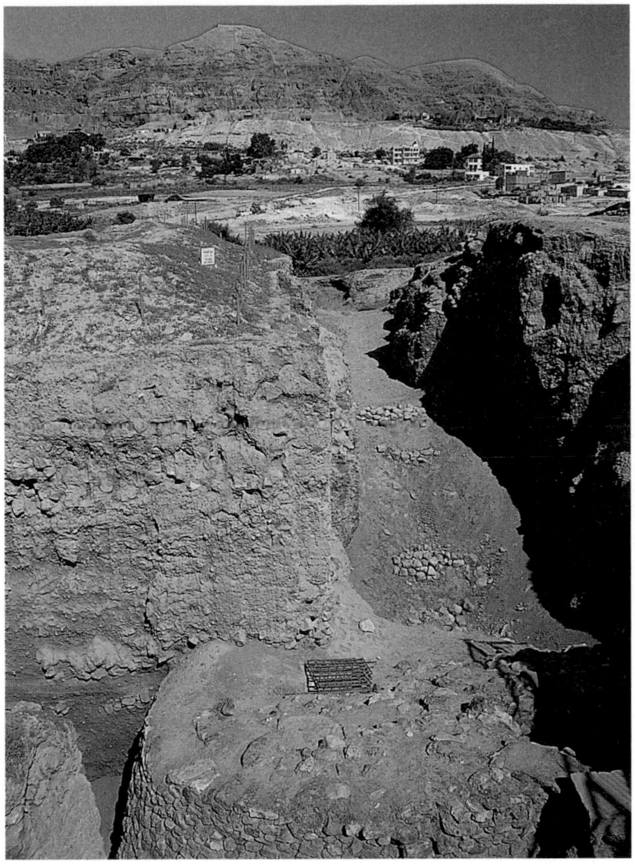

According to the book of Joshua, anyone attempting to rebuild the city would be considered accursed (Joshua 6:26). The archaeological evidence is unequivocal that, following Jericho IV's fall, one of the prime occupational sites in Canaan was abandoned as a ruin.

If, then, the fall of Jericho IV really is to be re-identified as the work of the Biblical Joshua, all hinges on exactly when this event might have happened. In this context, it is Bryant Wood who has again done some illuminating researches. Kenyon assumed that Jericho fell at the end of the Middle Bronze Age, because she found no examples of a certain imported Cypriote pottery distinctive of the Late Bronze Age. In Wood's view, she was wrong to make this assumption, since such pottery was most unlikely to be present anyway. The tiny sector of Jericho she excavated was a poor quarter whose inhabitants could not afford such expensive imports.

According to Wood, a pottery-dating specialist, not only is some of the Jericho pottery definitely from the Late Bronze Age, but also a series of scarabs found in Jericho's cemetery bear the cartouches of the 18th Dynasty pharaohs Hatshepsut, Tuthmosis III and Amenhotep III, the last generally dated 1391-1353 BC. So Jericho IV did not fall around the time of Ahmose, as Kenyon insisted, but anything up to two hundred years later, a finding corroborated by fragments from Jericho's destruction debris which have been carbon-dated to 1410 BC, plus or minus forty years[17].

One inference from this is that a longer period would have elapsed between the Exodus from Egypt and the victory at Jericho than the Biblically-prescribed forty years. This is no surprise, since Biblical chronological estimates are often more symbolic than reliable. Arguably, wherever Abel-Shittim was (and all we know is that it was just across the Jordan from Jericho), the group led by Joshua dallied there for some while, waiting for a moment of Canaanite weakness in order to pounce. That moment may have arrived when an earthquake shook the Jordan valley. A common accompaniment of such earthquakes is for the River Jordan to become blocked at Adam, or what is today Jisr-ed-Damiye[18]. Such occurrences match with uncanny exactness the Biblical account of Joshua's men making their 'miraculous' crossing of the Jordan:

A section of Jericho's walls as uncovered by archaeologists.

Right, above: Storage jars found brimming with grain indicating that Jericho IV fell at harvest-time, and without a prolonged siege. Below: Scarabs found in Jericho IV's cemetery, including one of Amenhotep III (c.1391-1353 BC), suggesting that the city fell as late as the 14th century BC.

The River Jordan winding its way southwards, between the Sea of Galilee (seen at top) and the Dead Sea. It is a matter of historical fact that in the vicinity of the book of Joshua's Adam, today Jisr-ed-Damiye, its flow has been repeatedly blocked by earthquakes, as in 1160, 1267, 1546, 1834, 1906 and 1927.

> The [Jordan's] waters coming down from upstream piled up in a single heap a great way off, at Adam, the town next to Zarethan; and those flowing downstream to the Sea of the Arabah (the Dead Sea) ran out completely. So the people crossed near Jericho. (Joshua 3:16)

The same seismically-triggered event which enabled Joshua and his men to cross the Jordan dry-shod may also have brought down Jericho's walls, allowing the invaders to swarm into the city and overcome the citizens just when they were in their greatest disarray.

If we are prepared to accept that the fall of some of the Canaanite cities should not be dated to Ahmose's time, but may have happened up to two hundred years later, it becomes easier to envisage something along the lines of a Joshua-led conquest, albeit with lesser numbers and continuity than the Biblical story suggests.

Although there can be no doubt that, after Ahmose, the Egyptians did subjugate Canaanite cities accessible to their chariots along the Way of the Sea, this is by no means incompatible with the Biblical record. The book of Judges is convincingly candid about the places that the Joshuahite tribes did not conquer:

> [The tribe] Manasseh did not dispossess [the inhabitants of] Beth-shan and its dependencies, or of Taanach . . . or the inhabitants of Megiddo and its dependencies; the Canaanites persisted in dwelling in this region . . . Nor did [the tribe] Ephraim dispossess the Canaanites who inhabited Gezer, so the Canaanites dwelt in their midst at Gezer . . . (Judges 1:27-33)

It so happens that at precisely these sites continuity of Canaanite occupation has been found between the end of the Middle Bronze Age and the Late Bronze Age. Any evidence of minimal destruction that does exist can be attributed to the Egyptians, in a way that is not possible at Jericho. Thus, in the case of Megiddo, the great Canaanite fortress city that stood at the northern end of the Way of the Sea, Egyptian textual sources show that Pharaoh Tuthmosis III laid siege to this around the mid-15th century BC, a hundred or so years after Ahmose. When Tuthmosis captured it after a seven months' siege, he preserved it and its Canaanite population essentially intact. Archaeological findings correspondingly indicate no level of destruction. Likewise, Beth-shan shows none of the savage Middle Bronze Age destruction level. At Taanach, although some signs have come to light of limited destruction at the end of the Middle Bronze Age, the town made a speedy recovery. Its proximity to Megiddo suggests that Tuthmosis simply took it over with minimum force, then allowed it to recover. As for Gezer, although excavations there were badly botched at the beginning of this century, Egyptian documentary evidence shows that it was still extant in the long reign of the 14th-century BC pharaoh Amenophis III, some two generations after Tuthmosis III. The archaeology seems to confirm this continuity of occupation.

Ironically, in all these cases the Canaanites survived because their cities were located along the Way of the Sea corridor. They were easily accessible to the Egyptians, who defeated them and then merely 'milked' them with the aid of garrisons, which also provided protection. A scribe's report dating from Tuthmosis III's reign explains how such Egyptian-controlled Canaanite territories should be taxed for their '[silver, gol]d, lapis, various semi-precious stones, chariots and horses without number'[19]. Conversely, it is precisely those cities which, according to the Bible, fell into the hands of the people who destroyed Jericho, that exhibit archaeological evidence of savage, seemingly-mindless destruction for destruction's sake.

Thus, in the case of the southern Canaanite town of Lachish (present-day Tell ed-Duweir) where according to the book of Joshua 'Joshua and all Israel . . . put it and every living creature in it to the sword' (Joshua 10:32), modern-day archaeological excavations show violent destruction of the last Middle Bronze Age city. At Debir, present-day Tell Beit Mirsim, where we are told that Joshua and his men left no one alive (Joshua 10:38), modern-day archaeological excavations show that its final Middle Bronze Age city was destroyed, and then abandoned for an appreciable period of time. At Hebron, just to the south of Jerusalem, we are told that Joshua and his men put 'its king, its dependencies and every living creature in it' to the sword. The archaeologists have found that this formerly populous Middle Bronze Age town suddenly ceased to exist and then lay abandoned for several centuries.

Such a striking pattern of destructions, of people repeatedly risking life and limb to take fine cities, only to leave them abandoned, tells its own story of unusual assailants who cared nothing for urban living. Arguably, therefore, it is no accident that this is precisely the picture that we have of Joshua and his followers at this time – individuals whose openly-avowed policy was to implement a 'curse of destruction' (Joshua 6:17), amounting to full-blooded genocide. As they pictured the Canaanites – 'they perform for their gods every abhorrent act that Yahweh detests, they even offer up their sons and daughters in fire to their gods' (Deuteronomy 12:31) – so they regarded it as their Yahweh-directed duty to:

> dispossess all the inhabitants of the land . . . destroy all their figured objects . . . destroy all their molten images . . . . demolish all their cult places . . . . take possession of the land, and settle in it. (Numbers 33:52-3)

It might now seem easy to attribute the destruction of Canaan's Middle Bronze Age cities to Joshua and his men. There is one problem, however. During this period, immediately after the Middle Bronze Age, Joshua's followers are all but invisible, archaeologically, as an identifiable, incoming people. As earlier mentioned, Gilgal was the within-Canaan base encampment from which they are supposed to have made their forays against Canaanite cities. This was also where Joshua apparently performed a fresh circumcision of his followers, because the rite had fallen into abeyance during the wilderness wanderings (Joshua 5:5). So far the site has eluded any firm identification.

The only other location firmly associated with occupation by the Joshuahite bands during their earliest years is the Abraham-associated hill-country town of Shechem. According to the Joshua account, it was the one Canaanite town which offered the incoming Joshua and his band no resistance (possibly because its inhabitants were family members who had stayed behind instead of going down into Egypt). This was where Joshua reportedly gathered a great assembly of the people before his death, to renew the covenant with their Yahweh (Joshua 24:1-29).

Egypt's 18th Dynasty pharaoh Akhenaten. His Canaanite vassals were repeatedly vexed by troublesome Habiru during his reign.

Archaeological findings have yet to provide us with clear evidence of incoming settlers whom we can firmly identify with Joshua and his band, but the reason for this lack of evidence may be simple. Although they took Canaanite towns, they did not occupy them themselves, but abandoned them and went back to their archaeologically-invisible tented encampments. In keeping with their non-urban inclinations, it is equally evident that wherever these tents were pitched, it was almost invariably in Canaan's central hill district, rather than on any flat or low-lying land where they might be vulnerable to Canaanite chariots. Indeed, this is explicitly stated in the first chapter of the book of Judges, where it remarks that although the tribe of Judah had 'made himself master of the highlands [or hill country], he could not dispossess the inhabitants of the plain, since they had . . . chariots' (Judges 1:19b).

It may be no coincidence that, according to the documentary record, marauding bands of 'Apiru, or Habiru, were making will o' the wisp-style raids in the environs of these hilly areas at precisely this time. When in 1887 a peasant women was digging beneath an ancient building just outside her village of el-Amarna in Middle Egypt, she came across a number of clay tablets dating from the time of the 14th-century BC pharaoh Amenhotep III and his famous successor Akhenaten. Now known as the Amarna letters, these included messages to the Egyptian court from Canaanite war-lord vassals, ruling with the 'protection' of garrisons of Egyptian soldiers. One such was from Shurwadata, responsible for the Hebron hill country region where Joshua and his men are Biblically said to have been active. He reported to Akhenaten:

> Let the king my lord learn that the chief of the Habiru has risen [in arms] against the lands which the god of the king, my lord, gave me; but I have smitten him. And let the king, my lord, know that all my brethren have abandoned me, and it is I and 'Abdu-Heba [a fellow war-lord] who fight against the chief of the Habiru.[20]

For his part, 'Abdu-Heba voiced similar alarm about the same marauding Habiru:

> Let the king . . . my lord, send out troops of archers [for] the king has no lands [left]. The Habiru plunder all the lands of the king. If there are archers [here] in this year the lands of the king, my lord, will remain [intact]; but if there are no archers [here] the lands of the king, my lord, will be lost.[21]

Particularly telling is a further remark by 'Abdu-Heba:

> Shall we do like Lab'ayu [the Canaanite prince responsible for Shechem], who gave the land of Shechem to the Habiru?[22]

Can it be coincidence that the very territory of Canaan Biblically said to have gone over most easily to Joshua and his band happens to be the one which, according to the Amarna letters, was being pillaged by Habiru? As emphasised earlier, it is important not to regard all textual references to 'Apiru, or Habiru, as being necessarily identifiable with the Biblical Hebrews or descendants of Jacob. After all, the Amarna letters are a single tranche of Egyptian correspondence that has survived by the merest chance amidst the huge amount of material lost. It would be the most enormous good fortune if this particular cache happened exactly to coincide with the time of the Biblical Joshua. In fact, Habiru would continue to be troublesome in the later reign of the 13th-century BC pharaoh Seti I, who reported them yet again in the hill country around Shechem, threatening the vulnerable Egypto-Canaanite city of Beth-shan, east of Megiddo[23].

Nonetheless, the Amarna correspondence confirms that as early as the 14th century BC the hill country of Canaan had fallen to will o' the wisp guerrillas, who were causing serious headaches for the urbanised Canaanites settled in their lot as law-abiding vassals of the Egyptians. It is, therefore, not too much to conceive that somewhere included among these predators were descendants of the 'sons of Jacob', who as defenceless refugees had fled Egypt. They had subsequently been through up to two centuries of itinerancy before gaining a new foothold in the land they believed divinely promised to them. And during this time they had developed guerrilla warfare skills in order to translate that promise into a reality.

All this must still be accounted the most fragile scenario for the timing and nature of the conquest of Canaan. Because of the long association of the preceding Exodus events with the later Ramessid period, it is also a scenario that even many maximalist scholars would shrink from endorsing. Nonetheless, its great virtue is that it restores the Biblical story of Canaan's conquest to a perfectly plausible historical context.

Furthermore (and most thankfully), the truly hard evidence for Jacob's descendants' arriving in Canaan is not far off, as we are just about to discover.

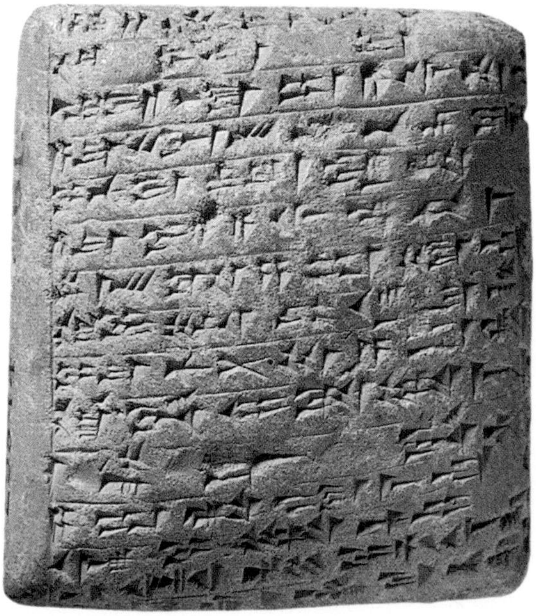

An example of one of the 'Amarna' letters from Canaanite vassal-kings, informing Akhenaten of their difficulties fighting 'Habiru' marauders in the Egyptian-contolled territories of Canaan.

7

'ISRAEL IS LAID WASTE'

As DESCRIBED in the Biblical book of Joshua, the conquest of Canaan was an aggressive, sharply-focused campaign, carried out by a single, very determined group of descendants of Jacob over a comparatively short period of time. It is natural, therefore, for us to look for a particular century of the 2nd millennium BC, of which we can say: 'That must have been when the "Israelites" conquered Canaan and created Israel.'

However, when we look at more recent and better documented history, the fallacy of expecting anything so clear-cut becomes all too evident. When, for example, did the English conquer England? Was it with the coming of the Celts (who spoke Welsh), the Romans (who spoke Latin), the Angles and Saxons (who spoke Danish), the Vikings (who spoke Norse) or the Normans (who spoke French)? These various 'conquests', by peoples who were rather more different from each other than the so-called Israelites from the Canaanites, were spread out over more than a thousand years. The emergence of the English people was so gradual as to be all but indefinable.

When the conquest of Canaan is seen in this light, it may begin to become clear why use of the word 'Israelite' has been avoided up to this chapter, when referring to those descendants of Jacob who theoretically entered Egypt during Jacob's lifetime, left it some centuries later during Moses' lifetime, and some time later still fought their way into Canaan during Joshua's lifetime. Even the Biblical account, edited and doctored as it is, acknowledges that it was a number of different tribes who took over allotted sectors of the former Canaan and its environs. Since textual criticism indicates that there were some amalgamations and divisions of these tribes[1], neither the official Biblical list of the 'sons of Jacob', nor their magic number twelve, should be regarded as historically unimpeachable. Any notion that they were all lineal descendants of Jacob whose parents left Egypt with Moses (and were theoretically, therefore, true Israelites) is likewise almost certainly wide of the mark.

Indeed, some Biblical scholars hold the view that the so-called 'Josephite' tribes – Ephraim and Manasseh – may have been the only ones to go down to Egypt and

Mount Tabor, as it looks today. According to the book of Judges, Deborah led here a coalition of the Israelite tribes, and routed the crack chariot force of the northern Canaanites.

back again. This may explain something (which the Bible does not) about how this collection of people, originally so timid that they reportedly travelled hundreds of miles out of their way into the Sinai desert to avoid opposing even very minor peoples, then lost 24,000 of their number in a terrible plague at Abel-Shittim (Numbers 24:9), could have transformed themselves into the book of Joshua's so-formidable and resourceful guerrilla army, ready and able to take on well-defended Canaanite cities. At the very least, we may suspect that some of the country folk who lived on the fringes of Canaanite towns resented the controlling Cananite warrior aristocracy, and allied themselves with people they recognised as their kin among the group returning from Egypt. This would go some way towards the 'peasant revolt' conquest theory of George Mendenhall, although far too much remains guesswork.

What we can be more sure of is the last chapter's provisional picture of at least some returning tribes first occupying Canaan's hill country. Here, they would have perpetuated much of their old nomadic way of life, then they would have moved down gradually into the more lowland areas and a more static mode of existence. All this now finds increasing support from both Biblical textual analysis and archaeology.

Here, one thing is especially difficult for us to appreciate. Having rendered themselves stateless by fleeing Egypt, and having then accepted the set of laws that Moses 'received' from Yahweh, these people managed to preserve the 'judges' system for governing themselves reportedly introduced by Moses and his Midianite father-in-law Jethro. In confirmation of this, the whole period from Joshua to the time of the monarchy is usually labelled the period of the 'Judges'. One astounding feature of these judges is evident from the Biblical text: they were neither aristocratic gentry, nor MPs or civil servants, but simply anyone, whether man or woman, priest or labourer, who had a recognised faculty for possessing, like the *nabi* Moses, some kind of 'direct line' to Yahweh.

Particularly revealing is what we read in Judges 4 of one such individual, apparently living a century or so after Joshua:

> Deborah, wife of Lappidoth, was a *nabi*; she led Israel at the time. She used to sit under the Palm of Deborah, between Ramah and Bethel in the hill country of Ephraim, and the Israelites would come to her for decisions. (Judges 4:4-5)

For anyone who might have supposed that feminism began in the 20th century AD, the picture is fascinating. We have an ordinary housewife, notable only for a certain 'psychic' gift, apparently acting as Lord Chief Justice for those who had ruthlessly taken Jericho a few generations before. As for this judge's 'Supreme Court', we read that it was a palm tree, high up on a hillside somewhere between two towns, the image taking on an appealing, homely quality. In the light of this information, it is hardly surprising that archaeologists have had such difficulty finding 'hard' evidence of the earliest occupation of Canaan by Israel, a people who apparently spurned solid buildings even for their court-houses.

This particular judge, Deborah, is interesting in many ways. Although she may seem rustic to us and difficult to place historically, from what we do know about her, she richly deserved the title some have given her as 'the most interesting woman in the Hebrew Bible'. It was apparently in her time that the Canaanites of the north, under their king Jabin and his general Sisera, took to cruelly oppressing and enslaving the region's Israelites. This inevitably recalls the near-contemporary Megiddo ivory depicting a Canaanite war-lord leading, tied to his chariot, two naked Shosu captives with what appear to be circumcised penises.

According to the book of Judges, Deborah, on the strength of insights received from Yahweh, decided to call an emergency muster of fighting men from all the tribes. When ten thousand men had been thus recruited, she urged the northern Israelite general Barak to do something that would previously have been unthinkable: engage the Canaanites with all their fearsome chariots in open battle. By divine inspiration, Deborah even apparently specified the ground where this engagement should take place: the Torrent of Kishon at Mount Tabor. This is identifiable as the Jezreel valley's still extant River Kishon, or Qishon, one source of which begins on the lower slopes of beautiful Mount Tabor, a few miles to the south-west of the Sea of Galilee.

With the redoubtable Deborah accompanying them, Barak and his men took up positions on Mount Tabor. There, they enticed the Canaanite general Sisera and his chariot squadron, then at their base at Harosheth-ha-Goiim, to come out to them.

At the place Deborah had specified, they charged down upon the Canaanites and utterly routed them. Fulfilling Deborah's prediction that Sisera would die by the hand of a woman, the Canaanite general reportedly took refuge in the tent of an ostensibly friendly Kenite. Here, the Kenite's wife Jael first poured him some milk and let him rest. Then, the moment he had fallen asleep, she hammered a tent-peg deep into his skull. Back at his capital Hazor, the Canaanite king Jabin, deprived of both his best general and his chariot force, was shortly afterwards 'utterly destroyed' (Judges 4:24).

The fact that the book of Judges' prose account is followed by a victory song, the 'Song of Deborah', adds special credibility to this Biblical episode. In common with the earlier 'Miracle of the Sea' victory song of Exodus 15, this represents not only one of the most powerful pieces of poetry in the entire Hebrew Bible, but also one of the oldest. The following extracts may convey something of its beauty:

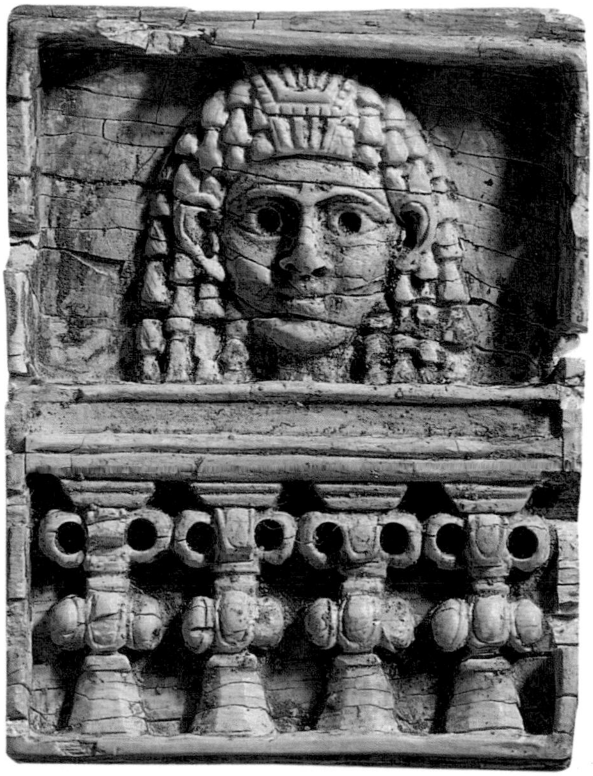

Both in the Bible, and in extra-Biblical sources, high-born Canaanitic women are typically described looking out of the window; the motif is similarly common in Canaanitic art.

Hear, O kings! Give ear, O potentates!
I will sing, will sing to Yahweh,
Will hymn Yahweh, the God of Israel . . .

In the days of Shamgar son of Anath,
In the days of Jael, caravans ceased,
And wayfarers went by roundabout paths
Deliverance ceased,
Ceased in Israel
Till you arose, O Deborah . . .

Then did the people of Yahweh
March down to the gates . . .

Then the fugitives went down against the nobles
The people of Yahweh went down against the warriors . . .

The stars fought from heaven,
From their courses they fought against Sisera,
The torrent Kishon swept them away,
The torrent Kishon that is the torrent Qedumin . . .

Most blessed of women be Jael,
Wife of Heber the Kenite,
Most blessed of women in tents,
He [Sisera] asked for water, she offered milk;
In a princely bowl she brought him curds
Her [left] hand reached for the tent peg
Her right for the workmen's hammer.
She struck Sisera, crushed his head,
Smashed and pierced his temple . . .

Through the window peered Sisera's mother,
Behind the lattice she whined:
'Why is his chariot so long in coming?
Why so late the clatter of his wheels?' . . ..
So may all your enemies perish, O Yahweh!

(Judges 5:3-31)

As generally agreed even by otherwise conservative textual scholars, the archaic language of this song indicates that it dates at least as far back as the 12th century BC, if not earlier[2]. Furthermore, when we try to set it in its correct historical context, we find at last some surprisingly encouraging signs that we can do so. For instance, the same ancient Egyptian 'itinerary maps' in Karnak's Temple of Amun that corroborated the book of Numbers' route northwards through Jordan, also serve to corroborate some of the Deborah story's place-names. One of these itineraries, that of the 13th-century BC Ramesses II, includes at the very point in Canaan where we would expect the Jezreel Valley and Mount Tabor region to be reached: 'Qerumin-Qishon of Ibn-Shimshon-Hadasht'.

As pointed out by the American scholar Charles R. Krahmalkov: 'Qerumin is actually the "Qedumin" that the Hebrew Bible gives as an alternative name for "Qishon" '[3], the interchange of 'd' and 'r' being a common spelling error. The 'torrent Kishon' is the already-noted River Qishon running through this region. The river most likely takes its name from the ancient town Qishon, today Tel Qaysun, that stands a mile south of Mount Tabor. 'Hadasht' is apparently the original, correct form of the 'Harosheth-ha-Goiim'[4], Biblically-featured as the base camp of Sisera and his men (Judges 4:13 and 16). This again is identifiable as today's Ayn al-Hadath, 5 miles north-east of Qishon/Tell Qaysun. As for 'Ibn', according to Krahmalkov this was none other than the Canaanite king whom the Judges text renders as 'Jabin', a time-honoured name for kings of this region. This is confirmed both by the book of Joshua, which records Joshua's defeat of an

The mound of Hazor as it looks today, showing typical Canaanite *glacis* defensive slopes. Excavations continue under the direction of the Israeli archaeologist Amnon Ben-Tor.

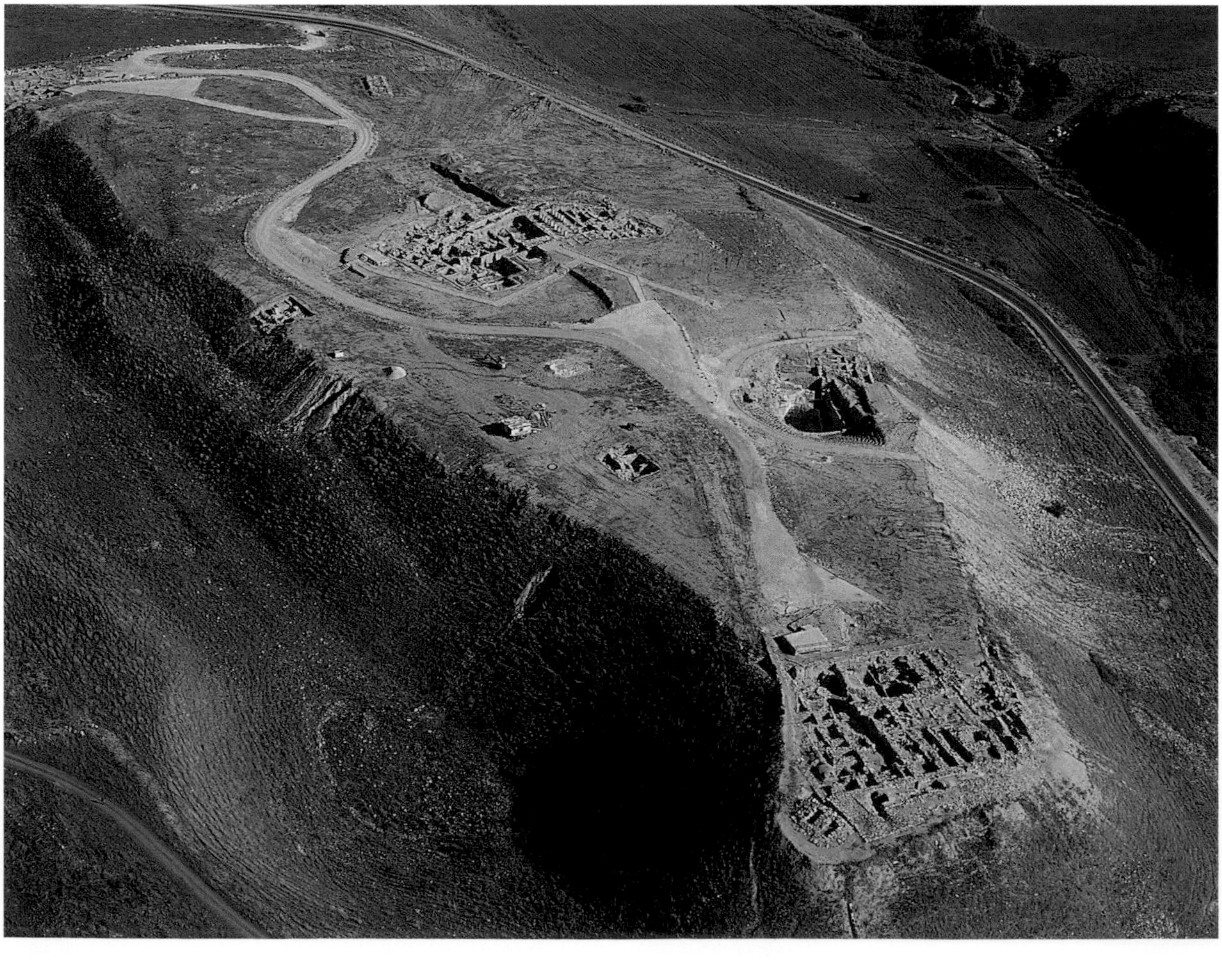

obviously earlier 'king of Hazor' of this name (Joshua 11:1), and by Israeli archaeologist Amnon Ben-Tor. He recently found at Hazor an 18th/17th-century BC cuneiform tablet inscribed 'to Ibni', i.e. 'to Jabin'.[5]

Furthermore, the Biblical text, which had earlier told us of Hazor's destruction by Joshua, makes clear that the city was recaptured by the Canaanites post-Joshua, only to fall again to Barak and Deborah. Given this, considerable interest must pertain to the generality of archaeological findings at Hazor itself. The location of this city, today a 25-acre mound just off the road running north from the Sea of Galilee, was first properly recognised by British archaeologist John Garstang back in the 1920s. Following his work, the famous Yigael Yadin carried out more definitive excavations during the 1950s. Work by Amon Ben-Tor continues to this day.

Obvious from all this is that Middle and Late Bronze Age Hazor was a major Cananite city with temples and a magnificent palace, which suffered a series of destructions culminating in one major catastrophe of *c.*1275 BC. During this, its cult statues were quite deliberately smashed. Such desecration would have been uncharacteristic of Egyptians (who would have feared that it might make them accursed), and completely unthinkable for rival Canaanites. So both Yadin and Ben-Tor have inferred that the true culprits were the Israelites, the chief difficulty being when they might have done this.

From our perspective it would make sense for it to have been the same destruction ascribed to Deborah and Barak in Judges 4:23. This would make Deborah approximately contemporary with Egypt's Ramesses II, the pharaoh still traditionally associated with the Egyptian oppression prior to the Exodus. But, whatever the date of Deborah and Barak's victory, this is far from the only intriguing element in this story. For, as is made clear in the ancient 'Song of Deborah', it was apparently not every Israelite tribe that answered Deborah's call to arms against the northern Canaanites. Those who did, thereby receiving much praise, are specified as Ephraim (Deborah's own tribe), Benjamin (Barak's tribe), Machir (the tribe that later becomes known as Manasseh), together with Zebulun and Naphtali (geographically associated with what would become Galilee). We are also told:

> Among the clans of Reuben
> Were great decisions of heart.
> Why then did you stay among the sheepfolds,
> And listen as they pipe for the flocks?
> Gilead tarried beyond [i.e. the other side of] the Jordan
> And Dan, why did he linger [*yagur*] by the ships?
> Asher remained at the seacoast
> And tarried at his landings . . .
> (Judges 5:15-17)

Such negative, self-critical information normally goes unmentioned unless it represents a true situation. As a result, it behoves us to ask what, historically, might have distinguished those tribes who did answer Deborah's call from those who did not, and what this might tell us about the state of the so-called Israelite occupation of Canaan in Deborah's time. In this regard, Numbers 32:1, as well as the 'Song of Deborah', both make clear that the Reuben and Gilead tribes (the latter better known elsewhere as Gad), were sheep-herders in the old style, living with their 'very large number of livestock' on the eastern side of the Jordan. As the American scholar Lawrence Stager has observed, such a livelihood would have imposed on them precisely the same symbiotic dependency upon the town-dwelling Canaanites that had prevailed in both the Abrahamic era and the Hyksos period in Egypt. This gave them very good reason to ignore Deborah's call.

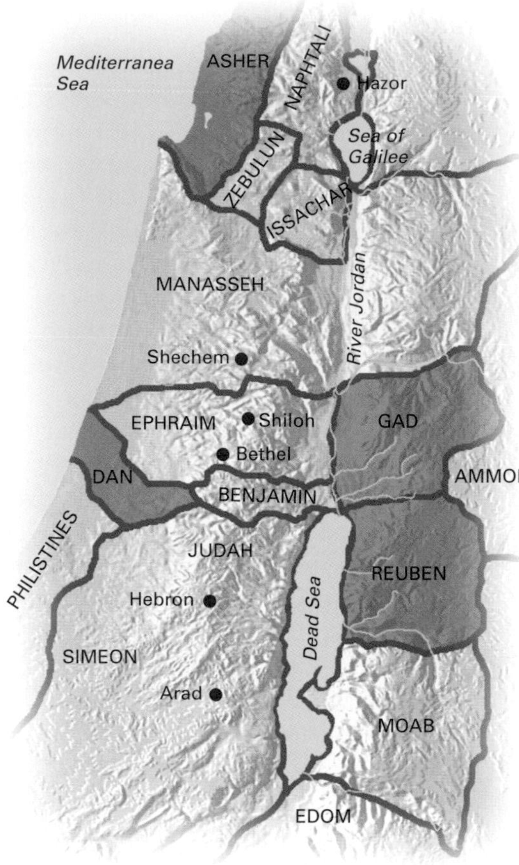

The Israel tribes who did – and did not – answer Deborah's call to arms. Those who did answer are shown in pale purple. Edom, Moab and the Philistines were not members of the twelve tribes, but are shown in their relative positions. Manasseh was known as Machir in texts such as the 'Song of Deborah'. The Gilead tribe referred to in Deborah's song is better known as Gad.

The tribes Dan and Asher may have had a similar dependency, though for a different reason. In Deborah's time, they apparently lived in the Mediterranean coastal region, while the 'Song of Deborah' refers to them as connected with the sea and ships. In the light of this, the likelihood is that they were not living freely in territory they had conquered, but instead employed in the coastal Canaanites' flourishing trading activities. This was a status quo that it was not in their interests to alter.

All interest focuses, therefore, on the Ephraim, Benjamin, Machir/ Manasseh, Zebulun, Issachar and Naphtali tribes. Clearly, they had no cause for goodwill towards the Canaanites, and we may regard them as the key movers in taking over Canaanite territory. As the Biblical record has already indicated, following their elimination of Jericho and other Canaanite fortified towns hostile to their infiltration, they took over the central hill country stretching from the Sea of Galilee to the Dead Sea. Apparently, this was where the two largest tribes, Ephraim and Manasseh, lived together as a single entity until, with increasing population, they had to split. They then took over and cleared some hitherto seemingly unusable forest terrain.

In this regard, some illuminating archaeological survey work has been done by a remarkable Israeli, Dr Adam Zertal. Trained mostly as a farm-worker until he decided to do a degree in archaeology at the age of 30, Zertal served as a paratrooper in the Yom Kippur War, during which an exploding shell injured his legs so severely that his doctors told him he would never walk again. Undeterred, he undertook for his doctoral thesis an exhaustive archaeological survey of the territory associated with the Manasseh tribe, painfully propelling himself on aluminium crutches throughout its 770 square miles. He noted each and every site with dateable historical remains, together with the site's height above sea-level, its water sources, vegetation, soil characteristics, etc.

From this work, which took him twelve years, Zertal identified 116 sites with remains dateable to the late Middle Bronze period of the Canaanites' heyday. Then came just 39 sites showing evidence of occupation during the Late Bronze Age period, then an escalation back to 136 sites for the subsequent Iron Age I period[6]. This clearly indicated that something very traumatic must have happened during the Late Bronze Age period, consistent with the fall of some big Canaanite cities in the wake of an Israelite influx.

Even more intriguing was the ecological pattern revealed. For, as Zertal found, whereas during the Middle and Late Bronze Age period, 43 per cent of the occupied sites were concentrated in the area's valleys, which had rich alluvial soil, only 19 per cent of the later Iron Age I/Israelite sites were found in this kind of terrain. Conversely, whereas a mere 13 per cent of the Middle and Late Bronze Age settlements farmed on mountain-type soil, 38 per cent of the Iron Age I sites did.

It would seem that the incoming Israelite people first settled in agriculturally less desirable upland or hilly areas, where their social units were small villages. Arguably, this was because the agriculturally-richer terrain down on the plains was still owned and controlled by the Canaanites from their fortified cities. As Zertal reasoned, the archaeological record unmistakeably confirmed the Biblical picture of the Israelites first occupying the hill country, before their military successes against the Canaanites enabled them to move into the more lowland areas.

But as Zertal has insisted, it would be wrong to assume from this that the Canaanites suddenly disappeared, as if the Israelites had rapidly and decisively swept them aside. It is more likely that in the earliest phase the still semi-nomadic 'sons of Jacob' settled in the hill country, where they initially retained their old tent-dwelling and herding ways. This is consistent with Deborah's so-homely court under a palm tree, and the Kenite Jael pouring Sisera's milk from a goatskin. As and when military successes allowed them to do so, they moved down into the valleys. It was only then that they became more agricultural, growing wheat and barley, also perhaps planting vineyards and cultivating olives. As we have already inferred, it was something they could have done only as a result of a certain symbiosis with at least some of the more rustic residents of Canaan.

Equally important, it is evident from both the Biblical and the archaeological record that by no means all was symbiosis. However much it may have been in the interests of some tribes to try to get along with the Canaanites, one point the Bible stresses is the fundamental religious difference between the two groups, for all their linguistic and other affinities. Biblically, Yahweh's explicit command had been to destroy Canaanite religious culture (Numbers 33:52-3). The archaeological evidence corroborates this, as earlier noted of the taking of Jericho. It is also arguably true of Deborah and Barak's victory at Hazor, where Canaanite religious statues were singled out for smashing.

Furthermore, the divide between Israelite and Canaanite cultures can be seen archaeologically even in the Israelites' shunning of pork. Although scholars used to claim that this Jewish religious practice was introduced only late in Biblical history, American archaeologist Lawrence Stager[7] has noted that despite the Israelites moving into ideal pig-grazing country around Ai, Raddana and Ebal, there is no archaeological evidence of their keeping these animals. When the archaeologist Israel Finkelstein excavated Shiloh, where Israelite clearly succeeded Canaanite occupation, he found that the incidence of pig bones in the post-Canaanite levels plummeted to virtually zero[8]. Conversely, excavations of coastal sites such as Ashkelon have revealed that there was a shift towards pig and cattle farming at around the same period, suggesting that Canaanite pig-farmers, dislodged by the Israelites from their former central hill country, moved with their animals to

A view of some of the Manasseh, early Israelite settlement terrain surveyed by Adam Zertal.

these Way of the Sea places. Here, Egyptian colonisation of coastal Canaan would have provided them with protection.

Such archaeological findings are intriguing for throwing light upon the historical background to the Biblical narrative. Their drawback is that they are silent. If a group of newcomers to a pig-farming district shun keeping these animals, it is likely that they were Israelite or proto-Jewish. But if no suitable inscription accompanies this evidence, we must still be cautious.

Thankfully, as we move a little further forward in time, the dearth of inscriptional evidence comes to an end. All too easily overlooked among the more dazzling treasures of Cairo's Egyptian Museum is a 7½-foot-high black granite stele that Sir Flinders Petrie unearthed at Luxor in 1896. It is important because it establishes a 'no later than' date for when the Israelites became a significant force in Canaan. Once part of the funerary temple of the 19th Dynasty pharaoh Merneptah, son of Ramesses II, this stele can be firmly dated to the fifth year of Merneptah's reign, around 1207 BC. Its crucial feature is its concluding lines, in which Merneptah boasts of all the foreign peoples he has subjugated:

> The princes are prostrate, saying 'Peace' . . .
> Canaan has been plundered into every sort of woe
> Ashkelon has been overcome
> Gezer has been captured
> Yano'am was made non-existent
> Israel is laid waste [and] his seed is not.

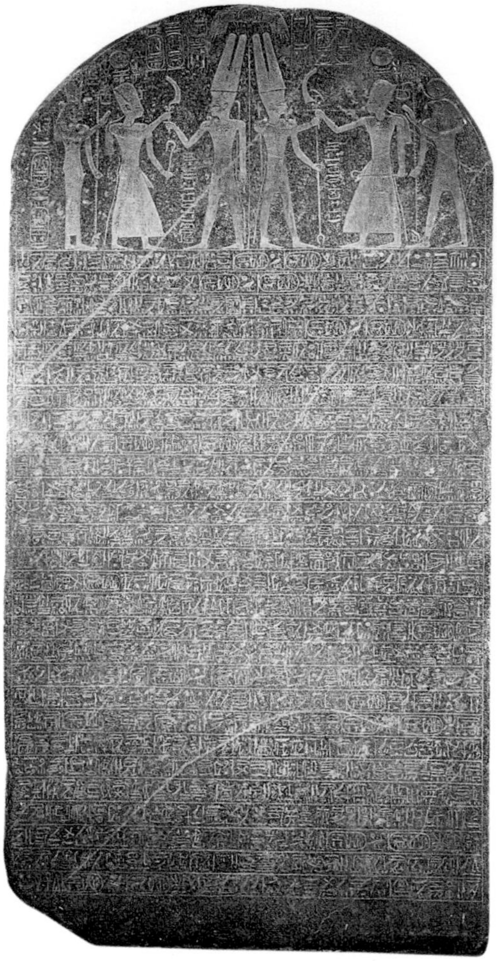

Egyptian stele of the late 13th-century BC Pharaoh Merneptah. The concluding lines read: 'Israel is laid waste [and] his seed is not.' This is the earliest document outside the Bible to mention the Israel people's existence as a significant force in Canaan.

A reasonable consensus of scholars has accepted this inscription as the earliest-known extra-Biblical recognition of the people of Israel's existence. It also establishes that they were occupying the land of Canaan. An important point here concerns ancient Egyptian hieroglyphs. Fundamental to writing any name in hieroglyphs is a so-called 'determinative', which makes clear whether it belongs, say, to a god, a man, a woman or a country. The Merneptah stele's determinatives for the Canaanite city-states of Ashkelon, Gezer and Yano'am are, in each case, a throwstick plus three mountains, conveying that each was a foreign territory. In the case of the name 'Israel', however, the determinative of a seated man, a seated woman and three hash marks[9] indicates this to be a people or ethnic group, rather than a territory name.

For the minimalists – those who try to minimise the Bible's historical veracity – this stele has long represented a stumbling block. For here is Egypt's pharaoh publicly boasting of his annihilation of this Israel people. And he sets the achievement alongside campaigns against some cities that we know, both Biblically and archaeologically, to have remained Canaanite. So whatever their earlier origins, the Israelites can no longer be dismissed as insignificant peasants. We can comfortably say that at least as early as 1207 BC or thereabouts, they were in their 'promised land' and, although they had not yet conquered it, they had become a significant force. This finding can only add support to our case that the Exodus from Egypt happened much earlier than the reign of Merneptah's father, Ramesses II.

However, thanks to some brilliant researches in the 1970s by American Egyptologist Frank Yurco, we may be able to push back this 'wasting' of the Israelites to a date even earlier than 1207, into Ramesses II's lifetime. While working on a survey of the inscriptions on the walls of the Temple of Amun at Luxor, Yurco became intrigued by a set of reliefs in the temple's First Court, or Cour de la Cachette. This comprised a series of scenes from a major military campaign, previously attributed to Ramesses II, later pharaohs having caused confusion by 'usurping' his name cartouches. But Yurco discerned, beneath the 'usurpings', that the true originating pharaoh was not Ramesses, but Merneptah. Furthermore, when Yurco was studying the inscriptions accompanying one scene that depicted a Canaanite city being stormed by the Egyptians, he noted that the city was Ashkelon, as mentioned on the Merneptah-Israel stele. This made him wonder whether the rest of the scenes in the reliefs might relate to the triumphs listed on that stele. When he carefully checked this out he found it confirmed, and many other scholars now support his insights.

The chief point of debate has accordingly switched to whether this campaign which laid Israel waste occurred during Merneptah's reign as pharaoh, or whether he may have waged it while still a prince, on behalf of his father who lived until he was around ninety. Greatly in favour of this latter idea is the fact that Merneptah was an old man unfit for the rigours of a military campaign when he succeeded his father. Another indication that the Israelites were already well-entrenched in Canaan as early as Ramesses II's reign is an Egyptian messenger's travelogue of this period. In this he describes the prosperity of the obviously still Canaanite coastal towns and valleys. But he also warns that the 'mountains of Shechem'[10] are occupied by a Shosu nomadic group called Isr, very possibly the Israelite tribe of Asher, who according to some Biblical passages settled first in the southern hill country of Ephraim[11] before moving to the northern coast.

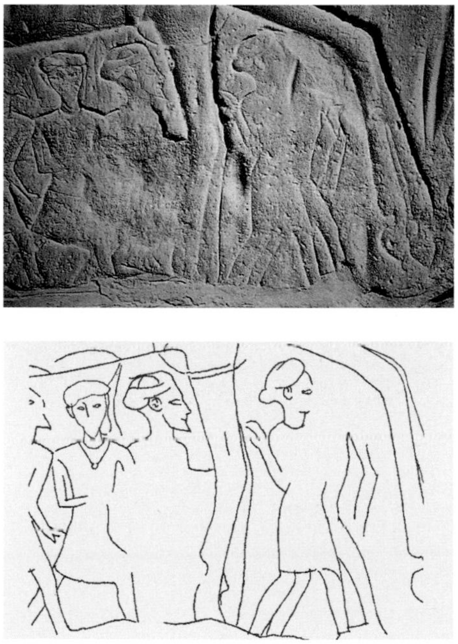

The earliest-known depiction of Biblical Israelites? In this detail from the Temple of Amun reliefs, Asiatics wearing turbans and short tunics are shown beneath Merneptah's horse.

Another fascinating aspect of the Cour de la Cachette reliefs is that they may provide the earliest-known data about the Israelites' physical appearance. Egyptian artists took a great deal of care in depicting foreign peoples accurately. The Canaanite males in the Cour de la Cachette scenes of the Egyptian capture of Gezer and Ashkelon, for instance, are consistently shown as bearded, with long hair tied in a headband, and wearing ankle-length tunics. Of considerable interest, therefore, is the very damaged scene that may be equivalent to the Merneptah stele's line about Israel being 'laid waste'. In this, several bearded, turbaned, short-tunicked warriors can be seen falling beneath the pharaoh's chariot wheels. Scholars tend cautiously to identify peoples wearing this kind of dress with the vague term Shosu, because that is how the Egyptians labelled them elsewhere. But in this context there is a good case for identifying these particular Shosu as Israelites in the throes of their being 'laid waste'. For Hollywood's makers of Biblical epics, the bad news is that, instead of the Arab kaffiyeh, almost universally worn by their extras, the real head-dress worn by Israelite males was more probably a turban. Also, instead of long, flowing garments, they more likely wore kilts, which as Scottish Highlanders can attest, are more practical than long robes for moving quickly and easily in hilly terrain[12].

Whatever the truth, it is ironic that history's first surviving reference to the people of Israel should speak of their extermination. For rather than being liquidated, as Merneptah boasted, the evidence suggests that the Israelites at this time were a people increasingly to be reckoned with. Yet if their tussle with the Canaanites was far from over, as later events would prove, their struggle with other more fearsome neighbours was only just beginning.

8

THOSE UNSETTLING PHILISTINES

TODAY, WE ARE used to living in solid-built houses. It seems natural to us, and we assume all too readily that a people like the Israelites would have wanted to move out of their traditional tents and into houses the moment they had the opportunity to settle down in their 'promised land'. But this is not necessarily how anyone brought up in tents would see it, any more than Amazonian Indians used to living naked may take to wearing clothes. As has been remarked by the Israeli archaeologist Avraham Negev:

> Tent-dwellers easily allocate a special tent for almost every function in their social life: a tent for the men, another for women, children, guests, storage space, etc. Moreover by moving the tent seasonally, problems of pollution are readily solved – in the best way known to the ancient world.[1]

Nevertheless, a shift is apparent as the repeated mentions of tent-dwelling and caring for flocks in the earliest Biblical books gradually and convincingly give way to references to housekeeping and the growing of crops. The book of Judges is transitional between the two life styles. For instance, after all the herd-keeping featured in Genesis and Exodus, Judges 6:3 speaks of the Israelites sowing wheat, while its chapter 8, verse 2, refers to their growing grapevines.

Archaeology supplements the picture, for the remains of humble village-clustered dwellings now emerge that even the more conservative archaeologists confidently call Israelite houses. They add, however, that the distinctive plan of these dwellings should not be thought exclusive to the so-called Israelite people. Indeed, this house-plan, dubbed the 'four-room house', became so characteristic during the next few centuries that it is clearly worth scrutinising for what it can tell us about an apparently new-found life style.

At the house's rear was a narrow back room that stretched the full width. As is evident from present-day Arab houses, it was most likely the men's parlour. There was a long middle room, which might include a cistern for water. This was where the domestic work, food preparation, cooking and weaving would have been done. Along either side of this, divided from it by lines of pillars, ran cobbled stalls

An artist's reconstruction of an Israelite house of the Judges period.

thought to have been used for indoors-reared livestock, such as 'stall-fed' calves (1 Samuel 28:24). Gaps between the cobbles allowed the animals' urine to drain away. Some dwellings seem to have had a ladder or steps providing access to an upper floor where the air would have been rather fresher than at ground level. Overall, the houses indicate occupants who are no longer the Shosu-type semi-nomadic herders of old, but are rooted to fixed locations and earning their living by agriculture.

Reflecting the same change of life style, instead of the goat-skin beverage containers used in the old days of tent-dwelling – and by the Kenite Jael when she poured Canaanite general Sisera his last drink (Judges 4:19) – the dwellers of the new houses are found to be using pottery vessels. These are of a simple, but by no means inelegant, 'collar-rim' type, which archaeologists designate as 'Israelite' in

The distinctive 'Israelite' collar-rim pottery often associated with Israelite houses of the Judges period.

much the same manner as they refer to the four-room houses as Israelite. Capable of holding between 10 and 15 gallons of liquid, and with a short, narrow neck rather like the collar of a crew-neck sweater (hence the term 'collar-rim'), these jars seem to have been used chiefly for water storage. Their very size indicates that the people who used them were now settled, rather than on the move.

Another characteristic of a people settling down is that they begin to build permanent monuments. In this regard, few constructions of this period are more intriguing than one discovered by Adam Zertal while doing his heroic survey work. On 6 April 1980, he and his small team were close to completing a survey of 3000-foot-high Mount Ebal, immediately to the north of ancient Shechem, when they came across a large heap of stones. This seemed nothing out of the ordinary, for Israeli farmers quite often pile up stones when clearing fields for planting, until they noticed a considerable quantity of surrounding ancient pottery fragments.

As they immediately recognised, the pottery type was Iron Age I, i.e. from c.1200-1000 BC, the generally-accepted date for when the Israelites emerged in Canaan. There was a puzzling feature, however – an absence of any sign of nearby settlement from this period. Because Zertal was so preoccupied with his survey, it took

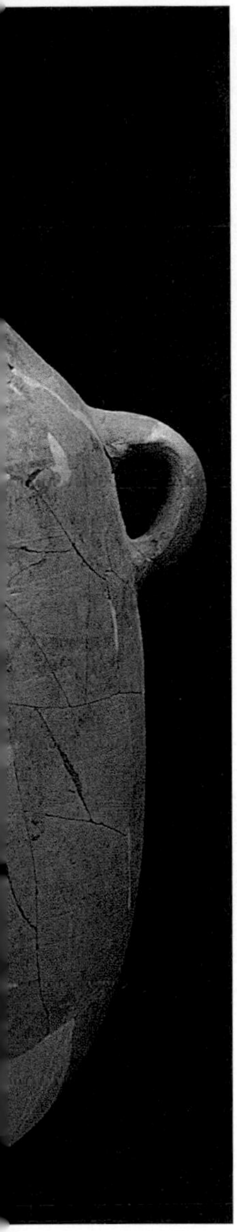

him two years before he began a proper investigation. When he did so his puzzlement only increased.

As he and his helpers dug away the surrounding earth, a curious rectangular structure made of unhewn stones came to light. It stood inside a stone wall, and was approached by a stepped entrance. Measuring 10 feet high by 30 feet long and 23 feet wide, and with corners oriented to the points of the compass, it contained a fill of stones, earth, wood ash and animal bones. On Zertal's own admission, it took him three seasons to recognise its function, and then only as a result of a remark by a casual visitor:

> I remember it vividly. It was a Thursday, the morning of October 13, 1983. A friend of mine, a young archaeologist named David Etam visited the site, and I gave him a tour. I was explaining the site to him, especially the difficulty we were having understanding the function of the strange central structure that had been filled. David interrupted me: 'Why don't you think the opposite? Why don't you think that the filling is the most important part, rather than the building?' For months we had been trying to understand the structure by thinking of the filling as secondary. We were concentrating on the outside structure. David's insight stunned me. I grabbed a Bible and opened it to Exodus 27:8 which describes the portable Tabernacle altar the Israelites were commanded to build in the wilderness: 'Make it hollow, with boards. As you were shown on the mountain, so shall it be made.'
>
> Then I went to a Bible encyclopaedia and looked under 'altar' and read as follows: 'The Tabernacle altar is described as having four walls: it was filled with earth and stones to its full height. On this filling the fire was burned. This construction method is well-known from Assyrian altars. That is why the altar is described [in the Bible] as being "hollow with boards".'[2] Suddenly it all became clear: the filling and the structure were together one complete unit – an altar![3]

And not just any altar. Into Zertal's consciousness came the words of Deuteronomy:

> Upon crossing the Jordan, . . . on Mount Ebal . . . you shall build an altar to Yahweh your god, an altar of stones. Do not wield an iron tool over them. You must build the altar . . . of unhewn [literally: 'whole'] stones. You shall offer on it burnt offerings to Yahweh . . . and you shall sacrifice there offerings of well-being and eat them . . . (Deuteronomy 27:2-7)

Corresponding to this is a passage from the book of Joshua. After its account of the destruction of the Canaanite city of Ai, it tells of precisely such an altar being erected on Mount Ebal. On it 'they offered . . . burnt offerings to Yahweh, and brought sacrifices of well-being' (Joshua 8:31).

One thing needs to be made clear. Although many scholars have supported Zertal in identifying this structure as the altar of Joshua 8, there have also been some doubters. For instance, the Israeli archaeologist Aharon Kempinski, after visiting the site for only an hour early on in Zertal's excavations, concluded that it was a former house converted into a watchtower.[4]

Strong indications do, however, exist that the Mount Ebal structure really was an altar. These include Zertal's finding of quantities of animal bones, as from sacrificial animals, among the fill. When Jerusalem's Hebrew University zoology department examined these, they identified them as the bones of young male bulls, sheep, goats and fallow deer, all of them animals that were regarded as acceptable for sacrifice.[5] More than that, they also established that most of the bones had been burnt on open-flame fires[6], exactly as if on a sacrificial altar. Furthermore, the structure's approach was via a ramp, conforming to Exodus 20:26's directions that the Israelites should not ascend altars by steps 'for fear you expose your nakedness'.

But if Zertal's discovery really was an altar, when was it built? A crucial find in this regard was unearthed deep amongst the fill: an Egyptian-style scarab of a rare type datable to the period during or shortly after the reign of Ramesses II (c.1290-1224).[7] This was followed by another scarab, to the north of the altar, datable to the same pharaoh's reign. Since the surrounding pottery confirms this dating, it is virtually certain that the altar was not built before the 13th century BC – in other words, slightly later than the period we have inferred as being the time of Joshua. At the very least, however, the Mount Ebal structure is the oldest Israelite burnt-offering altar found so far, and much the most complete.

Top: The stone structure on Mount Ebal identified by Adam Zertal as the altar built by the Israelites. Above: Reconstruction of the original altar.

Yet another mark of a people settling down is that they create cultic centres. The Ark, purportedly created out in the Sinai desert, would now surely need a safe home appropriate to its sanctity. The Biblical testimony is that Joshua's followers, after they arrived in Canaan, kept the Ark at Shiloh, a place-name that can be reliably located, thanks to the book of Judges' description of it as 'north of Bethel, east of the highway . . . from Bethel up to Shechem, and south of Lebonah' (Judges 21:19). Not only does this locate it in the central hill country which was the early Israelite heartland, but also a defunct Arab village called Seilun, 12 miles south of Shechem, preserves its name.

Thanks to this clue, its 8-acre tell was identified as 'early', by the pioneering American Biblical scholar Edward Robinson in the 1830s.

Later in the 19th century this site was explored more thoroughly by the archaeologically-inclined British Army engineer Sir Charles Wilson. During the 20th century it was properly excavated, first by a Danish expedition, then during the early 1980s by Israeli archaeologist Israel Finkelstein.[8] All this work revealed that a Canaanite sacred shrine had stood on the same site even before an Israelite takeover. Although there seemed to be no houses surrounding it, typically Canaanite *glacis*-type protective fortifications had been built for the shrine. Then, some time not before the 16th century BC[9], unidentified invaders set its buildings on fire. They acted so swiftly and ruthlessly that its cult objects were found still in their storerooms, with the mud-brick walls collapsed on top of them. Such destruction is so typical of the pattern noted of other Middle Bronze Age Canaanite sites, with valuable items again going unlooted, that Israelites have to be strongly suspected as the destroyers, though this cannot be considered proven.

But as archaeologist Finkelstein further discovered[10], after a lull during the Late Bronze Age period, when the Israelites were 'de-nomading' themselves, new buildings suddenly sprang up on the former *glacis*. Among the pottery found in these were collar-rim storage jars of the early Israelite Iron Age I type. Additionally, survey work of the surrounding area found that its population had dramatically doubled and trebled, a rate of growth much greater than that seen elsewhere. This strongly indicates that there was something special about living in Shiloh's environs at this time.

It is easy to guess what this was. For according to the book of Joshua, in the aftermath of the various victories over the Canaanites:

> The whole community of the Israelite people assembled at Shiloh and set up the Tent of Meeting there. The land was now under their control. (Joshua 18:1)

A reconstruction of the Tent of Meeting that is thought to have stood at Tell Shiloh.

It is apparent from the Bible that this Tent of Meeting included a Tabernacle, which housed the Ark containing the two stone tablets of the Law that Moses had brought down with him from Mount Sinai. This was also where the *nabiim* came to consult with Yahweh. Shiloh at this period was clearly the equivalent of the later Temple of Jerusalem. While it might seem surprising that a former Canaanite religious site was chosen for so sacred a purpose, arguably this was no different to early Christians commonly founding their churches on pagan sacred sites, or to Protestants during the Reformation equally commonly reusing churches that had belonged to the Roman Catholics.

Likewise, despite the obvious difficulties in determining the exact spot where the Tent of Meeting with its Ark might have stood at Shiloh, the Jewish scholar Asher S. Kaufman has made some very convincing deductions[11]. According to the Biblical description of how the double-chambered Tent was set up during the Israelites' travels[12], it was always surrounded by a large, rectangular, screened enclosure, which only priests were allowed to enter. This incorporated not only the Tent itself, but also an area for a portable sacrificial altar and the vessels needed to purify it. Because the animals intended for sacrifice were necessarily led into this enclosure and prepared there for slaughter, it had to be quite large even when 'on the road'. Its quoted Biblical

dimensions of 100 by 50 cubits are translatable as 140 by 70 feet, or more than the area of four tennis courts.

Shiloh's hilly terrain seriously limits the number of level sites capable of accommodating such an enclosure. The 19th-century British engineer Sir Charles Wilson, on visiting the site, identified an area he called a 'level court' about 160 yards to the north of the tell proper. This, he reckoned, was where the 'Tent' most probably once stood.[13] Forming a platform 400 feet long by 70 feet wide, it not only provides much the largest area of available level ground, it is also suitably aligned east-to-west, just as we are told the Tent of Meeting always was (Exodus 26:22; Numbers 3:23, 38). Kaufman supports Wilson's insights, and if both have deduced correctly, we may now be able to identify the spot on which the Biblical Ark stood during the years immediately following the Israelites' settlement in Canaan.

However, whether you are an individual, a family or a whole nation, it is one of life's ironies that just when you think everything is settling down, something or someone comes along to change it all. In the case of the Biblical Israelites, after they had settled in alongside the Canaanites, as well as successfully repelling camel-borne Midianites who harried them for a period, suddenly as if from nowhere a new and far more formidable threat emerged: the people Biblically called the Philistines.

It was only a couple of decades after Pharaoh Merneptah had boasted himself master of all the surrounding peoples that a mysterious but massive 'people explosion' burst upon the entire eastern Mediterranean. It is mysterious because its cause is by no means clear. Perhaps it was famine, drought, a climatic change triggered by a comet or a chain

Tell Shiloh as it appears today. In the foreground is the 'level court', on which the Tent of Meeting is thought to have stood.

Invasion of the Philistines. A relief of Pharaoh Ramesses III at Medinet Habu depicting his battle with the invading 'Sea Peoples', among these the *P-l-s-t*, Biblically better known as 'Philistines'.

of killer earthquakes.[14] Whatever the reason, it is quite certain that so-called Sea Peoples suddenly erupted in overwhelming force among the eastern Mediterranean's Late Bronze Age cities and city-states, in an arc stretching from Greece, through eastern Turkey, down to Crete and Cyprus, and into modern-day Israel. Even the powerful Hittite empire, with which the great Ramesses II had only shortly before concluded a treaty because he was unable to conquer it, was overrun. Hittite cities, including the great Hittite capital at Borghaz Köy, were pillaged and burned. Likewise, the formerly flourishing Canaanitic city-state of Ugarit was destroyed, never to emerge again. According to a last letter from its ruler, found still in the oven waiting to be baked:

> Thus speaks the king of Ugarit . . . Ships of the enemy have come, some of my towns have been burned and they have done wicked things in our country . . . Seven enemy ships have appeared offshore and done evil things . . . [15]

Whatever caused these Sea Peoples to go on the move, their general direction of advance was unmistakably southwards, towards Egypt, where Ramesses III (*c.*1194-1163) was then in his eighth year as pharaoh. This Ramesses built for himself a great mortuary temple at Medinet Habu near Thebes, today among the best-preserved of such temples. On its walls, reliefs depicting the great naval battle he fought with these Sea Peoples can still be seen, his own Egyptian soldiers distinguished by rectangular shields and bows, their adversaries by round shields and spears. In one part, Ramesses' scribes can be seen making a careful tally of heaped-up severed hands, their way, as earlier noted, of counting the dead. From this it might be inferred that the Egyptians scored a great victory.

However, the largest and the most magnificent papyrus to have come down to us from ancient Egypt also survives from Ramesses III's reign. It is the British Museum's Papyrus

Harris I, discovered in a hole in the ground at Thebes in 1855. And when we read between its lines, it becomes apparent that Ramesses III's battle with the Sea Peoples was more of a close-run thing than he cared too explicitly to admit:

> I [Ramesses] extended all the frontiers of Egypt and overthrew those who attacked them from their lands. I slew the Denyen in their islands, while the Tjekker and the P-l-s-t were made ashes. The Sherden and the Weshesh of the Sea were made non-existent, captured all together and brought in captivity to Egypt like the sands of the shore. I settled them in strongholds, bound in my name. Their military classes were as numerous as hundred-thousands. I assigned portions for them all with clothing and provisions from the treasuries and granaries every year.

It is apparent from this that Ramesses III averted what might otherwise have been a defeat as serious as the one his predecessors had suffered four centuries earlier from the Hyksos/Canaanites. But from his claim that he 'settled them [i.e. the Sea Peoples] in strongholds', it would seem that he was obliged to allow at least some of them to take over formerly Egyptian-controlled territories along the Canaan coast's Way of the Sea. Thus, the Sherden, for instance, are known to have settled around the middle section of this coast, with the Sikils (who feature with them on the Medinet Habu reliefs), at Dor just to the south, where they are known, archaeologically, to have constructed a fine new harbour[16].

However, our greatest interest concerns the P-l-s-t whom Ramesses claimed to have 'made ashes'. For although their fate goes otherwise unremarked in Egyptian sources, there can be no doubt that these were the people the Bible calls the Philistines, from whom we get the name 'Palestine'. It is from the book of Joshua, rather than any Egyptian or other Near Eastern source, that we learn that 'the five rulers of the Philistines have their seats at Gaza, Ashdod, Ashkelon, Gath and Ekron respectively' (Joshua 13:3).[17] And since all these places can be located today, either because they have kept their names, in the case of the first three, or because archaeologists have positively identified their sites, we know that they, too, were along the Way of the Sea corridor. They lived in the region between the central highlands and the Mediterranean coast which the Israelites had been unable to capture because the Egyptians 'protected' the incumbent Canaanites. Archaeologists have found Philistine remains succeeding Canaanite ones in

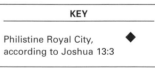

Left: A detail of captured P-l-s-t, or Philistines, from the Medinet Habu relief, showing their characteristic feathered head-dresses.

Commanding the former Egyptian-controlled Way of the Sea, now to become the 'Way of the Land of the Philistines', the coastal corridor south of present-day Tel Aviv that formed the Philistines' prime territory.

KEY

Philistine Royal City, according to Joshua 13:3 ◆

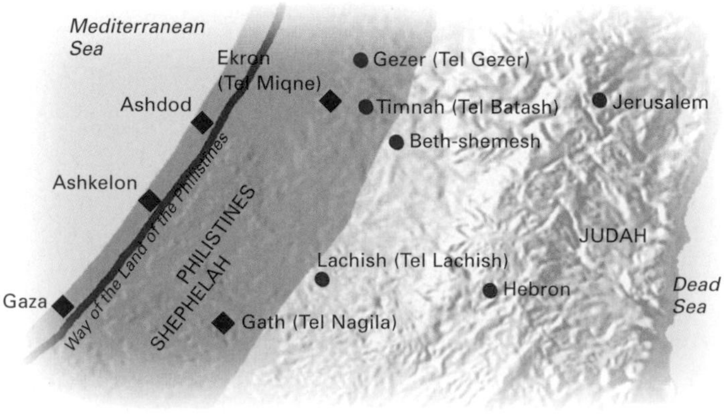

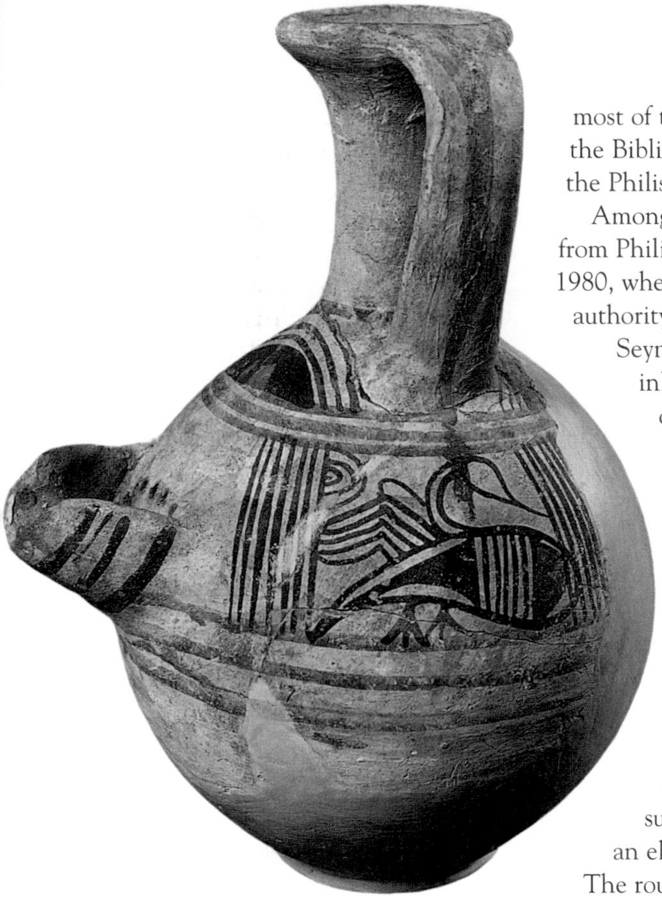

most of these locations, allowing us to check and flesh out the Biblical descriptions of the Israelite encounters with the Philistines.

Among the most revealing of these findings have been from Philistine Ekron. This site was thought to be lost until 1980, when Israeli archaeologist Trude Dothan, a world authority on the Philistines, in partnership with American Seymour Gitin, began seriously investigating a 50-acre inland mound known as Tel Miqne[18], 8 miles east of Ashdod.

From Dothan and Gitin's findings at Tel Miqne/Ekron, combined with those of other researchers at related sites[19], a picture of the Philistines has emerged that is very different from the crudity and boorishness our modern use of their name signifies. For instance, their town planning was excellent, contradicting any notion that they arrived as disorganised refugee-squatters. They laid out 'new towns' with straight, parallel streets evocative of the modern-day United States. Architecturally, their buildings, such as those at Tel Miqne, feature round hearths, an element previously unknown at Canaanite sites. The round hearth is, in fact, Aegean in its roots, as evident from excavations at Pylos and Mycenae, as well as from the pages of Homer.

Philistine pottery. Contradicting the Philistines' reputation, their pottery exhibits sophisticated shapes and designs, as in the case of this 'bi-chrome' pitcher, so called because of its distinctive red and black decorative motifs.

In pottery, the Philistines' taste was excellent. Although clay analysis shows that they made most of their potterywares on-site in Canaan, rather than importing them from elsewhere, the vessels' shapes and geometric and bird-motif decorations display characteristic Aegean styling. Microanalysis indicates they were used for beer, a beverage the Philistines seem to have been particularly fond of.

It is also very likely that the Philistines were literate. Certainly, Trude Dothan's husband Moshe, in his excavations at Ashdod, unearthed two seals with what may be Philistine writing on them (see overleaf). More recently, a clay seal impression[20] has come to light elsewhere, of the kind that would have been used to seal a papyrus document. It hints tantalisingly at the considerable amount of Philistine, Canaanite and probably Israelite writing of this period that has almost certainly been lost to us.

But the Philistine skill *par excellence*, recognised in the Biblical accounts and confirmed archaeologically, was probably their mastery of iron-working. Indicative of how rare and precious a commodity iron was at this period is the fact that the very oldest Philistine objects made of iron are invariably cultic rather than practical. Examples include ivory-handled iron knives excavated from the Philistine temples at Ekron and Tel Qasile. The Philistines' iron-working skills are also suggested in a

Philistine iron-working. A cultic knife found at Philistine Ekron.

passage from the Biblical book of Samuel, best quoted using the 17th-century 'King James' translation, for reasons that will become clear:

> There was no smith throughout all the land of Israel, for the Philistines said: 'Lest the Hebrews make swords or spears.' But all the Israelites went down to the Philistines, to sharpen every man his [plough]share and his coulter [the cutter in front of the ploughshare] and his axe and his mattock [pickaxe]. Yet they had a file [*pym*] for the mattocks and for the coulters, and for the forks, and for the axes, and to sharpen the goads. (1 Samuel 13:19-22)

Philistine writing? A stamp seal found at Philistine Ashdod, bearing an as-yet undeciphered inscription with so-called Cypro-Minoan characteristics.

An obvious point of interest here is that the Israelites are still featured as 'going down' to the Philistines, just as they had previously 'gone down' to the plain-based Canaanites. It indicates that they were still mainly confined to the hilly districts. Equally intriguing is their stated need to sharpen their ploughshares, re-affirming our earlier remarks concerning their life-style shift from pastoralism to land cultivation.

But there is a further detail which suggests that what we are being told, despite later editing, has a strong basis in historical truth. To the King James translators, and in fact to all other Biblical translators right up to the 20th century, the meaning of the Hebrew word *pym*, used in the Hebrew Bible only in this one passage, was 'file'. Then in 1903 an ancient bronze cube came to light in Jerusalem specifically inscribed with the Hebrew consonants *pym*. This discovery was followed four years later by the finding at Gezer of another 'pym', taking the form of a sub-spherical stone. A trickle of further specimens have come to light in more recent excavations. From the weight of these pyms, always precisely 0.275 ounces – i.e. two-thirds of the average common shekel weight of 0.413 ounces – it is obvious that the Samuel 13:22 pym was actually a balance weight for weighing out scraps of silver. The passage's true meaning, therefore, was that the Philistines charged the Israelites two-thirds of a shekel for sharpening their ploughshares and axes. Nor is this all. Since the use of these pyms had died out by the 7th century BC, the reference to a pym argues strongly that this part of the Biblical text originated far back in time, whatever later editing may have been applied to it.

Another point is apparent archaeologically: that there was very little intermingling between the Israelites up in the hill country and the Philistines on the coast. There is an almost complete absence of any Philistine pottery in the Israelite hill country, and likewise an almost total absence of Israelite-type collar-rim jars at Philistine coastal sites. The two peoples obviously kept their distance from each other. It is only from the Biblical record that we know anything of the serious hostilities between them.

Philistine weights and measures: a pym balance weight.

Thus, according to the fourth chapter of the first book of Samuel, nothing less than a pitched battle took place between the Israelites and the Philistines somewhere between Aphek and Ebenezer. The Israelites suffered so badly during what seems to have been a Philistine 'seek-out-and-destroy' mission that they deployed their ultimate 'weapon': the Ark. This did not protect them, however. The Israelites suffered a humiliating defeat, and the Ark itself was captured and taken away from them (1 Samuel 4:11). Reportedly, when a messenger brought back this bad news to the Ark's home base at Shiloh, Eli, the elderly priest-judge of the time, fell back heavily at the shock, broke his neck and died (1 Samuel 4:18).

Nor did the humiliation end there. Although the author of 1 Samuel could not bring himself to admit it, all the indications are that the Philistines then made their way to Shiloh and destroyed it. This may be inferred from the much later Biblical book of Jeremiah, which twice accredits Yahweh with threatening to inflict the fate of Shiloh on the Jerusalem Temple (Jeremiah 7:12-14; 26:6 & 9). This suggests that Shiloh lay in ruins in Jeremiah's time. Furthermore, from Israel Finkelstein's report of his Shiloh excavations, it is quite evident that the buildings with Israelite-type, collar-rim storage jars suffered destruction in a very serious fire. Their blackened bricks were found piled up to 3 feet deep in places.

It is not difficult to gauge how bitter a blow this must have been for the Israelites. According to 1 Samuel 3:1, 'in those days it was rare for Yahweh to speak; [and] *nabiim* were not numerous'. Yet somewhere, in one of the Israelite buildings on Shiloh's tell, was the place where the priest and *nabi* Samuel had had his famous experience of hearing someone calling him. As an acolyte of the judge and *nabi* Eli, Samuel at first supposed the voice to be Eli's, but eventually realised that the voice he was hearing was nothing less than the divine voice. Intriguingly, the very names 'Samuel' and 'Eli' suggest that these were Biblical individuals who still knew their deity as 'El' rather than 'Yahweh'. Whatever the case, their outrage at the loss, not only of their sacred sanctuary, but also of the Ark itself, from which they had heard the divine voice, must have been incalculable.

Yet as the Biblical account makes clear, any satisfaction the Philistines felt about capturing the Israelite Ark may have been short-lived. For all too soon they began to suffer disasters and plagues that seemed uncannily Ark-related. For instance, when they moved the Ark to Ashdod, it was quickly associated with the otherwise inexplicable collapse of a statue of their god Dagon. Then when they moved it to Gath, there was an epidemic of tumours which caused panic in the town. When they took it to Ekron, there was a further tumour outbreak, prompting them in desperation to ask their 'priests and diviners' for advice about what to do.

As noted earlier, the present-day archaeologists Trude Dothan and Seymour Gitin have been excavating Philistine Ekron/Tel Miqne. In one of its temples, they found a sacrificial knife made of iron, also a wheeled 'cult stand' which may have supported the statue of a god such as Dagon. Perhaps their most pertinent discovery, Biblically, has been the scapula of a cow incised with parallel lines along its upper edge. Such bones were popular among ancient Aegean peoples for precisely the kind of 'divining' the Philistines are said to have practised according to the Bible. Because the Ark was a cultic object, albeit one belonging to an enemy people, Philistine superstition would have regarded it as far too magical to be destroyed. This explains their ultimate decision to set it upon a cart, harness two milking-cows[21] to the cart, and then let the cows take the accursed object wheresoever its 'god' willed.

According to the Biblical account, the first place it reached in Israelite territory was Beth-Shemesh. This is another Biblical location that has been successfully identified in the form of a hillock called Rumeillah[22] directly east of Ekron. It lies at a convincing midway point between the Philistine-held Mediterranean coastline and the Israelite-held central hill country. Archaeological excavations there[23] continue to this day, the Iron Age or Israelite levels again being notable for an absence of pig bones. Apparently, at the time that Beth-Shemesh's locals saw the Ark being returned to them, they 'were reaping the wheat harvest in the plain' (1 Samuel 6:13). This is yet another indication of the change of life style, and to this day the region is a strong wheat-growing area.

Whatever credibility we may or may not attribute to this particular Biblical story, one thing is sure. Although the Ark was never restored to Shiloh (arguably because this was too vulnerable and had been too badly defiled), the Israelites did get it back, whereupon it lingered on as a Biblically 'historical' object for several centuries to come. Yet even if the Israelites' earlier humiliation had thus been eased a little, in order to enjoy the land they had been 'promised', they still needed someone very forceful to help them rid the country of the Philistines.

The book of Judges' closing chapters portray one man who at least came close to this: Samson, from the tribe of Dan. He was apparently brought up at Zorah, identifiable with the ruined Arab village Sar'ah, just north of Beth-Shemesh. According to the Biblical story, Samson went 'down' to Timnah (Judges 14:1), where he fell in love with and married the Philistine Delilah. Only very recently, Texan Baptist professor George L. Kelm, together with Israeli archaeologist Amihai Mazar, claimed to have found this Timnah.

The site in question, a flat-topped mound known as Tell Batash, stands at the bend of a stream called the Sorek, 5 miles east of the Tel Miqne we now know to have been Philistine Ekron, and 5 miles west of the Beth-Shemesh where the Biblical Ark allegedly crossed from Philistine into Israelite territory. From Kelm and Mazar's pottery finds at this location, they infer that it was settled by the Philistines a little after they moved into Ekron 'perhaps sometime between 1150-1100 BC'.[24]

As the Biblical Samson story goes on, Samson was cruelly betrayed by the Philistine Delilah. Apparently the long hair in which his strength lay was close cropped while he slept. Then he was blinded. His moment of revenge came when, in a superhuman show of returned strength, he managed to bring the Temple of Dagon at Gaza crashing down upon the three thousand Philistines assembled inside it.

Tell Batash has been identified as the Biblical 'Timnah' (Judges 14:1), where Samson met and married the Philistine beauty Delilah.

Whatever original truth this story may contain, at least some of it has degenerated into folktale. Although Philistine Gaza has yet to be properly excavated, it is certain that no Philistine temple yet discovered could possibly have accommodated anything like three thousand persons. This is another indication that the numbers in the early Biblical books have all too frequently been exaggerated. Nonetheless, one element of the Samson story still demands some serious attention: its description of Samson bringing down the temple by dislodging 'the two central pillars supporting the building' (see Judges 16:23-30). For temple architecture of around the 12th century BC commonly featured two massive columns in the centre of a temple's main hall supporting its roof, as in the 12th-century Canaanite temple at Lachish[25], and the later Solomonic Temple of Jerusalem.

Although Samson is best remembered for this last show of supreme strength, there is

another less well-known side to his career. For twenty years before his death, he served as a judge of Israel. He was one of that long line of divinely-inspired individuals, reputedly stretching back to the time of Deborah, of Joshua and ultimately of Moses. Each of them held this status for their lifetime only, without being able to pass it on to their children and grandchildren.

But given that even such a legendary strong man as Samson had failed to remove the Philistine scourge, was the time not right for the 'Israel' people to have a proper king, entrusted with the leadership of armies, as other nations had? As the Bible record makes clear, precisely such thoughts began to surface around the time of Samson's death. And if that is what people were beginning to think, surely the moment could not be far off when someone would come forward to fill such a role.

9

A KING MOST HUMAN

FOR THE STORY of how the people of Israel made their transition from free-living under divinely-guided judges to direct rule by divinely-anointed kings, the Bible's first book of Samuel is our prime authority.

Once again, as evident from analyses by Biblical scholars, we find that whenever this book was put together, its compiler drew from different, older sources – two in this case. According to the first, the formerly Shiloh-based judge Samuel was a staunch anti-monarchist convinced that any king would destroy the Israelites' traditional freedoms. According to the second, Samuel was a *nabi* divinely instructed to anoint Saul as king in order to save 'my people from the hands of the Philistines' (1 Samuel 9:16).

With regard to the Israelite people in Samuel's time, generally thought to have been around the end of the 11th century BC, it is clear, both Biblically and archaeologically, that there was very little unity among them. For instance, Samuel appears to have been 'nationally' revered. Yet even for him, his sphere of influence was probably limited to a circuit comprising Bethel, Gilgal, Mizpah and Ramah (1 Samuel 7:16), all hill-country locations clustered in a concentrated area just south of the ill-fated Shiloh. Territorially, there was still a great deal of jostling among the nationalities occupying different pockets of the land.

Thus, archaeologists excavating coastal Dor have found that the Sikil Sea People who had only so recently occupied the city[1] were dislodged some time around 1050 BC, seemingly by Canaanites recapturing it.[2] We noted that the Israelite coastal tribe of Dan enjoyed a symbiotic relationship with the Canaanites in Deborah's time. Apparently, however, they reached no such rapport with the incoming Philistines, and moved northwards to capture the previously inoffensive Canaanite city of Laish, renaming this Dan. Today known as Tel Dan[3], it is located in attractive forested terrain at the foot of Mount Hermon. Israeli archaeologist Avraham Biran's long-running excavations have shown that the Danites refortified the city's old and inadequate Middle Bronze Age walls. Both Philistines and southern Israelites of the Judah tribe seem to have suffered repeated harassment from Amalekites, a people of still undetermined (but most likely Arab)

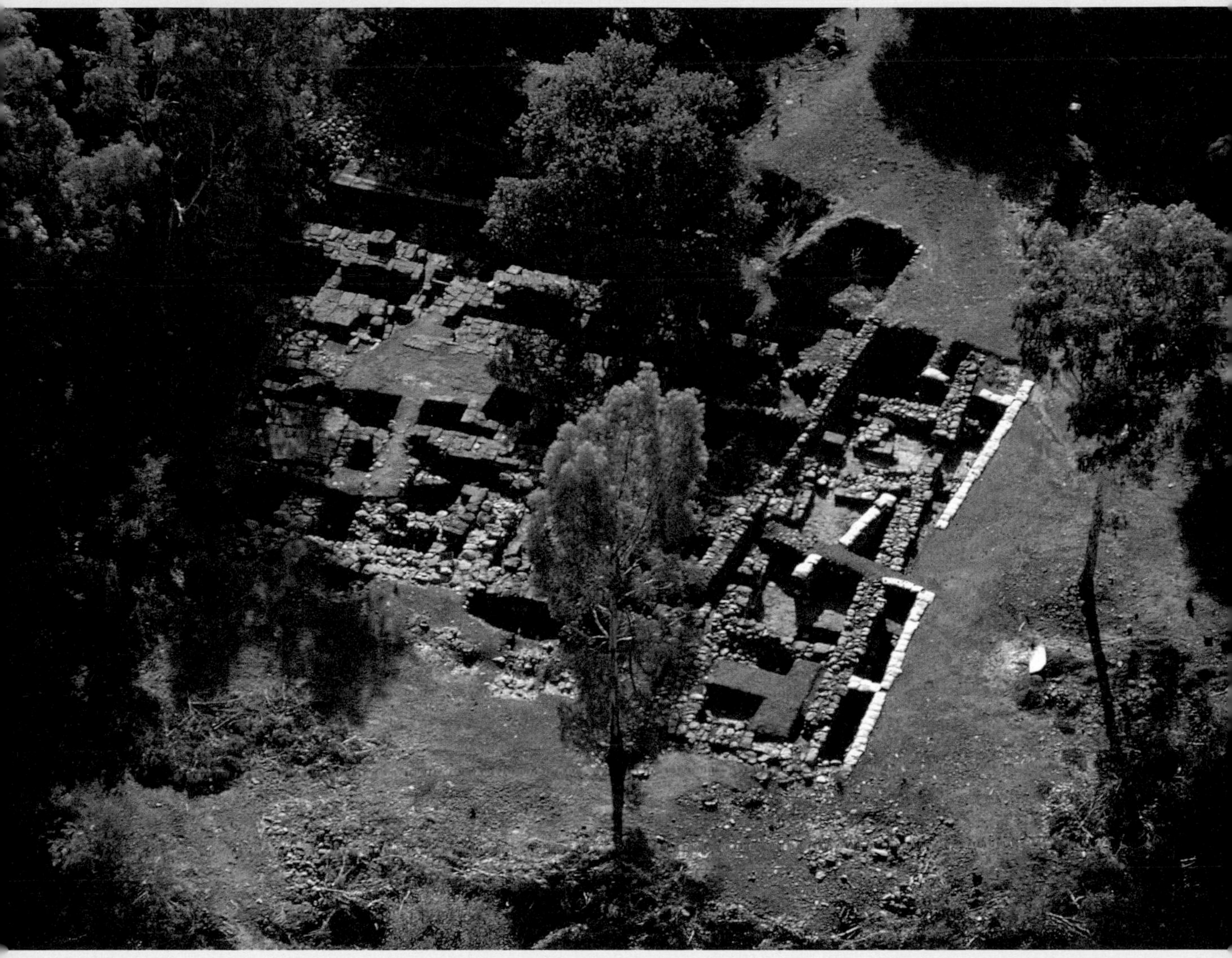

An excavated section of leafy Tel Dan, in present-day Israel's far north. This has been positively identified as Biblical Dan, formerly Canaanitic Laish.

origins who preyed upon the region between the Egyptian border and the Philistine coastal towns.

As for the Israelites' internal politics, they were apparently still very clannish within their tribal groups. About their religion Samuel is represented as alluding matter-of-factly to their 'foreign gods and Astartes'. It is clear, then, that a good number of them were worshipping in the old Canaanite way. This is corroborated archaeologically by a plenitude of Astarte-type fertility-goddess and other figurines of this period which have turned up in excavations. As for the Yahweh cult, anyone supposing that this bore any resemblance to present-day Judaism should read 1 Samuel 10's account of a band of *nabiim* 'coming down from the *bamah*, preceded by lyres, timbrels, flutes and harps . . . speaking in ecstasy' (1 Samuel 10:5). Not only was a *bamah* a Canaanitic-type cultic shrine or 'high place', but

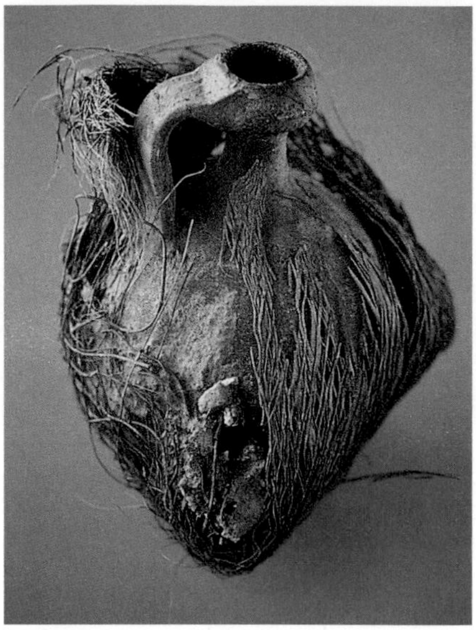

also this and later, similar passages evoke something very frenzied, ecstatic and 'pagan' in the way at least some of the supposed 'sons of Jacob' practised their religion at this time.

What was so special about Saul that people should have even begun to consider him seriously as the man who might bring some unity to this extraordinary mix of territories and peoples? In deference to minimalists, it must be acknowledged that, outside the pages of the Bible, there is not a jot of hard historical evidence that any Israelite king called Saul ever existed, although yet again this should not be considered as evidence for his non-existence. According to 1 Samuel 9:1, Saul was a Benjamite (i.e. from the very smallest of the twelve tribes), and his stronghold was Gibeah. This was identified in the 1930s by American archaeologist William Foxwell Albright as Tell el-Ful, the 'hill of beans', a few miles north of Jerusalem. Here, Albright found fortifications datable, from the accompanying pottery, to around the 11th century BC. There is a general consensus that this was where the Biblical Saul, assuming that he did exist, would have held his court.

Found very carefully buried at Qumran, this flask contained an unusual oil that may have been the special balsam used to anoint Israel's kings.

As conveyed by the Biblical account, Saul was anointed Israel's first king when the priest-*nabi*-judge Samuel poured oil over his head, a ritual that would be repeated at such ceremonies for the next thousand years. Fascinatingly, a recent find by Haifa University archaeology lecturer Joseph Patrich[4] may offer a glimpse – or more accurately, a sniff – of the special formula of oil used on these occasions.

During the 1980s, while systematically re-exploring the Qumran caves famous for the Dead Sea Scrolls, Patrich found, carefully wrapped in palm fibres and obviously very deliberately buried to a depth of 3 feet, a simple pottery juglet of a design datable to around the 1st century AD. The liquid inside was still partly fluid, and because of the container's ordinariness, it had to be the liquid that justified its so-careful burial. When this was analysed at Jerusalem's Hebrew University, it proved to be an oil of plant origin matching no variety known today. According to ancient documentary sources, Qumran and nearby Ein Gedi were cultivation centres for special trees with a sap used for making a very precious and secret balsam. The juglet's oil had long lost its perfume, but Patrich's theory is that it may have been the oil used for anointing Israel's kings.

Whatever the oil was that was used to consecrate Saul as king, it certainly brought him no special blessing. According to a bald Biblical summary of his reign, which has all the air of deriving from an earlier, lost chronicle, we are told that after he had secured his kingship over Israel:

> . . . he waged war on every side against all his enemies: against the Moabites, Ammonites, Edomites, the Philistines and the kings of Zobah; and wherever he turned he worsted them. He was triumphant, defeating the Amalekites and saving Israel from those who plundered it. Saul's sons were: Jonathan, Ishvi and Malchishua, and the names of his two daughters were Merab, the older, and Michal, the younger. (1 Samuel 14:47-48)

Aegean warriors on a 12th-century BC vase. Their weapons and armour match the Biblical description of the Philistine Goliath.

On the face of it, this might sound like an enviable record, suggesting that Saul reached out from his central highlands base to exert control over a territory extending into present-day Jordan. But his end was very far from enviable. According to the Bible, it was predicted by the dead *nabi* Samuel when 'conjured' by the mediumistic witch of Endor (a fascinating glimpse of ancient Canaanitic 'Spiritualist' practices).

Above: Ancient slingstones found at Khirbet el-Maqatir. Top: a diagram shows how these stones were deployed.

Reportedly at Mount Gilboa, a little to the south of Endor in present-day Galilee, Saul's three sons were killed in a fierce battle with the Philistines. Saul himself was so badly wounded that he and his armour-bearer took their own lives to evade an otherwise certain capture. As recounted in the first book of Samuel, the triumphant Philistines then 'placed his [Saul's] armour in the temple of Astarte; and they impaled his body on the wall of Beth-shan' (1 Samuel 31:10). In this regard, when American archaeologists during the early 1930s excavated Tell Beit She'an (the site of Biblical Beth-shan), just to the east of Mount Gilboa, they discovered the foundations of two temples. The more southerly temple still contained sufficient cultic objects to determine that it had, indeed, been a temple of Astarte.

Not only was Saul's resounding defeat an altogether most unpromising start for the new Israelite role of kingship, but it might also have meant the end of Israelite hopes of ever fully 'possessing' Canaan. However, a most exceptional individual was already waiting in the wings: David. To this day his name is the one that first springs to mind when asked to name a king of Israel.

David is, of course, universally famous for his toppling of the giant Goliath while he was still a youth, as described in 1 Samuel 17:

> A champion of the Philistine forces stepped forward; his name was Goliath of Gath, and he was six cubits and a span tall. He had a bronze helmet on his head and wore a breastplate of scale-armour, a bronze breastplate weighing five thousand shekels. He had bronze greaves on his legs and a bronze javelin [slung] from his shoulders. The shaft of his spear was like a weaver's bar, and the iron head of his spear weighed six hundred shekels, and the shield-bearer marched in front of him. . . . [Then David] quickly ran up to the battle line to face the Philistine. David put his hand into the bag; he took out a stone, and slung it. It struck the Philistine on the forehead; the stone sank into his forehead and he [Goliath] fell face down on the ground.
> (1 Samuel 17:4-7; 48-49)

This is fascinating as an account of Aegean/Philistine war gear, also of the usefulness of the slingstone[5] (which in the right hand had the range, accuracy and deadliness of any arrow[6]). For the story's many admirers, however, the disappointing news is that it has all the hallmarks of folklore, as is evident even from the Bible itself. For in one of the little-read supplements that appear at the end of the second book of Samuel, we learn that when the Bethelehem-born David was already an established king:

> . . . there was fighting with the Philistines at Gob and Elhanan . . . *the Bethlehemite killed Goliath of Gath*, whose spear had a shaft like a weaver's bar. (2 Samuel 21:19)

Arguably, therefore, while a very powerful Philistine called Goliath genuinely was killed by a young warrior from Bethlehem, that warrior was probably not David, but someone else born in his home town. It is a classic example of how easily stories become distorted.

Yet if this sort of thing is seized upon by minimalists as a reason for dismissing as legend virtually the entire Biblical story of David, this, in its turn, is very far from being justified. What can be gleaned of David's origins is often as confused as it is colourful. Nevertheless, it does also have a strong underlying ring of credibility and historicity. As recounted in 1 Samuel, David began as a warrior-courtier at King Saul's Gibeah court, and apparently was a very formidable one. It was on the strength of bringing to Saul the foreskins of two hundred Philistines whom he had slain – foreskins were the Israelites' equivalent of Egypt's amputated hands as a means of counting war-dead – that he was given Saul's daughter Michal as his marriage partner.

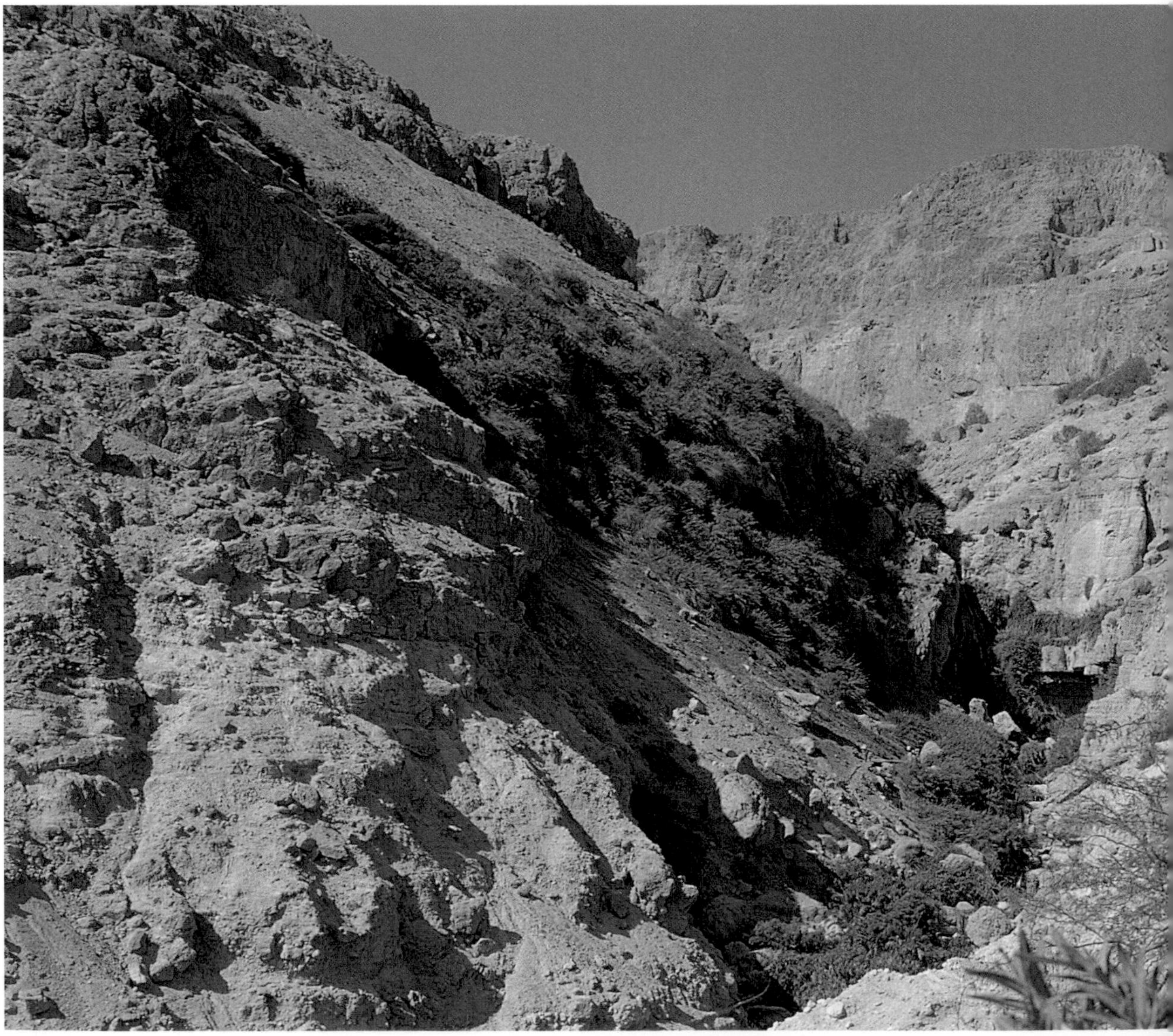

But relations seem not to have run smoothly between David and his royal father-in-law. Suspicious that David represented a threat to his throne (as he most probably did), Saul began to behave with hostility towards him, even trying to kill him. Concomitantly, the priest-*nabi*-judge Samuel, still licking his wounds following the Philistines' destruction of his Ark sanctuary at Shiloh, also fell out of Saul's favour. When after Samuel's death his fellow-priests, relocated at Nob just to the east of Jerusalem, declared themselves allied to David, Saul's response was to have them all massacred, bar one who managed to make his escape.

There had been no overt disloyalty on David's part. Even so, as was well-nigh inevitable, David and Saul became enemies. David became a hunted fugitive, living rough in a variety of remote locations, including caves at Ein Gedi by the Dead Sea, all the while gathering an increasing number of fighting men around him. If Gibeah was truly the northern stronghold of Saul, the Biblical record makes it clear that David's equivalent was the more southerly Ziklag. In what might seem an unlikely alliance, it was reportedly none other than Achish, king of the Philistine city of Gath, who gave Ziklag to David in return for services David and some 600 of his followers had performed for him as mercenaries in a struggle against the Amalekites. At first glance, this Philistine gift seems surprising, but it may well have been all too easy for Achish to give, because Ziklag was dangerously close to Amalekite territory. David and his men only had to be absent briefly for these marauders to raid it, and temporarily capture all its womenfolk, including David's two wives.

Where David hid? Ein Gedi, the spring-watered and cave-dotted region by the Dead Sea where the fugitive David hid from King Saul.

There is no scholarly consensus about Ziklag's present-day location, though some argue that it is Tell es-Seba, a modest but well-planned Negev fort-town of the 11th century BC.[7] Whatever the case, the Biblical account makes it clear that after Saul's defeat and death in the north, David established a new stronghold: the Judah tribe's capital Hebron and its surrounding villages (2 Samuel 2:1-3), i.e. the town where Israel's theoretical forefathers Abraham, Isaac and Jacob had their burial place. In Israelite tribal terms, David had now assumed command of the capital of his own ancestral tribe Judah. In accordance with this, it was here at Hebron that he was duly anointed 'king over the house of Judah' (2 Samuel 2:4), even though the deceased Samuel had purportedly anointed him earlier in Bethlehem (1 Samuel 16:13).

As head of a tribe that was almost the size of all the other Israelite tribes put together, David quickly increased his power. By contrast, in the more northerly kingdom, Israel proper, Saul's only surviving son, Ishbaal, presided over a decline that culminated in his assassination. Reportedly, after Ishbaal's death, the northern tribal leaders journeyed south to add to David's status by acclaiming him as king of their domains as well. At a single stroke, David found himself head of all the Israelite tribes, a position that was probably quite unprecedented if, as we have suspected, not all of the tribes ever went to Egypt.

Suddenly, the Philistines found themselves confronted with a former 'vassal', who now controlled a coherently unified empire that was potentially capable of toppling their own. Although they tried to act as quickly as possible for their own security, it was already too late. According to 2 Samuel 5:17-25, there were two skirmishes which may date from this period. The upshot was that the Philistines were chased back to Gezer. The phenomenon that was King David had already become too well-entrenched to dislodge.

As sceptics have never been slow to point out, almost all of this is based on Biblical reporting alone. None of it represents the slightest real proof that a King David ever even existed. Undeniably, no immediately contemporary monument has yet been found bearing David's name, nor is there any word about him in the annals of neighbouring Near Eastern peoples. Nonetheless, in 1993, a discovery was made concerning David's historicity, which meant that for once it is the minimalists who are on the wrong foot.

As we may recall, some time about the end of the Judges period, the Israelite tribe of Dan moved from the Mediterranean coast to an inland district of northern Galilee where they took over the former Canaanite town of Laish, which they renamed Dan. Israeli archaeologist Professor Avraham Biran has dug this Tel Dan site every season since 1966, but few moments have been more precious to him than one in 1993[8] when his surveyor Gila Cook happened to notice a broken fragment of stone. It was poking out from beneath a destruction layer known to derive from Dan's conquest by the Assyrians.

Attesting that 'King David' was no myth. An inscription of *c.*9th century BC found at Tel Dan, refers to the 'Beit David', or 'House of David', as a historical dynasty.

Taking a closer look at the stone Cook observed that it was inscribed with several lines of Palaeo-Hebrew, notable for each word being separated from the next by a dot, just as we put a space between each word. And since the Assyrian conquest had been in the 8th century BC, any stone found *beneath* its destruction layer had to be older than that. The mere discovery of such ancient Hebrew writing was important enough in itself.

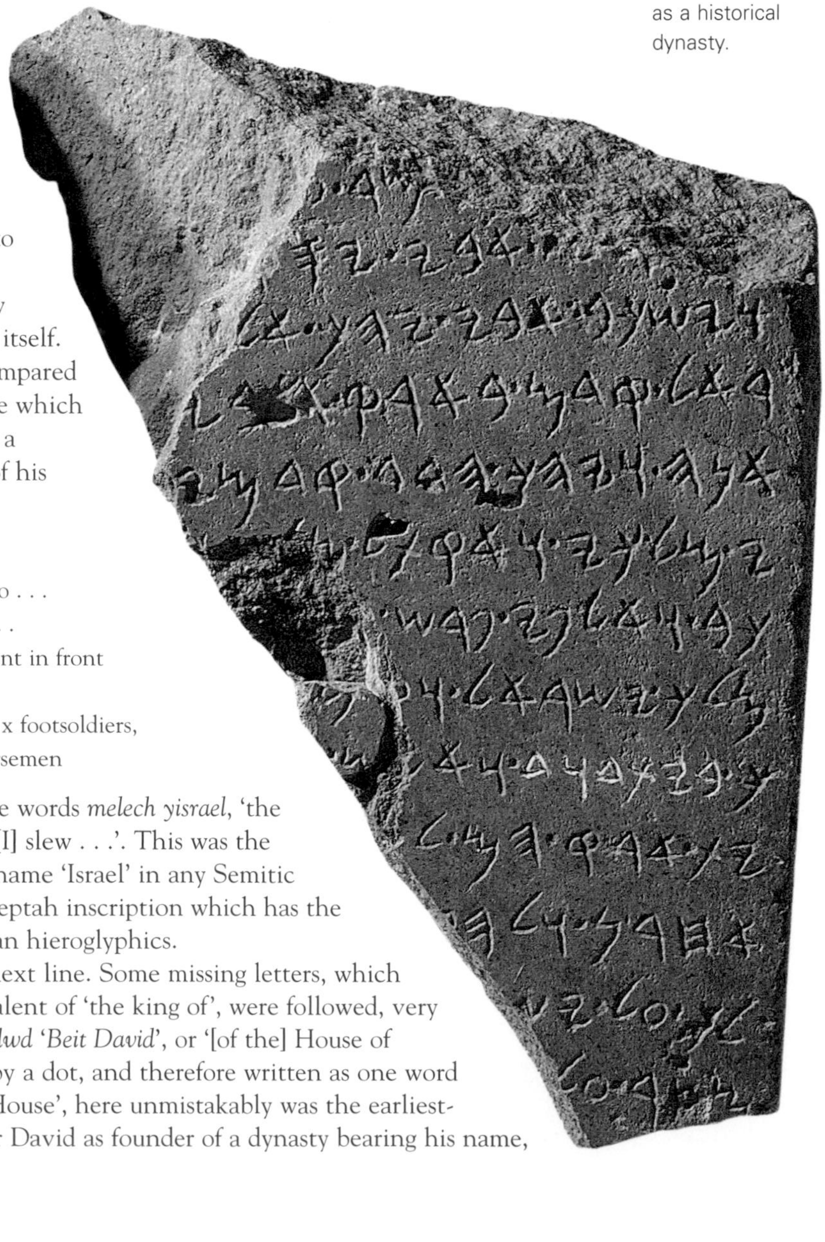

However, it was as nothing compared to the inscription's actual message which began uninspiringly enough with a monarch's all-too typical boasts of his victories:

> . . . my father went up
> . . . and my father died, he went to . . .
> . . . formerly in my father's land . . .
> I [fought] and [the god] Hadad went in front of me . . .
> . . . my king. And I slew of [them x footsoldiers, y cha-]riots and two thousand horsemen

Then on the eighth line came the words *melech yisrael*, 'the king of Israel', followed by 'And [I] slew . . .'. This was the oldest-known appearance of the name 'Israel' in any Semitic script, a counterpart to the Merneptah inscription which has the oldest example written in Egyptian hieroglyphics.

More important still was the next line. Some missing letters, which were probably the Hebrew equivalent of 'the king of', were followed, very legibly, by the Hebrew words *bytdwd* '*Beit David*', or '[of the] House of David'. Although not separated by a dot, and therefore written as one word rather as we might write 'WhiteHouse', here unmistakably was the earliest-known documentary evidence for David as founder of a dynasty bearing his name, just as related in the Biblical record. From a variety of clues, including the reference to the Aramean storm god Hadad, it is clear that the inscription cannot actually date from King David's reign. But specialists in ancient writing are confident that it dates to either the 10th or, at the latest, the 9th century BC, no more than two centuries after the original David's lifetime. At a single stroke the Tel Dan inscription has transformed the Biblical David from a figure who was almost as legendary as England's King Arthur to a firm historical personage.

As might be expected, the news of this discovery has not been well-received by the those who would minimise the Bible's historical accuracy. Danish Biblical scholar Niels Peter Lemche has gone so far as to suggest that someone faked the inscription, then planted it for Biran and Cook to find[9], rather in the manner of the Piltdown Man forgery. Only shortly before the discovery was made, Lemche's British counterpart, Philip Davies, had brought out a book arguing that there had never been an early Israel. He has taken a somewhat similar view to Lemche's.[10] A gross insult to Biran's integrity and professionalism, such attitudes are fortunately isolated, and not shared by the archaeological community at large.

Once such objections are set aside, we can say with some confidence that there genuinely was a King David. A variety of indirect clues, when taken in combination with the Bible text, tell us that someone very like the Biblical David must have existed in order to have had the political effects evident from archaeology. For one thing is certain from the generality of archaeological findings throughout present-day Israel. What had been a widespread Philistine presence was seriously pushed back towards the Mediterranean coast, never to regain its earlier dominance.

In the case of Philistine Ekron, for example, during the Judges/Iron Age I period this had occupied 50 acres, comprising a 40-acre lower city and a 10-acre upper city. In the 'Davidic' or Iron Age II period, which followed immediately afterwards, its large lower city was destroyed and all remaining Philistine occupation confined to the tiny upper city. It is difficult to associate this with anyone except the Biblical David.

David's greatest coup seems to have been taking the city of Jerusalem, which he made his capital. It was a wise and logical choice since it was geographically central to his new empire and had no previous ties with either his own Judahite tribe or the tribes of the north. In this instance, it was not Philistines he needed to dislodge, but Jebusites, a Canaanite-related people who, despite a misleading verse in Judges 1, seem to have been Jerusalem's continuous occupants.

Although the archaeological remains for Jebusite Jerusalem are meagre in the extreme, the Amarna letters of more than three centuries before show that even then, as 'Urusalim', it was a city of considerable importance. Under Egyptian suzerainty it controlled a sizeable territory from just south of Bethel in the north to Hebron in the south, and from the River Jordan in the east to the hills of the Shephelah in the west.[11] It had a palace occupied by a king, who was part of a dynasty. Its court included a professional scribe who wrote a series of letters on the king's behalf to Egypt's pharaoh.

How had Jerusalem remained uncaptured for so long? It seems that its geography protected it. Its most ancient sector, a 9-acre ridge south of what is today the Temple Mount, comprised a natural defence ditch of steep-sided valleys on three sides. But if this was the case, how did David succeed where those before him failed?

Here we come across one of the not uncommon instances of Biblical accounts that are difficult to comprehend at first, yet can be extremely rewarding when we do at last achieve some understanding. Both the Biblical Chronicles and second book of Samuel include stories of Jerusalem's capture. The second book of Samuel reads:

The king [i.e. David] and his men set out for Jerusalem, against the Jebusites who inhabited the region. David was told: 'You will never get in here . . .' But David captured the stronghold of Zion; it is now the City of David. On that occasion David said, 'Those who attack the Jebusites shall get up the *tsinnor*[12] . . .' (2 Samuel 5:6-9)

The Chronicles version, after saying much the same as the above, goes on:

Joab son of Zeruiah was the first man to go up, and became the chief. (1 Chronicles 11:4-7)

Two questions are inevitably raised. What is a *tsinnor*? And why might Joab have needed first to 'go up' it in order to bring about Jerusalem's capture? Even for those conversant with Hebrew, these questions are not easy to answer, since *tsinnor* is almost unique in the entire Bible. The only other instance is in a Psalm, in which it occurs in the context of rushing water:

Deep is calling to deep
by the roar of your *tsinnor*
all your waves and breakers
have rolled over me. (Psalm 42:8)

Such is the uncertainty that when nearly two thousand years ago the ancient scholar Aquila tried to translate the word into Greek, he chose *krounismos*, meaning a gushing out of water[13], while various subsequent attempts have included 'sewer', as suggested by a mediaeval Jewish exegete; 'gutter', as in the 17th-century King James Bible; 'watershaft', as in the Revised Standard Version Bible; 'tunnel', as in the present-day New Jerusalem Bible; and even 'penis', as ventured by German exegetical scholar G. Dalman.

The common denominator in these translations is the idea of some kind of conduit for conveying rushing water. In this context, one of Jerusalem's most time-honoured sources of water happens to have been the Gihon, or 'rushing' spring, which in Jebusite times gushed out from the eastern side of the rock on which Jerusalem stands. It featured an ancient interior conduit discovered by a 19th-century British Army engineer, Sir Charles Warren.

In 1867 Warren, then an army captain, visited the place where the spring would have emerged outside the city's walls in King David's time. Up in the roof, he happened to see

The Gihon Spring as it looks today, beneath medieval steps. In David's time, it gushed into a pool outside Jerusalem's walls.

a hitherto unnoticed cavity. When he and his sergeant Henry Birtles scrambled up into this, they found themselves inside a 40-foot shaft rising vertically upwards, which led to a passageway, then to an old chamber with a narrow chink to it. They squeezed through the chink and suddenly found themselves in an old Jerusalem street, with their original point of entry now way below them.[14]

As has been determined from subsequent Israeli archaeological and geological findings, by the late Yigal Shiloh, by Dan Gill[15] and most recently by Ronnie Reich and Eli Shukron[16], this shaft, now known as Warren's Shaft, adjoins a complex interior tunnel system, which Jerusalem's Jebusite inhabitants cut specially into the rock on which their city stood. This enabled them, even in times of siege by an enemy such as David, to draw their water safely from a large and only recently-discovered pool outside the walls, fed by the Gihon spring. But any tunnel leading from the inside to the outside of a city's walls also provides a way for a sneaky outside enemy to get in. As is now generally recognised, David's general Joab and an elite accompanying band almost certainly clambered up either Warren's Shaft or an adjoining conduit. In this way, they managed to capture Jerusalem with much the same daring as the Greeks showed at Troy with their Trojan Horse.

Certainly, whatever the means used to capture the city, it is historically undeniable that at a time consistent with that attributed to King David, formerly Canaanite/Jebusite Jerusalem changed hands. It became, quite literally, the royal 'City of David', the term by which Jews still affectionately refer to it.

Unfortunately, because of all the destructions Jerusalem has suffered in later centuries, combined with the way its building stones have been repeatedly used and reused, it has never been easy to find archaeological remains that belong indisputably to the city of King David's time. Nevertheless, while Jebusite Jerusalem is thought to have occupied a mere 9 acres atop the hill commanding the Gihon spring, David's city seems to have expanded northwards. The Biblical account[17] relates how, aided by craftsmen sent by his ally Hiram, king of the Canaanitic coastal city of Tyre, David had a palace built for himself from which he could look out over the roofs of Jerusalem's houses.[18] From this description it can be inferred that the palace must have been high up, most likely on the southern part of what has long been known as the Ophel, a natural ridge that leads to where David's son and successor Solomon built the First Temple.

According to 1 Chronicles 17:1, David's palace was 'a house of cedars', i.e. of cedar of Lebanon wood rather than stone. So we should not expect too much of it to have survived archaeologically. Even so, some once-massive towers, first discovered by Charles Warren, together with other surviving vestiges from this area, are now thought to come from its original approaches. There is also the enigmatic stonework known archaeologically as the Stepped Stone Structure (see overleaf), which thirty years ago Kathleen Kenyon dated to the 6th century BC. Thanks to more recent insights by Israeli archaeologists[19], this is now better understood as a support structure already extant by David's time. This would have provided 2800 square feet of extra flat space for whatever building was erected on top of it. In all logic, that building must have been David's palace. However, since the main area where the palace would have stood became absorbed into the vast platform of the present Temple Mount, there is currently no way of proving this.

As is evident from the Biblical record, King David's true legacy, even as recognised by those closest to his own time, was not one of grandiose monuments. Rather it lay in the fact that he was perhaps the most astute, and at the same time the most 'human', king of antiquity for whom we have documentary record. It is not for nothing that a recent Bible journal survey voted him the most interesting individual in the entire Hebrew Bible.[20]

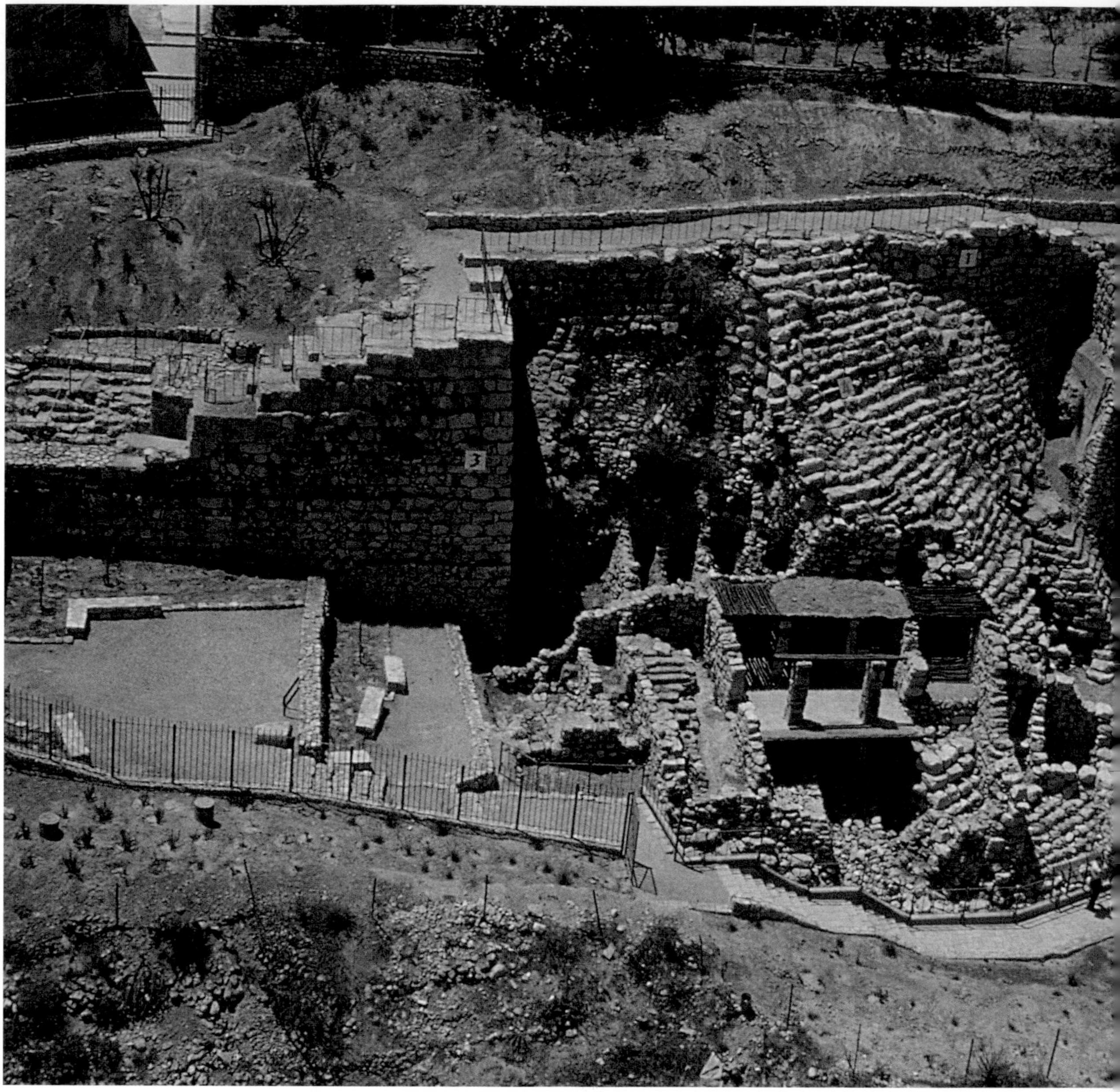

Thus, in domestic policy, instead of appointing one chief priest to be in overall religious charge of his empire, the Biblical record has it that he carefully appointed two. The first was Abiathar, descended from Moses, and the sole survivor of Saul's massacre of the Samuelite priests who had formerly been at northerly Shiloh. The second was Zadok, descended from Aaron, who hailed from his own former Judahite capital at southerly Hebron. This kept happy both the northern and southern parts of his new-founded empire. It was the same policy of neutrality between north and south that made him choose Jerusalem for his capital.

In foreign policy, it is evident that when absolutely necessary David could act with considerable ruthlessness. This showed against the Edomites of what is now Jordan. His general Joab reportedly waged a near genocidal campaign among them, killing 18,000 Edomites, plundering their land and stationing a permanent occupation force to maintain their permanent suppression (2 Samuel 8:11-14). We will see shortly that there

This 'Stepped Stone Structure' is known to have been extant in Jerusalem at the time of King David. It would have provided a support platform for a large building, possibly part of the royal palace.

was, in fact, a sound economic reason for this. In general, however, David's policy towards neighbouring states was far from following the 'exterminate every living thing' variety reported of his forebear Joshua. Instead, he chose tolerance and alliance wherever practical.

Thus, while he defeated the Jebusite former occupants of Jerusalem, he allowed them to stay in the city and made no attempt to destroy their houses and public buildings. Although he pursued the Philistines to the coast, he allowed them to maintain at least a modest presence there. For diplomatic purposes, he took numerous foreign princesses as wives. One such was apparently Maacah, daughter of 'Talmai, king of Geshur', who became mother of his son Absalom. Although the Geshurites might seem to be one of those 'lost without trace' Biblical names, in the event some recent excavations at Tel Hadar Geshur, east of the Sea of Galilee suggest that this may have been the actual Geshurite royal capital from which David's bride Maacah came.[21]

As for David's famous alliance with Hiram of Tyre, Hiram's so-called Phoenician culture, insofar as this is understood from archaeological findings, would have been as near Canaanite as makes little difference. Even so, David skilfully negotiated with him a trade deal, whereby Hiram sent him all the fine timber and skilled carpenters and stonemasons he needed for his palace (2 Samuel 5:11), while David provided Hiram with 'twenty thousand *kor* of wheat and twenty thousand *kor* of pure oil (1 Kings 5:25). These were commodities that the ancestrally herd-keeping 'sons of Jacob' could now apparently produce in considerable surplus.

By no means least of David's remarkable features is that, although the Biblical record is generally well-disposed towards him, it does not shrink from enumerating his faults with a candour that is unique from such an early period. Just as if he were a modern-day British or US politician whose misdeeds had come to media attention, we are told that he behaved in a particularly shameful way after committing adultery with the attractive Bathsheba, wife of his commander Uriah. Reportedy, he deliberately despatched Uriah to a dangerous battlefront, so that when the man was killed, he could have the lovely Bathsheba for himself.

Then, when Nathan, the *nabi* of the time, cleverly upbraided David for what he had done, instead of having Nathan immediately executed, as almost any other historical despot would have done, David had the humility to recognise that Nathan's accusations were well-justified. He sincerely repented the misdeed he had perpetrated.

Nor is this the only moment in which David is described as behaving in a manner which is very much more human than the god-like dignity normally attributed to monarchs of antiquity, and even those up to our own time. In order to give the Ark a proper permanent home for the first time since its days at Shiloh, David is supposed to have purchased some land for it. He then had it brought to Jerusalem from the private house at Gath where it had been kept. As we are told in 2 Samuel and 1 Chronicles, even while the Ark was in transit:

> David and all Israel danced before Yahweh [i.e. the Ark's 'occupant'] with all their might, with songs, lyres, harps, timbrels, cymbals and trumpets. (1 Chronicles 13:8)

Reportedly, at a further stage of the journey:

> David whirled with all his might before Yahweh with all his might, wearing a linen cloth. (2 Samuel 6:14)

On the Ark's arrival in Jerusalem itself, where apparently it was deposited in the traditional tent rather than a solid building, we are again told of David's 'leaping and whirling before Yahweh' (2 Samuel 6:16).

That such antics were regarded as undignified for a king, even in David's time, is evident from the reaction of Saul's daughter Michal. After 'watching from a window' (yet another instance of this), she greeted her husband with the words:

> Didn't the king of Israel do himself honour today? Exposing himself today in the sight of the slavegirls of his subjects, as one of the riffraff might expose himself? (2 Samuel 6:20)

When something as adverse on the face of it as this is chronicled, there is often a strong case that it has historical veracity. Supporting this, a fascinatingly similar wild dance, likewise in honour of what is supposed to be the Biblical Ark (although no outsider has been allowed access to examine it), is practised to this day by Ethiopian Jews claiming descent from a group who moved to Ethiopia many centuries ago. At their special Timkat ceremony, held annually at Axum in the Ethiopian highlands, a young man traditionally performs precisely such a dance in the midst of a host of people. They similarly leap and gyrate to music played on harp and flute, to the accompaniment of rhythms beaten out on tambourines and cymbals.

Furthermore, whether or not this ancient ceremony is in some way a time-capsule of David's original antics, in 1986 Avraham Biran, the Israeli archaeologist responsible for the discovery of the 'House of David' inscription, made another find. Also at Dan, he unearthed a little plaque depicting a male figure in a short tunic playing the lute and dancing. Because this was found beneath a Late Bronze Age stone floor, this figure can be dated reasonably reliably to some time around 1300 BC, i.e. three centuries before the time of David. Yet the costume matches that which we have inferred to be 'ancient Israelite'. As Biran himself has noted:

> . . . the first thing that comes to mind is the Biblical account of David dancing in front of the Ark when the Ark was brought back from the Philistines to Jerusalem.[22]

Found at Tel Dan, this plaque dates from *c.*13th century BC, and seems to depict a male dancer in a tunic, playing the lute while performing a spirited dance. The dance may be similar to that which King David reportedly performed before the Ark to celebrate its arrival in Jerusalem.

This leads us to the other aspect of music associated with David: the composition of a number of the Biblical Psalms. No fewer than seventy-three of these, or almost 50 per cent, have in their superscriptions in the Masoretic Hebrew manuscripts, the notation *ledawid*, usually translated as 'of David'. Thirteen of these carry additional information concerning when David theoretically composed them, e.g. Psalm 34, 'when he feigned madness in the presence of Abimelech'; Psalm 51, 'when Nathan the *nabi* came to him after he had come to Bathsheba'; and Psalm 56, 'when the Philistines seized him in Gath'.

In the older surviving Biblical manuscripts, however, considerably fewer of these Psalms are attributed to David. The likelihood is that, while some

Again evoking the pagan roots of David's dance, here a masked priest performs a similar dance for the goddess Isis, as depicted in a Roman fresco from Herculaneum. Note the horned altar, of which several examples have been found by Israeli archaeologists.

may genuinely come from his time, probably only a few are of his direct authorship. Also, some are adaptations from Egyptian and Canaanitic compositions. In the case of the latter, our prime source is a cache of tablets discovered at Ras Shamra, the former Ugarit. Despite being very fragmentary, the texts of these reveal that some verses from the Biblical Psalms are almost direct translations from earlier Ugaritic and thereby Canaanitic poems. Arguably, much subsequent so-called Hebrew music and verse has its origin in similar Canaanitic originals.

There is very little doubt, however, that David created a court climate in which the musical arts could flourish. At the same time, Israelite writing, in the form of chronicles and archives kept by professional scribes, began at least as early as his reign. David's court is specifically described as including a scribe and chronicler (2 Samuel 8:16-17). Again, these chronicles and archives may have been founded on practices established by Jerusalem's former Jebusite masters and their fellow Canaanites.

A noteworthy point about literary composition is the form in which the *nabi* Nathan conveyed to David the divine displeasure at his adultery with Bathsheba. It was via a parable, a highly sophisticated literary device that Jesus would use a thousand years later for teaching his disciples.

David may have been successful as a king and in establishing a significant empire. But, in its now characteristic way, the Biblical account does not omit the fact that he went through all sorts of family difficulties in his old age. For instance, his first-born son Amnon most cruelly raped his half-sister Tamar, David's daughter by his Geshirite wife Maacah. Absalom, Maacah's son, avenged this crime by killing Amnon. Absalom after first fleeing, then becoming temporarily reconciled with his father, died in a riding accident. One notable feature of the names of David's children is that they do not bear Yahweh suffixes as in the case of his commander Uri[y]*ah* and his chief scribe Serai[y]*ah*. This suggests that, thanks to David's foreign wives, the immediate members of his family may well have been rather less Yahwist than his army personnel and other aides.

Overall, however, David is recorded Biblically as having reigned very successfully for forty years as king, thirty-three of those from the new capital Jerusalem. When he died, it was apparently from natural causes, and it was only logical that he should be buried within his own City of David (1 Kings 2:10).

But where exactly within this was he laid? We can ignore what Jerusalem guidebooks call 'the Tomb of David' on Jerusalem's so-called Mount Zion, a location well

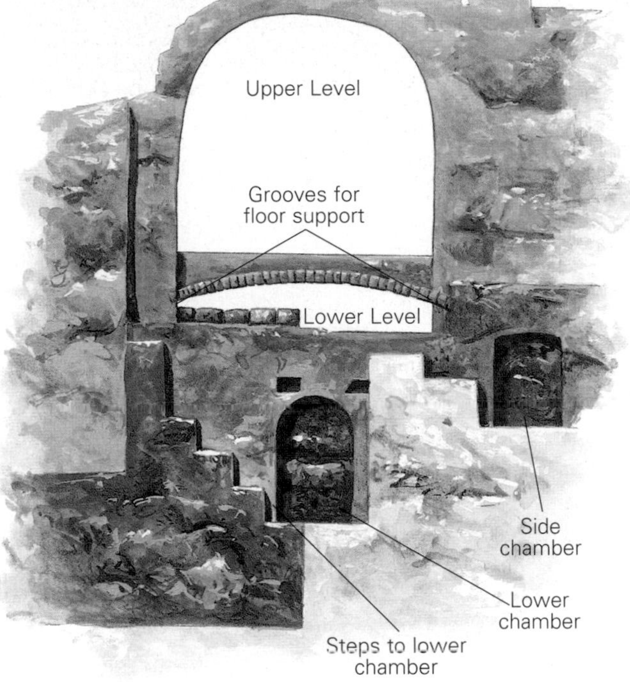

outside Jerusalem's walls as they would have existed in David's time. While in ancient times, ordinary citizens were usually buried outside a city's walls, royalty were an exception. For David's time, 'in the city of David' may be reliably inferred to mean somewhere on the hill on which the original Jebusite city stood. This is further narrowed down for us by the 5th-century BC Biblical writer Nehemiah[23], who described the Davidic Tombs as being on the southern part of this hill. From the 1st-century AD book of Acts we get a reassurance that David's tomb was still a Jerusalem monument then. While addressing a Jerusalem crowd, Jesus's disciple Peter was quoted as saying that 'his [King David's] tomb is still with us' (Acts 2:29).

Cuttings into bedrock are visible today down a path leading off Jerusalem's Kidron Road, and a little inside the surviving remains of the Jerusalem city wall of David's time. Labelled the Tombs of the Israelite Kings by the present-day guidebooks, most of these were excavated in 1913/14 by the French archaeologist Raymond Weill, who deduced that it was most likely here that David and his more immediate successors would have been buried. A particularly magnificent example consists of a long, artificially hewn tunnel 52 feet long, 8 feet wide, beginning at 13 feet high, then lowering to 6 feet. Although the front half has long been hacked away, ruining the original entrance, the back wall still features a carefully-cut, 6-foot-long depression in which either a body or a sarcophagus containing a body may have been laid. So was this where the mortal remains of King David were laid to rest?

Left: 'His [King David's] tomb is still with us', Jesus's disciple Peter is reported as saying in the book of Acts. The steps at the right of the picture lead down to a series of cuttings in the rock, thought to have been the tombs of King David and his descendants, referred to by several ancient authorities. Above: A cross-sectional drawing of the tomb thought to have belonged to David.

As with so much of the evidence we are dealing with, we are a long way from any certainty. British archaeologist Kathleen Kenyon doubted that the structures were tombs at all, suggesting that they might have been cisterns[24], while Nahman Avigad, the Israeli government's foremost excavator of Biblical Jerusalem, accepted their identification as tombs but cautioned that no 'evidence has been found to confirm that they belong to the Israelite period'.[25] Present-day Israeli archaeologist David Ussishkin also accepts the structures' identification as tombs, but he has expressed his doubts that the 'David' tomb could really have belonged to him, on the grounds of its poor architectural quality.[26]

However, as has been pointed out by *Biblical Archaeology Review* editor Hershel Shanks, the 'tombs' are at least in a convincing location. And from the fact that they are unlike tombs from significantly later periods, and that no one knows what a tomb of King David's time looked like, it is impossible to discount them as dating from his time. While hardly a conclusive argument, it is certainly the fairest assessment of the available evidence.

As all the world knows, King David's other claim to fame is that he was succeeded as king of Israel by the illustrious Solomon, the son born to him by that infamous marriage with Bathsheba, widow of the luckless Uriah the Hittite. Unlike David, King Solomon is credited in the Biblical record with having been a great builder. So does there survive any more hard evidence for him than there does for his father?

10

'IN ALL HIS GLORY . . .'

THE BIBLE REPRESENTS King David's successor Solomon as living in great magnificence, to the extent of marrying seven hundred foreign wives, including a pharaoh's daughter.[1] We might reasonably hope, therefore, that a contemporary inscription with his name might have survived, or at very least some reference to him in documents either from ancient Egypt or from other neighbouring peoples.

So far, however, such hopes have been in vain. Admittedly, the London antiquities collector Shlomo Moussaieff owns a seemingly ancient cylindrical seal[2] depicting a royal-looking personage on one side, and on the other the Hebrew letters *shin*, *lamed* and *mem*, unmistakably reading 'Solomon'. It was created in an Egyptian style generally fashionable in the Near East during the 1st millennium BC, and Moussaieff believes that it belonged to one of King Solomon's officials, who would have used it for sealing official documents. In this regard, the monarch depicted is certainly most interesting-looking, since beneath his long cloak-like outer garment he seems to be wearing a kilt of the kind we have inferred to be the original 'highland' Israelite mode of dress.

However, even if this seal really does date to the early 10th century BC, when Solomon is thought to have lived, we have nothing to check it against, since it is the only known example surviving from such an early time. Added to this, Moussaieff purchased it via a dealer who can only ultimately have procured it from someone who looted it. So we have no information regarding where it was found or in what archaeological context. Despite bearing the name Solomon, the seal has to be accounted evidentially near useless, at least until some similar specimen turns up via proper archaeological means.

As for the Bible's main information concerning King Solomon[3], although we are assured that it and much else is based on the lost 'Book of the Annals of Solomon'[4], arguably a chronicle kept by a scribe in Solomon's employ, much of the 1 Kings account of him has a folk-tale air, indeed rather more so than the equivalent stories about David. Typical are the famous stories of how the king resolved two prostitutes' quarrel over a baby and of the visit by the purported 'Queen of Sheba'. The latter has all the air of making Solomon sound important,

A seal bearing, on one side, the Hebrew letters *shin*, *lamed* and *mem*, spelling 'Shlomo', or 'Solomon'. If the seal is genuine, then the standing figure is probably a contemporary depiction of King Solomon.

yet has so far defied every attempt to pinpoint 'Sheba' either historically or geographically.

Accordingly, if we discard such material as impossible to check, the principal remaining 'hard' information is that Solomon built several substantial cities (1 Kings 9:15-22), thereby making a significant advance on the village life style of the Judges period; that he also built the famous First Temple in Jerusalem with the help of his father's old ally, Hiram of Tyre; and, not least, that he established a Red Sea fleet to go on trading expeditions, requiring a port somewhere on the Red Sea. Fortunately, all of these have at least some potential for being checked out, insofar as some physical evidence may have survived from them. There is certainly impressive archaeological evidence that someone, at some time around the Solomonic period, did a lot of work to rebuild and refortify the former Canaan's major cities. If, as the Davidic military successes indicate, the formerly disunited Canaan had become welded into one major state – a state so strong that Egypt was no longer able to walk into it and 'milk' it as part of its empire – then it would have been logical for a major effort to be put into remedying the defenceless state many of the cities had been in for a long time.

According to the Bible, it was Solomon who did this, unpopularly using forced labour to fortify 'Jerusalem . . . Hazor, Megiddo, Gezer . . . Lower Beth-Horon, Baalith, Tamar in the wilderness . . . [also] all of Solomon's garrison towns, chariot towns and cavalry towns' (1 Kings 9:15). As the editor/compiler of the first book of Kings also informs us, regarding Solomon's building programme in Jerusalem:

> All these buildings, from foundation to coping . . . were of choice stones hewn according to measure, smooth on all sides. (1 Kings7:9).

And, although in the case of Jerusalem there has been too much destruction for the archaeological evidence to be meaningful, in the cases of the other major cities mentioned, it is clear that major palaces and other public buildings were, indeed, constructed in this way. It was a remarkable upturn for a people who had only so recently graduated from tents to the modest four-room village house.

Thus, the northern city of Megiddo can be seen to have sprouted as many as three impressive palaces in the Solomonic period, with ashlars, or smooth-cut stones, used for these and other major buildings. Houses built around the city's perimeter had the city wall as their outer wall – a so-called 'casemate wall' style of building, reminiscent of the circles of wagons used in the 'Wild West' for defence against American Indians. And very fine city gates were built. When, some thirty years ago, the renowned Israeli archaeologist, the late Yigael Yadin, was excavating at Hazor, he discovered a cleverly designed six-chambered gate from the Solomonic period, flanked by a series of protective guardhouses. He then realised that similar examples had been found at Megiddo and Gezer, all remarkably corresponding to the fortifications of these cities as described in 1 Kings 9:15.

In fact, a fierce archaeological debate rages over these gateways. The present-day Israeli archaeologists Israel Finklestein and David Ussishkin attribute the six-chambered type to a later period, and argue that the Solomonic period had a simpler, two-chambered version. But for anyone trying to gain an overall picture, this is quibbling over trifles. It is clear, both Biblically and archaeologically, that the Solomonic period saw a powerful renaissance of building throughout the former Canaan, exactly as if this region now had an unprecedented unity and strong central control.

Added to this, some serious accompanying fortress-building work was in progress, clearly in order to hold on to the new assets. According to 1 Kings 9:18, one of the places specially built by Solomon was 'Tamar in the wilderness'. This has been reliably located 35 miles south of the Dead Sea in the Arabah, the arid corridor that runs north-south between the Dead Sea and the Red Sea.

Above: The Mound of Megiddo as it looks today, with (left) a model of how it may have looked in the Solomonic period. The area of the Solomonic city gates can be seen at the far right.

Recent excavations by Dr Rudolph Cohen[5] have revealed this as Israel's principal southern fortress city throughout the time it was ruled by kings, with walls at successive levels that were more massive than those of any other Israelite city except Jerusalem.

Solomon or someone very like him seems also to have built a string of similar fortresses right across the Negev desert.[6] Of these, Tel Arad in the Negev, although Biblically unnamed in connection with Solomon, has been particularly thoroughly excavated in recent years. At the Solomonic period level, it features not only casemate-type walls similar to those noted earlier, but also, and most notably, a temple of Yahweh, identified as such by an inscription on a piece of broken pottery.

Here, an important point has to be recognised. It was only at a later period of Biblical history that Jerusalem became designated the sole place which could have a Yahwist temple of its own. In all sorts of respects, this Arad temple was a modest construction based on the humble, four-room, Israelite house. Yet, as in the Solomonic period, it featured a sacrificial altar constructed of the Biblically-specified unhewn stone of Exodus 2:25, also tailored to precisely the measurements – '5 cubits long . . . 5 cubits wide . . . and 3 cubits high' – prescribed in Exodus 27:1. It is important evidence that much of what we regard as 'traditional' Israelite religion really was in place at this early time.

This leads us to ask what evidence might survive of that most famous of the Biblical Solomon's works: the Jerusalem Temple. Such was the importance of this that 1 Kings chapters 6 and 7 are almost entirely devoted to it. If we discard as later exaggeration the tens of thousands of craftsmen quoted as working on quarrying, dressing and erecting its stones (1 Kings 5), its stated dimensions – 103 feet (60 cubits) long, by 33 feet (20 cubits) wide, by 51 feet (30 cubits) high – sound modest enough to be reliable. Credibility is enhanced by the fact that later generations, up to the 6th century BC (when this Temple was destroyed by Babylonians), were able to check the dimensions for themselves.

The major difficulty, however, is the very fact that this First Temple was destroyed so long ago. Then its successor, the Second Temple, which was given a hugely enlarged supporting platform by King Herod the Great, was razed to the ground by the Romans in 70 AD. Added to that, when in the 7th century AD Arab Moslems arrived in Jerusalem to build their own Dome of the Rock and accompanying mosque on the then-empty

The earliest known 'Yahweh' Temple to have been discovered is at the Arad fortress in the Negev desert – one of a string built by King Solomon to protect his southern border.

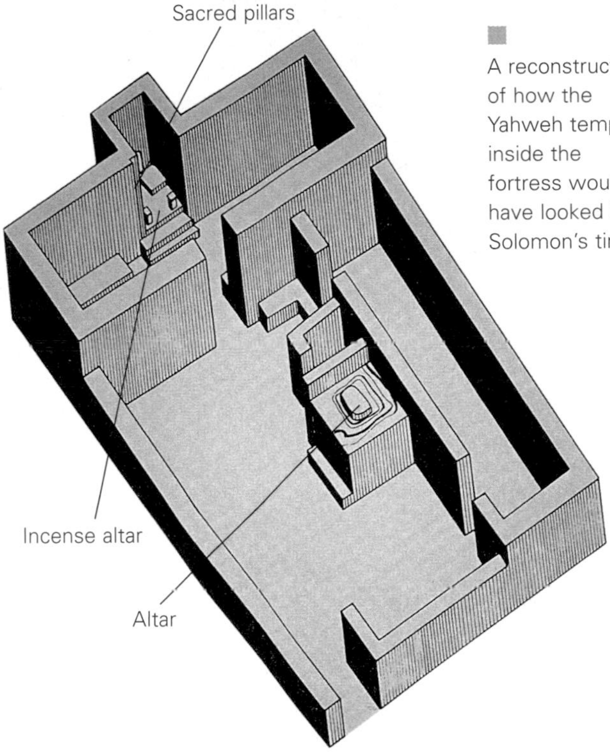

A reconstruction of how the Yahweh temple inside the fortress would have looked in Solomon's time.

platform, they made the site their second holiest after Mecca. To this day, any Israeli attempt to investigate it archaeologically provokes the most violent resistance.

Yet despite such impediments, clues to where Solomon's Temple might have stood on the surviving platform do remain. Thus, the book of Nehemiah, which substantially predates Herod's enlargement work, describes the Temple as having stood on a *birah*[7], or square, which, according to the *Mishnah*, measured '500 cubits by 500 cubits'[8], or 861 feet square. The present-day oblong platform is considerably longer, around 1500 feet. The extra length and new shape represent its major enlargement by Herod.

This has led British architect-historian Leen Ritmeyer to do some remarkable sleuthing. Merely by walking the present platform as if a tourist, Ritmeyer spotted a stone staircase at its north-western corner. He noticed that what looks like its bottom step is not as exactly parallel as it should be to the wall to which it leads. Closely examining the southernmost stone of this 'step', he noticed a boss on it. This betrayed the fact that it actually formed part of a buried wall of dressed masonry, which, since it was well inside the perimeter of King Herod's platform enlargement, had to be pre-Herodian. Moreover, this wall proved to be exactly parallel to the Temple platform's eastern wall, the one part of the original Solomonic platform that for geographical reasons Herod could not extend. Accordingly, when Ritmeyer measured the distance from this western wall line to the eastern wall and discovered it to be 861 feet – i.e. the *Mishnah*'s 500 cubits for the First Temple platform – he felt sure that it must be the section on which Solomon's Temple originally stood. A slight bend in the masonry at the southern end of the eastern wall, just

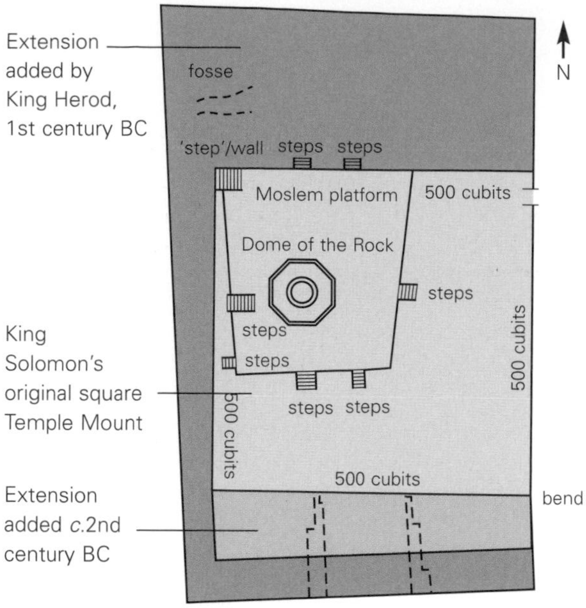

where Herod would have extended the platform from its south-eastern corner, confirmed this.

But where, on this section of the present platform, might the Temple building have been located? According to the Biblical account, Solomon's Temple had a three-part interior plan. The first part, a 10-cubit-deep porch or portico, in Hebrew *ulam*, featured two free-standing columns[9]. The second was a 40-cubit-long main hall[10], the *hekal*. The third was a 20-cubit, cube-shaped Oracle, or Holy of Holies, in Hebrew the *debir*, essentially an inner canopy inside which stood two 17-foot-high, sphinx-like cherubim made of wood. Beneath the wings of these reposed the already historic Ark, the seat of the divine voice for every *nabi* able to tune into it.

According to the Moslems, their Dome of the Rock's Holy of Holies – the es-Sakhra – marks the spot where Abraham so nearly sacrificed Isaac. So if the Solomonic Temple was built over this location, it is a matter of surprise that, as is evident from the present-day es-Sakhra, this did not stand centrally upon its original cube-shaped platform. However, as Ritmeyer discovered, the *Mishnah* actually resolves this seeming discrepancy. Having given the platform's measurements, it immediately states that the largest open space in Solomon's Temple was 'at the south, [its] second largest at the east, [its] third largest at the north and [its] least at the west.' This precisely matches Ritmeyer's reconstruction of the positioning of the Solomonic Temple. Not only does it confirm that the Temple was not built at the centre of the original platform, but also, as Ritmeyer points out, such specifications 'can be satisfied only if the Holy of Holies of the [Solomonic] Temple is placed over es-Sakhra.'[11]

What, then, can be gleaned by studying the present-day es-Sakhra? The site has suffered all sorts of vicissitudes over the centuries. It had a church built on it by Crusaders, only for this to be destroyed by Saladin's Moslems. Fortunately, however, today's Moslem controllers have cleared it back to its natural bedrock, and allow it to be viewed by the ordinary tourist, impeded only by a balustrade.

From this, it can be seen to bear a variety of scars, as from historical construction work. The key question is whether any of these can be identified as deriving from the site's theoretical occupation by Solomon's Temple. And here Leen Ritmeyer is again our guide, aided by some excellent overhead photographs. As he has pointed out, certain areas of the rock can be seen to have had cut into them what he calls 'flat receptacles for rectangular ashlars' – i.e. channels or trenches for the foundation stones of walls no longer there. Wherever this occurs – and a very distinct line runs across the es-Sakhra's southern part – the trench

Opposite: Ritmeyer's plan, locating the original square Mount of Solomon's Temple within the present Temple platform.

measures a consistent 10 feet wide. This corresponds precisely to the 6-cubit width that the *Mishnah* records as the original wall thickness of the Solomonic Temple's Holy of Holies. From this Ritmeyer claims he can reconstruct exactly where the walls of the Solomonic Holy of Holies must have stood in relation to the present es-Sakhra.

Particularly compelling, if Ritmeyer's reconstruction is correct, is a rectangular depression. Today, this is located in the northern part of the es-Sakhra, but according to Ritmeyer it would have been the dead centre of the Solomonic Holy of Holies:

> Converting its [i.e. the depression's] dimensions into cubits produces another rather startling fact. It measures exactly 1.5 by 2.5 cubits (2 feet 7 inches by 4 feet 4 inches, or 80 centimetres by 130 centimetres). These are the dimensions of the Ark of the Covenant the Lord told Moses to build in the wilderness (Exodus 25:10), the Ark that was ultimately placed in Solomon's Temple.[12]

As Ritmeyer explains, such a depression might well have been specially cut for the Ark: 'Such a sacred object could not be left to wobble about on the uneven surface of

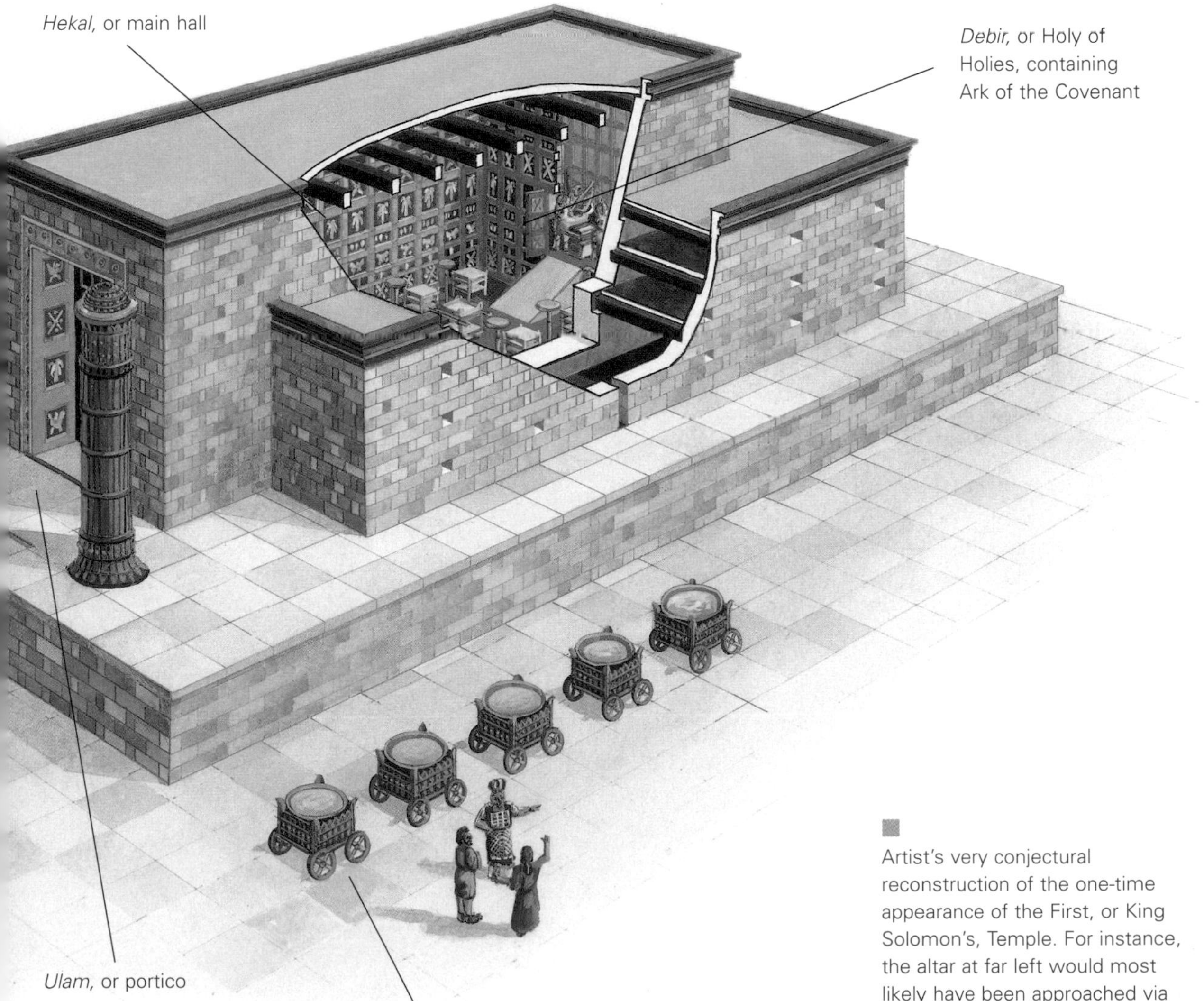

Artist's very conjectural reconstruction of the one-time appearance of the First, or King Solomon's, Temple. For instance, the altar at far left would most likely have been approached via a ramp rather than steps.

the Rock but would need a stable base on which to stand. The cutting of a flat basin such as this was the obvious solution.'[13]

Ritmeyer has even deduced why this depression, and thereby logically the Ark itself, is oriented with its short side facing the entrance to the Holy of Holies, in defiance of most reconstructions in which the Ark is set broadside on. In his words:

> A little thought reveals that this [i.e. with the short side facing] was the only way it could have stood. Otherwise the priests would not have been able to take out the staves or poles by which it was carried.[14]

This is readily corroborated from the Biblical text itself. The first book of Kings describes the 'winged sphinxes/cherubim in the Holy of Holies' as having their wings 'spread out over the place of the Ark', so that they 'shielded the Ark and its [carrying] poles *from above* [italics mine]'. It continues: 'The poles projected so that the ends of the poles were visible from the *hekal* [i.e. Main Hall] in front of the Holy of Holies but they could not be seen outside.'[15] To this the later editor of this text can be seen to have added: 'There they remain to this day.' This not only confirms Ritmeyer's deduction, but also indicates that although the editor/compiler of the 1 Kings text evidently lived

The es-Sakhra, or Rock, inside Jerusalem's Dome of the Rock. According to Leen Ritmeyer, traces of the foundations of the walls of Solomon's Temple can be identified, as on the plan (right), also a rectangular depression on which the Ark stood.

centuries later than the time of Solomon, he must also have lived before the Ark's disappearance from Jerusalem. As we will later discover, this was some time in the 7th century BC.

If, then, we can put together a picture of the Solomonic Temple's architectural details, despite the absence of physical remains, what can we also glean concerning its furniture and fittings? According to the Bible, one element of the furnishings consisted of:

> . . . ten *mechonot* of bronze. The length of each *mechonot* was four cubits and the width four cubits wide and the height three cubits. The structure of the mechanot was as follows: they had insets . . . and on the insets within the frames were lions, bulls and winged sphinxes/cherubim . . . Each mechanot had four bronze wheels and [two] bronze axletrees (1 Kings 7:27-30)

In this regard, the British Museum has in its collection a bronze cultic stand from Cyprus dating from only a century or so later than the Solomonic period. It corresponds so closely to the Biblical description of the Temple *mechonot* that there is general recognition that these must have been very similar.[16] During excavations of Philistine Ekron by Israeli archaeologist Trude Dothan, three eight-spoked bronze wheels were found at a Solomonic period level, together with a couple of other fittings. These are thought to have belonged to a similar cultic stand, the first of its kind to be found in Israel.[17] So there is nothing historically incredible about the Biblical description of the Solomon Temple's furnishings.

The other element in the Biblical description of Solomon's Temple's fittings concerns its walls, pannelling and gold overlay. The walls, we are told, were 'panelled . . . on the inside with planks of cedar . . . from the floor . . . to the ceiling (1 Kings 6:15). The floor itself was 'overlaid . . . with planks of cypress' (1 Kings 6:15). The cedar-wood altar in the *hekal was* 'overlaid . . . with gold'; the entire interior of the *debir*, or Holy of Holies, was 'overlaid with solid gold'; likewise the whole Temple was 'overlaid with gold'.[18]

This may sound like hyperbole. In the case of ancient Egypt's Temple of Amun at Karnak, however, an inscription specifically records that the New Kingdom pharaoh Amenophis III had this 'plated with gold throughout, its floor adorned with silver, [and] all its portals with electrum [a natural alloy of gold and silver]'[19]. In confirmation of this, the columns of Karnak's Temple of the Sacred Boat can be seen to have slits for holding the edges of such plating.[20] Similarly, the series of gold-plated shrines that protected Pharaoh Tutankhamum's sarcophagus, although these date from three centuries before Solomon, may well also give us an idea of how the Jerusalem Temple's Holy of Holies was once plated.

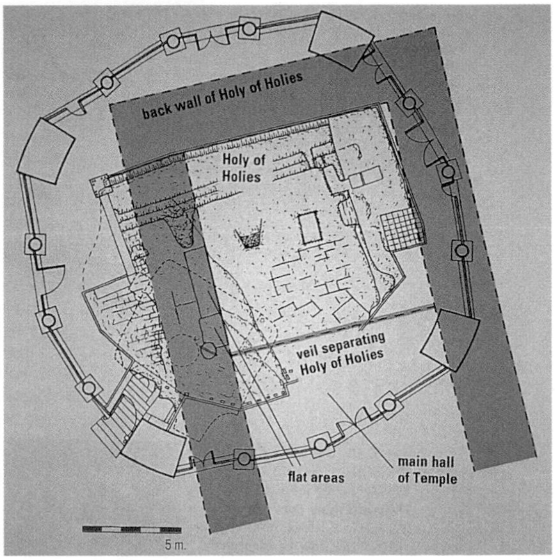

A necessary question arises here. How could Solomon, from a nation who so shortly before had been humble sheep-herders, have afforded all the luxurious materials needed for such ambitious building projects? A key to the answer is Solomon's father's old ally Hiram, king of the Canaanitic/Phoenician city-state of Tyre. Of the background to this alliance, the Bible text tells us that 'Hiram had always been a friend of David' (1 Kings 5:15). In like manner, the Bible tells us that

'Hiram kept Solomon provided with all the cedar and cypress wood he required, and Solomon delivered to Hiram twenty thousand *kor* of wheat as provisions for his household and twenty thousand *kor* of beaten oil' (1 Kings 5:24, 25).

Clearly, then, with regard to the fine-quality timber that Tyre had as its main natural resource, Hiram and Solomon had negotiated a mutually beneficial barter. But what about the gold with which so much of the Temple was plated? As the Bible makes clear, this did not come directly from Tyre. Instead 'Hiram's fleet . . . carried gold from Ophir' (1 Kings 10:11). Additionally, Solomon 'had a Tarshish fleet on the sea, along with Hiram's fleet. Once every three years the Tarshish fleet came in, bearing gold and silver, ivory, apes and peacocks' (1 Kings 10:22).

If only we knew where 'Tarshish' and 'Ophir' were, we might be the wiser. But this is not the case, despite many theories. The most we can be sure of is that Ophir is not just an invented name, for at Tel Qasile, in the environs of present-day Tel-Aviv, an 8th-century BC potsherd has been found bearing the inscription: '[G]old (of) Ophir. (Belonging) to Beth-Horon. 30 sh[ekels].' This is of great importance as the only known reference to Ophir surviving outside the Bible. Unfortunately, however, it fails to give us any greater clue than the Bible itself about where Ophir might have been located.

More rewardingly, the Bible does at least tell us the port from which those wanting to trade with Ophir set out. For in 1 Kings 9, repeated almost word for word in 2 Chronicles 8, we are told:

> King Solomon also built a fleet of ships *at Ezion-Geber, which is near Elath on the shore of the Red Sea, in the land of Edom.* Hiram sent servants of his with the fleet, mariners who were experienced on the sea, to serve with Solomon's men. They came to Ophir; there they obtained gold in the amount of four hundred and twenty talents, which they delivered to King Solomon. (1 Kings 9:26-28)

Solomon made 'ten *mechonot* ... each *mechonot* had four bronze wheels and [two] bronze axletrees' (1 Kings 7:27-30). A *c.*11th-century BC *mechona,* or laver-stand, from Cyprus resembles the Biblical description.

That this port was on the Red Sea, rather than on the Mediterranean, speaks volumes about why it was to Hiram of Tyre's considerable advantage to ally with Solomon, and to provide him with experienced mariners. For while Tyre's location as a busy Mediterranean sea-port gave Hiram all the access to the Mediterranean he needed, it was Solomon who commanded the land-route to the Red Sea. Arguably, this was thanks to King David's general Joab who had so savagely beaten the neighbouring Edomites into submission, as described in the last chapter. As Hiram would have been keenly aware, anyone who had the freedom of the formerly Edomite-controlled Arabah corridor to the Red Sea coast, and who possessed the necessary ships, had easy access to Africa to the south, also to Arabia and India to the east. Ophir with all its gold presumably lay somewhere among these places.

But where exactly was the Biblically-described 'Ezion-Geber . . . near Elath' port from which such trading expeditions to Ophir would have set out? From the list of the

places that Moses' followers stopped at in the course of their exodus from Egypt, we may recall Ezion-Geber. It was here that they camped after Moses had received the commandments on Mount Sinai (Numbers 33:35-6). Wherever this was, it had to be somewhere on the Sinai peninsula before Kadesh, which came next on the itinerary. Also, Deuteronomy 2:8 helpfully locates it at the end of the Arabah, the land-corridor from the Dead Sea extending southwards to what is today the Red Sea resort of Eilat.

From clues such as these, in 1933 the German spy Fritz Frank, posing as an archaeologist in order to survey the Arabah for future military purposes, tentatively identified as Biblical Ezion-Geber a low, wind-swept mound the Arabs called Tell el-Kheleifeh. It lies midway between Eilat and Jordanian Aqabah[21]. This seemed to be confirmed four years later by Rabbi Nelson Glueck, Frank's American counterpart. At the same site, Glueck found materials, accompanied by Solomonic pottery, that he interpreted as casting moulds, along with vast quantities of copper slag and a structure whose walls were discoloured green. This he identified as a blast furnace, complete with an impressive flue system. From such finds, Glueck hailed Tell el-Kheleifeh not only as Solomon's Ezion-Geber, but also as 'the Pittsburgh of old Palestine'[22], a vast 'copper refinery' that, he argued, would have contributed in very large measure to Solomon's alleged fabulous wealth.

How Solomon's Temple was originally gold-plated? Gold-plated shrine from the tomb of Tutankhamun.

But, although these interpretations by Glueck became widely accepted for more than two decades, in 1962 his former assistant Beno Rothenberg of Tel Aviv University published a paper showing that he had erred in almost every point. According to Rothenberg, Glueck's 'blast furnace' was in fact a large grain store, its green discoloration having come about when the building was destroyed by fire. What Glueck had interpreted as 'flue holes' were, in reality, the slots for holding the granary's wooden beams before these had gone up in flames. Traces of the charred timber were still evident in these. As for the so-called 'copper slag', this was pure moonshine on Glueck's part. Such was the cogency of Rothenberg's

'They (Solomon's ships) came to Ophir, there they obtained gold ...' (1 Kings 9:28). Proving that Solomon's 'Ophir' was no legend, a potsherd bearing the inscription 'Gold of Ophir . . . 30 shekels' was found near Tel Aviv.

arguments that in 1965 Nelson Glueck, to his considerable credit, publicly accepted that his interpretations had been fundamentally flawed.

But if Tell el-Kheleifeh was definitely not Ezion-Geber, where, assuming that it existed at all, could the original Solomonic Red Sea port of this name have been located? Even as early as 1956, Beno Rothenberg, together with a group of students and colleagues, made a promising survey of a small island known as Jezirat Faraun [Jeh-ZEE-raht Far-ROON], literally 'Pharaoh's Island', lying in the Red Sea just 300 yards off the Sinai coast, some 7 miles south of present-day Eilat. In particular, what had caught their attention were the remains of a low-level sea wall surrounding the island, also a small harbour, together with pottery suggesting that it had been frequented much earlier than the Byzantine period to which Glueck had attributed it.

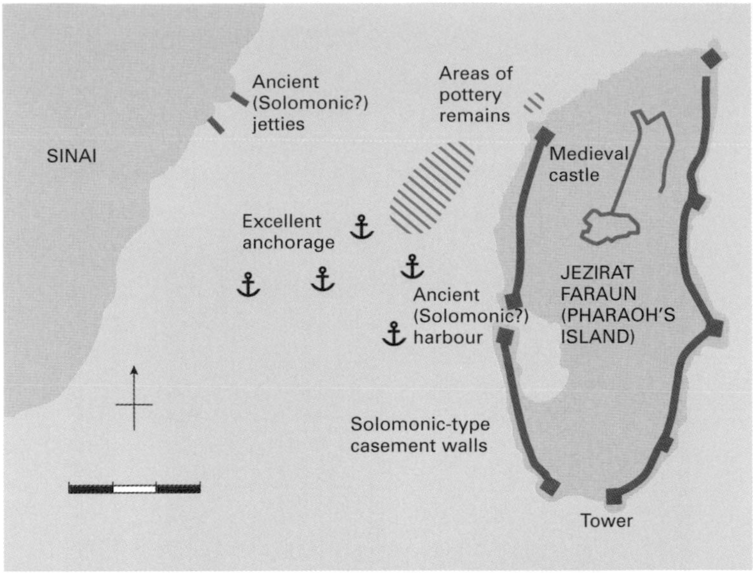

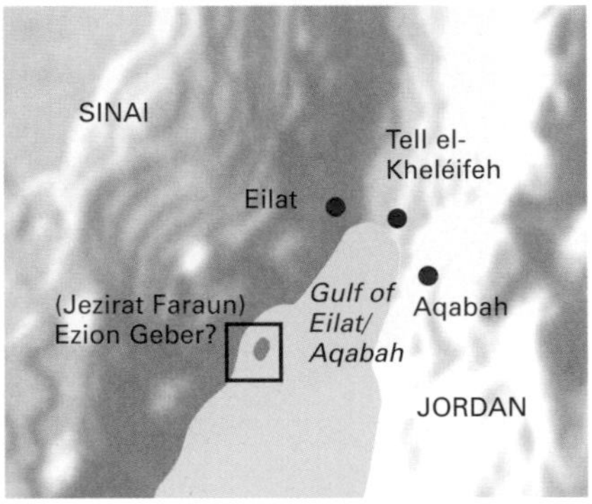

Top: Map of Jezirat Faraun, or Pharaoh's Island, thought to have been the Ezion-Geber port from which Solomon sent out naval expeditions to trade for gold. Above: Jezirat Faraun's location in the northernmost part of the Gulf of Eilat/Gulf of Aqabah.

In 1967, Rothenberg's interest was followed up by British architect and underwater archaeology pioneer Alexander Flinder. On visiting the island, Flinder was particularly struck by the calmness of the water between it and the Sinai mainland, even when elsewhere there were high waves whipped up by the winds and storms to which the region was prone. In Flinder's words: 'Any sailor would immediately recognise the area between the island and the shore as a natural anchorage.'[23] In fact, it is the *only* natural anchorage in this entire northern part of the Red Sea. The present-day ports of Eilat and Aqabah were both artificially constructed in much more recent times.

Like Rothenberg before him, Flinder was also intrigued by the island's perimeter wall. To him, it was quite obvious that someone, some time, had built this very strongly, complete with well-made towers. And there were indications of the same casemate-type construction we have already associated with Solomon. No less significant was a so-called pool on the island's western side, which turned out to be not a pool at all, but a one-time harbour. The original entrance to this, once also protected by flanking towers, had long ago become blocked by sand. When, in 1968, Flinder returned to Jezirat Faraun at the head of a British/Israeli three-week archaeological survey expedition, he and his team found two one-time mooring piers just outside this harbour, also, yet more revealingly, two stone jetties immediately opposite, on the Sinai mainland.

The obvious question, therefore, was: when were the harbour and fortifications first built? Although some scholars, following Glueck, continue to suppose that the island's tower fortifications, and thereby the harbour, were Byzantine, it is irrefutable that at least some of Jezirat Faraun's pottery[24] dates back to the Solomonic/Iron Age I period. Furthermore, as Flinder has cogently pointed out, the island corresponds extremely well with the sort of offshore location that Canaanitic/Phoenicians like Hiram specially favoured for their maritime bases. Thus, just as at Jezirat Faraun, Tyre has to its south a sandy sea-bed plateau creating very calm conditions between it and the mainland. And although Jezirat Faraun would have been only about half the size of ancient Tyre – its harbour proper, for instance, measuring only 180 feet by 90 feet – this is actually all that Hiram and Solomon would have needed. For as the Bible indicates, in the case of the Red Sea, the requirement was not for a day-to-day port as was the norm around the Mediterranean, but instead for a secure base from which a few irregular but potentially highly-profitable expeditions could be launched. Jezirat Fairaun would have fitted this bill perfectly.

Furthermore, if grain and oil were the commodities which these expeditions carried as barter against the gold, then arguably Tell el-Kheleifeh, with its granaries and what further expeditions have revealed as Solomonic-period, casemate-walled fortifications[25], may have been Biblical Elath. This may have represented a secure warehouse for the temporary storage of all export commodities before they were taken onwards to the port-island of Ezion-Geber, alias Jezirat Faraun.

But amidst all this, one thing cannot be overlooked. This is the profound change that must have come over so-called Israel to make all the temple, fortress and port building, and the related entrepreneurial and diplomatic activities, possible. Whereas King David had been the typical self-made man, roughened by having to live on occasion in a cave, and sufficiently careless about dress and manners to be unafraid of making a fool of himself in public, Solomon, his palace-reared son, clearly held great store by sophisticated outward show.

Also, whereas King David had been careful to be even-handed between north and south, appointing two separate chief priests in Jerusalem, one to represent the northern tribes, the other his own southern affiliations, Solomon coldly expelled the northern chief priest. Furthermore, he gave some of the northern tribes' territory to Hiram (1 Kings 9:10-11), and exerted markedly harsher work and food-supply levies on those living in the north than he did on his fellow southerners.

The dominion David took over had been village-based and religiously intolerant, with no expertise in the construction of major buildings and fortifications, no state-of-the-art weaponry and no significant precious-metals technology. Solomon re-fortified the former Canaanite cities, equipped himself with a sizeable chariot-corps on Canaanite lines and took to even further extremes his father's policy of intermarrying with foreign princesses. Many adhered to 'pagan' religions, many of them very Canaanitic. Not least, as builder of his religion's most sacred shrine – the Jerusalem Temple – he allowed and indeed encouraged 'pagan' craftsmen, supplied by the Canaanitic/Phoenician king Hiram, to do much of the work on this.

So it is quite apparent that, even in this heyday of the Israelite monarchy, an astonishing tolerance had crept in of the same Canaanitic and other pagan ways to which true Yahwist Israelites had been so violently opposed only a few generations earlier. For instance, a careful study of Syrian and Canaanitic 'pagan' temples of the period in relation to the Biblical description of Solomon's Temple, confirms Canaanitic influences upon the Jerusalem structure. An example is at Tell Tainat on the northern Orontes, where American archaeologists of the 1930s brought to light an 8th-century BC temple divided into three sections, just like the Jerusalem Temple, and with the same entrance-way twin pillars.

Likewise, the Biblical record informs us that Solomon's mother Bathsheba was the widow of a Hittite soldier, that the Court in which he grew up included numerous foreign princesses whom his father had married, that foreign mercenaries were used for his parents' bodyguards, and that many of the royal city's original Jebusite citizens still

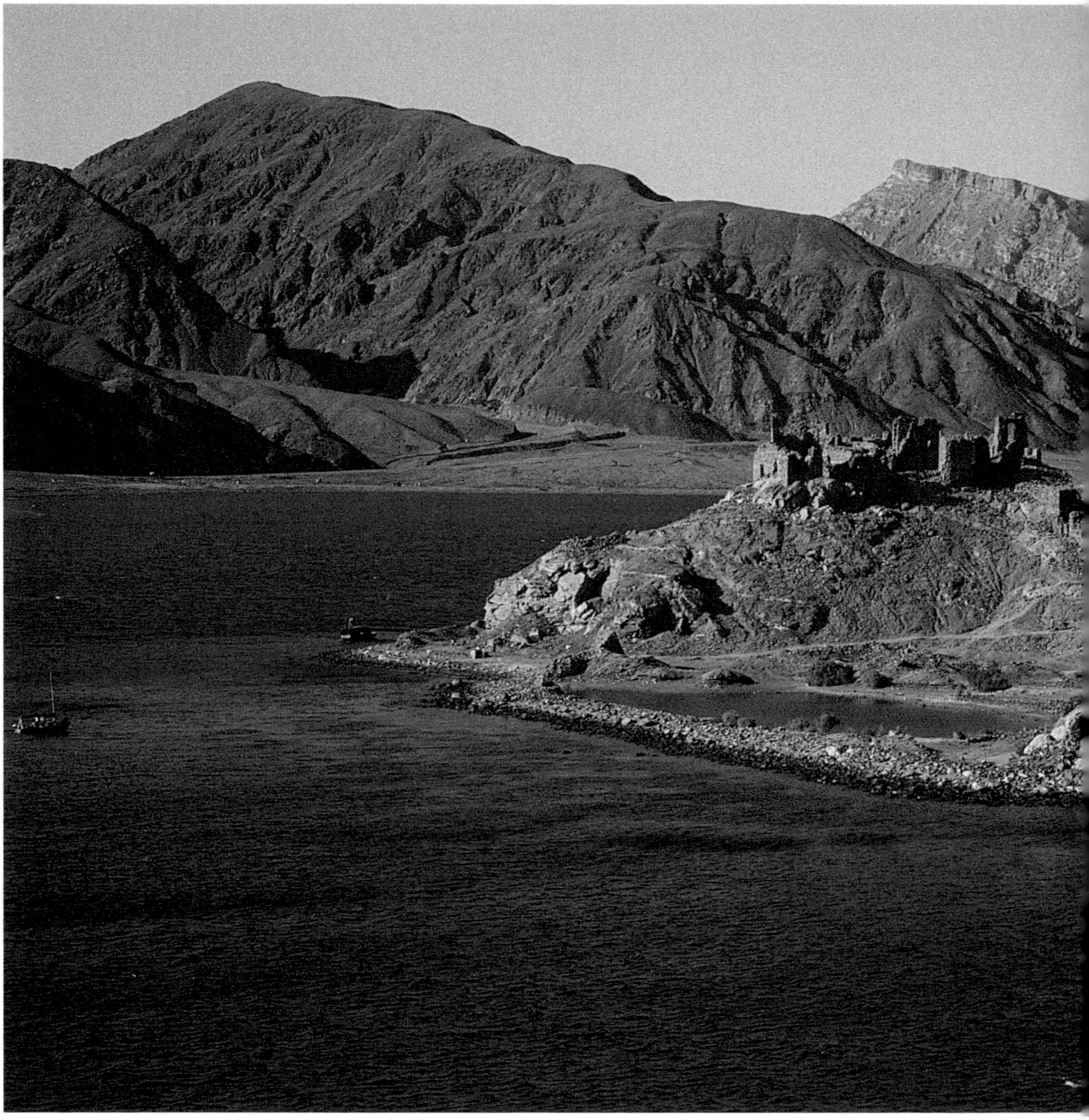

adhered to the traditional Canaanite religion. As for Solomon's own seven hundred foreign wives, we are told:

> In his old age, his wives turned away Solomon's heart after other gods, and he was not as wholeheartedly devoted to Yahweh his God as his father David had been. Solomon followed Astarte, the goddess of the Phoenicians, and Milcom, the abomination of the Ammonites . . . At that time Solomon built a *bamah* (high place) for Chemosh, the abomination of Moab, on the hill near Jerusalem and one for Milcom, the abomination of the Ammonites. (1 Kings 11:4-7)

Overall, then, the archaeological and Biblical picture of Solomon is of an individual who, reaping the benefits of his father David's military and diplomatic successes, had amassed unprecedented wealth and power for this new kingdom of Israel. Arguably, this

Jezirat Faraun, or 'Pharaohs Island', in the Red Sea off the Sinai coast. The fortress is medieval, but there are remains of casement-type walls typical of the period of Solomon.

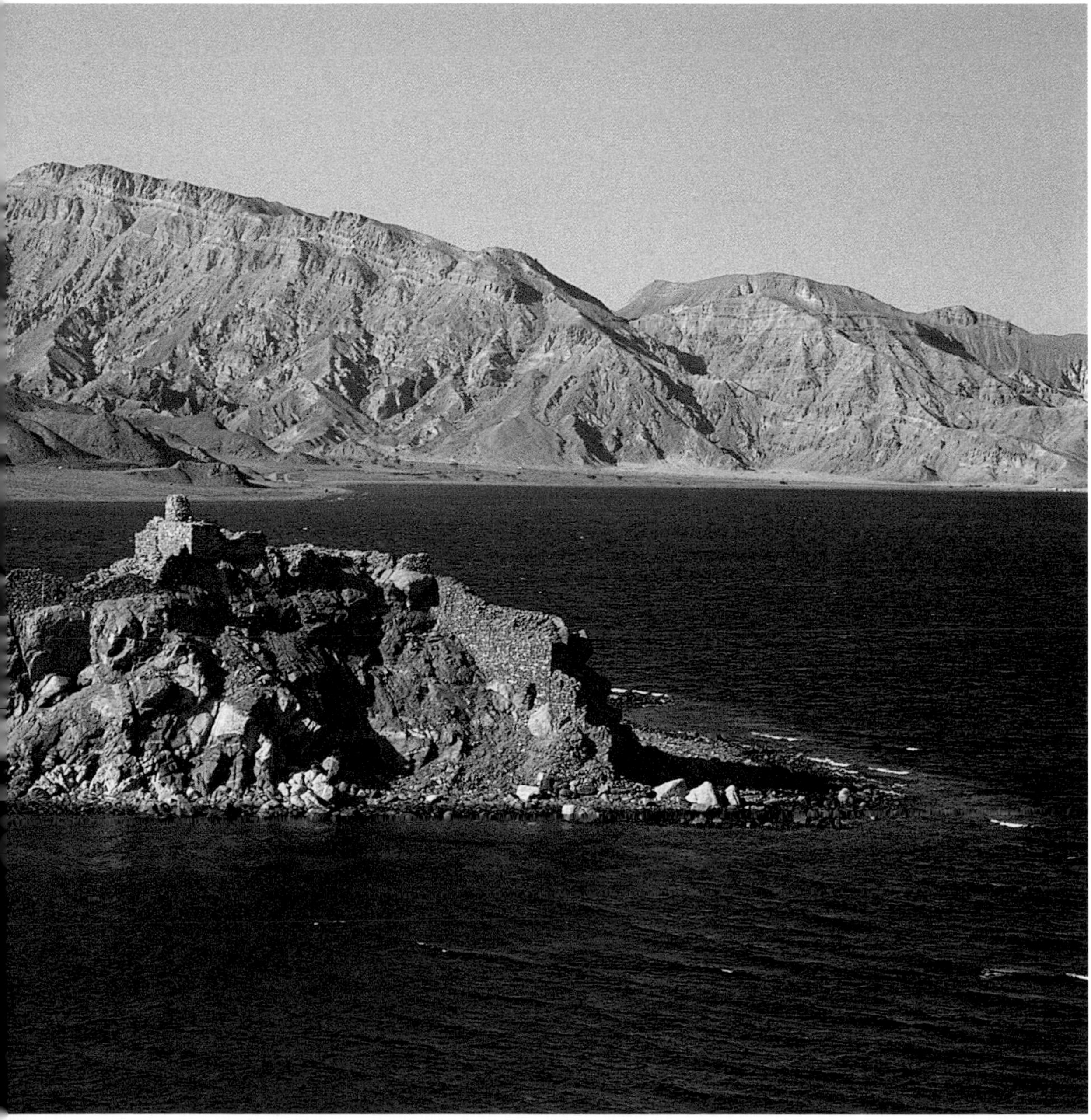

was a direct result of tolerating and embracing much of the Canaanitic way of life, as if there never ever had been any friction between it and the life style of the incoming Israelites.

But could such a status quo survive? Furthermore, what would Egypt and other major neighbouring states make of this upstart new empire rivalling theirs? Despite Solomon's reputed marriage to an Egyptian pharaoh's daughter, the fact that he built so many fortresses to protect his southern border suggests that it was from that direction he most expected any attack to come.

And although, when he died after a reign chronicled as forty years (1 Kings 11:42), his kingdom was still intact and apparently at peace, such attacks, both internal and external, would not be slow in coming forth.

11

A HOUSE DIVIDED

IT IS SOME MEASURE of both the internal divisions that Solomon's policies aroused and the firm control over these divisions he exerted in his lifetime that it was apparently only a matter of weeks after his death that his kingdom became rent asunder.

According to the book of Kings, when Solomon's recognised successor – his son Rehoboam – appeared at the old northern capital of Shechem, expecting to be formally crowned and making it clear that he would continue his father's policies, the northern tribal leaders formally and decisively severed themselves from any further ties with him and his southern dominions. With the cry 'Away to your tents, Israel!' (1 Kings 12:16) – an interesting indication that some of them were still more traditional herds-people than their southern counterparts – they sent Rehoboam scuttling back to Jerusalem as fast as his chariot would carry him. As for the tax official Rehoboam had brought with him, they contemptuously stoned him to death.

However, instead of the northerners reverting to their formerly so-revered judges system, they chose for themselves another king, Jeroboam. He was an already notorious political activist who, precisely because of his reputation, had been obliged to stay exiled in Egypt during much of Solomon's reign (1 Kings 12:1). On Jeroboam's acceptance of the northern throne, and on Reboboam's decision not to try to contest this, the country that had been so promisingly united and centralised throughout David and Solomon's long reigns simply split apart. From this point on, generally dated to 931 BC, Jeroboam's northern tribal territory became known as 'Israel' (the term Israelites thereby now carrying a quite different connotation), while Rehoboam's southern dominion was called 'Judah'. Although Rehoboam's House of David dynasty would enjoy sovereignty for several centuries longer than Jeroboam's, there was rarely much chance of the northerners returning to the southern fold. The rivalries were as bitter as those that have rent Yugoslavia in our own time. Symptomatically, from this point on, the two kingdoms reportedly kept separate chronicles – the 'Annals of the Kings of Israel' and the 'Annals of the Kings of Judah' – long-lost sources from which the present books of Kings and

Scene to make Solomon weep . . . Cartouches, or name boxes, representing just three of the 130 Canaanitic cities conquered by Egypt as a result of the national disunity after Solomon's death.

Chronicles were later compiled. Drawing upon these around the 7th century BC, the 1 Kings compiler/editor drily noted: 'Thus Israel [i.e. the north] revolted against the House of David [i.e. the Judahite south], as is still the case' (1 Kings 12:19).

The news that the formerly united Solomonic kingdom no longer had strong central control can hardly have been anything other than music to the ears of the neighbouring 10th-century BC monarchs. Pharaoh Shoshenq I had particular cause for rejoicing. Born in Libya, Shoshenq was the first Egyptian monarch for many a year with serious inclinations to expand his country's borders and with the military muscle to do so. According to the Biblical book of Chronicles, which refers to him as Shishak, in the fifth year of Rehoboam's reign, he 'marched on Jerusalem . . . with twelve hundred chariots and sixty thousand horsemen and innumerable troops who came with him from Egypt: Libyans, Sukkites and Kushites. He took the fortified towns of Judah and advanced on Jerusalem' (2 Chronicles 12:2-4).

Here we are fortunate to find a Biblically-described event clearly and unequivocally in the Egyptian record, for Shoshenq/Shishak and his successors added a colossal forecourt to the Temple of Amun at Luxor. Its adjoining so-called Bubastis Portal still bears Shoshenq's triumphal relief commemorating this very campaign. It features the cartouches, or name boxes, of some 130 different Canaanite cities that Shoshenq claimed to have conquered. All are set out in a logical, geographical order, each topped with a figure roped like a captive, among which appear Megiddo, Gaza and Beth-shan. Most of the towns guarding the routes along the Jordan Valley and the Negev also appear, including two 'fortress enclosures' called Arad.

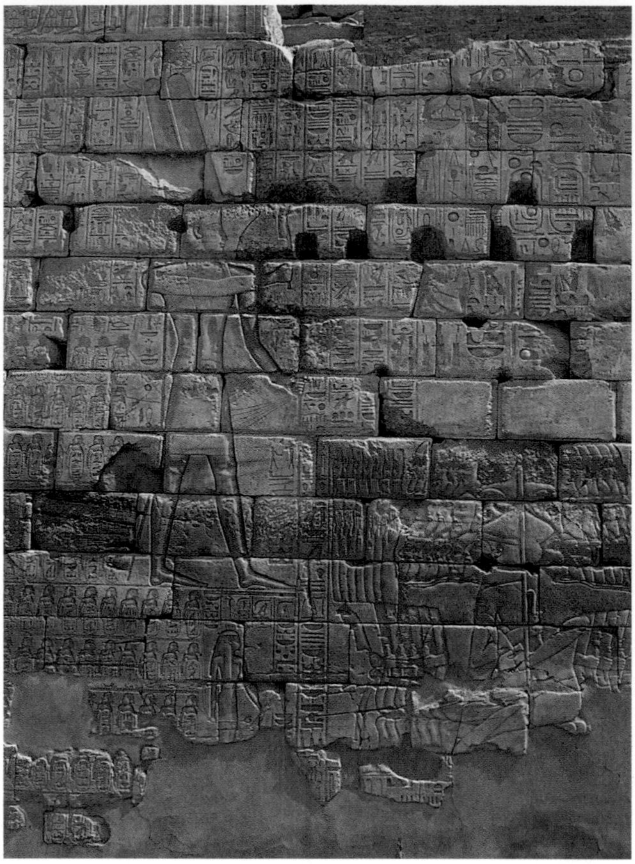

The Bubastis Portal, the vast triumphal relief Egyptian Pharaoh Shoshenq I erected at Luxor. It shows, bound to the god Amun, the Canaanitic cities that Shoshenq defeated in a campaign of *c.*925 BC.

That this was more than Ramessid-type empty boasting is apparent, for instance, from the excavations of Arad, the Negevite fortress with the Yahweh temple. Here, destruction by a devastating fire has been found at the late 10th-century BC level.[1] Shoshenq is thought to have reigned between 945 and 924 BC, and the Biblical dating of his invasion to Rehoboam's fifth year suggests that this was very close to the end of his reign. As a result, Arad's archaeologists are in little doubt that he was responsible for this particular destruction layer, also for similar elsewhere.

Yet from this it should not be supposed that Shoshenq indulged in destruction for destruction's sake. He obviously did not shrink from eliminating the Solomonic fortresses so recently built to check southern aggressors such as himself. But at Megiddo a once 10-foot-high, Egyptian victory stele erected by him[2] has been found. It indicates that he merely annexed this important city, while no doubt exacting a suitably punitive 'tribute' from it, just as his 18th and 19th Dynasty predecessors had done before him.

In this regard, there is another interesting feature. At the place on Shoshenq's Bubastis relief where we would expect the name Jerusalem to appear among the cities listed, it does not. Likewise, the Bible itself does not say that Shoshenq actually captured Jerusalem. It merely states instead that Rehoboam and his officers obtained 'some measure of deliverance', whereby the Egyptian king:

> . . . took away the treasures of the Temple of Yahweh and the treasures of the royal palace [and] . . . took away everything, . . . [including] the golden shields that Solomon had made. (2 Chronicles 12:9)

From this, we may infer that Rehoboam's 'measure of deliverance' was his buying Shoshenq off. It was an abject handing-over of the less sacred and more easily-disposable items from his royal palace and the Temple's treasury, in return for which the Egyptian pharaoh desisted from an all-out attack on Jerusalem. This would explain, for instance, the lack of any Biblical mention of the Ark being surrendered to the Egyptians, or of any loss of life among the city's inhabitants.

But what a 'buying off'! From what can be inferred of the scale of the treasures Shoshenq took away with him, there is every reason to believe that he had exacted an exceptionally heavy price from Rehoboam. It is also clear that Rehoboam's father Solomon really had been as wealthy in his heyday as the Biblical record suggests.

From our best chronological understanding, Shoshenq died only a year or so after his Canaan campaign, to be succeeded by his son Osorkon II. Of maximum interest here is an inscription on a granite pillar in a temple at Bubastis in the eastern Nile Delta. Dateable to between 924 and 921 BC, and therefore to the years immediately following Shoshenq's campaign of *c.*925 BC, this records that Osorkon made extravagant gifts to 'all the gods and goddesses of the cities of Upper and Lower Egypt'. The gifts amounted to a total of approximately 2 million *deben* of silver and 2.3 million *deben* of gold and silver[3], in modern-day measures something like 383 tons of precious metal, even by Egyptian standards an enormous amount of treasure. When we ask how and where Osorkon could have obtained such immense wealth after having reigned little more than three years, the answer is almost glaringly obvious. As has been pointed out by British Egyptologist Kenneth Kitchen:

> Barely five years earlier Osorkon's father Shoshenq had looted the wealth of Jerusalem. It seems unlikely to be a mere coincidence that almost immediately after that event Osorkon could dispose so freely of so much gold and silver. The vast amounts of Solomon's golden wealth may have ended up, at least in part, as Osorkon's gift to the gods and goddesses of Egypt.[4]

Nor is this all. In 1939, during his earlier-mentioned excavations at Tanis in the Nile Delta, the French archaeologist Pierre Montet found the tomb of Osorkon's co-regent son Shoshenq III, who had died before his father. Shoshenq III's sarcophagus was made of solid silver, the richest ever found in Egypt aside from Tutankhamun's, clear evidence that even after Osorkon had given so much to the Temple of Amun, there was still much treasure to spare. A major resurgence of building activity in Egypt, often an indication of sudden new wealth, can also be dated to the same time.[5]

Nor can there be any doubting the further serious 'knock-on' consequences of the swift division of Solomon's former territories. With regard to the northern, or Israel, kingdom, we may have some extra-Biblical documentation for its first king Jeroboam. At the beginning of the 20th century, the German archaeologist Gotlieb Schumacher, in the course of one of the first-ever excavations at Megiddo, unearthed a jasper seal superbly engraved with a roaring lion, inscribed '(belonging) to Shema, servant of Jeroboam', and thereby identified as having belonged to one of Jeroboam's officials.[6] Although the original, which Schumacher gave to the Turkish sultan in Constantinople, has most frustratingly disappeared, its genuineness is not in question, although the latest palaeographic opinion suggests that the Jeroboam of the seal was more probably the 8th-century BC Jeroboam II, rather than his earlier namesake.

Rather more definite, and not purely because we are Biblically told so, are some dramatic changes Jeroboam made to the prevailing religious practices in his new kingdom. They were apparently designed to discourage his

Facsimile of a jasper seal found at Megiddo in 1904, and since lost. It bears the inscription '[belonging] to Shema, servant of Jeroboam'.

subjects from being lured southwards on holy days to offer their animal sacrifices at the Jerusalem Temple, with its historic Ark as well as all its associations with the Judahite dynasty.

According to the Biblical account, Jeroboam ordered the making of two cultic 'golden calves' (or again more correctly, young bulls), inevitably reminiscent of the golden calf the refugees from Egypt had so controversially made in the Sinai desert. The first of these calves he had set up at the new national religious shrine, which he created at Dan in the northernmost part of his kingdom; the second was at Bethel, close to his southern border (1 Kings 12:28-9). Additionally, Jeroboam appointed his own independent priesthood from individuals not of the traditional Levite priestly descent, and also changed the calendar of religious festivals.

With regard to Jeroboam's choice of Dan for his northern sanctuary, this was, of course, the place where Israeli archaeologist Avraham Biran discovered the House of David inscription. A further finding of Biran's was that in the late 10th century, i.e. around Jeroboam's time, the city was given some impressive alterations befitting its status as a new or improved major religious centre. As can readily be seen from what the archaeologists have so far uncovered, an elaborate gatehouse complex was constructed of fine ashlar masonry, similar to that of the royal palaces at Gezer, Megiddo and Hazor. Immediately inside this was a small plaza featuring five standing stones corresponding to the Biblical *massebot*, together with twenty-five accompanying cultic jars and a low platform with a one-time canopy over it.[7] This corresponds closely with something we learn about later in the Bible: a Jerusalem '*bamah* (high place) of the Gates', which was suppressed as pagan by the 7th-century BC king Josiah (2 Kings 23:1-20). There can be little doubt that Dan's structure was of this kind.

Furthermore, in Tel Dan's north-western sector, not far from its attractive bubbling spring, Biran and his fellow archaeologists uncovered an imposing, platform-like masonry structure that can only have been the city's principal *bamah*, or 'high place' – as distinct from its gatehouse one. They also found a small, well-preserved altar with horns at its sides that was instantly reminiscent of the altar that King David's son Adonijah is said to have clung to for sanctuary, when he heard that Solomon and not he had been acclaimed as David's successor (1 Kings 1:50).

At Tel Dan, therefore, we can see confirmed in hard archaeological evidence the Biblical account of how King Jeroboam set up two religious sanctuaries in opposition to Judah with its Jerusalem Temple. An altogether more difficult task is how to interpret his intentions in setting up the 'young bull' statuettes and the *bamah*, or 'high places'. As we have already seen in our discussion of the 'golden calf' incident at Sinai, the young bull was a symbol of the Canaanite god Baal/El, and an

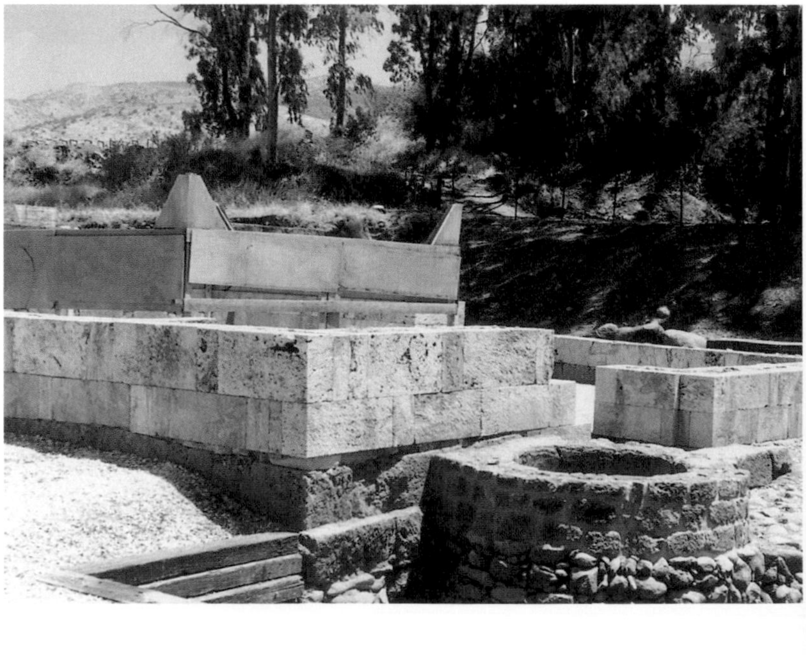

Recalling several Biblical references to horned altars (see also page 114), the horned altar uncovered at Tel Dan.

explicit-enough idol of the old Canaanite type to infuriate any follower of Moses. Yet something else is notable about the use of the name El. As already mentioned, the early books of the Bible were almost certainly editorially welded together from two or more independently-written, but similar, stories. In what scholars perceive as the northern, or Israel, kingdom's strand, El is the name given to the Biblical divinity.

So was it Jeroboam's policy to weld some kind of religious unity between the militant (and seemingly often military) Yahwists and the many traditional Canaanites who must still have formed a large element in his northern kingdom's population? Or was he Canaanite through and through? Biblically, we are told little more than what happened when Jeroboam's wife went to visit Ahijah, the *nabi* of the day. Ahijah, as Yahweh, roundly condemned the making of 'idols of cast metal' and predicted a swift doom for Jeroboam and all his line (1 Kings 14), a prophecy that was duly fulfilled.

Whoever compiled the 1 Kings account of this phase of Biblical history does not seem to have approved of the Israelite rebel Jeroboam. But neither did he have much good to say about Jeroboam's Judahite counterpart, Rehoboam. As we are told, Rehoboam 'did what was displeasing to Yahweh . . . He imitated all the abhorrent practices of the nations whom Yahweh had dispossessed before the Israelites' (1 Kings 14:22-24). The deviant practices of these 'dispossessed' and obviously Canaanitic nations were specifically enumerated. They had 'built themselves *bamah*, pillars and sacred *asherah* on every high hill and under every leafy tree'. They had also tolerated, if not positively encouraged, 'male prostitutes' (1 Kings 14:23 & 24).

Clearly, whatever may have been the state of what we may best term 'Yahwism', the old Canaanitic religion was still very much alive and kicking in both kingdoms. Both the Israel and Judahite monarchs played an uncomfortable juggling act between the two traditions. There is no better example of this than the events after Jeroboam's dynasty was usurped by an army general, Omri. On Omri's death, the Israel throne passed to his son Ahab, and to Ahab's now-notorious, Baal-worshipping queen Jezebel, daughter of the Canaanitic/Phoenician king of Sidon.

Ahab and Jezebel's reign is generally dated to c.874-853 BC, and as represented in the Bible they had their court at Samaria. This was where Ahab's father Omri had moved the northern capital, because its steep slopes on three sides made it naturally more defensible than the former capital Shechem. Under Jezebel's influence, Ahab reportedly erected at Samaria an altar to Baal in 'the temple of Baal' (1 Kings 16:31). He also apparently 'made an *asherah*' (1 Kings 16:33), i.e. a figure or post sacred to the goddess Astarte, reportedly the principal deity for 'Phoenicians' such as Jezebel (see 1 Kings 11:5).

All of this seems to have acted like a red rag to a bull for one of the most extraordinary figures of the entire Bible – the Yahwist *nabi* Elijah, a wild man accredited with bringing back to life a widow's dead child (1 Kings 17) and acknowledged as one of the greatest of those who professed to have Yahweh speak through them. In the face of Ahab and Jezebel's obvious Canaanite and pagan sympathies, Elijah's response was to challenge 450 *nabiim* of the Canaanitic god Baal and 400 of the goddess Astarte (1 Kings 18:19) to a showdown test on Mount Carmel. The object was to determine whose sacrifice would bring down fire from heaven. When the Baal and Astarte devotees abysmally failed, and Elijah's sacrifice dramatically succeeded, Elijah ordered his opponents' immediate massacre.

According to the Biblical account, Elijah also directly accused Ahab and Jezebel of murder and fraud for their part in illegally obtaining one of their subjects' vineyards. Reputedly, Jezebel 'wrote a letter in Ahab's name and sealed it with his seal' (1 Kings 21:8), as part of a plot to ensure that the vineyard owner would be stoned to death.

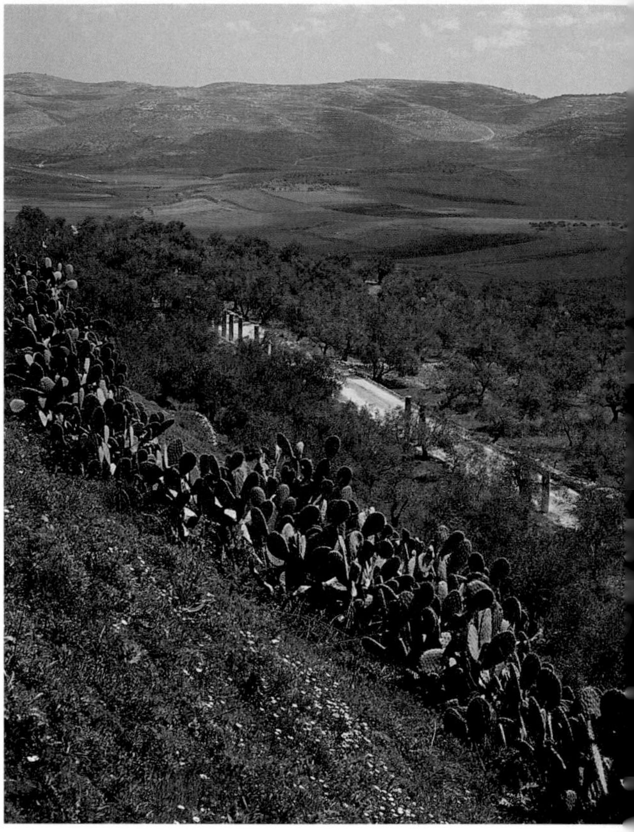

Intriguingly, a recently-discovered Phoenician style seal bearing palaeo-Hebrew letters *yzbl* may just conceivably have been Jezebel's own. Not to be overlooked, however, is the fact that while, in almost any other society, to accuse royalty of murder and fraud would have meant Elijah's immediate execution, the kingdom of Israel, seemingly following King David's example, was markedly more tolerant.

From the perspective of the editor/compiler of 1 Kings, it sounds as if the sole purpose of Ahab's reign was to 'vex Yahweh, God of Israel, [more] than all the kings of Israel who preceded him' (1 Kings 16:32-3). Yet the archaeological picture, as evident from excavations both at Samaria and at other northern cities[8], on the whole sheds a more favourable light upon Ahab and his colourful consort.

Concluding with a standard remark that much else about Ahab is recorded in the now-lost 'Annals of the Kings of Israel', the book of Kings' compiler mentions, very much as an aside, 'the ivory palace that he [Ahab] built and all the towns that he fortified' (1 Kings 22:39). From our present-day knowledge, this can only be accounted one of the Bible's greatest understatements. For as evidence of just how tasteful Ahab and Jezebel's 'ivory palace' must once have been, the archaeological excavations at Samaria have brought to light fragmentary ivories (see example, page 149), beautifully decorated with human and animal figures that must have been part of its wall and furniture decorations. Created in an Egyptian-Canaanitic style fashionable at that time, these show that whatever Ahab and Jezebel's ethics may have been, they were a couple with some culture and taste.

Samaria, the strategic hill chosen by Ahab's father Omri for the northern kingdom's new capital.

But this was far from all. For the Bible's similarly glancing mention of 'all the towns [that] he [Ahab] fortified' does scant justice to some prodigious construction work that Ahab seems to have implemented, particularly at Hazor and Megiddo, in order to protect these places against future destructions of the kind wrought by Pharaoh Shoshenq. As the archaeological record shows, someone – and from the historical perspective it must logically have been Ahab – replaced the casemate-type city walls of Solomon's time with walls of an altogether more solid construction. At Dor, following the destruction level attributable to Shoshenq, a monumental four-chambered gate with 6-foot-thick walls has been attributed to Ahab[9], likewise the rebuilding of its old harbour as a great fortified seaport.

Left: A recently discovered seal thought to have belonged to the Biblical Jezebel.

This indicates the harmony in which he co-existed with his seafaring Phoenician neighbours, just as David and Solomon had done with Hiram. If Finkelstein and Ussishkin are right, the six-chamber gateways at Megiddo, Hazor and Gezer that Yigael Yadin attributed to Solomon are more likely Ahab's trebly-protective reinforcements of the two-chamber gateways previously built by Solomon.

Additionally, both at Megiddo and at Hazor, Ahab can be seen to have initiated huge engineering projects to ensure that a water supply would always be accessible from inside the city's walls in the event of a siege. Because Megiddo, like Jerusalem, drew its water from a spring at the foot of the slope outside the city wall, but lacked any access to this from inside, an internal access tunnel had to be specially dug. Also, the old entrance to the spring outside the walls had to be impenetrably sealed, so that an enemy could not use, or interfere with, it from outside.

Both of these massive undertakings Ahab's engineers appear to have accomplished with distinction. Thanks to excavation and clearance by modern-day archaeologists, the visitor to Megiddo can now descend a steep flight of approach steps and at their base walk through a remarkable tunnel. This was evidently hacked through solid rock from two opposite directions, and there are indications that the diggers met in the middle and needed only a 3-foot correction to straighten out their course. A similar tunnel system can also be seen at Hazor.

Clearly, Ahab had a shrewd eye for improving his country's military capabilities, and this is borne out by far more than the Bible, which merely accredits him with some successes against the Aramaeans and Ben-Hadad, king of Damascus. When Megiddo was excavated by American archaeologists between the two world wars, they labelled two large pillared complexes on the city's north-eastern and south-western sides King Solomon's Stables. They supposed that this was where Solomon kept his Biblically-attested large chariot force, as well as the horses to draw these.

Engineering of Ahab's time. The impressive tunnel dug deep beneath Megiddo enabled water to be drawn even during time of siege.

However, the most recent thinking, as advanced by Israeli archaeologists such as David Ussishkin, is that if these are indeed stables (and there is lively debate on this[10]), they are more likely to have been King Ahab's work. What is historically definite is that Ahab built up a very impressive chariot force, as evident from a limestone stele found at Kurkh on the Tigris. This records how the Assyrian King Shalmaneser III tried to extend his territories *c.*853 BC. He was checked, however, at Qarqar on the Orontes river by a coalition of twelve kings, headed by the earlier-mentioned Ben-Hadad of Damascus, with further military support from Aleppo, Hamath and Ammon and, most notably, '2000 chariots [and] 10,000 infantry of Ahab the Israelite'.[11]

The stele's reference to Ahab represents the earliest direct contemporary mention of any king of either Judah or Israel in any document outside the Bible. The stone has further value. Although Shalmaneser claimed to have been victorious, the Biblically-evident fact is that Ahab survived to fight another day. Also, the Assyrians' own tacit admission that they were deterred from campaigning for another three years suggests that

Ahab's chariots had proved genuinely formidable. The 2000 chariots accredited to him were not only a hundred more than Damascus's and Hamath's put together, but also eight hundred more than the Egyptians had been able to muster for Shoshenq's entire invasion of three generations earlier.

Furthermore, although the Biblical compiler/editor, for reasons best known to himself, ignored the battle of Qarqar and Ahab's part in it, he did record the manner of Ahab's death. The king died in a chariot, fighting the Aramaeans, and it seems to have been the death of a hero. Although he knew he had been mortally wounded, Ahab reportedly refused to leave the battlefield. Instead, in order to bolster his forces' morale, he had himself:

> . . . propped upright in his chariot facing Aram [i.e. the Aramaeans]; the blood from his wound ran down into the hollow of his chariot, and at dusk he died. (1 Kings 22:35)

Not least of the fascination here concerns the chariots. Up to and including David's time, the chariot did not even begin to feature as part of any Israelite battle line-up – according to the Bible, it was Solomon who built up a royal chariot force. By Ahab's time, however, it had clearly become the major fighting machine, just as it had long been under the former Canaanite regime. It had become an icon, rather like the motor-car today. Even according to the Bible, when the fiercely Yahwist Elijah came to depart from this world, it was in a 'fiery chariot' that he was described as being taken up to heaven.

If the Shalmaneser III stele is an important landmark in positively establishing King Ahab as a figure of history, another monument providing similar evidence from around the same time is the so-called Moabite stone, or Mesha stele. The discovery of this was particularly colourful. In 1886, at Dhiban (Biblical Dibon) in Moab on the eastern side of the Dead Sea, local Bedouin showed medical missionary F.A. Klein an interesting-looking black basalt tablet they had found. Klein was so intrigued by its ancient-looking inscription that he verbally agreed to buy it, even though it was too heavy for him to take away immediately.

Unfortunately, neither Klein nor any other European would see it again intact. For the elaborate collection arrangements so roused the Bedouins' suspicions that they demanded ten times the original price. Then, while the negotiations were still in progress, they attacked an Arab sent to make a paper 'squeeze' of the tablet's inscription. This individual only just managed to snatch the paper away before fleeing for his life. Hearing that local Turkish troops were about to be sent against them, the Bedouin angrily threw the tablet onto a fire and doused it with cold water, shattering it into numerous pieces which they divided among them. Ultimately, it took patient bargaining on the part of French scholar Charles Clermont-Ganneau and Britain's Captain Charles Warren (of Warren's Shaft), before fifty-seven fragments representing two-thirds of the original were eventually retrieved. Now safely in the Louvre, Paris, the portions that are

More than seven feet high, this stele of Shalmaneser III describes him fighting a coalition that included '2000 chariots and 10,000 infantry of Ahab the Israelite'. This is undoubtedly the Biblical Ahab.

still missing have fortunately been almost completely reconstructed thanks to the paper 'squeeze'.

The efforts of Clermont-Ganneau and Warren proved worthwhile. For even though the Moabite stone has now been available to scholars for more than a century, its thirty-four lines of 9th-century BC Canaanitic/old Hebrew script still represent one of the oldest, longest and most Biblically-meaningful inscriptions ever discovered anywhere in and around present-day Israel.

As the key portions of the text read:

> I am Mesha, son of Chemosh . . . , king of Moab, the Dibonite. My father reigned over Moab thirty years and I reigned after my father. And I made this high place for Chemosh in Qorchah . . . , for he saved me from all kings and caused me to triumph over my enemies. Omri, king of Israel had oppressed Moab for many days, for Chemosh was angry with his land [i.e. the people of Moab]. And his [i.e. Omri's] son succeeded him, and he also said: 'I will oppress Moab.' In my days he spoke [thus], but I have triumphed over him and his house, and Israel has perished forever. . . . And I built Baal-meon, and made a reservoir in it, and buil[t] Qiryathan [Kir-haraseth]. Now the men of Gad had dwelt in the land of Ataroth from of old, and the king of Israel had built Ataroth for them, but I fought against the city, took it, and smote all the people . . . And Chemosh said to me, 'Go, take Nebo from Israel,' and I went by night, and fought against it . . . , and took it and smote all of them, 7000 men, [boys], women, [girl]s and maidservants . . . And I took from there th[e ves]sels of Yahweh and dragged them before Chemosh.'[12]

The Moabite stone, or Mesha stele. Recording a victory of King Mesha of Moab over Israel, this both illuminates and corroborates events for which the Biblical text is otherwise our sole authority.

The inestimable importance of this inscription is that it illuminates and corroborates so much that we otherwise hear of only from the Biblical text. Self-evidently, its author was King Mesha of Moab, whose god, we are told, was Chemosh. It was for this very god, specifically described as 'the abomination of Moab', that King Solomon reportedly 'built a *bamah* on the hill near Jerusalem' (1 Kings 11:8). Likewise, Mesha's information that Chemosh 'was angry' and needed to be appeased reminds us of innumerable similar Biblical instances where such anger is attributed to the Israelite god Yahweh.

Also important is the stone's clear and unequivocal naming of King Ahab's father Omri as king of Israel. Together with Tel Dan's House of David inscription and the Shalmaneser III stele's reference to 'Ahab the Israelite', this represents one of the very earliest extra-Biblical namings of any king of either Israel or Judah. Indeed, the naming of Israel as a kingdom, previously so elusive, is prolific throughout this tablet's text. Also very precious is the tablet's reference to the Israelite tribe of Gad. This is the first-known mention of them outside the Bible. The stele places them 'from of old in the land of Ataroth', i.e. north of Moab's northern border, which conforms to the territory Biblically said to have been allotted to them: 'The Gadites rebuilt Dibon, Ataroth, Aroer . . . [etc] as

King Mesha's spectacularly lofty capital Kir-haraseth, subsequently the Crusader Krak des Chevaliers.

fortified towns or as enclosures for flocks' (Numbers 32:34). Furthermore, in the tablet's King Mesha we find an individual accorded a full chapter of Biblical text, who proves to have been firmly historical.

In 1 Kings 3, Mesha features as a sheep-breeder ruler who ill-advisedly rebelled against Israelite oppression. This happened during a rare period when unity was restored between Israel and Judah after Ahab and Jezebel's daughter Athaliah married King Jehosaphat of Judah's son Jehoram. Reportedly, the armies of the two kingdoms combined, with some equally rare help from the Edomites. They invaded Mesha's Moab from the south, crushed all resistance and turned up menacingly before the very walls of his capital Kir-haraseth (the Qiryathan of the Moabite stone). This is readily identifiable as modern-day Jordan's spectacularly-located Kerak, or Krak des Chevaliers, overlooking the Dead Sea from a height of 4000 feet. At this point, holed up with what remained of his army, and with supplies running low, Mesha in his desperation reportedly:

> . . . took his first-born son, who was to succeed him as king, and offered him up on the [city] wall as a burnt offering. (2 Kings 3:27)

We are reminded of the dark Canaanitic rite of child sacrifice glimpsed in the Arkhanes finds (see page 28), as well as the grim Egyptian depiction of children's bodies being dangled from the walls during Merneptah's siege of Ashkelon (see page 49). In the case of Mesha, the god to whom the child was being offered was Chemosh. Clearly, in desperate circumstances, the compulsion to child sacrifice, and in particular to sacrifice a first-born son, was deeply rooted in the psyche of many Canaanitic peoples. The intriguing element in this instance is the besieging armies' superstitious response. The 2 Kings text continues:

> A great wrath came upon Israel, so they withdrew . . . and went back to [their own] land.

As present-day Jewish scholars point out, 'great wrath' is probably a very inadequate conveying of the Israelites' reaction. The original Hebrew *ketsef*, or *qesef*, indicated the most profound shock, horror and indignation. And certainly, whatever their exact

emotions, to Mesha's would-be attackers there was something utterly spell-binding about this act. Despite having tramped arduously long distances to reach his high stronghold, they simply abandoned their hostilities and returned home, striking testimony to the extraordinary power that ritual magic still held for the 1st-millennium mind.

The Bible text appears, then, to record accurately something of the humiliations that Mesha's Moab underwent at the hands of the Israel kingdom's Omrid dynasty during and immediately following King Ahab's reign. For its part, the Moab stone records some of Mesha's ultimate acts of revenge for these humiliations. The two accounts are therefore complementary.

Particularly important for us, however, is the Mesha stone's reference to 'vessels of Yahweh', indicating that these belonged to an Israelite settlement at Mount Nebo (reputedly where Moses was buried), against which Mesha perpetrated one of his acts of revenge. For it is here, for the first time in any known extra-Biblical inscription or text, that we find the divine name YHWH, or 'Yahweh', spelt in Palaeo-Hebrew just as in the Hebrew Bible texts, and featuring very specifically as the divinity of a Yahwist/Israelite community some 20 miles north of the Moabite border. Biblically, this community seems to have been so minor that it rates never a mention in the text that has come down to us, and exactly where it lived has not been located. What is remarkable is that something of this kind has been recorded on the Moabite stone, dating as this does at least as early as c.840 BC. Although the old Canaanite Baal and Astarte cults undoubtedly continued in the Israel and Judahite kingdoms, this evidence shows us that the Biblical worship of Yahweh was also quite definitely there alongside them.

But what did the future hold for it? Such was the pro-Yahwist bias of the compilers of the Biblical books of Kings and Chronicles that they have almost certainly grossly understated the achievements of Israel and Judah monarchs such as Ahab who favoured the old Canaanitic religion. As indications of such unsung progress, just as Ahab had reinforced the fortresses of the north, so some counterpart in Judah stoutly rebuilt its southern defences, as at Arad. Here, the walls of this period average 12 feet thick, and feature a markedly steepened approach slope.[13] When the book of Kings records that a Judahite ship was wrecked at Ezion-Geber, it also mentions that Israel's king Ahaziah offered his Judahite counterpart the help of his sailors (1 Kings 22:48-9). This indicates not only that Israel was a seafaring nation – of which we might otherwise have been unaware, but for archaeological findings of Ahab's harbour-construction at Dor – but also that the Solomonic-type Red Sea trading expeditions were most likely beginning again. Supporting this, a contemporary seal found at the very inland Israel capital of Samaria, depicts a ship, owned apparently, from the seal's inscription, by 'Oniyahu' or 'ship of Yahweh'. From all these indications, we gather that for a brief period there may have been promise of a return to a new David-Solomon-type united kingdom under the Israelite king Jehoram and his Judahite counterpart Ahaziah.

A model of a cargo boat of the period, based on a tomb painting in Thebes.

However, Yahweh, as he was given voice by the *nabi* Elijah's successor Elisha, seems to have had other plans. Spurred on by a whisper from Elisha, another of the era's oft-mentioned chariots was waiting in the wings. And this was one which carried a rider who was about to shed well over seventy times more blood than just an Ahab's.

12

FATEFUL CHARIOT

THE ROLE OF A YAHWIST *nabi* was to act as a voice for his deity. But it is by no means clear how the Israelites and Judahites conceived of their Yahweh during the Kings period, particularly given that no original Biblical manuscript of any kind survives from this early time. Adding to this uncertainty, finds from the tiny Arab village of Khirbet el-Kom, 8 miles west of Judahite Hebron, suggest that the Yahweh of this period might even have had a female counterpart, just as the Canaanite El had his Astarte/Asherah. In a tomb excavated at this location there is an inscription accompanying an incised hand which seems to say:

> Blessed be Uryahu by Yahweh
> and by his Asherah, from his enemies he saved him,
> . . . and by his Asherah
> . . . and by his Asherah.

The Israeli archaeologist Ze'ev Meshel has discovered corroborating evidence that there was some such blessing, linking Yahweh with Asherah. Excavating at Kuntillet Ajrud, a one-time way-station for those travelling between the Red Sea and Kadesh-barnea, he found dozens of inscriptions datable to the late 9th or early 8th century BC. One of them clearly reads: 'I bless you by Yahweh of Teiman and by his Asherah.' Another, with some strange-looking figures, has the inscription: 'I bless you by Yahweh of Samaria and by his Asherah.' The specific mention of Samaria in the latter inscription shows that the formula was one used by people in the northern as well as the southern kingdom.

Despite the fact that the deity name Asherah occurs some forty times in the Hebrew Bible, even the most authoritative Biblical translations tend to fudge or gloss over its meaning, often translating it into something innocuous-sounding such as 'sacred pole'. Yet as we learned in our discussion of Canaanitic religion, it was indisputably either a physical totem of the Canaanite goddess Astarte in tree or pole form, or a nude figurine, or a breast-lifting bust of her atop a short column, of which thousands of Kings-period examples have been found throughout ancient Israel and Judah. Or it denoted the very goddess herself.

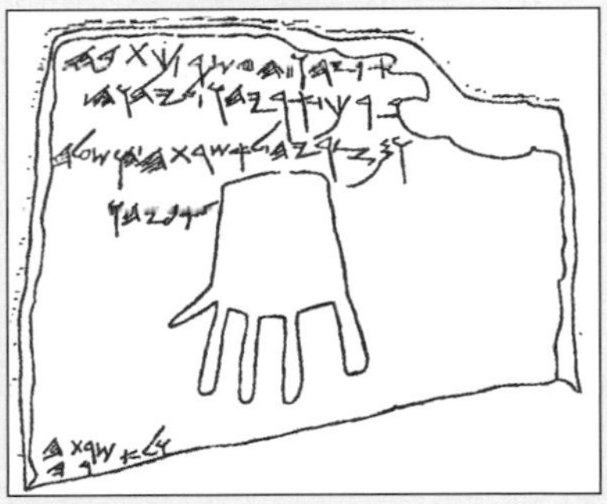

Seen at right, two inscriptions from the monarchy period that link Yahweh with the pagan goddess Asherah, or Astarte. Crude statuettes of the goddess (as above) were still widely popular.

All of which reminds us that, although archaeologically we can be certain that Yahweh was a deity who was already greatly revered at this period, no one should assume from this that for Israelites and Judahites he had yet become the exclusively monotheistic divinity of later Judaism. Still less can we be sure that he had acquired that deity's later, more benevolent attributes.

One thing we do have is a graphic example of just how *mal*evolent a 9th-century BC Yahweh could be, certainly as given voice by a *nabi* such as Elisha. We find this in what we learn Biblically of the extinguishing of the hitherto promising alliance between Ahab's son, King Jehoram of Israel, and his young brother-in-law, King Ahaziah of Judah.

As the Biblical books of Kings and Chronicles now relate quite monotonously of almost all the kings of Israel and Judah around this time, both Jehoram and

Ahaziah did things 'displeasing to Yahweh'. In their case, this seems to have been little worse than the fact that they tolerated the old Canaanite religion. Yet it was this which apparently sealed their fate. Around 841 BC, both monarchs were together fighting the still troublesome Aramaean King Hazael at Ramoth Gilead, the same town where Jehoram's father King Ahab had been killed in the same cause, when Jehoram became wounded and temporarily withdrew. He crossed the Jordan to Jezreel, a royal city where his mother Jezebel and other members of his family were staying, leaving his army still at Ramoth Gilead. Ahaziah seems to have been concerned for Jehoram and, presumably during some kind of lull in the fighting, went to Jezreel to visit him there.

This meant that both Jehoram and Ahaziah had journeyed some distance from the protection of their armies, and Elisha apparently seized upon it as a Yahweh-given opportunity to purge the country of the, to him, so-detestable regime. Reportedly, he summoned one of his acolytes and gave him a flask of what we have already learned was the special 'king-making' oil. He ordered the acolyte to take it to Jehoram's fiercely Yahwist chariot commander, Jehu, then still on the front-line at Ramoth Gilead. There the acolyte took Jehu to one side and, pouring the oil over his head, pronounced:

> Yahweh, the God of Israel, says this: 'I have anointed you king of Yahweh's people, of Israel. You will strike down the family of Ahab your master; and I shall avenge the blood of my servants the *nabiim* and all Yahweh's servants, on Jezebel and on the whole family of Ahab. I shall destroy every manjack of Ahab's family . . .'[1] (2 Kings 9:6-8)

Jehu, hardened soldier as he was, was evidently not the kind to ignore such instructions, emanating as they did from a revered *nabi* whom he and others believed to voice their god's direct orders. After imparting the news to his chariot troop and duly having himself acclaimed by them, he got back into his chariot and with the troop behind him headed full-tilt for Jezreel. There he met Jehoram and Ahaziah, each of them riding in a chariot, and almost the moment he was within speaking distance he drew his bow. As Jehoram, perceiving the danger, turned to flee, Jehu unhesitatingly shot him through the heart. Then, as the astonished Ahaziah of Judah in his turn wheeled to get away, Jehu's men seriously wounded him. Although he managed to escape to Megiddo, he too died soon after.

Even the assassination of not one but two kings failed to appease the blood-lust now roused in Jehu. As earlier mentioned, Ahab's widow, the Yahwistically-reviled Queen Mother Jezebel, was in Jezreel. The moment she showed herself, in classic Canaanitic style, at a high window, regally attired, and with her eyes made up with mascara, Jehu ordered her to be seized and thrown down into the street below. He then drove his chariot over her blood-spattered corpse (2 Kings 9:30-37). Next it was the turn of Ahab's seventy sons, brothers to Jehoram, who at that time were being educated at the royal capital Samaria. Jehu gave orders that each and every one of them should be killed, and for their decapitated heads to be brought to him at Jezreel (2 Kings 10:1-5). Next, he had the forty-two brothers of King Ahaziah of Judah slaughtered (2 Kings 10:12-14). Lured into his clutches by a trick, all the priests of Baal/El from throughout Israel were murdered, then all that were left of the House of Ahab, together with other notables and priests (2 Kings 10:11). Meanwhile, in Judah, the Israel-born Queen Athaliah, for reasons best known to herself, went on a killing spree of her own to further eliminate Judah's dynasty, missing just one infant prince who became King Jehoash. Jehu's coup was thereby effective fully only in Israel.

Whatever we may make of this extraordinary bloodbath, for the details of which we are totally reliant on the Biblical record, there is one definite fact about Jehu: he became

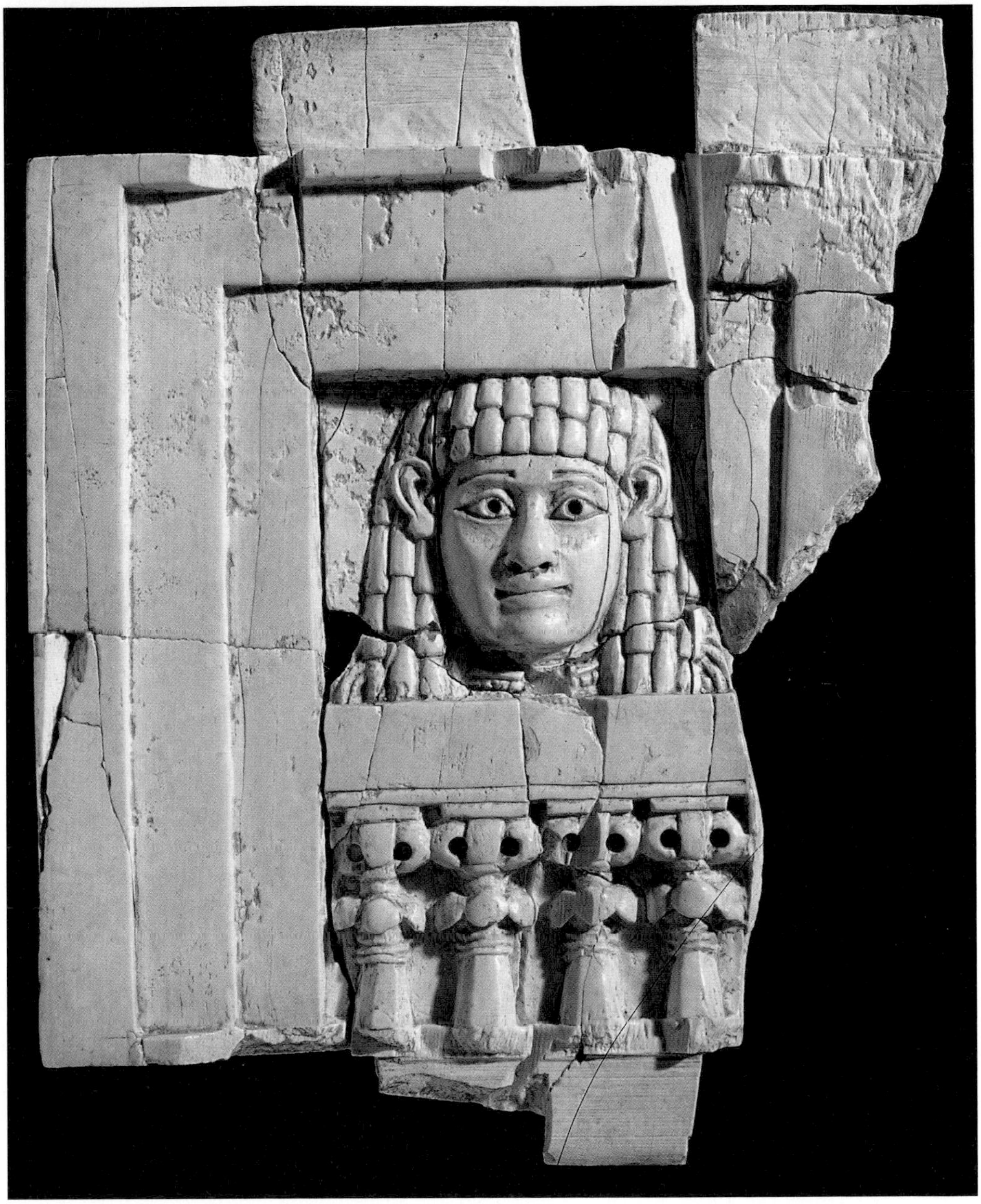

'Jezebel ... made up her eyes with mascara, adorned her head, and appeared at the window' (2 Kings 9:30). The 'woman at the window' is the commonest motif among Canaanitic ivories, and appears to have been charged with sexual-religious overtones. This example is from Samaria where Ahab and Jezebel had their ivory palace.

king of Israel in its aftermath. He is also the first and indeed only king of either Israel or Judah throughout the monarchy period, whose artistic likeness may have come down to us from a contemporary source.

When, in the mid-1840s, the great founding father of Assyriology, Austen Henry Layard, was excavating at Nimrud he came across a magnificent obelisk in limestone. It had scenes of tribute being brought to the Assyrian king Shalmaneser III, the same monarch whom Israel's King Ahab had fought so valiantly at the Battle of Qarqar. Thanks to Britain's good relations with the Turkish Sultan of the time, this obelisk was shipped to the British Museum. In the second row of its scenes, the typically amply-bearded Shalmaneser is shown standing majestically before a man sporting a much lesser beard and wearing a turban-like cap on his head. He kneels at Shalmaneser's feet, abjectly kissing the ground. As generally agreed by modern-day experts, the cuneiform inscription accompanying this scene reads:

Tribute of Ia-ú-a [Jehu], son of Omri. Silver, gold, a golden bowl, a golden beaker, golden goblets, pitchers of gold, tin, staves for the hand of the king, [and] javelins, I [Shalmaneser] received from him.[2]

Modern scholars are essentially agreed that the abjectly-kneeling figure must be either the mass-murdering King Jehu himself, firmly identified as Israel's king by the 'son of Omri' description (despite no hard evidence that Jehu was actually of that line of descent[3]), or an emissary visiting Shalmaneser's court on his behalf. An interesting incidental feature is that this scene seems also to provide a reliable guide to the Israelite costume at this time, showing a long robe for both Jehu and his male retinue. In the case of both Elijah[4] and Elisha[5], we are told Biblically that on occasion these men needed to 'hitch up their clothes' in order to run. So we may infer that male attire had in general lengthened from the old pre-monarchy days. This was, no doubt, yet another consequence of the effective 'merger' from King David's time with the theoretically displaced Canaanites/Phoenicians and their fashions and trappings.

The obelisk, which can be ascribed with some confidence to 841 BC, tells us more. For all his Rambo-like seizure of power, King Jehu at that date was actually a quite abject vassal of Shalmaneser's. For some 50 per cent of the Lower Galilee archaeological sites of this period show an otherwise unaccounted-for layer of destruction. This suggests either that Shalmaneser directly invaded Israelite territory in a move that has gone unmentioned in the Biblical record, or that the destruction was Aramaean and that Jehu allied with Shalmaneser to overcome this menace.

Either way, Jehu became an Assyrian puppet, whiling out a largely-undistinguished reign of some thirty years, during which he at least outlived Shalmaneser. The latter's successors then became too preoccupied with problems closer to home to have much interest in him. As further evidence of both the Israel and Judahite kingdoms' weakness during his time, the Bible and archaeological findings alike show that peoples neighbouring the old Davidic/Solomonic empire took their opportunity to break free and wreak whatever vengeance they could on their former oppressors.

Thus, the previously cooped-up Philistines and Arabs invaded and plundered Judah[6], which may well account for yet another destruction of the Arad fortress at around this time[7], while the Edomites, whom King David's general Joab had so ruthlessly suppressed, likewise broke away. There is also evidence that many of those time-honoured allies – the Canaanite/Phoenician inhabitants of Tyre – were forced around this time to quit their city. They moved all the way across the Mediterranean to found Carthage in what is now Tunisia, as well as to Tharros in Sardinia. And despite having very good reason to remain at peace with each other for mutual support, Israel and Judah failed even in this. In 796 BC, Jehu's descendant Jehoash reportedly took an army southwards to fight his counterpart King Amaziah of Judah and defeated him at Beth Shemesh. He then broke into Jerusalem and raided the gold and silver in the Temple's treasury.

Yet, as so often happens in history, resurgence followed set-back. Not long after, during the reigns of Judah's reputedly leprous King Uzziah (783-742 BC) and Israel's Jeroboam II (786-746 BC), harmony was restored between the two kingdoms, bringing in some overdue fresh prosperity. As the Israeli archaeologist, the late Yigal Shiloh, found during eight seasons of excavating the City of David sector of ancient Jerusalem, 8th-century BC Jerusalem quadrupled its size, to 150 acres, compared to its 37 acres of just two centuries earlier. This made it six times larger than any other city in either Israel or Judah.

Furthermore, Shiloh took a rare and seemingly insignificant-looking piece of Jerusalem stonework from this period, and managed to reconstruct it as having once

The earliest known depiction of a Biblical king? The usurper Jehu, or one of his emissaries, prostrates himself before the Assyrian king Shalmaneser III, as depicted on the 'Black Obelisk' found at Nimrud. The depiction, together with that of Jehu's tribute-bearers (below), provides information on Israelite formal costume of the period.

formed part of a window balustrade decorated with most elegant columns. This offers only the merest glimmering, but it does convey at least something of what an architecturally splendid city Jerusalem would have been during Uzziah and Jeroboam II's time. It also makes us aware of the extent to which later destructions have prevented us from properly appreciating this.

This time of peace and prosperity seems also to have had accompanying benefits for general education, as is evident from one discovery of recent decades that has never been given the attention it deserves, largely because it was made in what is now Jordan, not Israel. In March 1967, a Dutch expedition led by Professor Henk J. Franken was excavating at Deir Alla, a hillock north of the Jabbok river which was a significant 10-acre Israelite city in the 8th century BC. As they were working, an Arab foreman happened to notice traces of ancient lettering written in ink on some tiny fragments of plaster his workers were just about to throw away. The lettering was only visible because the fragments were wet from some recent rain. Duly alerted, and conscious that a further heavy rain-shower might destroy other pieces not yet spotted, Franken and his team immediately covered everything in the vicinity. Then they began painstakingly sifting every inch of the location, successfully retrieving a considerable quantity of other lettered fragments. These were apparently from a long inscription. It was written in black ink, set within columns and framed in red. It had once decorated the plastered wall of the building they had been excavating. From the accompanying pottery, also from carbon-dating, Franken and his team dated the building to the same 'prosperous' 8th-century BC period of Kings Uzziah and Jeroboam II, interpreting it as most probably a teaching centre.

A fragment of window balustrade (top) from 8th-century Jerusalem. Israeli archaeologist Yigal Shiloh based his reconstruction (above) on a detail from the 'woman in the window' ivory (see page 149).

The Palaeo-Hebrew writing was by far the finest example of Biblical script surviving from this early period, effectively an 8th-century BC Dead Sea Scroll. But even more fascinating than that was its content. After piecing this together, jigsaw-style, from all the broken fragments, the translators read:

> Inscription of [Ba]laam [son of Beo]r, the man who was a seer of the gods. Lo, the gods came to him at night and [spoke to] him
>
> According to these wor[ds], and they said to [Balaa]m, son of Beor, thus: 'There has appeared the last flame, a fire of chastisement has appeared!'[8]

From this and similar surviving passages, all evidently from an early religious text otherwise lost to us, there can be no doubt that 'Balaam, son of Beor' is the same *nabi* of this name who features in the Biblical book of Numbers. As the Biblical version runs, Balaam was hired by the Moabites to curse Israel while they were still en route from Egypt to the promised land, but instead of complying, he pronounced a blessing upon Israel:

> Word of Balaam, son of Beor
> Word of the man whose eye is true

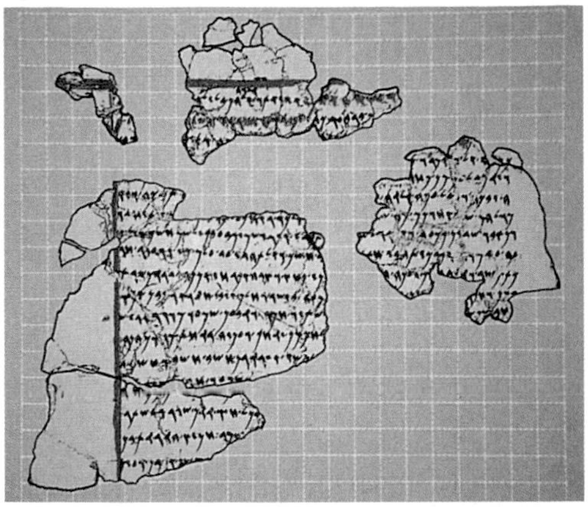

Part of the Balaam text from an earthquake-shattered plaster wall at Deir Alla, pieced together to convey its original appearance.

Word of him who hears God's speech
Who beholds visions from the Almighty . . .
(Numbers 24:3-4)

The Deir Alla text does not reproduce what the Bible says about Balaam, nor does the Bible feature Balaam in the way that he appears in the Deir Alla text. Even so, scholars are generally agreed that whoever was responsible for the building bearing the inscription must have shared with the Bible's originators some common traditions about Balaam that were already old even in the 8th century BC.

This is not all. The Biblical book of Amos has come down to us from this same 8th-century BC Uzziah/Jeroboam II period. It was written by a traditional Yahwist *nabi*, self-described as 'one of the shepherds of Tekoa', locatable in Judaean wilderness country near Bethlehem. Of course, Amos's original manuscript has not survived. It is nonetheless the first and oldest book in our Bible to derive from a clearly-identifiable, indisputably-historical author. One great value of the Deir Alla Balaam inscription is that it gives us a glimpse of how Amos's original text might have looked.

Even this is far from all. For as Franken and his fellow archaeologists came to realise, the Deir Alla centre with the Balaam text on its walls came to a very abrupt and dramatic end about the middle of the 8th century, seemingly as a result of an earthquake. The plaster fragments owed their preservation to the collapse of the wall on which they had been written, the severity of this causing some pieces to be scattered up to 20 feet away. Archaeologists have found similar damage to buildings from around the mid-8th century BC as far afield as Gezer, Hazor and Samaria. The shock must therefore have extended over hundreds of square miles. In which regard, what do we read in the very opening lines of the Biblical book of Amos?

Words of Amos . . . The visions he had about Israel, in the time of Uzziah king of Judah and Jeroboam [II] king of Israel, *two years before the earthquake*. (Amos 1:1)

Clearly, then, a major earthquake *did* happen in the reigns of Uzziah and Jeroboam, Amos's royal contemporaries. Equally clearly, the book of Amos, even in the several-generations-removed manuscripts by which it came down to us, must embody some eyewitness reporting from its time. In this respect, it may be more valuable than the more directly 'history' books of Kings and Chronicles, because of their later compilers' heavy editing of early sources that have long been lost to us.

In the same light, particularly bearing in mind the glimpse of 8th-century Jerusalem's architectural sophistication gained from archaeologist Yigal Shiloh, we may regard as accurate reporting Amos's vivid and highly critical description of the Canaanitic-type luxury life enjoyed during Uzziah and Jeroboam II's reign by those he calls the 'Israelites . . . who dwell in Samaria' (Amos 3:12). In his words:

They lie on ivory beds,
lolling on their couches
feasting on lambs from the flock
and on calves from the stalls . . .
They drink [straight] from the wine bowls,
and anoint themselves with the choicest oils . . . (Amos 6:4-6)

In characteristic *nabi* fashion, as if Yahweh were speaking through him, Amos painted a similarly vivid picture of the Canaanitic-style religious ceremonial he saw practised around him. He clearly found this just as abhorrent:

> . . . I spurn your festivals
> I am not appeased by your solemn assemblies
> If you offer me burnt offerings . . .
> I will not accept them
> I will pay not heed
> To your gifts of fatlings
> Spare me the sound of your hymns
> And let me not hear the music of your lutes. (Amos 5:21-23)

Amos's fellow *nabi* Hosea, who lived only a little after his time, struck a similar theme in the Biblical book that bears his name, accusing the Israelites of deserting their Yahweh by offering 'sacrifice on the mountaintops' and burning incense 'on the hills, under oaks, poplars and terebinths' (Hosea 4:12-13). In a clear reference to the known Canaanitic practice of sacred prostitution, closely related to the Astarte cult and archaeologically attested by sexually explicit cultic figurines found at Dor and elsewhere[9], Hosea railed against the Israelites' daughters for 'playing the whore' and their men likewise for 'offering sacrifice with sacred prostitutes'. With regard to the Ephraimites, the tribe that occupied the territory including the sacred heartlands of Shiloh and Bethel, Hosea accused them of both Baal worship and idolatrously making 'molten images, idols, by their skill, from their silver' (Hosea 13:1-2).

A clear and unequivocal picture emerges from all this. Despite King Jehu of the bloody chariot's apparently fervent Yahwism, the Israel and Judahite kingdoms were still very strongly Canaanitic in both their general culture and their religious ritual. This trend continued into the reigns of Uzziah's Judahite successors Jotham (750-731 BC) and Ahaz (731-716?).

In his private 'museum', the London antiquities collector Shlomo Moussaieff has, as well as his 'Solomon' seal, a clay seal impression. It is less than half an inch wide, with an inscription set on three lines reading: *'l'hz.y/hwtm.mlk./yhdh'*, which translates as 'Belonging to Ahaz (son of) Yehotam [i.e. Jotham] King of Judah'.[10] From scientific analysis there is general agreement that it is genuinely derived from the Biblical King Ahaz's time, and is thereby the first positively-known seal impression for a Biblical monarch. It even bears on its left edge a fingerprint that may be Ahaz's own, together with impressions of the texture of the papyrus document it sealed and the string with which this was tied.

Seal impression inscribed 'belonging to Ahaz [son of] Yehotham King of Israel'. Generally recognised as genuine, this is thereby the oldest uncontested seal of a Biblical monarch.

For the editor-chroniclers of the Biblical books of Kings, Ahaz was little better than his predecessors. Reputedly, he still 'sacrificed and made offerings at the *bamah*, on the hills and under every leafy tree' (2 Kings 16:4). Canaanite-style, he

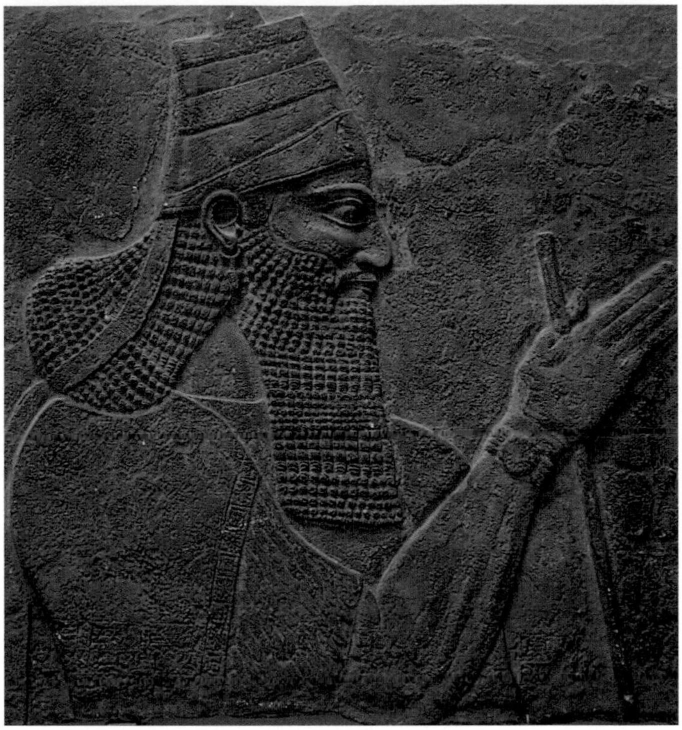

The Assyrian Tiglath-pileser, to whom the Judahite king Ahaz paid tribute, from Tiglath-pileser's palace at Nimrud.

also 'consigned his son to the fire, in the abhorrent fashion of the nations which Yahweh dispossessed before the Israelites'.

To the further fury of the Biblical compilers, Ahaz apparently had a new altar built for the Temple of Jerusalem, based on one he had seen in Damascus while visiting Assyria's Tiglath Pileser III. This monarch is well-known archaeologically from reliefs of his military campaigns against the Aramaeans and others, excavated at Nimrud. In his surviving annals, Tiglath-pileser specifically boasted of having received tribute from Ahaz, whose name his scribe rendered as Ia-u-ha-zi, or Yeho-ahaz, showing that its full form, not given in the Bible, included the divine name Yahweh, even though he followed the Biblically-disapproved deviant Canaanitic practices.

Politically, from the viewpoint of the citizens of Jerusalem's immediate well-being, Ahaz's lip-service to the Assyrians, as well as his adroit 'gift' to Tiglath-pileser of an impressive amount of silver and gold from the Temple treasury, may have bought some valuable breathing space. For, although the obvious Judahite weakness encouraged the Edomites to retake Elath (2 Kings 16:6), and in alliance with the coastal Philistines to overrun the Shephelah and the Negev (2 Chronicles 28:17-18), destroying the Arad fortress yet again, the Assyrians were successfully persuaded to hold off a direct attack on Jerusalem for at least a few decades more.

For those living in Israel, in the north, however, there was no such postponement. Boasting in one of his annals that 'I overwhelmed him . . . and he . . . fled like a bird alone', Assyria's Tiglath-pileser as early as 738 BC forced Israel's King Menahem to pay tribute to him (2 Kings 15:19-20). This led in 733 BC to a revolt by Menahem's successor Pekah. That revolt Ahaz of Judah adroitly declined to join, causing Pekah and the king of Damascus to join forces against him. When Ahaz duly appealed to Tiglath-pileser for aid, the Assyrian monarch had the excuse he needed to invade Israel, swiftly capturing Hazor and Galilee and much else. With classic Assyrian ruthlessness he deported large numbers of Israelites to Assyria as slaves (2 Kings 15:29). This was dramatically confirmed by excavations in Lower Galilee, which reveal a large gap in occupation in the late 8th-century BC period.[11]

But in a manner all too typical of Israel's dynastic foibles, one Hosea, not to be confused with the *nabi* of that name, reportedly seized this moment of national weakness to assassinate Pekah and instate himself as king. He apparently had some encouragement from Tiglath-pileser, whose annals record:

> They [i.e. the Israelites] overthrew their king Pekah and I placed Hosea as king over them.[12]

As an interesting 'souvenir' of Hosea's reign (732-722 BC), a 1-inch-long, oval-shaped seal recently turned up at auction at Sotheby's, New York and was acquired for London collector Shlomo Moussaieff. It was inscribed in Old Hebrew, 'Belonging to Abdi, servant of Hosea'. Unlike the earlier-mentioned Ahaz seal, it includes (in breach of Moses' second

commandment), a depiction of its owner Abdi (a name identical with the 'Obadiah' of King James and other Christian Bibles), whom we may guess to have been one of the chief ministers of the Israel king Hosea.

Abdi is represented bare-chested in the Egyptian style, wearing a long kilt, also in the Egyptian style, and holding a papyrus sceptre, with a winged disc at his feet. These are further indications of strong Egyptian influence, all of which correspond rather neatly with what the Bible tells us about King Hosea's Israel and the way it came to be swallowed up by Assyria.

For according to 2 Kings 17:4, when Tiglath-pileser died in 727 BC, Hosea first began paying tribute to his successor Shalmaneser V. But he then rather rashly decided to test the latter's grip by withholding further payment and sending envoys instead to ancient Egypt's 14th Dynasty rulers at their then-capital Sais (2 Kings 17:4). Was the Egyptian-inspired Abdi of the Moussaieff seal perhaps one of those envoys?

Whatever the answer, no one, least of all Israel's Hosea, could afford to treat the Assyrian menace so lightly. Forebears of Iraq's Saddam Hussein and his generals, the Assyrians were one of the most warlike and callously punitive peoples the world has ever seen, whose monarchs graphically displayed on their palace walls scenes of their cruelty towards those they vanquished, flaying their defeated enemies alive, impaling them on stakes and cutting out their tongues.

Egyptian fashion at the Israel kingdom's court. Inscribed 'Belonging to Abdi [or Obadiah] servant of Hosea', this seal appears to have belonged to an official of king Hosea of Israel. It shows strong Egyptian influence – symptom of a time when, according to the Biblical record, the court of Israel was seeking alliance with Egypt for support against the threat of Assyria.

One who certainly saw it all coming was the *nabi* Micah, author of at least part of the Biblical book that bears his name. His historicity is evident from the similarly historical Jeremiah, a century later, who referred back to Micah's prophecies (Jeremiah 26:17-19). He is self-described as given to wandering 'stripped and naked' (Micah 1:8), like his contemporary Isaiah. Speaking for Yahweh, Micah declaimed:

> I will turn Samaria into a ruin . . .
> I will tumble her stones rolling into the valley . . .
> All her sculptured images shall be smashed . . .
> I will make a waste heap of all her idols
> For they were amassed from prostitutes' earnings
> And to prostitutes' earnings they shall return. (Micah 1:6-7)[13]

And so it came to pass. Testifying to King Omri's shrewd recognition of the Samaria site's strategic strengths two centuries before, it took the Assyrians three years of determined siege before the Israel capital fell to them. But when they succeeded, they duly led off its inhabitants for enforced resettlement 'in Halah on the Habor, a river of Gozan, and in the cities of the Medes' (2 Kings 17:6). The Assyrian side of the story is told in the records of the reign of Shalmaneser's successor Sargon II:

> I besieged and conquered Samaria, led away as booty 27,000 inhabitants, forming from among them a regiment of fifty chariots . . . I crushed the tribes of the . . . Arabs who live far away in the desert and who knew neither overseers nor officials and who had not brought tribute before to any king, and I deported their survivors and settled them in Samaria.[14]

Sargon's policy was to switch conquered peoples forcibly from one territory to another, so that their internal squabbling strengthened his own rule. Could he have realised, one wonders, how much this would continue to cause trouble more than two and a half thousand years later?

Whatever the answer, the northern kingdom that had been called Israel abruptly ended with the usurper Hosea, and from his time on the ten Israelite tribes theoretically comprising this kingdom became 'lost' forever. At that same moment, there ended the world that produced what Biblical scholars now know as the 'E' strand in, or the Israel kingdom's contribution to, the texts of our present-day Bibles.

Whatever the future held for the people of the Bible's tenure over their promised land, that future now lay almost exclusively with the southerners of Judah.

Typical Assyrian cruelty: impaling their captives on stakes, a precursor of crucifixion.

13

When the Assyrian Came Down

SO VIGOROUSLY DID the Assyrians renew their empire-building activities towards the end of the 8th century BC that even in Judah the danger did not take long to resurface. In 716 BC the Judahite throne passed to a promising 25-year-old called Hezekiah. Throughout his early years the Assyrian menace loomed constantly larger, with the famous Isaiah, the consultant *nabi* to Hezekiah's court, ever on the side of caution.

However, in the case of Hezekiah, there was an important difference between him and virtually all his royal predecessors: the Biblical compilers did not castigate him for doing things 'displeasing to Yahweh'. Instead, as the Kings compiler approvingly remarks: 'He did what was pleasing to Yahweh, just as his ancestor David had done' (2 Kings 18:3).

So what was it that King Hezekiah did right? Enthusiastically, the Kings compiler tells us that he:

> . . . abolished the *bamot* (i.e. the high places), smashed the pillars and cut down the Asherah. (2 Kings 18:4)

In other words, he banned the traditional Canaanite-type of religious worship. Immediately after, we are also told that he:

> . . . broke into pieces the bronze serpent that Moses had made, for until that time the Israelites had been offering sacrifices to it; it was called Nehushtan. (2 Kings 18:4)

From our perspective, we might suppose that the destruction of any relic associated with the *nabi* Moses would have been regarded with horror by a true Yahwist. But the editor/compiler of 2 Kings seems to have been of a faction with no such qualms. Likewise meeting with his clear approval was Hezekiah's order to Yahwist Judah and Jerusalem: 'You must worship before one altar and on that alone offer incense.' This could only have meant a major upheaval for the whole Yahwist religious world. The sacrificial altars that had existed at centres outside Jerusalem, such as the one we noted at the Arad fortress, were to be

Menace at its height: Assyrians attack Lachish, from a relief in Sennacherib's palace at Nineveh.

banned in favour of Jerusalem's Temple, which would now have total exclusivity.

This was no idle decree, and even archaeology can show us that it was positively implemented, as at the Arad fortress. Here, the excavators at the level[1] they dated to the 8th century BC revealed that the temple's whole courtyard was suddenly covered over with a fill 3 feet thick, thereby burying its altar and making this redundant, though the temple's usage as such otherwise continued. Likewise at Tell es-Seba, the site some identify as King David's Ziklag, Israeli archaeologist Yohanan Aharoni found some well-dressed stones embedded in a late 8th-century BC rampart, which when reassembled formed a 5-foot-high horned altar, which someone had carefully dismantled and buried in the rampart, in Aharoni's view again as a result of Hezekiah's reforms.[2]

Hezekiah seems very forthrightly to have outlawed the old Canaanite religious practices, to have profaned at least one historic souvenir of Moses, and to have centralised Yahwist worship so aggressively that Jerusalem's Temple and its priesthood could now control the whole show. The evident approval of the books of Kings' compilers most likely indicates their own close ties to those behind the reforms.

Evidently, then, Hezekiah was no shrinking violet when it came to acting decisively. At a time when he needed all the unity and loyalty he could get, he risked alienating a sizeable proportion of his own people, and he would take an even greater risk in defying the Assyrians. Yet, as we are about to see, he survived all these hazards remarkably well.

The first wave of Assyrian assault, directed by Sargon II, came in 712 BC, four years after Hezekiah's accession to the Judahite throne. Fortunately, this was foreseen, and the coastal Philistines, Moabites and Edomites all sensibly combined with Hezekiah, despite their traditional enmities, to put up a strong, though by no means fully effective, resistance.

The first thirty-nine chapters of the Biblical book Isaiah are thought to have been genuinely by Hezekiah's contemporary the *nabi* Isaiah. And just as the *nabi* Amos's Biblical book proved helpful to us about the history of a generation earlier, so these chapters of Isaiah help us with the history of this period. Thus, thanks to Isaiah's chapter 20, we learn that this first attack, concentrated on the Philistines, was led by an Assyrian commander called 'the Tartan'. Although long perplexing to Bible translators, this term features as '*turtanu*' in 9th- to 7th-century BC cuneiform texts and refers to one of the Assyrians' highest military ranks.[3] In the same sentence, Isaiah also tells us that the Assyrians 'attacked and took' Philistine Ashdod. This event is again independently corroborated in the Assyrian annals, which enable us to date it to 712/711 BC. Further illuminating the Biblical information is a relief on the walls of Sargon's palace at Khorsabad depicting Ashdod's sister city, Philistine Ekron, while it was being besieged this same year.

A clay prism recording the annals of Sennacherib.

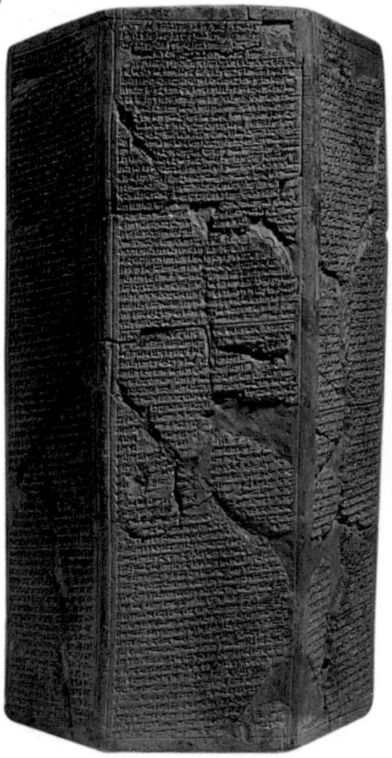

The real test of Hezekiah's mettle came, however, with a renewed attack by Sargon's son and successor Sennacherib in the year 701 BC. Of the preliminaries to this, as recorded on the Assyrian side, our chief source of information is a six-sided clay prism found at Nineveh in 1830 by British army colonel R. Taylor, and now in the British Museum.

From this and related sources, we learn that Sennacherib's ire was first roused when he received word that the Phoenicians of Tyre and Sidon, the Philistines of Ashkelon and Ekron, together with Hezekiah of Judah, were combining against him in collusion with ancient Egypt's up-and-coming Nubian King Shabaka. Sennacherib's response was first to defeat Tyre and Sidon's King Lule, obliging him to flee to Cyprus. Then one wing of his army moved southwards into Trans-Jordan to collect tribute from the chiefs of Ammon, Moab and Edom, while another did the same in the Philistine territories, during which Ashkelon's King Sidka was defeated and taken off to captivity. King Shabaka of Egypt did his best to co-operate by sending a troop northwards to help the allies, but the moment these learned that two victorious Assyrian armies were converging on them they withdrew southwards again. All of which meant that Hezekiah and his Judahites were suddenly left to face the might of Assyria alone.

Of this confrontation the 2 Kings compiler's version is a masterpiece of compression:

> In the fourteenth year of King Hezekiah, King Sennacherib of Assyria marched against all the fortified towns of Judah and seized them. (2 Kings 18:13)

A horned altar from Tell es-Seba which, when found, had been carefully dismantled. According to its excavator, Yohanan Aharoni, this was done in response to King Hezekiah's religious reforms in the late 8th century BC centralising all sacrifice at Jerusalem.

Although the British Museum prism's Assyrian version, written as if spoken by Sennacherib, provides rather fuller information, even it is brief and almost laconically matter-of-fact:

> I [Sennacherib] besieged and captured forty-six of his [Hezekiah's] strong walled cities, and the small cities of their environs which were without number, by the spanning of a ramp, the approach of siege engines, the battling of infantry, breaches, breaks and storm ladders. Two hundred thousand, one hundred and fifty persons, small and great, male and female horses, asses, mules, camels, oxen and sheep and goats without number I brought out from them and I counted as spoil.

In the event, it is archaeology that provides a fuller but no less devastating picture. Thus, at that so-front-line Arad fortress in the Negev, whose temple Hezekiah had only recently deprived of its altar, the excavators found evidence of yet another massive destruction. They unhesitatingly ascribe it either to Sennacherib or to one of his allies. It is a similar story at Beth-Shemesh, which Hezekiah appears to have specially provisioned with rations supplied in *'l'melech'*, or 'belonging to the king', jars found among its ruins. The archaeological findings are again of massive destruction by Sennacherib. Likewise at Timnah, where the excavators found an unburied human skeleton lying amidst the broken fragments of another thirty *l'melech* jars.

In fact, throughout Judah the only city, apart from the capital, that seems to have put up significant resistance was Lachish, which had earlier been massively re-fortified as a last pre-Jerusalem line of defence. Although the Biblical chronicler does not even mention its defenders' efforts, certainly Sennacherib accorded them star-rating in the

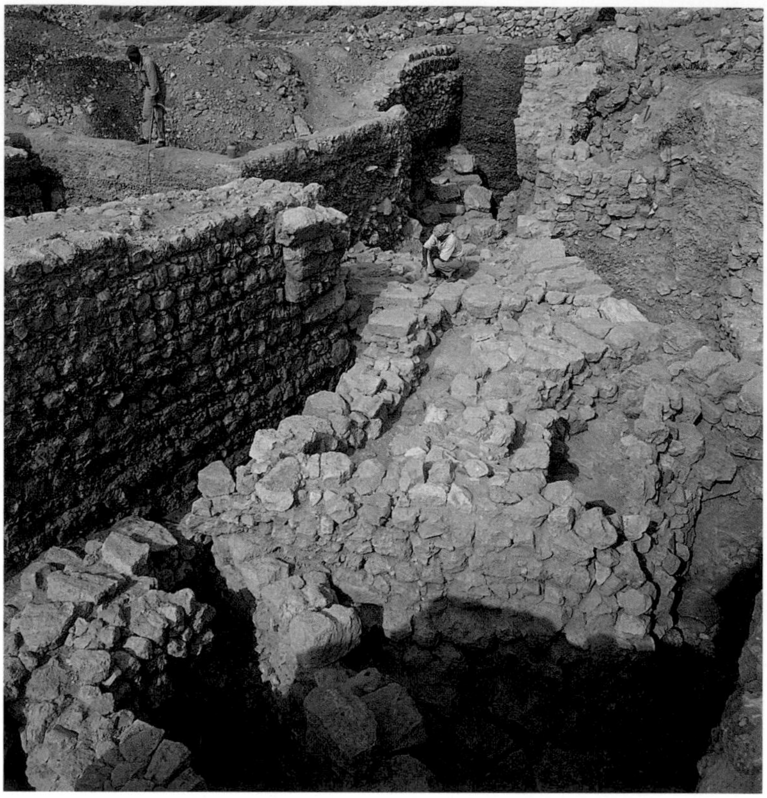

reliefs with which he decorated his palace at Nineveh. He had himself depicted surveying the scene from a hill, as his army remorselessly deployed their formidable repertoire of ramps, battering rams and heavily armoured foot-soldiers amidst a hail of arrows and firebrands coming from the beleaguered city. In the face of such a determined onslaught, even Lachish could only hold out for so long. As the same reliefs graphically record, those of its citizens who did not die during the fighting found themselves led off helplessly to slavery.

Following this, all that now separated Sennacherib from the complete subjugation of the former Israel and Judah was Hezekiah's Jerusalem. Living within Jerusalem's walls at this time was a population archaeologists estimate at some 25,000 people.[4] Here, all the evidence suggests that Hezekiah had prepared for this circumstance exceptionally well.

Hezekiah 'pulled down houses to strengthen the wall [of Jerusalem]' (Isaiah 22:10). Excavations in Jerusalem by Israeli archaeologist Nahman Avigad revealed this massive wall of the time of Hezekiah.

Specifically with regard to Jerusalem's walls, the compiler of the Biblical book of Chronicles recorded that Hezekiah:

> . . . acting with determination . . . repaired all the damaged parts . . . , built towers on it, [and] constructed a second wall on the outer side . . . (2 Chronicles 32:5)

Supplementing this information, the *nabi* Isaiah tells us that Hezekiah had necessarily 'pulled houses down to strengthen the wall' (Isaiah 22:10). Confirming this, Israeli archaeologist Nahman Avigad, in the course of his excavations of the old Jewish Quarter, uncovered a massive 130-foot stretch of city wall, partly built directly onto bedrock, and partly on top of houses only recently constructed. The dating of the pottery in these houses provided clear evidence that the huge wall was part of this same Hezekiah-directed fortification effort.[5]

With sieges in mind, Jerusalem's citizens' internal access route to the city's external Gihon spring had already been long-established. Hezekiah seems to have carefully thought out how he might take things a step further, and positively prevent the Assyrians, or any future besieging armies, from gaining access to this water supply. According to 2 Chronicles, he:

> . . . consulted his officers and warriors about sealing off the waters of the springs outside the city, and they supported him. So a large number of people were called out to block all the springs and cut off the watercourse flowing externally. 'Why' they said 'should the kings of Assyria find plenty of water when they arrive?'[6] (2 Chronicles 32:3-4)

The Biblical compilers are frustratingly vague about how Hezekiah might have carried this out. For the 2 Kings editor/compiler, it was sufficient to tell us that the details were recorded in the now long-lost 'Annals of the Kings of Judah'.[7] His 2 Chronicles counterpart offers little more, merely remarking that Hezekiah 'stopped the upper outlet of the Gihon and directed this straight down to the west side of the City of David' (2 Chronicles 32:30). Thankfully, fresh light has been shed, due to a chance discovery made more than a hundred years ago, but only properly understood more recently.

In 1880, when Jerusalem was under Turkish rule, some boys cooling off in what is now the rather unsavoury Siloam Pool swam deep into its water-filled feeder tunnel, to discover on its walls an interesting-looking old inscription. Although they crudely hacked this off for sale as an antiquity, it survives in Istanbul's Archaeological Museum. It represents the most first-hand evidence possible of an achievement of Hezekiah's that might otherwise have gone unrecognised. According to its Palaeo-Hebrew text:

> This was the account of the breakthrough. While the labourers were still working with their picks, each toward the other, and while there were still three cubits to be broken through, the voice of each was heard calling to the other, because there was a *zdh* [split?] in the rock to the south and to the north. And at the moment of breakthrough the labourers struck each toward the other, pick against pick. Then the water flowed from the spring to the pool for 1200 cubits. And the height of the rock above the heads of the labourers was 100 cubits.[8]

As scholars now generally accept, this inscription was a group of Jerusalem engineers' own private memorial to their feat in digging this tunnel on Hezekiah's orders. Their task was to reverse the direction of the Gihon spring. Instead of this gushing out into a special pool in the Kidron valley, where Sennacherib's troops could take advantage of it, it would flow in the opposite direction, emerging inside Jerusalem's walls, thereby creating the Siloam Pool. Exhaustive surveying by Israeli geologist Dan Gill has further revealed that these 8th-century BC engineers plugged with huge quantities of rock the old fissure through which the Gihon had formerly exited, so that Sennacherib's army would be unable to capture Jerusalem by the sneaky method used by King David.

Despite such careful preparations, it is clear from the Biblical chronicling that Hezekiah suffered considerable personal anxiety at the prospect of all these efforts being put to the test. His anxiety was so great that, apparently even before Lachish fell, he belatedly sent Sennacherib a handsome 'tribute' of all the gold and silver he could muster from his palace and the Temple's treasury, and enquired what price the Assyrian

The palaeo-Hebrew inscription that was discovered in the Pool of Siloam in 1880. It has helped to explain how 'Hezekiah's tunnel' was built.

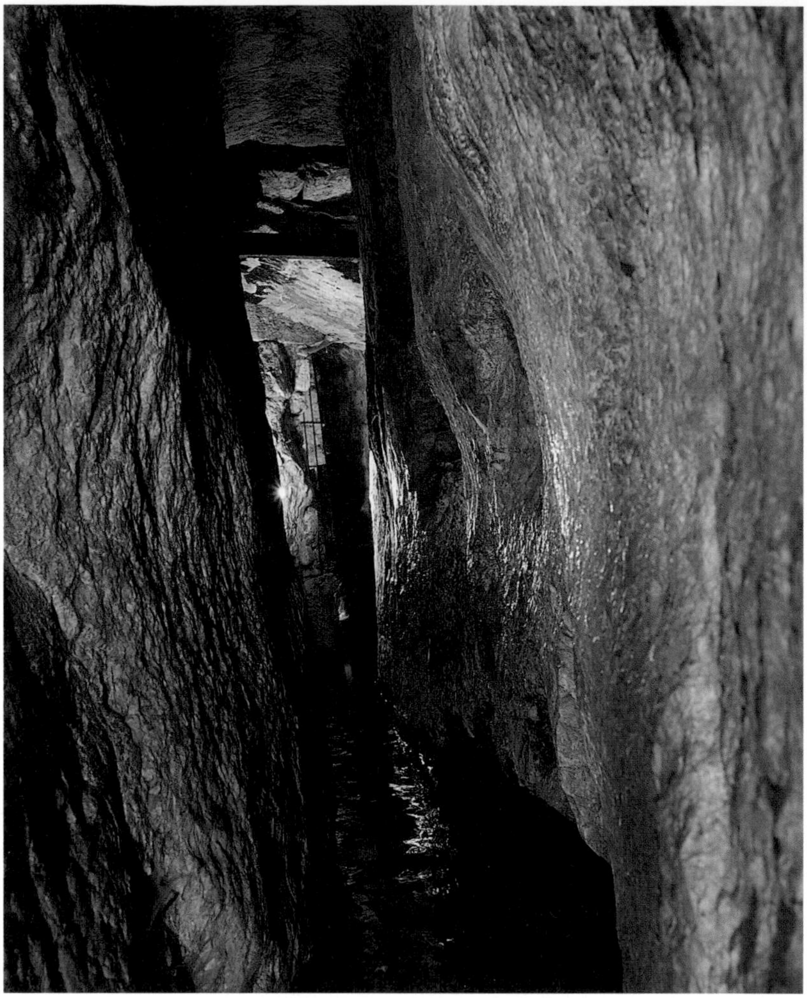

might put on sparing Jerusalem.

By now, however, Sennacherib was reportedly in no mood for anything other than Jerusalem's total surrender. To this end, according to 2 Kings, he sent ahead from Lachish to Jerusalem a 'strong force', headed not only by the already-mentioned 'Tartan', but also by two other top army commanders – the 'Rab-saris' and the 'Rab-shakeh' (2 Kings 18 17), authentic ranks that are again confirmed from cuneiform texts. Stationing themselves provocatively just outside Jerusalem's walls, these grim-looking generals loudly addressed the Jerusalemites in their own language, warning them that any divine protection promised by Hezekiah was useless, and that nothing could now save them from 'the king of Assyria's clutches' (2 Chronicles 32:11). After their departure, a personal letter came from Sennacherib to Hezekiah, pointing out the foolishness of having hoped for help from Egypt. The Assyrian delivered a further taunt: since none of the gods of the other peoples he had subjugated had managed to save them, why should Hezekiah's Yahweh be any different?

The Jerusalem tunnel, now known as Hezekiah's tunnel, by which Hezekiah's engineers diverted the Gihon spring to flow inside, rather than outside, Jerusalem's walls.

For what happened next, we have only the compilers of Kings and Chronicles to rely upon. Reportedly Hezekiah, who had earlier dressed himself in nothing more than sackcloth, 'took the letter . . . . went up to the Temple of Yahweh [i.e. the Temple Solomon had built] and spread it out before Yahweh' (2 Kings 19:14). The compilers indicate that the king was directly before the historic Ark in the Temple's Holy of Holies.[9] Then, clearly in deep, deep distress, he prayed: 'Save us from his [Sennacherib's] clutches, I beg you.'

Living, as he was, with the *nabi* Isaiah on close call, Hezekiah did not have long to wait for his Yahweh's response, as 'received' by Isaiah in the classic *nabi* manner. After a vigorously Yahwistic fulmination against Sennacherib for all his arrogance, Hezekiah was divinely promised:

> He [Sennacherib] shall not enter this city [Jerusalem]
> He shall not shoot any arrow at it
> Or advance upon it with a shield
> Or pile up a siege mound against it.
> He shall go back by the way he came
> He shall not enter this city. (2 Kings 19:32-3)

Surely it was wishful thinking, in the face of any army so fearsome and so repeatedly successful as that of Sennacherib. Yet whatever else we may believe or disbelieve in the Bible's pages, what happened next is a matter of firm history. On the same British Museum prism that carries the boasting about the forty-six Judahite cities the Assyrians had stormed and captured, and about the 200,000 Judahites who had been carried away as slaves, Sennacherib could only lamely say of Hezekiah: 'I locked him up like a caged bird in the midst of Jerusalem, his royal city.' Given that it was the aim of any besieging army to get itself inside the 'bird's cage' and to ransack it for all it was worth, this represents an unmistakable admission on Sennacherib's part that he had failed to take Jerusalem. Self-evidently, Hezekiah had managed to keep him 'locked out'. But how?

According to the 2 Kings compiler, the answer lay in the hand of Yahweh:

> That night an angel of Yahweh went out and struck down 185,000 in the Assyrian camp, and the following morning they were all dead corpses. So King Sennacherib . . . broke camp and retreated. (2 Kings 19:35-36)

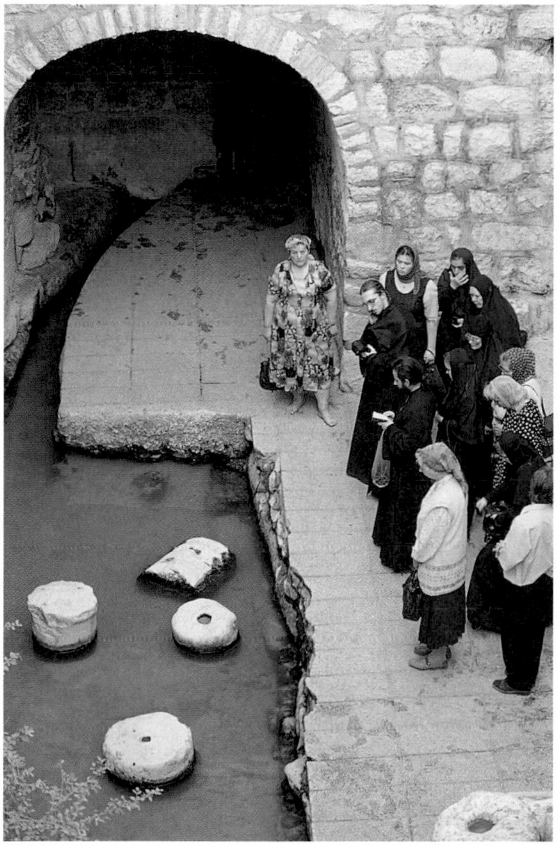

The Pool of Siloam, created by Hezekiah's diversion of the Gihon spring, as it looks today.

Lord Byron's famous 'Destruction of Sennacherib' poem has, of course, imbued this incident with an immortality all its own. But for any rationalist historian the Biblical information is totally inadequate. It leaves us either to reject the whole story, or at a complete loss to explain how so many tens of thousands[10] in so large and successful an army could have died so suddenly and so mysteriously. Unless . . .

What if, when Hezekiah's engineers so cleverly diverted the Gihon spring's water (as we now know they did), they left a quantity of water outside the walls in the recently-discovered old pool[11], just where they knew Sennacherib's army would drink from it most thirstily when they arrived, hot and dusty, after marching the 25 mostly-uphill miles from Lachish? And what if that same water, in any event no longer fresh because of its isolation, had become adulterated? We don't necessarily have to suspect poison. A few rapidly-multiplying bacteria of the wrong kind may have been quite enough for a devastatingly lethal epidemic. Pure speculation, of course. And if the ruse was deliberate, it was the sort of thing that would work only once. But surely it was also just the circumstance that might well have stopped Sennacherib's hosts dead in their tracks, without, true to Yahweh's promise, a single arrow being fired or shield raised?

Whatever the answer, this episode would have carried a painful lesson for Sennacherib that the Judahites' Yahweh could work some extremely powerful magic, and needed to be treated with respect. In which regard, it is again a matter of history that Sennacherib never made any further attempt against Jerusalem, even though he lived another twenty years. The House of David could therefore linger on for at least a while longer.

Nonetheless, for Hezekiah's successors, there was yet another and even more dangerous enemy waiting just beyond their horizon.

14

Succumbing to Babylon

HEZEKIAH'S JERUSALEM had survived the Assyrian invasion. Even so, much of its surrounding territory had fallen to the invaders, and temporarily at least the city lay like a lone island amidst a sea of ruin.

Thus Sennacherib, on the British Museum prism, declared of the Judahite cities he had successfully taken 'from the midst of his [Hezekiah's] land': 'I gave them to Mitinto, King of Ashdod, Padi, King of Ekron, and Silli-Bel, King of Gaza.'[1] In other words, he appointed the previously all-but-vanquished coastal Philistines to police these on his behalf. Archaeologically, this can be seen to have been implemented, as at Beth-Shemesh between Jerusalem and the coast, where the formerly thousand-strong Judahite population simply disappeared (no doubt mostly deported as slaves). Even those few who crept back were forced out again, and their water-reservoir was sealed off to discourage further attempts.

As for Jerusalem itself, it seems that even Yahweh's spectacular successes against the Assyrians failed to persuade those adhering to the old Canaanite religion to change their sympathies. The staunchly Yahwist Hezekiah had done his best to stamp out the Canaanitic religious practices, but when he was succeeded around 687 BC by his twelve-year-old son, Manasseh, the Biblical account tells us that Manasseh positively undid all of his father's work.

In the words of 2 Kings:

> He [Manasseh] did what is displeasing to Yahweh, following the abhorrent practices of the nations that Yahweh had dispossessed before the Israelites. He rebuilt the *bamot* (high places) that his father Hezekiah had destroyed, he erected altars for Baal and made an Asherah as Ahab king of Israel had done. He bowed down to all the host of heaven and worshipped them and built altars for them in the Temple of Yahweh . . . He built altars for all the hosts of heaven in the two courts of the Temple of Yahweh. He consigned his son to the fire; he practised soothsaying and divination and sorcery, and consulted ghosts and familiar spirits . . . The sculptured image of Asherah that he made, he placed inside the Temple concerning which Yahweh had said to David and his son Solomon: 'In this Temple . . . I will establish my name forever' . . . Moreover, Manasseh put so many innocent persons to death that he filled Jerusalem [with blood] from one end to the other. (2 Kings 21:2-16)

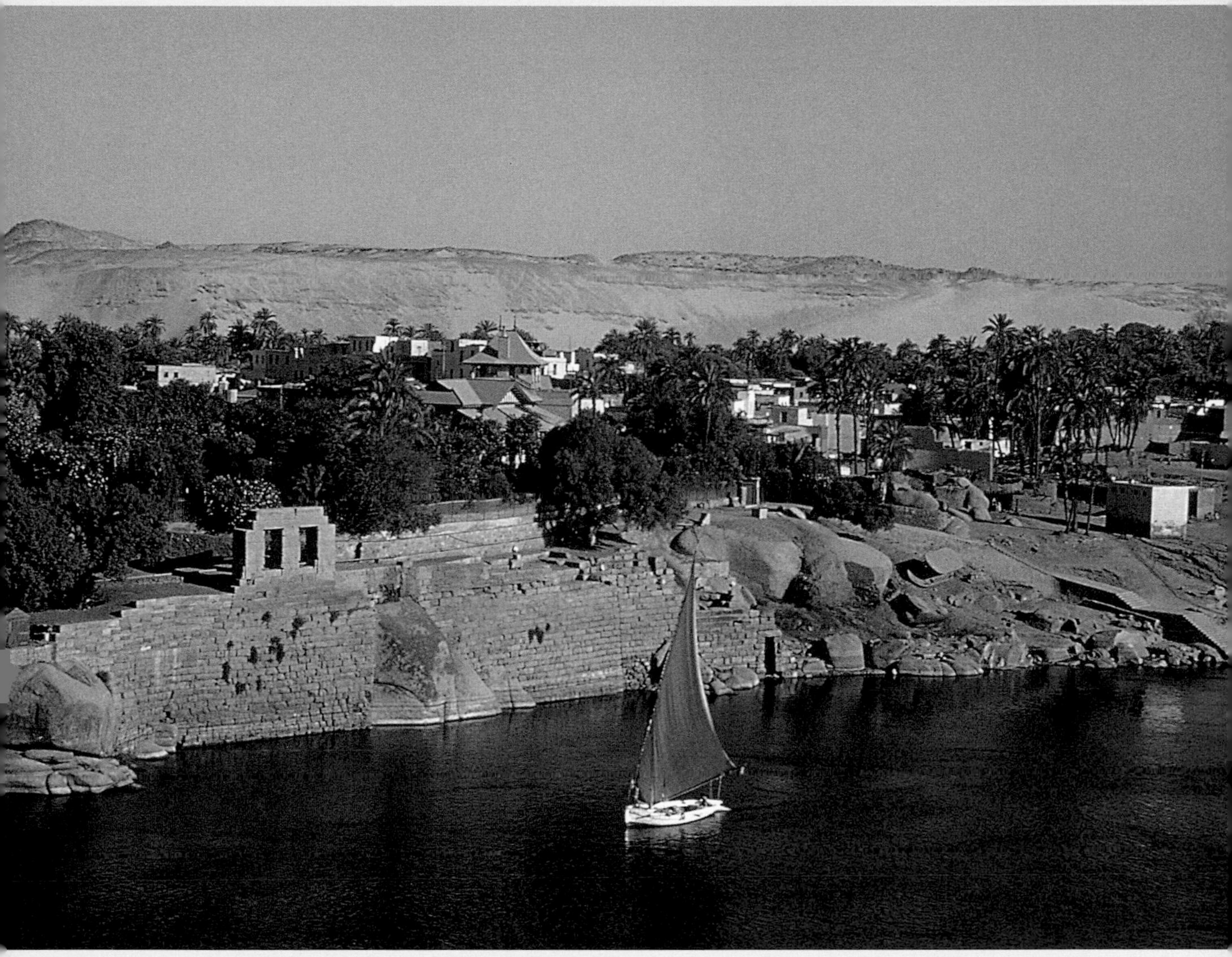

Elephantine Island, near Aswan, where in Manasseh's time a colony from Jerusalem built a Temple of Yahweh (and where they may have taken the Ark).

According to the compilers of both Kings and Chronicles, the very Canaanitic-minded Manasseh reigned for fifty-five years. The compilers do not name the 'innocent persons' he murdered during this long and otherwise largely unknown period. But the fact that they provide no information about contemporaneous Yahwist *nabiim* suggests that these must have been high on Manasseh's 'hit list'. An oblique reference in the book of Jeremiah, composed half a century later, that 'your sword has devoured your *nabiim* like a ravening lion' (Jeremiah 2:30), may well refer to an otherwise unrecorded massacre.

Why, after his father's staunch Yahwism, the young Manasseh should have swung so violently in the opposite direction is impossible to answer adequately in the light of our present knowledge. Conceivably Yahwism, with its Habiru mercenary roots, remained the minority, army men's cult through much of the monarchy period, while the women were largely responsible for controlling and perpetuating the sex-charged Canaanitic religion. A possible hint at this comes from the 2 Kings chronicler. Immediately before he enumerates Manasseh's 'abhorrent' religious practices, he remarks darkly that: 'His mother's name was Hephzibah' (2 Kings 21:1).

Certainly, the Bible chroniclers' most intense disgust was aroused by Manasseh's act of building altars for pagan gods in the two outer courts of Solomon's Temple: the *ulan* and *hekal*. Even worse, he erected a sculpted image of Astarte in what seems to have been the Temple's *debir*, or Holy of Holies, where the Ark of Yahweh normally reposed. Many of the preceding Judahite kings had followed Canaanitic ways, but as Professor Menahem Haran of Jerusalem's Hebrew University has pointed out, despite these and the recently discovered 'Yahweh and his Asherah' inscriptions, there is no direct evidence that anyone before Manasseh had ever used the Temple for worshipping Asherah/Astarte or any god other than Yahweh.[2] The fact that the Ark remained in the Temple up to Manasseh's time is established by his father Hezekiah's anguished prayer before it at the time of the Assyrian siege.

Another fact has to be faced. It is precisely from Manasseh's time onward that all mentions of the Ark as a still extant object mysteriously disappear from the Bible. When the Yahwist *nabiim* were killed, the Ark's role for them as an inspirational 'oracle' would have died likewise. Even so, it seems highly unlikely that it would have been destroyed, since as we noted earlier, even the Philistines were too superstitious to try anything so likely to provoke divine vengeance. Yet, it is equally unlikely that Jerusalem's Yahwists would have allowed their sacred Ark to stay anywhere near a statue of Asherah/Astarte in all her defiling nudity. So the question arises: if the Ark was genuinely removed from the Jerusalem Temple sometime during Manasseh's reign, where was it taken and by whom?

A 5th-century BC letter found at Elephantine Island, which specifically mentions 'the Temple of YHW the God which is in Elephantine'.

In this regard, one of the least-known Biblical discoveries from the first decade of the 20th century was a finding by German archaeologists of a quantity of ancient papyri. These were written in Aramaic – i.e. the everyday language of Hebrew peoples – in the unlikely location of a tiny Nile island called Elephantine, near Aswan in Egypt's deepest south. Together with similar papyri acquired by New York journalist Charles Wilbour and others, these so-called Elephantine Papyri comprise the correspondence and legal papers of a colony of Hebrew mercenaries who first arrived at Elephantine Island some time during Manasseh's reign. They came to Egypt to help Pharaoh Psammetichus I (664-610 BC)[3] fight the Nubians to his south.

One fascinating discovery from this correspondence is confirmed by excavations on Elephantine Island currently being conducted by the German Archaeological Institute. This far-flung Hebrew colony was not only Yahwist (suggesting that it may have offered its services to Psammetichus quite independently of Manasseh), but also built its own temple of Yahweh on the island. There can be no doubt about this since one of the papyri, datable to 407 BC and preserved today in Berlin's State Museum, specifically complains of the very recent destruction of 'the temple of Yahweh the god which is in Elephantine'.[4] Furthermore, today's leading Jewish papyrologist, Bezalel Porten[5], collating the papyri's various references to this edifice, has determined that this temple had a cedar roof just like its Jerusalem counterpart, that it matched its dimensions very closely and was also oriented to Jerusalem.

From clues of this kind, British journalist Graham Hancock has argued persuasively that these mercenaries took the Ark with them from Judah to Elephantine Island, and there built a replica Jerusalem Temple for it. After this temple was destroyed in the 5th century BC, the Ark was taken by their descendants to Ethiopia, where, according to Hancock's theory, it remains to this day in a closely-guarded sanctuary in the ancient Ethiopian capital of Axum.[6] Supporting this, an ancient community of Jews subsequently journeyed to and settled in Ethiopia, as the Falashas, maintaining many archaic religious practices there. These include the 'dance of David', the practice of animal sacrifice and performing ceremonies celebrating their possession of the original Ark. Unfortunately, however, until we know exactly what it is that is kept at Axum, the theory must remain just that.

Wherever the Ark may have been taken, for Yahwists the one source of new hope on Manasseh's death was the grandson who succeeded him. Josiah not only reinstated the pro-Yahwist religious reforms of his great-grandfather Hezekiah, but also went substantially further, initiating for Jerusalem and its environs a religious reformation hardly less iconoclastic and violent than that of 16th-century Europe.

Thus, Josiah apparently 'cleansed' the Jerusalem Temple and associated sites of all the idolatrous and pagan objects that Manasseh had introduced. Specifically, in the words of the 2 Kings compiler:

> [He] ordered Hilkiah [with] the priests next in rank . . . to bring out of the Temple all the objects which had been made for Baal and Asherah [Astarte] and all the host of heaven. He burned them outside Jerusalem in the fields of Kedron . . . [he] tore down the altars made by the kings of Judah on the roof [of the Temple] . . . and the altars made by Manasseh in the two courts of the Temple of . . . [he] desanctified the *bamot* (high places) facing Jerusalem, to the south of the Mount of Olives, which Solomon king of Israel had built for Astarte the abomination of the Sidonians, for Chemosh the abomination of Moab and for Milcom the detestable thing of the Ammonites . . . As for the altar in Bethel [and] the 'high place' made by Jeroboam . . . that altar too and the *bamah* he tore down. (2 Kings 23:4-13, 15, 19)

Josiah also apparently disrupted, and in some cases actually took, the lives of the Canaanite religion's many functionaries:

> He suppressed the idolatrous priests whom the kings of Judah had appointed to make offerings at the high places . . . He tore down the cubicles of the male prostitutes in the Temple of Yahweh at the place where the women wove veils for Astarte . . . [he] also did away with the necromancers and mediums, the household gods and idols, all the detestable things that were to be seen in the land of Judah and Jerusalem. (2 Kings 23:5, 7, 24)

Manasseh had apparently reintroduced the Canaanite-style practice of child sacrifice at its traditional site called the Tophet immediately to the south-west of Jerusalem. Josiah positively outlawed this, closing down:

> . . . the Tophet which is in the Valley of Bet-Hinnom, so that no one might consign his son or daughter to the fire of Molech. (2 Kings 23:10)

Josiah also seems to have gone substantially further than Hezekiah in centralising all Yahwist worship in Jerusalem, apparently having:

> . . . brought all the priests from the towns of Judah [to Jerusalem] and decommissioned the 'high places' where the priests had been making [sacrificial] offerings. (2 Kings 23:8)

Even today, the scars of the 16th-century Reformation are visible all over England, with mediaeval monasteries abandoned to ruin, and the old cathedrals and churches stripped of their one-time statuary and ornament. In the same way, the Biblical Josiah's reforms have left their mark in the archaeological record. For instance, British archaeologist Kathleen Kenyon, in the course of her 1950s Jerusalem excavations, found a cave a few hundred yards south of the Temple Mount containing several dozen broken Astarte/Asherah figurines and similar objects. These are generally thought to derive from Josiah's savage suppression of the Canaanitic cults.

The nature of Josiah's reforms of Yahwism are also indicated by archaeologists' findings at the Arad fortress. During Hezekiah's reforms, its Yahwist temple had been deprived of its altar but had otherwise been maintained. Excavations revealed, however, that it was not rebuilt following Sennacherib's destruction. Instead, it was completely closed down. The two incense altars that had stood on its steps were reverently laid on their sides and covered over with earth to conceal all traces of the location's former use. Thereafter, as again evident from the archaeological record, it was used for ordinary habitation.

According to the 2 Kings compiler, it was only in the eighteenth year of Josiah's reign, when he was still merely twenty-six (he succeeded at the age of eight), that all these reforms were introduced. This raises the question: what exactly was it that prompted him to embark on the reforms at that particular time? Biblically, the answer is straightforward enough. Because of Manasseh's long reign, and the thoroughness of his suppression of Yahwism, much of the Yahwist mode of belief had been all but forgotten, until the seemingly accidental discovery in the Jerusalem Temple of a hidden 'scroll of the *Torah*'. When Hilkiah's scribe Shaphan brought this scroll to Josiah and read it to him, the king was reportedly overwhelmed by the number of Yahwistic commandments that were currently being flouted, and the dire consequences that were said to arise from this flouting. He resolved that something must be done, and swiftly.

Intriguingly, his first move was to summon the most revered *nabi* of his time, clearly one who had survived Manasseh. She was a married woman called Huldah who 'lived in Jerusalem in the new town' (2 Kings 22:14). Huldah told him that because of his conscientiousness he would live to be buried in a Jerusalem that was still free. However, for the people of Judah as a whole, a 'great disaster' was looming as Yahweh's punishment for their having 'forsaken me [Yahweh] and made offerings to other gods' (2 Kings 22:17). Anxious to mend matters as much as possible, Josiah reportedly ordered 'the entire text of the *Torah* scroll which had been found in the Temple of Yahweh' to be read out to 'all the inhabitants of Jerusalem, and the priests and *nabiim* – all the people, young and old'. Following that, he implemented his radical programme of religious reforms.

So, what exactly was this *Torah* scroll that had purportedly been found somewhere in the Temple? For today's Jews, the word conveys the entirety of what Christians call the Old Testament, but it would be wrong to believe that this scroll incorporated every book of our present Bibles written up to Josiah's time. As modern-day Biblical scholars recognise, the one earlier Biblical book that makes significant reference to the *Torah* is Deuteronomy. Since Deuteronomy's first commandment is for sacrifices to Yahweh to be made at a single place, there is surely a link between this and King Josiah's closing down of all the places of sacrifice except the Jerusalem Temple? In this light, even conservative Biblical scholars agree that at least part of our present Bible's book of Deuteronomy was also part of the scroll 'discovered' in Josiah's reign. Arguably, this had been composed by a still faithful Yahwist shortly before or during King Josiah's minority.

Furthermore, as the same scholars are generally agreed, Deuteronomy should not be thought of on its own. Instead, it seems to have been one of a group of books, the others being Joshua, Judges, 1 and 2 Samuel and 1 and 2 Kings. All of these have the appearance of having been compiled and arranged into a unity at one specific time, from earlier texts such as the 'Book of the Wars of Yahweh', the 'Annals of the Kings of Israel' and the 'Annals of the Kings of Judah'.

Have we now, in or around King Josiah's reign, reached the time of some of the mysterious Biblical editor-compilers whom we have repeatedly alluded to? Certainly, the signs are there. One indication lies in 1 Kings 13 which tells a story of the 10th-century BC King Jeroboam of Israel. He was just about to offer a Canaanitic-type sacrifice at Bethel, when a 'man of God from Judah' reportedly came up to him with the prediction from Yahweh:

> A son shall be born to the House of David, *Josiah by name*, and he shall slaughter upon you the priests of the shrines who bring offerings upon you' (1 Kings 13:2).

This 'prophecy' unmistakably reflects its fulfilment in 2 Kings 23:15-17, when King Josiah reportedly destroyed the same Bethel altar and burnt the bones of those who had offered sacrifices on it, suggesting that the earlier passage was 'written in' in King Josiah's time.

Underscoring the entire editing and compiling of the two books of Kings is a good-bad rating for each king of Judah and Israel. This culminates in the rating of Josiah, who was like 'no king . . . before' (2 Kings 23 25), an assessment reflecting Deuteronomy's closing words that Moses was like no other *nabi* who came after him (Deuteronomy 34:10). It is true that 2 Kings incorporates history up to and including Jerusalem's fall to the Babylonians a quarter of a century later, but it also includes repeated references to Jerusalem landmarks that are still extant 'to this day', even when the Babylonians are known to have destroyed these. This suggests that the post-Josiah material was simply added on. Overall, Biblical scholars recognise such a similarity of language and other traits between the books of Deuteronomy, Joshua, Judges, 1 and 2 Samuel and 1 and 2 Kings, that they now almost routinely refer to these as the Deuteronomic or Deuteronomistic History. They regard their 'history' content as having been compiled and edited from different strands of earlier material – some Israelite, other Judahite.

If we can identify the time, can we perhaps identify the compiler? Here some compelling sleuth-work has been done by the American Biblical scholar Richard Elliott Friedman.[7] He has pieced together textual clues such as the Deuteronomistic editor-compiler's favouring of the priests of the old, disestablished shrine at Shiloh, his revering of Samuel, his dislike of King Solomon for erecting shrines to foreign gods, his favouring of Josiah and the assumption that he lived partly in Josiah's reign. Putting these together, Friedman has identified him as none other than the *nabi* Jeremiah, author of the Biblical book of the same name.

The very first verse of the book of Jeremiah states: 'The words of Jeremiah . . . the word of Yahweh came to him in the days of Josiah . . . king of Judah'. So Jeremiah certainly *was* contemporary with Josiah, though he would outlive him. Furthermore, Jeremiah's own Biblical book shows him to have been pro-Shiloh. He was the only *nabi* Biblically to refer to this shrine. He was also the only *nabi* to refer to Samuel, equating Samuel and Moses as his people's greatest historical figures. As Friedman has further remarked: 'Parts of [the Biblical book of] Jeremiah are so similar to Deuteronomy that it is hard to believe that they are not by the same person.'[8]

Once we take this insight on board, we are able to gain some extraordinarily close glimpses of the milieu in which a significant portion of the Bible came into being. Only comparatively recently several clay *bullae* of Josiah and Jeremiah's time came to light. Some simply turned up on the antiquities market, but others thankfully were discovered archaeologically. Among the latter, some specimens excavated by the Israeli archaeologist, the late Yigal Shiloh, are particularly interesting. They came from Jerusalem's 'Stepped Stone Structure' area (see page 112), at a level just below that of the Babylonian destruction, and therefore chronologically as close to Josiah and Jeremiah's time as makes no difference.

A bulla, or seal impression, identifiable as having belonged to the 'Gemariah, son of the secretary Shaphan' of Jeremiah 36:10.

The first of these is inscribed in palaeo-Hebrew, 'Gemaryahu son of Shaphan'. This immediately reminds us that it was a Shaphan, secretary to the priest Hilkiah, who was described as bringing the newly-discovered *Torah* scroll to Josiah and reading it to him. Biblically, however, we can get even closer than this. This is because names ending in the Palaeo-Hebrew 'yahu' are effectively the same as those that end in 'iah' in English Bible translations. So this humble *bulla*'s 'Gemaryahu' can have been none other than the Biblical 'Gemariah son of the secretary Shaphan'. It was in his room 'in the upper court, near the new gateway of the Temple of Yahweh' that Jeremiah's predictions of Jerusalem's impending doom were reportedly read out during the reign of King Josiah's son Jehoiakim (Jeremiah 36:10).[9]

Likewise identifiable from a Biblical text is a *bulla* (also found in the Stepped Stone Structure), inscribed: 'Belonging to Azaryahu, son of Hilkiyahu', i.e. 'Belonging to Azariah, son of Hilkiah'. Hilkiah, we may recall, featured in 2 Kings as the Temple priest who discovered the *Torah* scroll. Once again, we can get even closer than this. In the book of Chronicles' listing of the Jerusalem Temple's high priests for this period we find:

> Shallum fathered Hilkiah, *Hilkiah fathered Azariah*, Azariah fathered Seraiah, Seraiah fathered Jehozadak, and Jehozadak went into exile (1 Chronicles 5:39 – or 6:13 in some versions).[10]

This *bulla* must therefore derive from a seal once owned by the Biblical 'Azariah son of Hilkiah'.

Among the *bulla* specimens that have surfaced via the antiquities market – and almost certainly looted from the same Stepped Stone Structure – one is inscribed: 'Belonging to Yerahme'el/son of the king'. This may be confidently identified as having belonged to King Jehoiakim's son Jerahmeel. He features in the book of Jeremiah as the person sent to arrest Jeremiah and his secretary Baruch after King Jehoiakim had angrily rejected Jeremiah's prophecies of Jerusalem's downfall (Jeremiah 36:26).

A bulla identifiable as having belonged to the Baruch, son of Neriah, who features repeatedly in the book of Jeremiah as Jeremiah's secretary.

Most interesting of all, however, are two that bear the same three-line inscription 'Belonging to Berekhyahu son of Neriyahu the scribe'. Since 'Berekh' is simply a palaeo-Hebrew rendering of the 'Baruch' of our English-language Bible, and 'son of Neriyahu' may be transliterated 'son of Neriah', the owner of the original seal from which these two impressions came must have been the 'Baruch son of Neriah' repeatedly mentioned in the book of Jeremiah as Jeremiah's secretary. For instance, in chapter 32,

'Baruch son of Neriah' is asked to safeguard a deed of land purchase (Jeremiah 32:12-16). In chapter 36, he features writing down Jeremiah's prophetic utterances and reading these to the people. And in chapter 45, he is identified as the secretary who took down the Biblical book of Jeremiah at Jeremiah's dictation. Because they emerged on the antiquities market, the authenticity of these *bullae* cannot be guaranteed. Nonetheless, scholarly doubts are largely non-existent because they are so readily comparable with those found by the legitimate archaeologists.

If, thanks to finds of this kind, some key people behind key portions of our Bible are now beginning to assume real life, it is surely fitting that the oldest surviving text of any passage in our Bibles should also have surfaced from this period. In 1979 the Israeli archaeologist Gabriel Barkay was excavating some ancient burial caves overlooking the Hinnom Valley, just to the south-west of the Old City of Jerusalem, when to his surprise he found one that was undisturbed. It contained the bones of at least ninety-five people, some with pottery, arrowheads, pieces of gold and silver jewellery buried alongside them. But Barkay's most spectacular find in this cave was a pair of small cylindrical scrolls made of pure silver. Although insignificant-looking when first found, the largest no more than 4 inches long, they were both found to bear eighteen lines of Palaeo-Hebrew script when unrolled, including the words:

> May Yahweh bless you and keep you
> May Yahweh cause his face to shine upon you and grant you peace.

'May Yahweh bless you and keep you
May Yahweh cause his face to shine upon you and grant you peace.' (Numbers 6:24-26)
The oldest ancient inscription bearing a Biblical text, these words were inscribed on the 4-inch silver scroll (seen at right), one of a pair found in 1979 in a burial cave south-west of the Old City of Jerusalem.

As palaeographic specialists are generally agreed, the date when these words were incised on the scrolls can be no later than the late 7th century BC, i.e. the time of Jeremiah. Since they are none other than the 'priestly blessing' of Numbers 6:24-26, still used in both Jewish and Christian liturgies, they are by far the oldest portion of Biblical text yet discovered. They also suggest that the Biblical book of Numbers may also have been extant at the Jeremiah period, although the sceptical alternative that the words were a popular oral blessing later incorporated into the Biblical book cannot be discounted.

For posterity Jeremiah would be best remembered as the *nabi* par excellence who most publicly and exhaustively predicted Jerusalem's impending destruction, not by either of its former enemies – the Assyrians or the Egyptians – but by an entirely new menace: the Babylonians. The known historical facts are that in 626 BC, more than 500 miles east of Jerusalem, a Chaldean-born army commander called Nabopolassar suddenly overthrew his Assyrian overlords and made himself king of Babylon. Together with his son Nebuchadnezzar, Nabopolassar set about rebuilding Babylon as capital of a mighty new empire. When to the Assyrians' further discomfort another new threat – the Medes – appeared, it was natural for the two new menaces – Babylonian and Mede – to combine forces. In 612 BC they attacked and destroyed the Assyrians' vast metropolis of Nineveh, mopping up all further resistance during the following three years, until the Assyrian menace was completely eliminated.

King Josiah, now in his late thirties, must inevitably have been one of many who rejoiced at this news. Unfortunately for him, however, in the very same year, Pharaoh Necho II turned up in Judah at the head of a more impressive-looking Egyptian army than had been fielded in centuries. Taking advantage of Assyrian decline, Necho's father Psammetichus I had greatly revived his country's clout as a superpower. During some form of confrontation with the Egyptians at Megiddo, Josiah was killed by an arrow (2 Kings 23:29-35; 2 Chronicles 35:30-36:4). Compounding this disaster, Necho took Josiah's eldest son Jehoahaz hostage, and demanded that Jerusalem's citizens pay him tribute via Josiah's younger son Jehoiakim, who was obliged to take over in his elder brother's stead.

However, in 605 BC, Babylon's Nebuchadnezzar resoundingly defeated Necho II's Egyptians at Carchemish on the Euphrates river. The *nabi* Jeremiah colourfully remarked upon this victory in what we now know as his book's chapter 46. An emboldened Nebuchadnezzar, now king in succession to his father, then swept southwards to attack the pocket of Mediterranean coastal towns that were still Philistine. Jeremiah duly pronounced:

> The day . . . is coming for ravaging all the Philistines
> For cutting off every last ally of Tyre and Sidon . . .
> Baldness has come upon Gaza
> Ashkelon is destroyed . . . (Jeremiah 47:4-5)

These words were matched by real-life events checkable outside the Bible's pages. Thus, with regard to Philistine Ashkelon, a fragmentary Babylonian Chronicle records that Nebuchadnezzar 'marched to the city of Ashkelon and captured it . . . [also] captured its king and . . . turned the city into a mound and heaps of ruins'.[11] Likewise, direct archaeological excavations at Ashkelon have revealed that its formerly prosperous metropolis suffered at this time a sudden and overwhelming destruction that can only have been inflicted by Nebuchadnezzar and his Babylonians. One skeleton, discovered among smashed pottery, vitrified brick, charred wheat and collapsed roofs, was that of a Philistine woman in her mid-thirties who had clearly been trying to hide behind some storage jars. When found, her legs were still contorted and her left arm raised as if to ward off a club blow.

After Ashkelon, Nebuchadnezzar's next target was Philistine Ekron, where the earlier-mentioned Dothan and Gitin excavations have revealed that this too was devastated, apparently during the same campaign. Although Nebuchadnezzar failed in his attempt to go on and conquer Egypt as well, he nevertheless established a strong claim right up to its border. As a result, Judah's King Jehoiakim had no alternative but to transfer to Babylon the tribute he had only recently been paying to Egypt. As recorded in the Babylonian Chronicles[12], a further battle between Egypt and Assyria took place in 601 BC. This time the fighting went sufficiently in Egypt's favour for Jehoiakim to change his allegiance back to Egypt once again – with disastrous consequences.

In the winter of 598 BC, just three months after Jehoiakim had been succeeded by his son Jehoiachin, Nebuchadnezzar arrived in person before Jerusalem's walls at the head of a Babylonian army every bit as ominous-looking as that of Sennacherib and his Assyrians just over a century before. In these circumstances, Jehoiachin, apparently yet another Canaanitic-inclined monarch who 'did what is displeasing to Yahweh', stood little chance.

According to the Babylonian Chronicle[13] on the 'the second day of the month of Addaru' (16 March 597 BC by our reckoning), Nebuchadnezzar seized 'the city of Ia-a-hu-du' ['Judah', i.e. Jerusalem], 'captured the king', 'appointed there a king of his

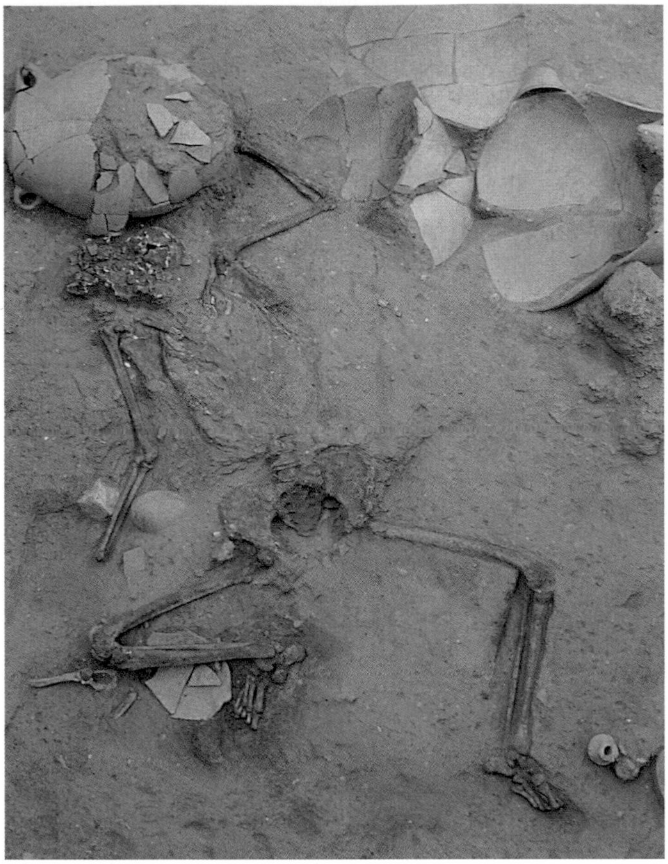

heart, received its heavy tribute and sent it to Babylon'. This puts a date to a story told much more fully in the Biblical version:

> King Jehoiachin of Judah, along with his mother, and his courtiers, commanders and officers, surrendered to the king of Babylon . . . [who] brought [them] as exiles from Jerusalem to Babylon . . . [together with] all the able men, to the number of seven thousand – all of them warriors, trained for battle – and a thousand craftsmen and smiths. (2 Kings 24:12, 15-16).

With regard to the 'heavy tribute' that the Babylonian Chronicle tells us Nebuchadnezzar carried off with him, we are told Biblically that this included 'all the treasures of the Temple of Yahweh and the treasures of the royal palace' (2 Kings 24:13). The lack of any specific mention of the Ark may indicate that this had, indeed, been spirited away earlier. Archaeology has provided a fascinating corroboration of King Jehoiachin and his retinue's imprisonment in Babylon. In the early part of the 20th century, when the German archaeologist George Koldewey was excavating Babylon's site in present-day Iraq, among the many cuneiform tablets he found was a ration list. This was worded:

'Ashkelon is destroyed.' (Jeremiah 47:4-5) The skeleton of a young woman, clubbed to death during the Babylonian destruction, was found exactly where she fell.

> To Ya'u-kinu [Jehoiachin] king of the land of Yahudu [Judah], 26 pints [of oil] for Ya'u-kinu, king of the land of Yahudu, 3¾ pints for the five sons of the king of the land of Yahudu, 6 pints for eight men, Yahduites [i.e. Judahites] – for each one three-quarters of a pint. By the hand of Kanama [scribe].[14]

As generally agreed, this can only have been a scribe's account of the food and drink the Babylonians allowed King Jehoiachin and the mini-court of five sons and eight courtiers who shared his imprisonment. Similarly deported at this time, though almost certainly not as a member of this court, was the priest-*nabi* Ezekiel. The whole of his Biblical book seems to have been written from the same circumstances of exile in Babylon.[15]

Despite the deportation of so many of Jerusalem's highest and most influential individuals, along with so much of the city's material wealth, even this was not the Judahite capital's last hour. There is no suggestion that the city was destroyed at this point. Instead, we learn that it staggered on for a few more years under Jehoiakin's Babylonian-appointed uncle Zedekiah. Jeremiah also was still around, voicing ever grimmer and more unpopular prophecies.

Just as we might expect, the neighbouring peoples whom the Judahites had oppressed in the past now saw their opportunity for revenge. The Edomites, for instance, who had already considerably improved their status in the wake of Sennacherib's conquests, now grabbed yet more territory for themselves, much to the disgust of Jeremiah's fellow-*nabi* Obadiah:

The Lord Yahweh says this . . .
On that day, when you stood aloof
while aliens carried off his goods
when foreigners entered his gates
and cast lots for Jerusalem
you were as one of them. (Obadiah 1:11)

Archaeology yet again confirms this Biblical picture. For from the Arad fortress that was rebuilt after Sennacherib's destruction, broken bits of pottery have survived with the last records of its apparently still staunchly Yahwist commander Eliashib. Among these is a partly lost message to him from a neighbouring fortress, which specifically warns:

To Eliashib . . . The word of the king is incumbent on you for your very life!
Behold I have sent to warn you today [Ramat-Negeb] has to be defended
lest Edom should come there.

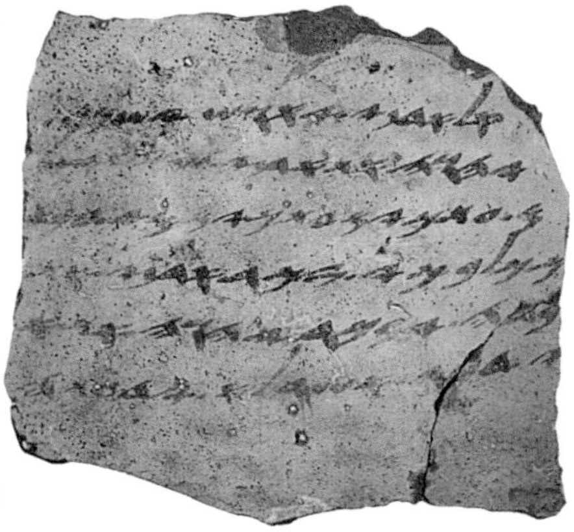

Grim testimony to Judah's last hours. An army commander's last messages, written on a potsherd shortly before the fall of Lachish.

According to Jeremiah, Lachish was still free from the Babylonians during Zedekiah's time (Jeremiah 34:7). British archaeologist James Starkey excavated there in the mid-1930s, and found on the 'guard room' floor, immediately below a burnt layer attributed to Nebuchadnezzar, a complete cache of the commander Ya'osh's similar last messages. Among these was one from a fortress clearly within fire-beacon range of Lachish:

And let my lord know that we are watching for the fire-beacons of Lachish, according to all the indications which my lord has given, for we cannot see Azekah.[16]

From this message it would seem that Azekah had just fallen to the Babylonians. And Lachish, which had held out so staunchly against Sennacherib, followed in its turn, as Starkey's 'burnt layer' findings graphically showed. A fascinating feature of the messages found at both Arad and Lachish is that their handwriting is fluent, as from a people long versed in writing. Furthermore, vocabulary and grammar specialists adjudge the messages' language to be virtually indistinguishable from that of the Jeremiah-compiled Deuteronomistic History books. It is also apparent that, whatever religion prevailed in the royal palace at Jerusalem, these army outpost commanders were staunchly Yahwist. Eliashib certainly was, and one of Ya'osh's messages concludes: 'May Yahweh cause my lord to hear news of peace, even now.'

Jerusalem was, of course, the Babylonians' ultimate prize, and when, as recorded in 2 Kings, even their puppet king Zedekiah 'rebelled against the king of Babylon', the stage was set for the final showdown. The Babylonian army had apparently never relinquished its encampment before Jerusalem's walls. Around 587 BC, it began besieging in earnest, until 'famine had become acute in the city; there was no food left for the common people' (2 Kings 25:2). As

Prisoners are taken away after the Assyrian assault on Lachish.

A Jerusalem toilet seat of the period immediately before the city's fall. The accompanying faecal matter showed the starving inhabitants were reduced to eating wild plants and weeds.

poignant evidence of this, Israeli archaeologist Yigal Shiloh, in his excavations of the same Jerusalem Stepped Stone Structure from which the Jeremiah-period *bullae* came, unearthed two immediately pre-Babylonian stone toilet seats.[17] Scientific analysis of the accompanying faecal matter revealed an unusually high proportion of wild plant residue, a correspondingly low proportion of cultivated vegetables, also unusually large numbers of intestinal tapeworm and whipworm eggs. This led scientists to conclude that Jerusalem's starving inhabitants had been reduced to eating the roots and leaves of wild plants, with the whipworm indicating very poor sanitation, as if there had been no clean water for washing even these crisis foodstuffs.

Zedekiah and his army, in their desperation, apparently attempted a breakout under cover of darkness, but the Babylonians caught up with them near Jericho. A now merciless Nebuchadnezzar reportedly had Zedekiah's sons 'slaughtered . . . before his eyes, then Zedekiah's eyes were put out. He was chained in bronze fetters and brought to Babylon' (2 Kings 25:7). Then the final curtain fell upon Jerusalem itself:

> Nebuzaradan, commander of the guard and a member of the king of Babylon's staff, entered Jerusalem. He burned down the Temple of Yahweh, the royal palace and all the houses of Jerusalem. The Chaldaean troops . . . demolished the walls surrounding Jerusalem [and] deported the remainder of the population left in the city [except] . . . some of the poor country people left behind as vineyard workers and ploughmen.[18] (2 Kings 25:8-12)

The Israeli archaeologist Nahman Avigad and others, in the course of their City of David excavations, have found much that adds detail to the harsh reality behind these Biblical words. They have unearthed what must clearly have been, up to the time of the Babylonian conquest, one of Jerusalem's most imposing defence towers. It still survives to a height of 27 feet. At the foot of this, just outside the ancient city wall, they came across a layer of charred wood, ashes and soot in the midst of which lay five arrowheads. Four of these were of a 'flat iron' type known to have been used by the defending Judahites. The fifth was of Scythian triple-winged design, as used by the Babylonians and by the mercenaries they recruited to fight on their behalf.

As only the most inadequate testament to the glory that had been pre-conquest Jerusalem, carbonised fragments of some wooden furniture from this period came to light in the course of the same excavations. Many of these pieces bear the hallmarks of having been finely carved by expert craftsmen. The variety of woods from which they have been made tells its own story. Olive, almond, terebinth, Tabor oak, evergreen oak, cypress, Jerusalem pine, poplar, acacia, tamarisk and sycamore, all represent the use of Judahite home-grown timber. But boxwood, too, has been found, indicating that even during the late Judahite period there were trade links with what are today southern Turkey and northern Syria.

On Nebuchadnezzar's direct orders the entire city of Jerusalem went up in flames in one of the most thorough urban destructions the ancient world had ever seen. We need be in no doubt that Jerusalem's fall to the Babylonians in 586 BC was as calamitous an end to its near five-centuries-old Judahite monarchy as Samaria's to the Assyrians had been for the Israelites nearly a century and a half earlier. Historically, it represented the end of the so-called First Temple period, with the Temple burnt beyond repair. It also marked the effective end of the ancient Hebrew language as its people's spoken tongue.

But, however dark this hour must have seemed, with so many Judahite inhabitants, including now Jeremiah and Baruch, transported to enslavement in Babylon, a new and surprisingly formative phase of Biblical history was just about to begin.

15

IF I FORGET YOU, O JERUSALEM

ONE THING IS remarkable about the period of 'Babylonian captivity'. After all the earlier religious discord, during which the deep-rooted Canaanitic religious practices so often prevailed as the status quo, a massive disaster like this might have been expected to bring about Yahwism's complete extinction, especially after Nebuchadnezzar had killed off Jerusalem's high priests. The Judahites transported to Babylon were now plunged into a totally pagan environment, lacking their traditional places of worship. Few would ever see their homeland again. The period of captivity also saw the end of the old Hebrew language, which was discarded in favour of the Near East's widespread lingua franca Aramaic. Inscriptions would now appear in the square letters of present-day Hebrew.

Yet, as even the most minimalist of Biblical scholars readily acknowledge, those who had been uprooted managed, even while exiled, to retain the distinctiveness that set them apart from the general run of ancient peoples. They also clung tenaciously to the belief in their divine right to the land from which they had been so brutally plucked. Clearly, they managed to take with them and preserve a considerable amount of documentation pertaining to their historical past. More than that, they succeeded in sublimating and sanctifying their recent sufferings in writings so packed with soul-searching that foreign nations, even millennia into the future, would absorb them into their own cultural heritages.

These are undeniable facts, evidenced by the same writings' editing, translation and multiplication by the thousand million into the books we call Bibles. But we also have to accept that this so-seminal 'Exile' phase was one we know very little about. Biblically, the books of Kings and Chronicles end with the fall of the Judahite kingdom in 586 BC. And when the story is taken up again in the subsequent books of Nehemiah and Ezra, neither written until the following century, some fifty essentially unrecorded years had elapsed. During these years, all the key people, such as the *nabi* Jeremiah and his secretary Baruch, who featured so vividly just before the fall of Jerusalem fairly obviously died. Archaeology can tell us little of this time. Moreover – and this must have been a huge object-lesson for the exiles – the mighty Babylonians, who had been responsible for the Judahites'

Epitomising the might that had crushed and scattered Jerusalem's Judahites, a lion sculpted in brick relief, from Babylon's imposing Ishtar Gate.

enslavement, had been defeated in their turn by an altogether more humane new world power – the Persians.

Neither the Assyrians nor the Babylonians had ever, by their policy of forcible deportation, totally denuded the populations of the old Israel and Judah kingdoms. Although the surviving texts of the books of Jeremiah and 2 Kings disagree about how many Judahites were carried off in 586 BC – according to Jeremiah 4600, according to 2 Kings 11,600 – neither figure is overwhelming, and both are therefore the more credible for it. As has been pointed out by the Israeli archaeologist Gabriel Barkay[1], Galilee, Samaria and the Negev were left virtually unaffected. At sites excavated in Benjaminite territory only just north of Jerusalem, no Babylonian destruction levels have been found. The same is true to the south, while as the Bible indicates and archaeology confirms, even in Jerusalem itself a

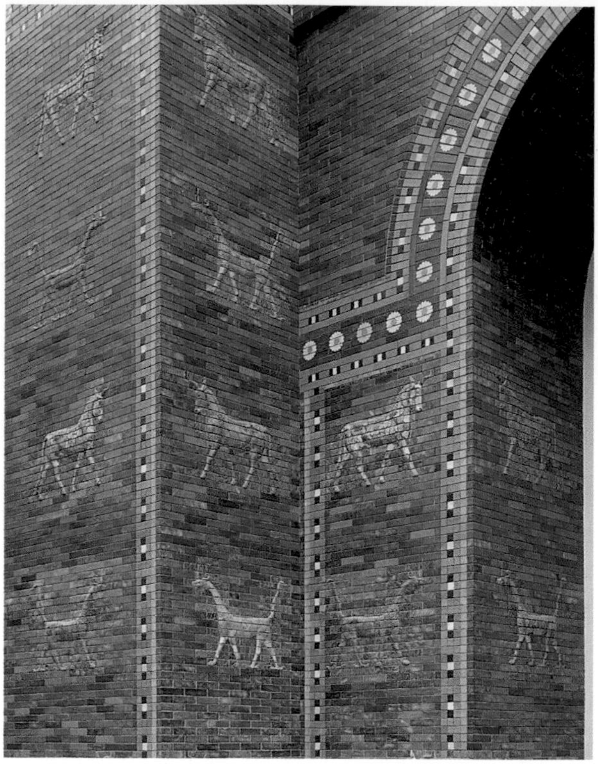

meagre population remained, perpetuating the same pottery styles as formerly used.

Nevertheless, as the Bible record also makes clear, those who were taken to Babylon represented the highest-born and the most intellectual of their time. Their spiritual and literary calibre is very evident from what we glean of them Biblically during the period of the Babylonian Exile. Thus, from a 'looking back' passage in the book of Zechariah, who wrote *c*.520-517 BC, we learn that they imposed five annual fast days upon themselves.[2] This was obviously an attempt to appease Yahweh after the punishment he had inflicted upon them, as they saw it, for the Canaanitic monarchies who had so displeased him. The Biblical book of Lamentations most likely represents their required reading on those fast days, vividly recollecting the privations of besieged Jerusalem: 'My priests and my elders expired in the city as they searched for food to keep themselves alive' (Lamentations 1:19). It also personalises the city's humiliation, using almost identical imagery to that which Christians would later associate with Jesus's sufferings:

The Ishtar Gate was one of Babylon's eight gates with which the Judahite would have become familiar. It has been reassembled in the State Museum, Berlin.

Look, Yahweh and consider
how despised I am!
All you who pass this way
look and see
is any sorrow like the sorrow
inflicted on me . . . ? (Lamentations 1:12)

Although the historical *nabi* called Isaiah lived in the reign of Hezekiah, and most likely authored the first thirty-nine chapters of the Biblical book bearing his name, it is also quite obvious from the Biblical book that Isaiah's next sixteen chapters, and in particular its four famous Suffering Servant passages, must have been written around the period of the Babylonian captivity. And the author must have been someone from the same school as the Lamentations author:

I have not resisted
I have not turned away
I have offered my back to those who struck me
my cheeks to those
who plucked my beard
I have not turned my face away
from insult and spitting. (Isaiah 50:5,6)

Particularly evocative is a further 'revelation of Yahweh' extract from the Isaiah passages written at this time. Some five centuries into the future, Galilee's best-known son would see it as pertaining to himself:

Like a sapling he grew up . . .
Like a root in arid ground

He had no form or charm to attract us
No beauty to win our hearts
He was despised, the lowest of men
A man of sorrows, familiar with suffering
One from whom, as it were,
We averted our gaze
Despised, for whom we had no regard
Yet ours were the sufferings
He was bearing
Ours the sorrows he was carrying . . .
Ill-treated and afflicted,
He never opened his mouth,
Like a lamb led to the slaughter-house . . .
He was given a grave with the wicked,
And his tomb with the rich. (Isaiah 53:2-9)

Clearly, Psalm 137 must also be attributed to this period. Unmistakably set in Babylon, it must have been added to the already extant psalms that the exiles had brought with them from their homeland:

By the rivers of Babylon
We sat and wept
At the memory of Zion . . .

If I forget you, O Jerusalem[3]
May my right hand wither!
May my tongue remain stuck to my palate
If I do not keep you in mind.

Yet life during the Exile was not necessarily all wailing and gnashing of teeth. Despite or because of having been among the first to be exiled, the priest-*nabi* Ezekiel was able, in his famous vision of the Valley of Dry Bones, to look forward to a resurrection of 'Jacob's captives' in the form of a return to their land. Later in his book, at a moment he recorded as 'fourteen years to the day' after Jerusalem's fall, he described how he was 'shown' a vision of the Jerusalem Temple rebuilt. He was able to relate its exact specifications down to the tiniest detail (Ezekiel 40-44).

Under Amel-Marduk, who succeeded Nebuchadnezzar *c.*562 BC, Babylonian attitudes towards their captives softened, as acknowledged even by the Judahites themselves. According to the very last verses of 2 Kings, unmistakably written during this period, Amel-Marduk released the Judahite King Jehoiachin after thirty-seven years of imprisonment, treating him 'with kindness' and allotting him 'a seat above those of the other kings who were with him in Babylon', also guaranteeing his daily upkeep 'for the rest of his life'. When the historically-minded Nabonidus succeeded to the Babylonian throne five years later, one of his pet projects was restoring Ur's ancient ziggurat and initiating a lot of copying of ancient archives. Although despised by many native Babylonians, this task may well have provided some not too uncongenial employment for the more historically-minded among the exiled Judahites.

Even so, the Lamentations author could not hide his longing for the day when the Babylonians might receive, in their turn, the same sort of sufferings that had been inflicted on them:

Daughter of Babel, doomed to destruction
A blessing on anyone who treats you as you treated us . . .
Treat them [the Babylonians] as you have treated me
For all my crimes. (Lamentations 1:22)

Accordingly, there can be no doubting the Judahite delight in the events of 539 BC. By this time, Babylonian military might had lost much of its former edge. In that year, Cyrus the Great, King of Persia, having previously eliminated first the Medes, then the Lydians, walked into Babylon virtually unopposed. After that, not only did he behave more magnanimously towards the Babylonians than they had ever behaved towards the peoples they conquered, but he also promised liberty and renewal to those same conquered peoples. With typically Persian religious syncretism and tolerance, Cyrus ascribed his victory to the Babylonian god Marduk (counterpart of the Canaanites' Baal). On a cuneiform cylinder preserved in London's British Museum, he declared:

> I entered Babylon as a friend, and . . . established my royal residence in the palace of the princes amid jubilation and rejoicing . . . My numerous troops walked around Babylon in peace. I did not allow anybody to terrorise . . . With regard to the inhabitants of Babylon . . . I improved their dilapidated housing, thus eliminating their main grievances . . . I [also] restored to the cities on the other side of the Tigris their hitherto long-ruined temples together with the images [of deities] they had contained and arranged permanent new buildings for them. I also gathered up their one-time inhabitants and returned them to their homelands.[4]

It was not uncommon for conquering kings to make promises of this kind, and similar examples survive from as far back as the 3rd millennium BC. The difference in Cyrus's case was that he seems genuinely to have meant these things. The Biblical book of Ezra begins with an account of him not only encouraging the Judahite exiles to go back to their homeland, but even unstintingly handing back to them all the Temple's precious gold and silver vessels that Nebuchadnezzar had looted:

> The inventory was as follows: thirty golden bowls for offerings; one thousand and twenty-nine silver bowls for offerings; thirty golden bowls; four hundred and ten silver bowls; one thousand other vessels. In all, five thousand four hundred vessels of gold and silver. (Ezra 1:7-11)

A clay cylinder, found at Babylon, details King Cyrus of Persia's munificence to those peoples previously subjugated by the Babylonians.

Intriguingly, the Ark was not included in this inventory. Even more intriguingly, no one at the time asked why. Since no accusation was levelled either at the Babylonians for destroying it, or at the Persians for withholding it, the only reasonable inference is that it had already disappeared before either of these conquests. All of this tends to support, rather than diminish, Graham Hancock's case that the Ark was spirited away to the Elephantine Temple at Aswan, perhaps as far back as the time of Manasseh.

Whatever the answer, only a little less puzzling is what we are *not* told of the old Judahite monarchy's fate at this time. As noted earlier, King Jehoiachin, a mere eighteen-year-old when the Babylonians captured him in 598, had spent the subsequent thirty-seven years in prison, then whatever remained of his life as a house guest of the Babylonian court. Although we are nowhere told when he died, this must have been before Cyrus's takeover of Babylon, because there is no record that Jehoiachin took part in any subsequent return to Jerusalem. Instead, it was two men of the house of David – Sheshbazzar and Zerubbabel – who reportedly led the exiles back.

In fact, a later Biblical compiler seems to have muddled two lists of returnees from Babylon: one dating from the reign of Cyrus, the other more than a hundred years later in the reign of Artaxerxes. Since Zerubbabel features in the latter list he probably belonged to Artaxerxes' time, while Sheshbazzar was the 'blueblood' contemporary of Cyrus. In any case, these 'royals' were given such scant attention that the inference has to be that the monarchy, whether Israelite or Judahite, had lost most, if not all, of its former allure.

Indeed, nearly everything to do with the first wave of exiles returning from Babylon seems to have been low key. Although we are told that one of their first ambitions was to erect an altar to Yahweh on 'its old site', fear of 'the people of the country' apparently hampered them (Ezra 3:3). This suggests that those who had stayed behind did not necessarily welcome their return.

Certainly, the incumbent Jerusalemites were offended when the returnees spurned their offer to help to rebuild the Temple on the grounds that those who had stayed behind were not theologically pure enough. These wrote to Cyrus's successors warning that if Jerusalem ever was rebuilt, the returning grandees would almost inevitably try to break away from the empire and set up on their own. From these same embittered non-exiles the so-called Samaritans sprang. They created a rival Yahwist Temple on Mount Gerizim, the sister mountain to Mount Ebal, flanking Shechem/Nablus, and followed slightly differing versions of the Five Books of Moses. Five centuries later, when the Galilean Jesus told his famous parable of the 'good' Samaritan, the deep indignation aroused by the very concept of a 'good' Samaritan was founded on this same disaffection.

Another even more volatile source of local strife was the Edomites. They had moved into land that had been Judahite before Jerusalem's fall and had prospered. They had also built a capital at Maresha, just 4 miles to the north-east of Lachish. They had no inclination to relinquish any of their hard-won territory. As 'Idumeans', the new name by which they were known in this region, they would provoke hatred every bit as strong as that for the Samaritans.

Because of such hostility, it was not until 516 BC, by which time Darius the Great (521-486 BC) had succeeded as emperor, and the Persian empire extended from North Africa to India, that the rebuilding of Jerusalem's Second Temple reached even its dedicatory phase. Reportedly, 'many of the older priests, Levites and heads of families, who had seen the first Temple, wept very loudly when the new foundations were laid before their eyes' (Ezra 3:12). As previously, this Second Temple had a high priest of the Aaronid line. But as a passage in the later Talmud tells us[5], the new version had no Ark, nor the winged sphinxes that had protected the Ark, nor the Urim and Thummim that had formerly been used for oracular purposes.

In the event, several decades went by with very little further progress. Jerusalem remained a backwater place, in sharp contrast to the cities of the Mediterranean coast where, with Persian encouragement, the Canaanite/Phoenicians seem to have flourished once more. At formerly Philistine Ashkelon, which had been so savagely destroyed by the Babylonians, as well as at Dor to the north, the Persian period is represented archaeologically by occupational levels that are between 6 and 10 feet thick. They are replete with Phoenician inscriptions and pottery.[6] Inland, by contrast, in the province that the Persians knew as Yehud (i.e. Judah), the Persian-period archaeological strata have been described as 'very thin if not ephemeral'.[7]

All this, however, was about to change. It is clear that by the second half of the 5th century BC, those of Judahite descent, who had not returned to Jerusalem but had stayed on in Babylon and other major centres of the Persian empire, were enjoying lives of considerable culture and prosperity. Babylon, as may be recalled, had been left intact when Cyrus conquered it, and continued as a flourishing metropolis even under his and

Persian soldiers, shown in a relief from the entrance to the royal palace at Susa. Troops such as this reportedly accompanied Nehemiah on his mission back to then Persian-controlled Jerusalem.

his successors' rule. There is every reason to believe that the antiquarian interests of its last Babylonian king, Nabonidus, as well as the advanced religious and social attitudes of the current Persian overlords, profoundly influenced those of Judahite origins who were socially well-placed within this milieu.

Certainly, by the time the second wave of people of Judahite ancestry made their return in the mid-5th century BC, some among them had used the time of Babylonian captivity to do major work in codifying their historical past. It was this that fired them to return to the land of their ancestors, and to do all the right things for the Temple and for Jerusalem in general.

Most particularly, in 445 BC, during the reign of Artaxerxes I (465-424 BC), a high-ranking official called Nehemiah, then resident at the Persian royal court at Susa, was told by fellow Judahites of Jerusalem's parlous state. He petitioned Artaxerxes to be allowed to return to his ancestral city to conduct major refurbishments, accompanied by a group of fellow-exiles with the appropriate skills to carry these out. As a trusted royal servant he was duly allowed to do so, and even granted 'an escort of army officers and cavalry' (Nehemiah 2:9) for the group's protection.

The Biblical account of this venture is vividly and authoritatively written in the first person, and includes much accurate topographical detail. It is thought to have been compiled from an actual memoir of Nehemiah's. Of his arrival in Jerusalem, he related:

> After I had been there three days, I got up during the night with a few other men . . . taking no animals with me other than my own mount. Under cover of darkness I went out through the Valley Gate towards the Dragon's Fountain as far as the Dung Gate, and examined the wall of Jerusalem where it was broken down and its gates burnt out. Then I crossed to the Fountain Gate and the King's Pool, but it was impassable to my mount. So I went up the Valley in the dark, examining the wall . . . then went in again through the Valley Gate . . . without the officials knowing where I had gone or what I had been doing. (Nehemiah 2:11-16)

This reconnoitre duly completed, Nehemiah called a meeting of all the 'priests, the nobles, the officials and others', none of whom so far knew anything about the purpose of his mission. He explained to them, in his words, how 'the kindly hand of my God had been over me, and the words which the king had said to me'. He then urged upon them the need to 'rebuild the walls of Jerusalem and put an end to our humiliating position' (Nehemiah 2:17-18).

Nehemiah gained the city elders' trust and support for this rebuilding. The Biblical book carrying his name then provides an impressively detailed account of how this work was apportioned out section by section, among different groups of the existing citizens and those he had brought with him:

> Eliashib the high priest with his brother priests . . . rebuilt the Sheep Gate . . . and proceeded as far as the Tower of the Hundred and the Tower of Hananel . . . The sons of Ha-Senah rebuilt the Fish Gate . . . Joiada . . . And Meshullam . . . repaired the gate of the New Quarter . . . Malchiah . . . and Hashub . . . repaired . . . as far as the Furnace Tower/(Tower of the Ovens) . . . Hanun and the inhabitants of Zanoah repaired the Valley Gate . . . Malchijah . . . repaired the Dung Gate . . . Shallum . . . repaired the Fountain Gate . . . also the wall of the Pool of Siloah, adjoining the king's garden, as far as the steps going down from the City of David. After him, Nehemiah . . . carried out repairs from a point opposite the Davidic Tombs to the artificial pool and the House of the Champions . . . Palal . . . carried out repairs in front of the Angle and the Tower projecting from the king's Upper Palace by the Court of the Guard and after him Pedaiah . . . carried out repairs to a point by the Water Gate to the east and the Projecting Tower. After him the men of Tekoa repaired another section in front of the Great Projecting

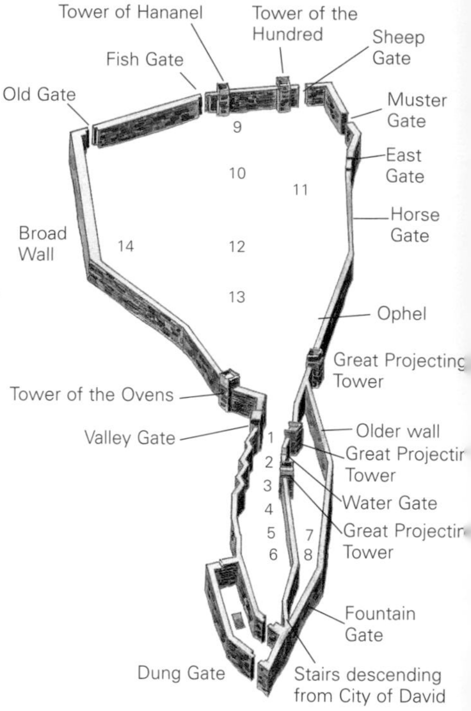

1 King's Upper Palace 2 Azariah's house
3 Benjamin and Hashub's house
4 Eliashib's house 5 Climb to armoury
6 Champion's house 7 Artificial pool
8 Davidic tombs 9 Upper chamber of the corner 10 Hall of Temple slaves and merchants 11 Meshullam's chamber
12 Zadok's house 13 Priests' houses
14 Jedaiah's house

The Jerusalem Nehemiah knew. In the foreground is the area of present-day Jerusalem occupied in Nehemiah's time. The map shows the principal topographical features mentioned by Nehemiah. Note the Davidic tombs, matching the location of those featured on pages 116-7.

> Tower as far as the wall of the Ophel. From the Horse Gate onwards repairs were carried out by the priests . . . Malchijah . . . repaired as far as the Hall of the Temple slaves and merchants, in front of the Muster Gate, as far as the upper room at the corner. And between the upper room and the Sheep Gate repairs were carried out by the goldsmiths and the merchants.
> (Nehemiah 3:1-32)

One particularly important feature of this account is that it starts and finishes with the Sheep Gate. It is self-evidently a description of Jerusalem's perimeter as this existed, albeit in ruin, *c.*440 BC. As a result, it is possible to trace almost exactly on present-day Jerusalem where each feature would have been. By referring back to Nehemiah's original night-time reconnoitre, we can even determine that he must have begun this from the western side of the city, moving southwards from the Valley Gate down to the Dung Gate. Then having reached the walls' southernmost point, he proceeded northwards to Fountain Gate. After this he found the way impassable because of the amount of rubble.

Intriguingly, this rubble appears to have marked the point where, in 587 BC, the resistance to the Babylonians had been greatest. It lay in the environs of the so-called Great Projecting Tower and the Water Gate, which as Nehemiah's account makes clear, opened into the 'king's Upper Palace'. More than a century of archaeological excavations of this area, from Charles Warren in 1867 through to ongoing work by Eilat Mazar, have progressively revealed at this location a large gate-complex comprising two towers, with an inner gate-house behind these. In Eilat Mazar's opinion, this complex is most likely the same as Nehemiah's Water Gate, which once opened into the 'king's Upper Palace' (Nehemiah 3:25).[8]

According to Nehemiah's Biblical account, the restoration work took only fifty-two days. The feat was all the more impressive since the workers were repeatedly harassed by hostile surrounding peoples, including 'the Arabs, the Ammonites and the Ashdodites'. It was in all these peoples' interests for Jerusalem to remain as defenceless as it had been since Nebuchadnezzar. At Nehemiah's urging, the repairers reportedly kept their weapons close to hand at all times, enabling them to rally instantly whenever Nehemiah's personally-blown trumpet-call alerted them to a fresh raid. In Nehemiah's own words:

> Neither I, nor my brothers, nor my attendants, nor my bodyguards, ever took off our clothes; each one kept his spear in his right hand. (Nehemiah 4:17)

This account of how one inspired leader gave Jerusalem's citizens new self-respect, and set about rebuilding the city after the ruin Nebuchadnezzar had inflicted upon it, must be regarded as one of the most historically authoritative books in the Bible. However, from the Biblical point of view, the story of the book of Nehemiah is also inextricably linked with the name of another person of almost equally heroic stature: Ezra.

For just as Artaxerxes had given Nehemiah the authority and resources to rebuild Jerusalem's physical fabric, so Ezra, Biblically described as a priest, scribe and direct descendant of Aaron (Ezra 7:5), was accorded equivalent spiritual authority. He was provided with 'a number of Israelites, priests, Levites, singers, gate-keepers and temple slaves' to employ as functionaries, with gold and silver for sacrifices, and with a royal warrant authorising him to teach 'the *Torah* of your God . . . to those who do not know it'. He could impose fines, imprisonment and even death on those who transgressed.

So what was it that Ezra, in his turn, accomplished? According to the American Biblical scholar Richard Elliot Friedman, Ezra had brought together even before arriving in Jerusalem a now very substantial collection of 'scriptural' material. This included the earlier combined Yahweh (J) and El (E) strands from which Genesis and Exodus were composed, the third 'Priestly' strand of the same books which had emerged in the days of Hezekiah, the lost 'Book of Generations' (from which all the King James Bible's famous 'begat' passages come), and a document listing the places where the Israelites stopped in the wilderness. All of these he had woven into a coherent whole, adding only a few elements important to his own day. Also, to the Five Books of Moses – Genesis, Exodus, Leviticus, Numbers and ending in our present book of Deuteronomy – he added the Deuteronomistic History comprising, besides Deuteronomy itself, the books of Joshua, Judges, 1 and 2 Samuel and 1 and 2 Kings. Therefore, whatever Biblical books may or may not have been extant before Ezra's time, around 440 BC something closely resembling a major portion of our present Bibles had been 'canonised' by him and set in place.

No less interesting is a special 'convention' Ezra arranged. On what was already a holy day in the seventh month (our September/October), he assembled all the 'men, women and children old enough to understand' in front of Jerusalem's Water Gate, and there read to them from a dais 'the Book of the *Torah* of Moses which Yahweh had prescribed for Israel' (Nehemiah 8:1-8). In the history of how the Bible came to us, this was one of *the* great moments, recognised as such even in Ezra's time. The people, having received this reading with great emotion, were then encouraged to go away and celebrate by feasting to their hearts' content.

The following day, the heads of families were invited to read for themselves from 'the words of the *Torah* . . . that Yahweh had prescribed through Moses'. This feast day became incorporated in the Jewish calendar as the feast of Succoth (Shelters or Tabernacles), commemorating the time during the Exodus wilderness years when the Israelites had been obliged to 'live in shelters'. The institution of the feast in Ezra's time is evident from information in the book of Nehemiah that this rite had not been observed 'from the days of Joshua . . . till that day' (Nehemiah 8:17). The requirements of our present Bible's Leviticus 23:33-44 must, therefore, have been brand new in Ezra's time. This part of Leviticus, at least, had only just been put together, arguably by none other than Ezra himself.

Scholars will no doubt argue for many decades to come about how much of the Bible Ezra may personally have invented while he was in Babylon, and how many ancient and original materials he already had to hand from which to make an intelligent compilation. It is, however, very apparent that this historic assembly of the people before the Water Gate marked the moment when the Jewish religion as we know it today came into being. From now on, and for the very first time in the course of our study, we can legitimately call these people 'Jews'.

This depiction, from the west wall of the synagogue at Dura-Europos, is thought by some to be of Ezra, who effectively brought what we now know as the Hebrew Bible, or Old Testament, into being.

It is also not too difficult for us to understand how Nehemiah and Ezra were able to impose themselves so strongly at this time, in a way that even kings such as Hezekiah and Josiah had failed to do. After all, they were governors on Artaxerxes' behalf of the province the Persians termed 'Yehud' – Judaea. The pervasiveness of the power they represented is evident from the many jars with stamp impressions bearing this name that turn up at sites excavated in the formerly Judahite region. Also, because of Ezra's background as an Aaronid priest, his high ranking within the Persian empire would have had the effect of enhancing the Jerusalem priesthood's own status.

There is eloquent archaeological evidence of how strongly Nehemiah and Ezra imposed themselves. At site after site to which the exiles returned during the post-Exilic period, the Astarte/Asherah-type figurines that had been so popular during the previous centuries are simply not found at the Persian-period levels, and are never heard of again. Seemingly, the formerly powerful Canaanitic religion did not just wither away and die out throughout 'Jewish' territories. It was positively made to die, despite the Persian overlords' general tolerance. Thus, when excavating at Tel Dor on the Mediterranean coast, the Israeli archaeologist Ephraim Stern found two pits where all such figurines had been collected and thrown at what seems to have been the end of the 5th century BC, i.e. Ezra and Nehemiah's time. This was apparently a formal ritual burial of the old religion, following which such figurines disappeared, except in areas, such as Idumea, Philistia, Phoenicia and Galilee, that were still predominantly controlled by pagans.[9]

In the same way, the Jerusalem Temple, which was now the sole recognised location for offering sacrifices, went from strength to strength, whereas the *bamah*, or 'high place', sanctuaries formerly used for public sacrifices, whether Yahwist or Canaanitic, disappeared. The only exceptions were the Samaritan temple on Mount Gerizim, whose adherents remained in schism with the rest of the Jewish world, and the Yahwist temple at Elephantine, which Egyptian priests of the god Khnum destroyed in 410 BC. The island's Jewish population left, seemingly for Ethiopia, shortly afterwards.

Not everything that Nehemiah and Ezra introduced was received with equanimity. Their ban on Jews intermarrying with other races and taking foreign wives, as both David and Solomon had done, definitely provoked dissent. Some of the dissenters even turned to the Samaritans.

However, in the process by which the old Yahwist religion became transformed into today's Judaism, there was no more seminal time than this. The enlightened attitudes of Nehemiah and Ezra's Persian masters are not to be underestimated in this context, nor the way in which these may have subtly influenced the transformation.

Thus, we may recall how the book of Genesis's Creation story has some unmistakably Persian touches. Even the wrathful old Yahweh himself seems to have undergone a radical change of character, arguably under the same influences. Throughout much of the earlier books of the Old Testament, he featured as an extremely angry divinity. Even the book of Nahum, theoretically written only a century and a half before Ezra, begins with the words:

> Yahweh is a jealous
> and vengeful God
> Yahweh takes vengeance
> He is rich in wrath. (Nahum 1:2)

Yet of Ezra we are told that 'the *kindly* hand of God was over him' (Ezra 7:9), recalling Nehemiah's first-hand account of the speech he delivered to the Jerusalemites: 'I told them how the *kindly* hand of my God had been over me' (Nehemiah 2:18). Likewise, only a few verses into Nehemiah's book, he is represented as speaking specifically of Yahweh as 'the great and awe-inspiring God who keeps a covenant of faithful *love* with those who love him and obey his commandments' (Nehemiah 1:5). It is true that in our present Bibles these words appear in Exodus 20:6, linked to Moses' Ten Commandments. But it is also hard to avoid the impression that they are out of kilter with most of the early Biblical Yahweh's others actions and sentiments. Like much else, they may derive from some editing at this Persian period.

It is apparent, then, that from the time of Ezra onwards, the people we can now call Jews had already taken on the characteristics which separate them from other peoples right up to the present day. They now regulated themselves not to intermarry with other peoples. Instead of their worshipping many gods, mostly linked to the local city, as other people did, they had their one Yahweh, whom they regarded as omnipresent everywhere. They already had their prohibitions on eating certain kinds of food, and they set aside certain days as holy, on which they would refrain from normal work.

One fact greatly increased the chance of these things achieving permanence. So far as we can tell from the sparse surviving information, the tolerant Persian period seems to have been an unusually settled one for the people newly united in their religion. It was no coincidence that in the eyes of the editors who assembled our Bibles, it was the Persians, almost alone of all their foreign neighbours, who are consistently represented in a favourable light.

But even the benevolent Persian Empire could offer no *real* permanence. For once again the world of the Near East was about to undergo a dramatic political change.

16

WHEN PRIESTS FOUGHT AND RULED

A SUPERB MOSAIC discovered at Pompeii (see overleaf) has probably the most masterly depiction of a battle scene to survive from the ancient world. In the right-hand foreground, an ornate chariot with huge wheels, drawn by two magnificent black horses, whirls in retreat, while its obviously regal, Eastern-looking commander looks back in fear and bewilderment. To the scene's left, we see where his anguished eyes are directed. A clean-shaven young European, bare-headed, tousle-haired and wearing a Medusa-decorated breast-plate, is determinedly urging forward his spirited horse (detail, right). Although the mosaic carries no inscription, the battle is almost certainly Issus, the man in retreat Darius III, King of Persia, and the determined young European Alexander the Great.

At the Battles of Issus and Gaugamela in 333 BC, Alexander so resoundingly defeated Darius and his Persians that shortly afterwards the recently repatriated Jews, along with many other subject peoples, became part of a new, even larger empire, now controlled by Greeks. Although Alexander himself was dead within ten years, his generals divided up his conquests among them. The Persian province of Yehud, formerly Judah, fell to the able and energetic Ptolemy Soter as part of a territory ruled from Egypt.

In the canonical Bibles used by both Jews and Protestants, this period goes essentially unchronicled. Yet from other, mainly historical, sources we know that it was a particularly formative time, when the Jewish way of life and worship, which had been so recently restored to the country of its roots, grew an unexpected, fresh and prolific shoot in Greek Egypt.

Before his death, Alexander the Great had asked a highly imaginative young architect, Deinocrates, to design a great new capital bearing his name on the site of the former Egyptian city of Rhacotis in the Nile Delta. So successful was this Alexandria that it swiftly became the Mediterranean's busiest international entrepôt, its warehouses bulging with goods from all parts of the world. When Ptolemy Soter took it over, he set out to exploit its potential yet more fully, and recruited thousands of able Jews from Yehud to help him with this task. That Ptolemy's 'recruitment' involved at least a degree of coercion is evident from the excavations

Victorious Alexander. Detail from the Pompeii mosaic depicting the Battle of Issus (see overleaf).

at the former Philistine seaport Ashkelon where archaeologists have found a clear destruction layer dating to his time.[1] However, the Jews thus relocated were soon not only prospering, but also multiplying.

Before long, Alexandria had the world's largest expatriate Jewish colony. As a result, many Alexandrian Jews, together with similar Jewish expatriates in other parts of the new Greek empire, found themselves growing up in a milieu where the Ezra-prescribed Jewish religion and scriptures dominated their lives, but their everyday spoken language was Greek, now the new lingua franca. It may have been as early as the reign of Ptolemy II Philadelphus (284-246 BC) that Alexandria's Jews felt impelled to initiate their *Torah*'s translation into Greek. They commissioned what became known as the Septuagint (a variant upon the Greek word for 'seventy'), after the seventy-two Jewish scholars said to have been brought

Persia's Darius III wheels in flight before Alexander the Great's advance. As a result of Darius's defeat, the Persian province of Yehud passed to Greek rule.

from Jerusalem to work on it. Although the Septuagint's development was probably more extended than the stories of its origin suggest, one thing is certain. As in Babylon, the Alexandrian Jews' geographical distance from Jerusalem strengthened their devotion to their scriptures and heritage. Thus, they prayed facing the direction of Jerusalem, they punctiliously paid a requisite half-shekel a year for the Jerusalem Temple's upkeep, and they regularly journeyed to Jerusalem to offer up an animal sacrifice, much as today's Moslems visit Mecca.

As for the Jews still in Jerusalem, this period of very relaxed hegemony from Greek-controlled Egypt seems to have been something of a golden age. Arguably, our best witness to this is a book that appears in the Bibles of Roman Catholics and Eastern Orthodox, but not those of Jews or Protestants, as Ecclesiasticus, or the Wisdom of Ben Sira.

According to this book's introduction, its original author 'Jesus [or Joshua] Ben Sira Eleazar of Jerusalem'[2], had 'long devoted himself to the reading of the *Torah*, the *nabiim*

and other books of the fathers'[3]. This information is provided by his grandson, apparently living in Egypt in the 38th year of Ptolemy Euergetes[4], i.e. 132 BC. The grandson tells us that he is translating into Greek reflections by his grandfather that were 'originally written in Hebrew'.

We have good grounds for trusting that a Hebrew original really did exist, from which Ben Sira's Egypt-based grandson would have made his later translation. In 1896, two Scottish-born twins, Agnes Lewis and Margaret Gibson, returned to Cambridge from collecting ancient manuscripts around the Near East. One scrap they had obtained in Cairo was quickly and enthusiastically identified by their Jewish scholar friend Solomon Schechter as coming from Ecclesiasticus and written in Hebrew.[5] It was, of course, far too much to hope that this scrap was Ben Sira's original. The handwriting showed that it dated from around the 11th century AD, and sleuthing by Schechter eventually traced its origins to a Cairo synagogue's *genizah*, or repository, of this period. However, during

the 1960s further Hebrew-language scraps from Ecclesiasticus came to light both among the Dead Sea Scrolls and from Masada. These were reliably datable to the 1st century BC, so that Ecclesiasticus's composition sometime before Ben Sira's grandson's lifetime in the mid-2nd century BC could hardly be doubted.

Although Ben Sira's work may not be among the most original or compelling of Biblical books, it does have great value in telling us of the Jewish religion in Jerusalem at the time when he lived. While giving a potted history of his people, Ben Sira makes it clear, exactly as the Deuteronomistic History does, that his people's kings, 'apart from David, Hezekiah and Josiah', all 'heaped wrong on wrong' (Ecclesiasticus 49:4). As a 3rd-century BC resident of Jerusalem, he referred knowingly and authoritatively to Hezekiah's engineering achievements: 'Hezekiah fortified his city and laid on a water-supply inside it; with iron he tunnelled through the rock and constructed storage tanks' (Ecclesiasticus 48:17). Of Josiah he remarked: 'He took the right course, of converting the people, he rooted out the iniquitous abominations' (Ecclesiasticus 49:3). With the exception of the book of Daniel – for reasons that will later become apparent – he refers to every book of the Hebrew Bible, providing crucial confirmation that its canon had already been essentially completed by his time.

Beneath the Temple Mount lies an underground water cistern known as the Great Sea, seen here in a 19th-century painting by William Simpson. This may have been the 'reservoir as huge as the sea' described by Ecclesiasticus's author Jesus Ben Sira.

In determining exactly when he lived, a crucial clue is that he ends his potted history of 'our ancestors in their successive generations' with a clearly authoritative first-hand account of 'the High Priest Simon, son of Onias'. This figure is identifiable as the Simon II, son of Onias III, historically known to have been High Priest between around 220 and 195 BC. In the absence of any Jewish king, he was the Jerusalem-based Jewish people's highest-ranking leader below the incumbent Ptolemy.

According to Ben Sira, this Simon the High Priest was a vigorous builder who 'repaired the Temple during his lifetime and in his day fortified the sanctuary. He laid the foundations of double depth, the high buttresses of the Temple precincts. In his day the pool was excavated, a reservoir as huge as the sea' (Ecclesiasticus 50:1-3). Intriguingly, beneath the Temple Mount is a massive ancient underground water cistern, known to this day as the Great Sea. Frustratingly inaccessible to archaeologists, as a result of Moslem religious and political sensitivities, this is conceivably the very reservoir that was dug during Simon son of Onias's time.

With regard to Simon son of Onias's performance of his public duties as High Priest,

which Ben Sira self-evidently witnessed and in which he may have assisted in some capacity, the picture painted is one of great magnificence:

> How spendid he was . . . when he emerged from the curtained shrine . . . like fire and incense in the censer, like a massive golden vessel encrusted with every kind of precious stone . . . when he took his ceremonial robe and put on his magnificent ornaments, when he went up to the holy altar and filled the sanctuary precincts with his grandeur . . . when all the sons of Aaron [i.e. the Temple priests] in their glory, with the offerings of the Lord in their hands, stood before the whole assembly of Israel.' (Ecclesiasticus 50:5-13)

Ben Sira likewise waxed lyrical about the music which accompanied such ceremonial:

> Then the sons of Aaron would shout and blow their metal trumpets, making a mighty sound ring out as a reminder before the Most High, and immediately the people all together would fall on their faces to the ground in adoration of their Lord . . . and with the cantors chanting their hymns of praise. Sweet was the melody of these voices. (Ecclesiasticus 50:16-18)

Fascinatingly, archaeological evidence for these trumpets came to light in 1969 at the foot of the south-western wall of the Temple Mount. An incomplete inscription (see overleaf) was found on a large piece of balustrade, which must once have been at the top of the same wall. It reads 'to the place of the trumpeting', and while it dates from the time of the later King Herod the Great's aggrandisements of the Temple, it makes clear that trumpeting was integrally associated with Temple ceremonial.

An air of worldly-wise contentment pervades Ben Sira's writings. Although he apparently had his moments of stress, he also had the fortune to live in a comparatively settled period, certainly when compared with what had gone before and with what would come after. He was probably still alive in 198 BC, when the Ptolemy of the time was defeated in battle by his Seleucid rival, Antiochus III of Syria. One result of this was that Yehud passed from Egypt-based Greek to Syrian-based Greek control. But even this seems initially to have had comparatively little effect on the local Jews' everyday life.

It would be a different matter, however, in 175 BC, by which time Ben Sira had almost certainly died, when Antiochus IV Epiphanes succeeded to the Seleucid throne. Our Biblical source, albeit one as 'apocryphal' as Ecclesiasticus, now becomes the books of 1 and 2 Maccabees. Like Ben Sira's, these two books were rejected for the Jewish Bible canon (and therefore subsequently for the Protestant one), but were included in the Roman Catholic and Eastern Orthodox Bibles. The great value of these Maccabees books is that they are replete with historical detail much of which can be checked out point for point from other ancient sources, such as the works of the highly respected 1st-century AD Jewish historian Josephus.

By all accounts, Antiochus Epiphanes, who had himself portrayed with Alexander the Great-like good looks on his coins, had his sights set on making Greek culture in all its aspects universal throughout his empire. One of his first moves in this direction might have seemed innocent enough. He encouraged a faction of pro-Greek Jews to build a gymnasium in Jerusalem. However, this was far more divisive than the provision of a recreation centre might suggest. The Greek gymnasium was a well-appointed all-male social club where, while the elders watched and talked politics, the younger bloods performed their exercises, as Greek custom required, stark naked. For the culturally prudish Jews, this was not only embarrassing in itself, but their all too conspicuous circumcisions made it doubly so. This impelled some to undergo a painful surgical procedure to disguise the unsightliness, something that Ben Sira, had he been alive at the time, would certainly have found contrary to the spirit of his beloved *Torah*.

An inscription reading 'To the place of the Trumpeting' was discovered on a wall of the Temple Mount (top). The drawing (above) reconstructs the Temple balustrade where the inscription was located.

Then, in 169 BC, Antiochus used the pretext of quelling a disturbance to enter Jerusalem in overwhelming strength. Reportedly, he strode arrogantly into the Temple that High Priest Simon, son of Onias, had so recently embellished. He did not even respect the sanctity of its inner sanctuary. He flagrantly looted the sanctuary, removing 'the golden altar and the lamp-stand for the light with all its fittings, together with the table for the loaves of permanent offering, the libation vessels, the cups, the golden censers, the veil, the crowns and the golden decoration' (1 Maccabees 1:21-23). Two years later, his general Apollonius followed this up by pillaging Jerusalem itself, destroying many of its houses.

Next, on the pretext of refortifying Jerusalem, Antiochus constructed a near-impregnable fortress called the Akra, in which he installed a garrison looking out directly onto the Temple, and able to control anything in its vicinity. The intention behind this became all too clear in the winter of 167 BC, when he decreed that from thenceforth the Temple should be dedicated to the Greek god Zeus. It would have Zeus's statue erected in it, pigs would be sacrificed on its altar, and all normal Jewish-style sacrificial procedures would be prohibited. He further forbade the possession of copies of the *Torah*, and banned both circumcision and observance of the Sabbath day, imposing the death penalty on anyone who flouted these injunctions. In the case of women who insisted on their sons being circumcised, he ordered that they should be executed 'with their babies hung round their necks'.

Nothing could have been more calculated to incite Jewish fury, yet militarily Antiochus was so strong that outright insurrection was suicidal. Accordingly, subtler forms of protest had to be used. One was allegory, finding its greatest expression in the works of a brilliant but otherwise unknown contemporary publicist, who wrote what we now know as the Biblical book of Daniel. The writer of Daniel ostensibly set his story in Babylon, with its culmination in the time of Nabonidus's hedonist son Belshazzar. But from a variety of historical clues, not least a scattering of Greek words, scholars are

generally agreed that the book's author wrote it around 167 BC, in direct reaction to Antiochus. He presented the issues of his present under the cover of those of the historical past, much as the crypto-Catholic Shakespeare would do in his history plays more than a millennium and a half later.

Looking into the far future, Daniel predicted, *nabi*-style, the coming of a mysterious 'Son of Man' who would appear on 'the clouds of heaven' and eventually create an everlasting kingdom of 'rule, honour and kingship' with 'all peoples, nations and languages . . . his servants' (Daniel 7:13-14). However, his chapter 11 contained 'prophecies' that were unerringly close to events actually happening in Antiochus's time. As for the book's central theme of God's kingdom being restored by a stone destroying a mighty statue, this inevitably recalled David's legendary toppling of Goliath with a stone. The Goliath in this instance was the so-offensive effigy of Zeus that Antiochus had erected in the Jerusalem Temple.

Antiochus IV Epiphanes styled himself on Alexander the Great and tried to impose Hellenistic culture upon the Jews.

But who might be the David, who dared to step out of line and present an overt physical challenge to the military might of Antiochus? One tactic initially attempted, with considerable heroism, was passive resistance. According to 1 Maccabees, a band of a thousand Jews, including women and children, 'went down to the desert' where they would live in total obedience to the *Torah* even if attacked on the Sabbath. They were followed, however, by 'a strong detachment' of the Seleucid forces. Deliberately choosing a Sabbath, the Seleucid troops slaughtered them all, even though their victims 'offered no opposition; not a stone was thrown, [and] there was no barricading of the hiding-places' (1 Maccabees 2:32-38).

This is one of the first occasions on which we hear of such extreme passive resistance by Jews. Inevitably, for some people at the time, the idea that you adhered so strictly to *Torah* Sabbath observance that you could not even defend your life seemed self-defeating. Since the High Priests had been Jerusalem's effective rulers before Antiochus, we should perhaps be not surprised that the first violent resistance came from one of this ilk.

According to 1 Maccabees, the priest in question was Mattathias of the House of Hasmon. In 167 BC, he killed a fellow Jew who was about to offer an animal sacrifice in a village outside Jerusalem, thus contravening Josiah's rule that made all such sacrifices exclusive to the Jerusalem Temple. Mattathias followed this up by assassinating the royal official who was officiating at the same ceremony. Then he fled with his five sons to that traditional refuge: the hills. Already elderly, he died not long after.

The Greek custom of naked exercising made any participating Jews, with their circumcisions, embarrassingly conspicuous.

Although minimalist scholars such as Philip Davies have suggested a certain improbability in this episode, there can be no doubt that Mattathias's sons full-bloodedly took up armed rebellion, making daring guerrilla attacks on any Seleucid troops they came across. Under the leadership of Judas (called Maccabeus, the Hammer, hence the books of Maccabees), they routed every Seleucid expedition sent against them so successfully that at last they were able to enter Jerusalem unopposed.

Only the garrison in the hated Akra continued to hold out against them, as it would do for decades to come.

They were less concerned about this garrison's sporadic attacks, than about the Temple which Antiochus had so arrogantly violated. As related in the first book of Maccabees:

> There they found the sanctuary deserted, the altar desecrated, the gates burnt down, and vegetation growing in the courts as it might in a wood or on some mountain, while the store-rooms were in ruins. They tore their garments and mourned bitterly . . . Judas then . . . selected priests who were blameless and zealous for the *Torah* to purify the sanctuary . . . They discussed what should be done about the altar of burnt offering which had been defiled, and very properly decided to pull it down, rather than later be embarrassed by it . . . They, therefore, deposited the stones in a suitable place on the hill of the Dwelling to await the appearance of a *nabi* who would give a ruling about them. (1 Maccabees 4:46)

It is a point of no little interest that, however much these Jews detested the pagan objects that had defiled their Temple, an accompanying deep-rooted superstition demanded that they should not destroy them out of hand. Just as hoards of Canaanite-type Asherah statuettes have been found carefully buried, so now we are told that the stones of the detested Greek altar were deposited 'in a suitable place'. The same thinking prevented them from destroying their own old and discarded scripture rolls. Instead, they shut them up in so-called *genizeh*, like the one in which Solomon Schechter found that the Hebrew Ecclesiasticus scrap had been kept.

Equally interesting is the information that there was apparently no one at this time who could speak for Yahweh in the manner that the *nabiim* of earlier centuries had done; hence the remark that they would 'await the appearance of a *nabi* who would give a ruling'. It is clear from this that although the book of Daniel probably dates from this time, and appears in our Bibles among the books of the so-called 'prophets', it was not the work of a *nabi* as such. To the contemporary mind, a new *nabi* was certainly expected, someone who would once again speak for Yahweh, but he had not come yet.

These issues aside, for Judas Maccabeus and his fellow rebels the important outcome was that they had gained the foothold in Jerusalem they needed. Despite repeated Seleucid attacks, they set about restoring all of the Temple that had fallen into ruin. They dedicated its new altar 'to the sound of hymns, zithers, lyres and cymbals', following which they indulged in eight days of celebrations, including the setting up of a new feast day. Judas was killed in battle with the Seleucids in 161 BC, after which his brother Jonathan took up the struggle in his stead. Jonathan tried diplomacy as a means of persuading the Seleucid monarchy to recognise him, and succeeded to the extent that they officially appointed him High Priest and governor of Jerusalem and its surrounds. However, a Seleucid general treacherously captured and killed him in 143 BC, whereupon his mantle passed to yet another brother, Simon, who without further reference to the Seleucids, took over the same roles.

According to 1 Maccabees, the Seleucid garrison had held out all this while in the Akra. Under Simon's rule, however, they were forced to surrender because they were unable to get food:

> . . . prevented as they were from coming out and going in to the countryside to buy and sell, [they] were in desperate need of food, and numbers of them were being carried off by starvation. They begged Simon to make peace with them, and he granted this, though he expelled them and purified the Akra from its pollutions. The Jews made their entry on the twenty-third day of

the second month in the year 171[6] [i.e. 141 BC] with acclamations and carrying palms . . . chanting hymns and canticles . . . (1 Maccabees 13:49-51)

It is from the later Jewish historian Josephus that we learn that Simon demolished the hated Akra. The first book of Maccabees supplements this with the information that Simon then 'fortified the Temple hill on the Akra side, and took up residence there with his men' (1 Maccabees 13:52).

With the Akra's fall, Jerusalem was properly returned to Jewish control for the first time since the Babylonians, and a formal council duly acclaimed Simon 'High Priest and General and Ruler of the Jews'. It is interesting that, although there must somewhere have been descendants of the House of David – as is evident from the subsequent surfacing of Jesus of Nazareth in Galilee – we hear nothing of their joining forces with the Hasmoneans, as Judas Maccabeus's dynasty was known. Nor do we hear of them intermarrying with the Hasmoneans, or of any other way in which they might have tried to win back power for themselves.

There is one possible reason for the absence of a movement of this kind. Simon Maccabeus, as the first of his line with real dynastic recognition, seems to have been highly popular. Thus, 1 Maccabees includes a hymn celebrating the way in which he had given his people back their national identity:

He [Simon] sought the good of his nation
and they were well pleased . . .
He took Joppa and made it a harbour
gaining access to the Mediterranean Isles
He enlarged the frontiers of his nation
keeping his mastery over the homeland . . .
He conquered Gezer, Beth-Zur and the Akra
ridding them of every impurity . . .
The people farmed their land in peace . . .
The elders at ease in the squares . . .
He strove to observe the *Torah*
and gave new splendour to the Temple
enriching it with many sacred vessels. (1 Maccabees 14:4-15)

The picture of Simon's rule, then, is one of renewed prosperity. It is also characterised by an evangelism for what we can now call the Jewish religion, free of the Canaanitic taint that had so often prevailed under Judah's House of David. Thus, of Simon's capture of Gezer, we are told that he first expelled the former inhabitants from the city, then 'purified the houses which contained idols . . . [then] settled in it people who observed the *Torah*' (1 Maccabees 13:47-8). As evidence of Simon's status as monarch in all but name, he issued coins, carefully conforming to the second commandment of Moses by omitting his likeness from them, even though such portraiture was the norm for most other coin issues of this time.

But how long would such a 'royal' priesthood, however competent militarily and administratively, be able to stay popular as rulers of the Jews? And how long would it be before a new superpower arose intent upon absorbing Yehud into its empire, just as the Assyrians, the Babylonians, the Persians and the Greeks had all done before? Even as Jesus Ben Sira's grandson was putting the finishing touches to his translation of his grandfather's words of wisdom – words clearly penned before anything of the Antiochus-Maccabee conflict had erupted – a new predator was in the wings, waiting to pounce.

17

TRUE TIME OF THE SCROLLS?

WITH THE WRITING of the book of Daniel, datable to around 167 BC, every book of the present-day Hebrew Bible, or Protestant Old Testament, had been completed. Yet with the exception of the 7th-century BC silver scrolls bearing the text from the book of Numbers, no Biblical manuscript, or even scrap of a manuscript, has survived that is datable to any time significantly earlier than the first half of the 2nd century BC. However, from this point onwards all at last begins to change, thanks to the discovery of the now world-famous Dead Sea Scrolls – though even with these, the task of dating them with any kind of exactness has been far from easy.

The first Dead Sea Scrolls were found in 1947 when a Bedouin boy minding goats in the Wadi Qumran, on the north-western edge of the Dead Sea, idly tossed a stone into a cave and heard some pottery breaking inside. Clambering into the cave to investigate, he and a companion discovered a number of rolls of decaying leather with writing on them. Some lay among the pieces of pot he had just broken; others were tucked away inside still-intact clay jars. As, with much cloak-and-dagger, these scrolls drifted piecemeal onto the antiquities market, the first scholars to study them became increasingly excited. They recognised the scrolls as Hebrew-language religious texts dating from approximately a thousand years before any others known up to that time. Among them was a magnificent scroll of Isaiah, 22 feet long and designed to be continuously unrolled and rolled up again as reading proceeded. There were portions of other books, also from the canonical Hebrew/Old Testament Bible, while further manuscripts were obscure and hitherto unknown.

During the next few years, the caves around Qumran were all intensively combed by amateurs and professionals alike, while archaeological excavations were carried out on nearby ruins supposed to be those of a monastery where the scrolls originated. This was widely thought to have belonged to the early Jewish Essene sect. From these endeavours a bewildering array of further manuscript fragments came to light, now collectively representing every book of the Hebrew/Old Testament Bible except Esther, but again including other

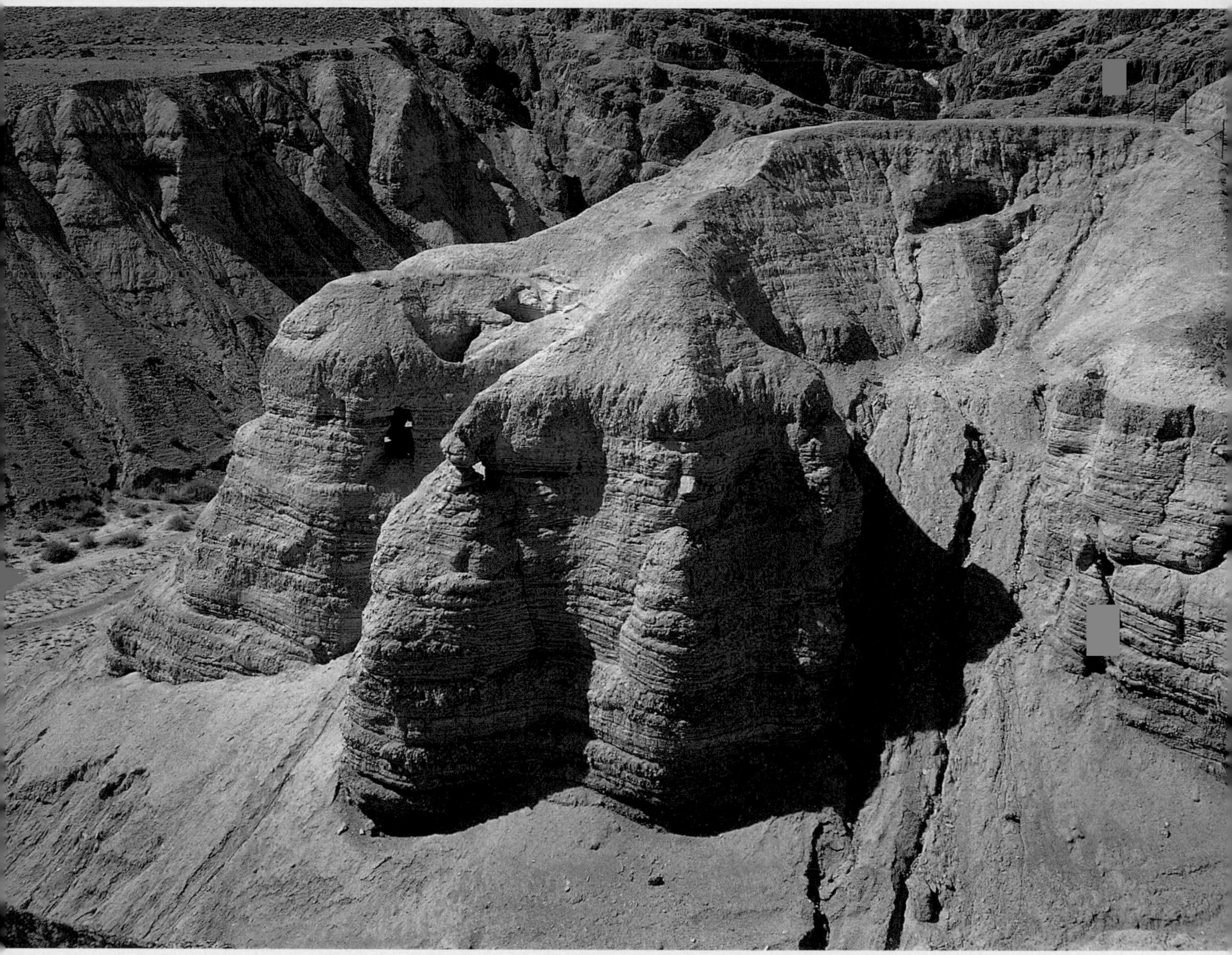

The terrain of Qumran, by the Dead Sea, where the famous Dead Sea scrolls were discovered.

books that were unknown and non-Biblical. Because Qumran at that time was under Jordanian rule, evaluation of these fragments fell mainly to a coterie of scholars based at East Jerusalem's École Biblique, led by French Dominican monk Père Roland de Vaux. De Vaux, who had also excavated the so-called Essene monastery, decided not unreasonably that all access to them should be denied to outsiders, until he and his team had had a chance to produce a definitive publication.

The task was undeniably huge, like an immensely difficult jigsaw puzzle. But when de Vaux died in 1971 he had not got close even to writing a report on his excavations of the 'Essene monastery', let alone to publishing the scrolls. As recently as 1991, his successors had published a mere hundred of the five hundred texts they controlled, compared with the nearly-complete publication of the three hundred in other hands. As is evident from photographs of the École Biblique team at work, they thought nothing of smoking cigarettes while poring over tiny, tinder-dry text fragments. Their overall supervision was so poor that some material, including the earliest-known portion of the book of Daniel, simply disappeared without explanation.

To make matters worse, their chronically-slow release of hard factual data, combined with the fact that the texts of non-Biblical content were highly cryptic and difficult to pinpoint historically, all helped to generate wild speculation. Sensationalist authors Michael Baigent and Richard Leigh charged the Vatican with deliberately suppressing the scrolls' publication because they contained material that was damaging to Christianity.[1] Even accredited scholars, such as American Robert Eisenman and Australian Barbara Thiering, pondered over individuals who were cryptically referred to in the scrolls as a 'Teacher of Righteousness' and 'Man of Lies', and confidently identified these with early Christian leaders such as Jesus's brother James and the apostle Paul. They thereby created a widespread impression that the scrolls dated predominantly from the 1st century AD.

Thankfully, however, as recently as 1992 some very determined lobbying[2] resulted in access at last being opened up to photographs of all still unpublished scroll material. Gradually, this has revealed not only the utter spuriousness of the Baigent-Leigh allegations, but also the very first real clues to the scrolls' true historical background. In particular, it is now becoming clear that they belong not so much to the 1st century AD, as argued by Eisenman and Thiering, as to the 1st century BC. This means that the mysterious 'Teacher of Righteousness' and 'Man of Lies' can have nothing to do with early Christian leaders. Two other initial assumptions, widespread even among the most academically orthodox, seem to have been equally unfounded: that the scrolls belonged to the Essene monastic sect and that the ruined Qumran complex had been their 'monastery'. Instead, the case is growing for ascribing both the scrolls and the Qumran ruins to the aristocratic Jerusalem-based priests we have already met. Led by Judas Maccabeus and his brothers' House of Hasmon, they were called Sadducees at this period, a name almost certainly derived from the High Priest Zadok of 2 Samuel 8:17.

How did the priestly Sadducees come to be associated with the scrolls? It will be recalled from the last chapter how studiously the 2nd-century BC Hasmonean family of high priests avoided calling themselves kings. This policy was continued even by the original Mattathias's grandson John Hyrkanos I, when he succeeded his father Simon in 135 BC. He waged military campaigns in Samaria and Edomite Idumea which were so successful that he created an independent Jewish empire virtually as large as that of the old kings David and Solomon. He even converted the formerly pagan Edomites to Judaism. Yet Hyrkanos chose to style himself no more than high priest.

But around 104 BC Hyrkanos's sickly son Judah Aristobolus succeeded as high priest on the death of his father, and arrogantly proclaimed himself king as well, the first Jew to do so since before the Babylonian Exile. Although Aristobolus died within a year, his brother Alexander Jannai, on his succession, did the same. Some of his surviving coins bear on one side a Greek inscription 'Alexander the King', and on the other in Hebrew '*Yonathan ha-melech*' (Jonathan the King). The latter was clearly Jannai's adopted Hebrew royal name. There is, however, clear evidence that not everybody favoured Jannai's adoption of this status. On other of his surviving coins, below the inscription '*Yonathan cohen gadol*' (Jonathan the High Priest), the accompanying Jonathan the King wording has been very deliberately erased.

In this regard, those who most opposed the Sadducee Jonathan or Jannai are known from historical sources to have been the Pharisees. They were a group behind the gradual introduction of altar-less synagogues as local religious meeting houses in place of the banned provincial temples.[3] Their leaders were not animal-sacrificing priests, as were Jannai's colleagues at the Jerusalem Temple, but instead lay rabbis recognised for their religious wisdom. The Pharisees were so angry at Jannai's royal pretensions that they even asked the Seleucid King Demetrius III Eukairos of Syria to help them against him. The bad news for them was that when Demetrius duly fought Alexander Jannai in a battle near Shechem, it was Jannai who won the day.

By way of reprisal, the Sadducee Jannai ordered eight hundred of the Pharisee rebels to be crucified in the centre of Jerusalem, followed by a massacre of their wives and children. He watched the grisly spectacle 'cup in hand . . . reclined among his concubines'.[4] Although crucifixion's origins are obscure, Jannai seems to have been the first Jewish leader to have used this hideous and excruciating mode of execution upon his fellow Jews. Certainly, his action guaranteed the Pharisees' most intense hatred of him and his Sadducee party from this time on.

Scroll 4Q448 – one that speaks approvingly of the repressive and unpopular pro-Sadducee Alexander Jannai (King Jonathan).

In this context, new insights are emerging from and about the Dead Sea Scroll fragments. At least two of their texts not only name the harshly repressive 'King Jonathan' Jannai, but they also do so with a surprising degree of approval. Scroll fragment 4Q448, from the cave first discovered by the Bedouin goatherd, takes the form of a prayer for 'King Jonathan'. It likens his earthly kingdom to the kingdom of God, and asks blessings for his welfare.[5] Another scroll, known as the 'Commentary on Nahum', again names him and dubs him, approvingly it seems, as the 'Lion of Wrath', who 'used to hang men alive [as it was done] in Israel'. It is an unmistakable reference to his crucifying of the eight hundred Pharisees. The same scroll derides Jannai's luckless victims as 'Flattery Seekers'. Clearly, its author was referring to the Pharisees. He was evidently anti-Pharisee and thoroughly approved of Jannai's actions. In turn, this suggests that the members of the Scrolls sect were either actual Sadducees or so strongly in favour of Jannai's monarchy as made little difference.

But this is not all. According to the 'Commentary on Nahum', Jannai's day is past and the 'Flattery Seekers' are currently holding sway. This enables us to pinpoint its date quite closely, for historically there was only one time when this happened.[6] This was in the period immediately following 76 BC, when Jannai died and his then-sexagenarian wife, Salome Alexandra, succeeded him. Under Salome's rule, the Pharisees enjoyed unprecedented royal favour, to the extent that there were even some executions of Sadducees. Salome Alexandra also thoughtfully appointed her pro-Pharisee son, Hyrkanos II, as high priest. For the Pharisees, there was again bad news: this period of favour would be short-lived. When Salome died in 67 BC her more hot-headed and pro-Sadducee younger son, Aristobulus II, immediately declared war on his pro-Pharisee brother, turning the tables once more.

With findings of this sort, the idea that the scrolls belonged to the obscure monastic Essenes, an idea that was shaky and had little substance even when the scrolls were first discovered, has begun to fall apart. From all that is historically known of the Essenes, mainly from the early Jewish historian Josephus and the Roman author Pliny, they were as anti-Sadducee as the Pharisees. They had gone out into the desert specifically to get

away from the laxity and corruption of Jerusalem's ruling Sadducee establishment. The Dead Sea Scroll known as the 'Manual of Discipline', from its writing definitely datable to the 1st century BC, again suggests that a link with the Essenes is unlikely. Seemingly the scroll-keepers' foundation document, it is difficult to equate with Essene practices. Furthermore, there is nothing that specifically identifies the Qumran 'monastery' as an Essene desert hideaway. Despite a continuing lack of any proper excavation report[7], the discovery of women and children buried in its large cemetery (still largely unexcavated), as well as of money stashed under its floors, hardly equates with the strict celibacy and dedication to poverty of the Essenes. Ownership by the Essenes becomes even more unlikely in the light of the so-called Copper Scroll. Uniquely, this was written on copper, seemingly to preserve it from insect infestation. It consists of directions for finding buried treasure on a scale that was conceivable only for the Sadducee-controlled Jerusalem Temple, in the environs of which some of the items were purportedly hidden.[8]

In short, while it would be wrong to suggest that the issues involved are resolved, there is a growing body of opinion that the scrolls originated as part at least of the library of the Temple of Jerusalem's priestly rulers: in other words, the Sadducees. It may have been hidden at Qumran, most likely during one or other of the Jewish revolts in the first two centuries of the Christian era.

That possibility adds greatly to the significance of the canonical Hebrew Bible books that are represented with such near-completeness among the discovered scrolls. Whatever their status, whether as single fragments or complete scrolls, no fewer than 175 of the scroll texts are from books found in our present-day Bibles. Seventy of these

Top: Graves at Qumran, among them ones of women and children, suggesting that the Qumran community were not celibate Essenes. Above: The mysterious Copper Scroll.

belong to one or other of the first five Biblical books, i.e. Genesis, Exodus, Leviticus, Numbers and Deuteronomy. There are forty-eight scrolls of the *nabiim*, or 'prophets', with the book of Isaiah by far the most popular among these. Fifty-seven are from the Psalms and the historical writings.

These oldest-known Biblical texts have one absolutely crucial feature. Although dating from shortly before or around the beginning of the Christian era, which makes them a thousand years older than the texts previously available in Hebrew, they show just how faithful the texts of our present Bibles are to those from two thousand years ago and how little they have changed over the centuries. Two Isaiah scrolls, for instance, contain the Isaiah text almost exactly as it is in our present-day Bibles, including the sections not regarded as being written by the original Isaiah.

Although there are, as we might expect, some minor differences, these are mostly the interchange of a word or the addition or absence of a particular phrase. For example, whereas in present-day Bibles Isaiah 1:15 ends, 'Your hands are covered in blood', one of the Dead Sea pair adds, 'and your fingers with crime'. Where Isaiah 2:3 of our present-day Bibles reads, 'Come, let us go up to the mountain of Yahweh, to the house of the God of Jacob', the Dead Sea Scroll version omits, 'to the mountain of Yahweh'. Such discrepancies are trifling, and there can be no doubt that the Biblical books someone stored away so carefully at Qumran two thousand years ago were as close to those we know in our present Hebrew and Old Testament Bibles as makes no difference.

We also have clear evidence that this was a serious library built up over several generations. It comes from the varying dates ascribed to different Dead Sea texts by palaeographers. The handwriting quirks of unimportant ancient manuscripts that carry

One of the two near-complete Isaiah Scrolls from the Dead Sea Scrolls. The texts show that the received texts of our present-day Bibles were preserved with remarkable fidelity.

a date, such as receipts and letters, have helped the palaeographers to determine the date of more important ones that do not, such as the scrolls. In their opinion, while some scroll texts conceivably date as far back as the 3rd century BC, most date to the 1st century BC, with just a few from the 1st century AD. Interestingly, the scrolls' owners do not seem to have been so punctilious that they insisted on everything being in Hebrew/Aramaic. The contents of the first cave to be discovered included two Greek manuscripts of the book of Leviticus, one of the book of Numbers and two of Deuteronomy. All this makes it more important to determine who originally owned these ancient Biblical books, and exactly when and why they stored them away.

Whatever the answer, the 1st century BC was an era in which, despite the Pharisees, the Temple's Sadducee, or high priestly, masters went from strength to strength, aided, if anything, by the next major shift in world-power politics. For following the successes of predecessors who had earlier eliminated both the Carthaginians and the Greeks as rivals, in 64 BC the Roman general Pompey conquered Syria. Then, while Pompey went off campaigning elsewhere, his commander Aemilius Marcus Scaurus, in Damascus, happened to hear of the conflict between the pro-Pharisee Jerusalem High Priest Hyrkanos and his pro-Sadducee brother Aristobulus. At the time, Aristobulus was on the wrong foot, withstanding siege by his brother on the highly fortified Temple Mount.

Scaurus marched his troops south, relieved Aristobulus – not without cost – then went back to Damascus. He alerted Pompey that Jerusalem was ripe for the picking, and within a matter of months Pompey was before the city's walls. He found the inhabitants as divided as ever. This time Aristobulus's supporters put up a stiff resistance on the Temple Mount, while the pro-Pharisee Hyrkanos, largely at the urging of his wily Idumean (or Edomite) courtier Antipater, opted for a diplomatic surrender. In the event, it took the Romans three months to fight their way onto the Temple Mount. When they did so, on a holy day, they duly massacred all the supporters of Aristobulus they found inside. Curious to learn more about the religion of this strange people, Pompey reportedly strode into the Temple's Holy of Holies, to find it, to his acute disappointment and puzzlement, a small, empty room, with not even a window.

Because Hyrkanos had earlier surrendered to him, Pompey reinstated him as high priest and puppet king, under the watchful eye of a Roman occupying force led by Scaurus. Our interest now turns to another Dead Sea Scroll text, only recently made available: the so-called 'Annalistic Calendar'. This contains references to Salome (under her Hebrew name Shelomyziyon), the mother of Hyrkanos and Aristobulus, as well as to Hyrkanos and Aristobulus's feud. It also mentions the death of Aemilius, i.e. the Roman general Aemilius Marcus Scaurus; this leads us to yet another Dead Sea Scroll, the 'Commentary on Habbakuk'.

The commentator likens the Chaldaeans or Babylonians mentioned in the 6th-century BC Biblical book of Habbakuk to the *Kittim* of his own time – *Kittim*, although applied Biblically to both Greeks and Romans, in this instance is generally agreed to mean Romans. He argues that just as the Babylonian conquest in the 6th century had been due to Israel's sins at that time, so the present Roman conquest was due to the sinfulness of two individuals of his own time: a 'Wicked Priest' and a 'Man of Lies'. Once the scrolls' authors are identified as Sadducee, it becomes easy to identify the 'Wicked Priest' as the Rome-supported pro-Pharisee High Priest Hyrkanos and the 'Man of Lies' as the Pharisee party's then leader.

In short, the Dead Sea Scrolls, and their Bible book contents, are emerging more and more convincingly as the library of a pro-Hasmonean, pro-Sadducee, anti-Pharisee group. In the light of these findings, the hitherto mysterious characters such as the

The site of the Herod Temple as it looks today. The Temple buildings have long been swept away and replaced by two of the holiest Moslem shrines: the golden-domed Dome of the Rock, occupying the site of the Temple 'Holy of Holies'; and the silver-domed El-Aqsa mosque, occupying the site of Herod's Royal Stoa.

'Wicked Priest' can be correctly identified and placed in their true historical context. In this case, it follows that the ingenious attempts, such as those of Robert Eisenman and Barbara Thiering, to associate them with early Christian leaders must now be considered wrong.

The coming of the Romans was certainly not the end for the Sadducees. Although Aristobulus and his two sons had been led off to imprisonment in Rome, all three managed to escape, setting off a fresh uprising in and around Jerusalem. At this point Hyrkanos's Idumean courtier Antipater began to show his colours. Forcefully crushing the rebellion, he persuaded the Romans so strongly of his usefulness that when Pompey was toppled by Julius Caesar in 48 BC, it was Antipater who was put in charge of the province the Romans now called Judaea. When he died of poisoning in 43 BC, his two sons, Phasael and Herod, jointly inherited the province. Phasael soon fell victim to yet another recapture of Jerusalem, this time led by Aristobulus's son Mattathias Antigonus, in alliance with an up-and-coming neighbouring power – the Parthians.

This left Antipater's second son Herod still at large. Knowing that as a despised Idumean, he could expect no help from the Jewish populace, he lost no time in making his way to Rome. There, his father's reputation stood him in such good stead that the Senate formally appointed him their king of Judaea. They then despatched him at the

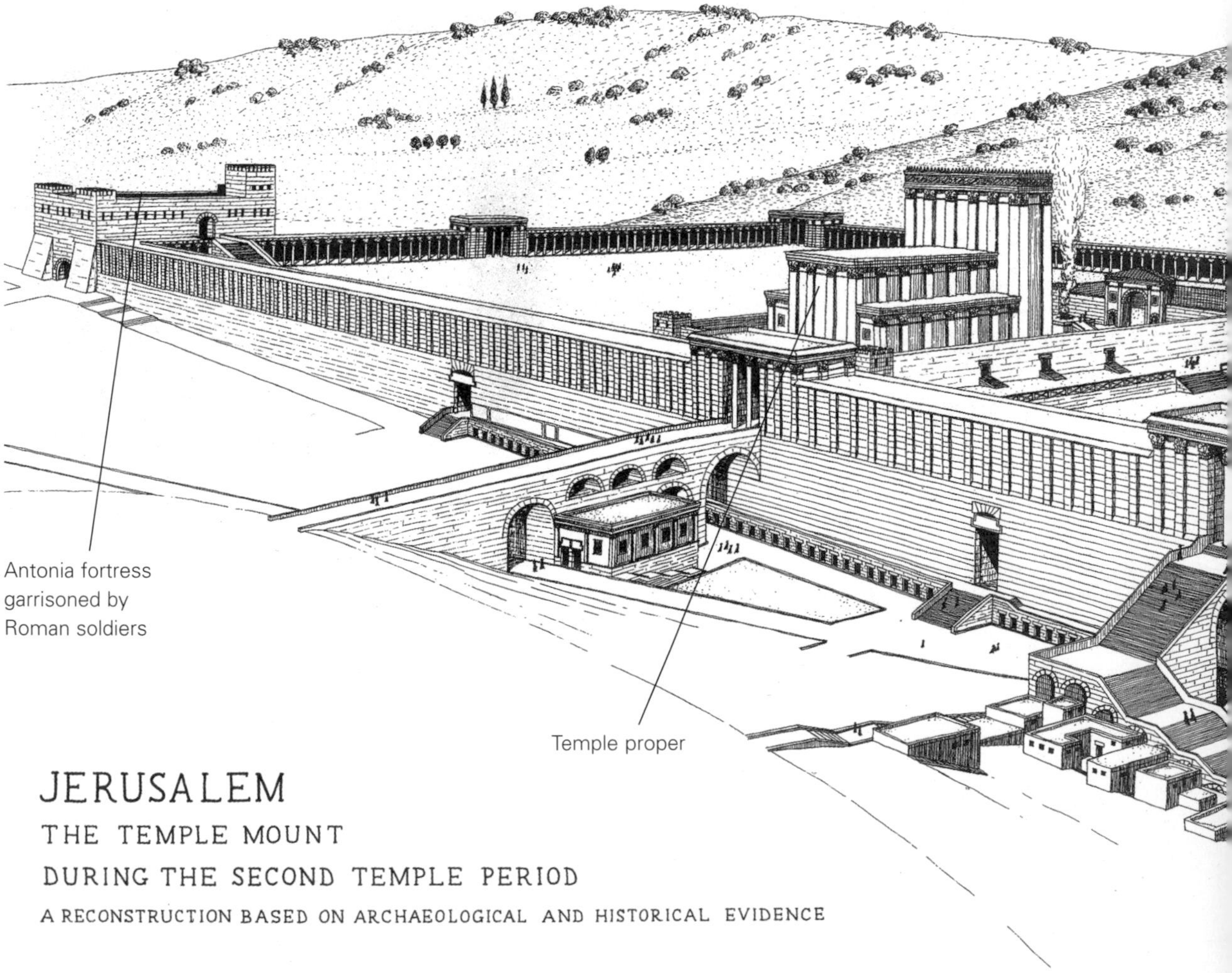

JERUSALEM
THE TEMPLE MOUNT
DURING THE SECOND TEMPLE PERIOD
A RECONSTRUCTION BASED ON ARCHAEOLOGICAL AND HISTORICAL EVIDENCE

head of a sizeable army to recapture the recalcitrant province. It took Herod two and a half years, until 37 BC, before he and his army finally succeeded in doing so. But he then had the satisfaction of knowing that he, a despised Idumean, had become king of Judaea, i.e. king of the Jews, in both fact and name.

At this point, he began to show his mettle, and by no means to the detriment of the ostensibly defeated Sadducees. In all sorts of ways Herod was a tyrant. He surrounded himself with spies and informers, and systematically liquidated anyone he considered potentially dangerous to him, including his wife and two of his sons. But there was one respect in which he could only warm the hearts of Sadducee priests and high priests. Among numerous grandiose building projects, he put in hand as his pièce-de-resistance the enlargement and aggrandisement of Jerusalem's Second Temple, doing so on such a massive scale that it became a genuine wonder of the world. As noted earlier, he created a vast platform, almost double the original area, by extending the Temple Mount's northern, western and southern sides. He faced this with blocks of dressed masonry which were so huge – up to 70 tons apiece – that most are still in place. On top of this, he threw up a dazzling array of fresh buildings to surround the Temple proper.

Frustratingly, not a single block of either these buildings or the Temple itself remains in situ. But thanks to excellent modern-day reconstructions, such as one by

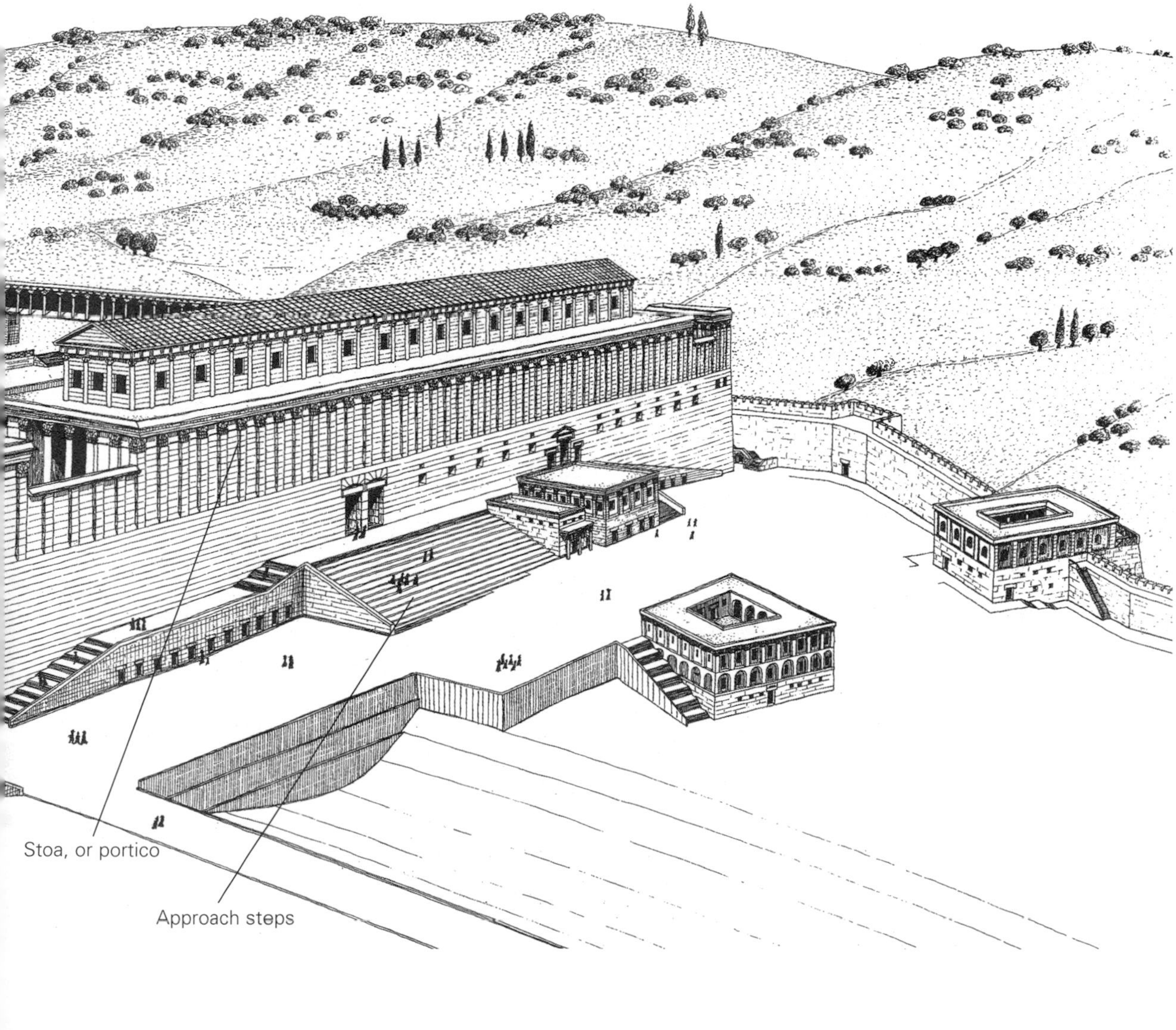

A reconstruction by Leen Ritmeyer and his wife Kathleen of Jerusalem's Second Temple, as lavishly enlarged and aggrandised by King Herod the Great.

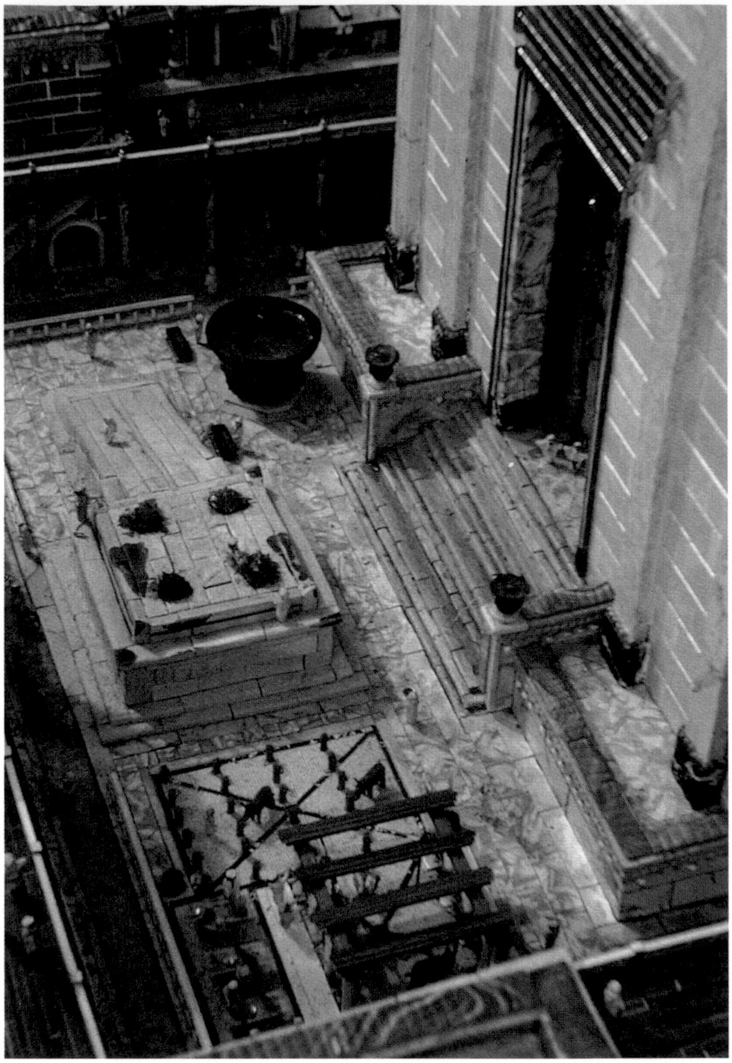

architect-artist Leen Ritmeyer, and another by British model-maker Alec Garrard, both of whom have drawn upon every possible clue to the original's appearance, something can still be gleaned of what a vast powerhouse the Temple was.

After ascending a vast flight of steps, the worshipper first entered an enormous stoa, or portico, supported by columns so wide that it took three men with outstretched arms to encircle them. Here, he would have been assailed by stallholders, eager to sell him any of the animals the priests deemed acceptable for sacrifice. These ranged from prime cattle to pigeons, depending upon how rich or poor the worshipper was. Also competing for his attention were money-changers, offering to change his pagan Roman currency into the special aniconic coins (coins without an image on them) that were acceptable within the Temple's precincts. This 'Yahweh money' he would have been able to pay into the new and magnificent Treasury, successor to those that had been so repeatedly looted by earlier predators, from the Egyptian Sheshonq, to the Babylonian Nebuchadnezzar, to the Macedonian Antiochus Epiphanes.

The Temple sacrifical area, from Alex Garrard's model of the Herod Temple.

Then, with whatever animal he brought for sacrifice, the worshipper would cross a vast square, possibly accompanied by family and friends, all chanting prayers and singing psalms. They would make their way towards the Temple proper, where they would join others with their animals. In the inner part reserved for them, the priests would slaughter each animal according to the prescribed rites, then pour some of the blood at the base of the altar and all around the altar. There were twenty-four posts specially designed to accommodate the heads of the hoofed animals, and eight pillars for the hanging of their carcasses. When the sacrificial animal was dead it would be butchered, then parts of it immolated on a huge altar with four fireplaces, at least two of which were always kept burning, with a third in reserve. Not that the meat was wasted. Much would be consumed by the officiating priests and their attendants. To wash their hands from all the blood, they had a vast 'laver', resting on twelve huge lions, the water of which was changed daily. Behind all of this stood the Holy of Holies, seat of the invisible Yahweh, to be entered by no one except the incumbent high priest.

Such a vast undertaking, 'out-Solomoning' King Solomon and employing many thousands both on its building and upkeep, could only aggrandise the Sadducee high priests who controlled it. Its very scale ratified and reinforced their monopoly over *the* central place for all Jewish worship – the only place where sacrifices were allowed to be made. Ultimately, then, Herod's forceful take-over had worked very much in their favour, and it was not at all in their interest to do anything to rock this status quo.

And at face value, tyrant though Herod was, the Jewish people in general could hardly have seen better days than throughout his long reign. The Roman regime for which he acted as agent was on the whole civilised and not overly harsh, bringing a peace from outside aggression similar to that enjoyed under the Persians. And surely the religion of Yahweh was in fine shape. There was the Temple's grandeur, its handsome and richly decorated buildings gleaming in the sunshine, its superbly robed priests processing for the regular ceremonies, its trumpet calls, its choruses sung by choirs, its savours of animals being offered up on the great altar before Yahweh's Holy of Holies. If you had been sinful, you paid your special Temple money for an animal to be slaughtered and immolated as part of this 'Grand Central' Religion Factory. Then you could go back home, content that you had done all that Moses' ancient *Torah* demanded of you.

But was there something incomplete, something lacking, in all this show? By modern standards, the Jews were seemingly far more advanced than other civilisations around them, for they had a religion that did not involve the veneration of man-made images. Yet even so, was the ritualistic slaughter of helpless animals by men in fancy costumes really what 'God's kingdom' was all about? The *nabiim* of old had often suggested that it was not, specifically targetting this very world of Temple sacrifices. Moreover, some had spoken of a Messiah, an anointed one, who would bring in a 'kingdom of God' of a very different kind to that ruled by a Herod.

Thus, in the 6th century BC, Jeremiah had put a very explicit prophecy into the mouth of Yahweh:

> Look, the days are coming when I shall make a new covenant with the House of Israel and the house of Judah, but not like the covenant I made with their ancestors the day I took them by the hand to bring them out of Egypt . . . This is the covenant I shall make with the house of Israel when those days have come . . . *Within them* I shall plant my *Torah*, writing it *on their hearts*. Then I shall be their God and they will be my people. (Jeremiah 31:31)

It is quite clear from other hints that Jeremiah's New Covenant was expected to take the form of a person. Indeed, if Jeremiah was responsible for the book of Deuteronomy, as we have suggested, then he explicitly put into the mouth of Moses the words:

> God will raise up for you a *nabi* like myself, from among yourselves, from your own brothers; to him you must listen . . . I will put my words into his mouth and he shall tell them all I shall command him. (Deuteronomy 18:15, 18)

Likewise Daniel, at the time of Antiochus Epiphanes' so-terrible oppression, had looked forward to the coming of one 'as it were a Son of Man', on whom would be conferred 'rule, honour and kingship', 'an everlasting rule which will never pass away' (Daniel 7:13-14).

Yet, whereas before the Babylonian exile there had been Yahwist *nabiim* aplenty, despite the Canaanitic kings' repeated attempts at their suppression, these had fallen strangely silent in the centuries since. This was in spite of predictions that there really would be a future *nabi*, none other than an Elijah returned, who would recognise and anoint the Messiah-to-be. So if all this was to be believed, when and how might this new Elijah appear? Likewise, when and where might this 'Son of Man' make his entrance upon the stage of history?

Some time around the decade that the world now knows as 10 BC to AD 1[9], the Bible story was about to begin its most dramatic and controversial chapter yet.

18

THE COMING OF THE 'NEW COVENANT'

HOPEFULLY, IT will have been perfectly possible thus far for Jewish readers to accept and approve this book's quest for the history that lies behind the pages of the Bible we share. While clearly not directed towards fundamentalists of any denomination, its whole thrust has been to argue that the Hebrew Bible, alias the Christian Old Testament, has sufficient basis in historical fact to command serious respect. Now, however, we run the unavoidable risk of spoiling this agreement by going on beyond their Bible into books they do not recognise as Biblical at all. These are the books of the Christian New Testament – or, to use a term that fits better with the *nabi* Jeremiah's prophecy, the New Covenant.

As this has come down to us, in a canon that parallels in many ways that of the Hebrew Bible, the New Covenant consists of twenty-seven books. These comprise four gospels (broadly, collections of sayings interspersed with quasi-biographical narrative), one history (the book of Acts, apparently by the same author as the Luke gospel), one piece of visionary writing (the book of Revelation) and twenty-one letters to individuals and groups, fourteen of these attributed to one author: the reportedly Pharisee-educated[1] Paul. As canonically received, all these books were written in Greek, which the Romans had perpetuated as their empire's lingua franca, but in each case the author seems to have been of some kind of Jewish origin. Furthermore, without exception, all have their springboard in one most remarkable Jew. According to the books' authors, he lived only shortly before they set pen to papyrus. He was a Galilean, or northerner, called Jesus.

Whatever stance people who count themselves as non-Christians may take about Jesus, it is a very weak argument indeed to contend that he never existed, as one London University professor of German has claimed in no fewer than three books on this theme.[2] As already seen in the case of the Hebrew Bible, or Old Testament books, the discovery of the Dead Sea Scrolls provided Biblical manuscripts, or portions of them, that dated in some instances from as little as three centuries after the time when they were originally composed. This is a considerably better record than the eleven centuries that separates our earliest manuscript copy of Tacitus's *Annals* from the Roman era of its origination. Yet

Remains of a synagogue at Capernaum, a Galilean town closely associated with much of Jesus's early ministry.

even the scrolls' proximity in time to their originals pales when compared with that of the early documentation for Jesus.

In Manchester University's John Rylands Library is a papyrus scrap of the John gospel that was found in Egypt. Its writing firmly dates it to the early 2nd century AD, therefore within a century of the period between around AD 30 and 36 during which Jesus is thought to have died.[3] Papyrus portions of several non-canonical gospels, including that of Thomas, also date from that century. The Chester Beatty Library in Ballsbridge, Dublin, houses thirty pages from the gospels and the book of Acts, eighty-six out of an original ninety-nine pages from the letters of Paul, and one-third of a copy of the book of Revelation, all dating to the early 3rd century AD or thereabouts. Also dating from this period are substantial portions of a papyrus book of the John and Luke gospels, acquired during the 1950s by the Swiss collector

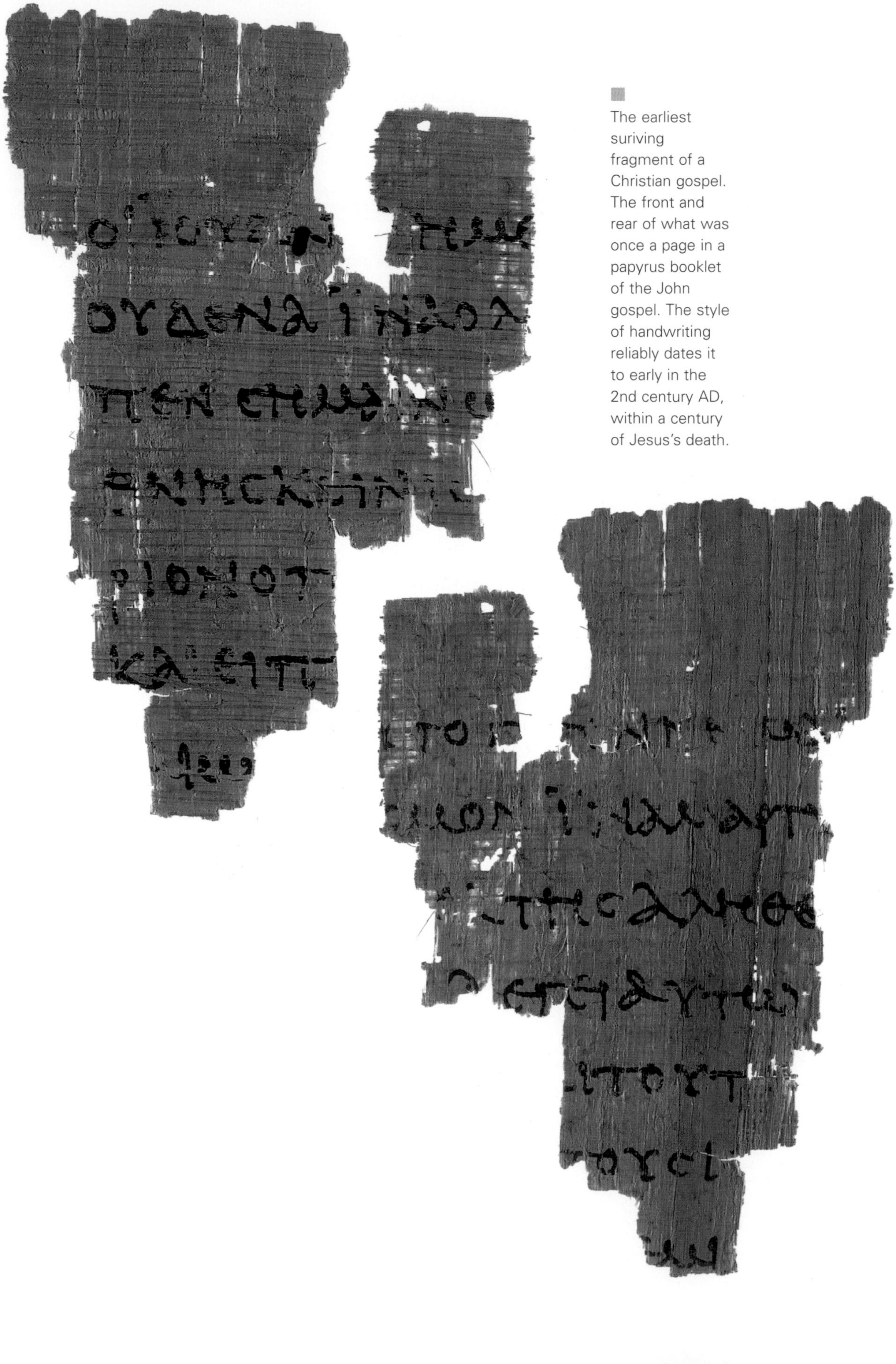

The earliest suriving fragment of a Christian gospel. The front and rear of what was once a page in a papyrus booklet of the John gospel. The style of handwriting reliably dates it to early in the 2nd century AD, within a century of Jesus's death.

Martin Bodmer. All in all, no fewer than eighty-eight gospel fragments survive that are reliably datable to within three centuries of Jesus's lifetime, along with two hundred and seventy-four full vellum codices for the next seven centuries. Their texts show much the same integrity to the 'received' versions in Christian Bibles as the Dead Sea Scrolls do to their Jewish equivalents. Another fascinating aspect to them is that, unlike ancient Judaism's cumbersome scrolls, mostly written on one side of long rolls of expensive animal skin and clearly designed to be kept in a formal religious repository, these New Covenant texts were written on both sides of cheap papyrus sheets and made up into easily portable books, just as we understand them today.

Furthermore, quite independently of any Christian attestation to Jesus's historicity, the Roman historian Tacitus, writing at the beginning of the 2nd century, mentioned followers of Christ being put to death in Rome during the reign of the emperor Nero (AD 54-68). This is clear evidence that even within a generation of Jesus's death, his cult had spread sufficiently to disturb the very capital of the Roman Empire. Under his Jewish-language name Yeshu, which means 'Yahweh saves' (the same name that the English language Old Testament renders as Joshua), Jesus is also referred to in supplements to the Jewish *Mishnah* compiled around this same time[4], albeit not altogether favourably. Likewise, the writings of Tacitus's Jewish contemporary – the Pharisee-educated Josephus, born within a year or two of Jesus's death – make it clear that he, too, knew of Jesus, even though his surviving mention of him has undoubtedly suffered some tampering by later Christian copyists.[5]

But even if we can be sure that the documentation concerning Jesus is just about as ancient as you can reasonably expect, what about the authority of its reporting, particularly in the case of its key sources – the four gospels? Here, we have to acknowledge that the gospels have not come down to us as we might ideally have wished them to, neatly accompanied by each author's credentials. In fact, we cannot even be sure that the true authors were those under whose names the gospels appear in our Bibles, since these names were not integral to the texts, but added later on.

Thus, scholars are generally agreed that because the Matthew gospel shows dependency on that of Mark, it cannot have been written by the tax-collector Matthew listed as one of Jesus's direct disciples. They believe this even though, according to an ancient tradition, this same disciple did write down Jesus's sayings in their original Aramaic, and these were then translated and incorporated into the gospel bearing his name. In the case of the Luke gospel, the best that even ancient tradition can say is that Luke was a companion of Paul and had never known Jesus directly. In the case of the Mark gospel, ancient tradition attributes this to John Mark, who was again apparently not a direct eyewitness of the events described, but merely an associate of one who was – Peter.

The John gospel was purportedly written by the original disciple John, son of fisherman Zebedee, but has long been rejected as such by modern-day scholars. In this case, however, some serious argument has surfaced for a return to its traditional attribution. In the teeth of fierce earlier objections that no Galilean fisherman's son could ever have written the Greek of the John gospel, the late Dr John Robinson (of *Honest to God* fame) argued that its language, replete with terminology special to fish traders, is precisely the language we might expect from a successful tradesman's son operating in a society where Greek was the lingua franca.[6] His view is finding increasing support archaeologically. For example, Greek inscriptions have been found even in otherwise very Jewish tombs and, as we saw, even some of the Dead Sea Scrolls' Biblical texts were written in Greek.

In short, the gospels, like many of the Old Covenant books, do undeniably include much work of editors who were not present at the events described. Arguably, however, they also contain substantial portions of sayings and narratives recorded by individuals who genuinely did witness, at first hand, the events of the life and death of Jesus, and should be respected for this.

But even if this is acknowledged, to what extent can these documents be said to be truly reliable? This question is particularly important, bearing in mind that much of their content, not least the purported miracles attributed to Jesus and the events associated with his death, put a strain on credulity that is far more violent than in any of the later and more historical Old Covenant books.

We have to face the fact that the gospel writers' prime intention was not biographical. As a result, they are undeniably weak in certain aspects of Jesus's biographical history, particularly with regard to the circumstances of his birth and early life.

Thus, of the four gospels, only two – the Matthew and Luke ones – contain any kind of birth story, and these are seriously contradictory. In the Matthew version, Jesus was purportedly born during the reign of the very Herod the Great (Matthew 2:1ff) whose Temple building we discussed in the last chapter. If this were true, Jesus would have been born before 4 BC, the year when Herod is historically known to have died – in which case his true two-thousandth anniversary passed unnoticed! In fact, there is general scholarly recognition that the 6th-century AD Byzantine monk Dionysius Exiguus, who devised the Christian calendar, must have miscalculated.

Another factor undermines the Matthew gospel's general credibility regarding Jesus's birth. This is its claim that King Herod ordered every male infant in Bethlehem and its environs to be killed (Matthew 2:16). For while such an act was by no means unthinkable of Herod, the fact is that other historical authorities such as Josephus, who exhaustively chronicled Herod's misdeeds, know nothing of this particular atrocity. Furthermore, the Luke author seriously conflicts with the Matthew author by stating that Jesus was born at the time that the Roman governor Quirinius held a census. This could not have happened until AD 6, the first year that Judaea came under direct, as distinct from indirect, Roman rule. Adding a further complication, whereas the Luke gospel describes Jesus's parents as making a long journey from their home in Nazareth, Galilee, 70 miles south to Bethlehem in order to comply with this census (Luke 2:4), the Matthew version represents them as already being Bethlehem residents (Mathew 2:1-8). If we believe Matthew, it means that Luke's famous 'no room at the inn' story could never have happened.

With respect to Jesus's birth stories, the sensible view is to set them aside as shaky add-ons. The one birth element that does seem definite is that Jesus's ancestry was traceable to King David. The Matthew and Luke gospels provide full, though differing, genealogies (Matthew 1:2-17; Luke 3:23-38). The Mark gospel describes a blind man acclaiming Jesus as 'son of David' (Mark 10:47, 48). The Pauline letters also allude to his descent from David (Romans 1:3; 2 Timothy 2:8), despite their scant information on other aspects of Jesus's earthly life. Finally, the John gospel reports contemporary debate over the scriptural requirement that 'the Messiah must be descended from David[7] and come from Bethlehem, the village where David was' (John 7:40-42).

In their genealogies, the Matthew and Luke authors somewhat illogically traced Jesus's descent from David via his father Joseph, despite both birth stories insisting Joseph was not his real father. Whatever the reason for that was, it would be interesting to know more about his recent royal ancestors and why they had apparently chosen to live in such obscurity – in Joseph's case, far to the north of his ancestral Judah – during the post-Exilic period. But this eludes us, as does any meaningful information about Jesus's childhood and early manhood, despite the popularity of some baseless modern-day claims that he lived in India and suchlike.

One fact about Jesus is altogether less contested. When he emerged into the public spotlight sometime around AD 30, he like many others at that time received a baptism from the first real *nabi* to have appeared in centuries: John the Baptist. All four gospel writers refer to this John at some length. The Luke author in Acts reports that his teaching had been carried as far as Alexandria and Ephesus. So, quite independently, does the Jewish historian Josephus[8] in a passage that modern-day Jewish scholars are happy to acknowledge as free from Christian scribal tampering.

John the Baptist seems, then, to have been a genuine historical figure. He apparently spurned comfortable housing and clothing, and chose instead to live out in the desert wearing nothing more than 'a garment made from camel-hair with a leather loin-cloth round his waist' (Matthew 3:4), an attire that specifically emulated Elijah's (2 Kings 1:8). Reportedly, he was both anti-Sadducee and anti-Pharisee (Matthew 3:7). His message, just like that of the earlier *nabiim*, was the futility of trying to appease Yahweh by offering empty animal sacrifices. For him, the key requirement was sincere repentance, symbolically ratified by a baptism of total immersion in the waters of the River Jordan, recalling the way in which Elijah's acolyte Elisha cured the leprous Naaman the Syrian.

However, there was a key difference between John the Baptist and all his *nabi* predecessors. It had apparently fallen to him to be the 'forerunner', foreseen by the Babylonian-exiled second 'Isaiah' five centuries earlier, who would proclaim: 'Prepare a way for the Lord, make his paths straight' (Isaiah 40:3), and whom the *nabi* Malachi would later describe as a second Elijah (Malachi 3:23). John seems to have believed that in his own lifetime the 'one who is to come' would appear as a king of Israel to end all previous kings. According to the John gospel, it was John the Baptist's disciple Nathanael who first accorded Jesus that title, immediately after John baptised him. The rite had, therefore, been a form of royal anointing.

Another fact is consistent in all the gospels, evoking no contradiction: that Jesus and his parents had been living for some while in northern Galilee. This neatly suits a remark made by the original 8th-century BC Isaiah, immediately before his famous 'people that walked in darkness' verses, that the Messiah would come from 'Galilee of the nations' (Isaiah 8:23). We cannot be totally sure that Jesus ever lived in the very tiny Galilean village of Nazareth, for the gospel references to this may derive from their authors' mistaking the description 'Jesus the Nazarene' for a reference to Nazareth, rather than to the *nezer*, or root, of King David. But Jesus's associations with Capernaum, a little over 20 miles from Nazareth, are unmistakable. This town on the shores of the Sea of Galilee is closely intertwined with much of his early ministry.

As conveyed in the Matthew and Mark gospels, it was at Capernaum, and specifically at the house where his disciples Simon Peter and Andrew lived, that Jesus reportedly healed Simon Peter's mother-in-law of a fever (Matthew 8:14-15; Mark 1:19-21). Matthew 4 refers to Jesus going to live in Capernaum after leaving Nazareth. The Mark gospel describes Jesus as entertaining a sizable gathering of disciples, tax collectors and sinners in what sounds like a reasonably substantial residence at Capernaum (Mark 2:15). As for the gospel of John, its chapter 6 has Jesus and his disciples rowing across the Sea of Galilee to Capernaum very much as if they were returning home (John 6:15).

Intriguingly, therefore, while Nazareth's location has always been identifiable, even though the present Arab town has little that is meaningful in the way of ancient remains, Capernaum's whereabouts became lost. Then, in the 1860s, the British Army engineer Charles Wilson, earlier noted for his insights concerning Shiloh, identified it with a site by Galilee's waterside that the local Arabs called Kfar Nahum. Here, Italian archaeological excavations revealed the foundations of an octagonal church that

Byzantine Greeks had built in the 5th century. The octagon was known to denote a site regarded at that time as especially holy.

Furthermore, below the church foundations, the remains of an ancient private house came to light. It seemed to have been a conventional dwelling in the 1st century AD, but was remodelled in subsequent centuries into a house-church. Its walls still bore ancient Aramaic, Syriac and Hebrew inscriptions: 'Lord Jesus Christ help your servant' and 'Christ have mercy'.[9] It seems to have been this same house-church about which the Christian Abbess Egeria wrote as early as AD 380: 'In Capernaum the house of the prince of the apostles has been made into a church with its original walls still standing. It is where the Lord cured the paralytic.'[10] From the fact that this Capernaum house was regarded with such exceptional reverence by Christians of the very earliest period, there is a real possiblity that this was the very dwelling once owned by Jesus's disciple Peter's family, and that Jesus himself once walked its very floors.

An aerial view of Capernaum on the shores of the Sea of Galilee.

The information in the Mark gospel that Jesus taught in the Capernaum synagogue (Mark 1:21) raises a further question about whether anything of this building might also have survived. It has an additional source of interest. According to three of the gospels, it was built, rather unusually, by a locally-based Roman centurion or royal official whose servant Jesus reportedly cured of an illness (Matthew 8:5-13; Luke 7:2-9; John 4:46-53). In this regard, archaeologists have found evidence of Roman military presence in Capernaum in the form of a long bathhouse, of positively non-Jewish design, that almost certainly belonged to the garrison commanded by Jesus's centurion. They have also found the still well-preserved columns of a substantial Jewish synagogue (see page 213). Although its architecture dates it to the 4th century AD, it is reliably thought to stand on the foundations of an earlier synagogue, which would have been the one Jesus attended.

Jesus is described as teaching, and reading from the *Torah*, in Pharisee synagogues (Luke 4:15-22), also as teaching in the Sadducee-controlled Temple in Jerusalem (John 7:14). However, he seems to have been happiest addressing open-air gatherings of ordinary folk from the flourishingly agricultural region that 1st-century AD Galilee is independently known to have been. The venues were sometimes hills, sometimes desert, sometimes the lakeside. Apparently, Jesus's hearers repeatedly sought him out, rather than he them.

The octagonal foundations mark the site of the house thought to have been owned by Peter and his family at Capernaum.

Equally characteristic, it appears that those he chose as disciples were not Sadducee priests, or Pharisee teachers, or any of the recognised intelligentsia of his time. Instead, among other seeming nobodies, he picked out a number of fisherfolk of the kind who plied their trade from Capernaum and similar small towns bordering the Kinneret, or Sea of Galilee. These fishermen must have been comparatively well-off, for the gospels indicate that the fishing boats operated by Jesus's disciples were substantial five-man-crew vessels. They were easily

capable of carrying over a dozen adults, plus a heavy cargo of fish, and would have needed significant capital to build. Modern-day archaeology has done much to corroborate this, thanks to the discovery of just such a fishing-boat, a mere 3 miles from Capernaum and dating from around Jesus's time. It came to light as recently as January 1986, when a drought caused an unusual drop in the Sea of Galilee's water level.

Retrieved from the mud in a remarkable rescue operation, and now successfully preserved in a special museum[11] close to where it was found, this vessel was originally 26 feet long. It was capable of being both sailed and rowed by a crew of five: four rowers and a helmsman. Although it would be wrong to suggest that it was one of the actual fishing boats in which Jesus moved around the Galilee region, it must at the very least resemble these closely. It, therefore, helps us to flesh out the very real social and geographical context of the Jesus of history.

As for Jesus's teachings recorded in the gospels, again these have the ring of deriving from someone who genuinely lived, rather than an invented mythical figure. While Jesus's sayings and parables were self-evidently rooted in all that *nabiim* had been teaching for centuries – the parable, for instance, one of Jesus's favourite teaching vehicles, had been used at least as far back as the time of King David – they have a distinctiveness to them that bespeak a very individual human being.

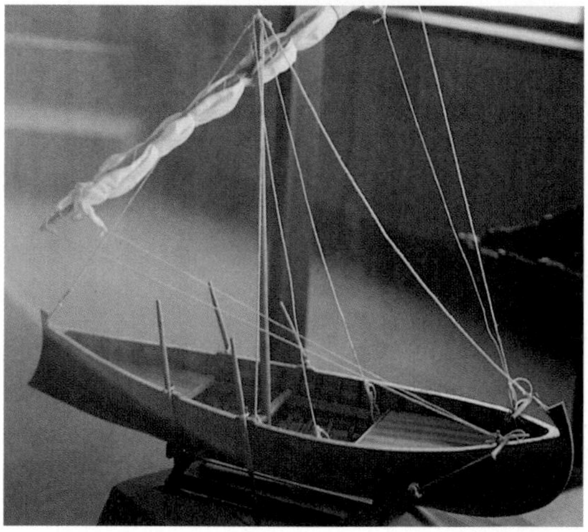

For instance, they show familiarity with a rustic background redolent of the agriculturally-prolific Galilee region. Within a single chapter of the Luke gospel (Luke 13), Jesus is depicted as knowing how to revive a barren fig tree (vv6-9), being sensitive to farm animals' need for watering (v15), being aware of the remarkable growth propensity of mustard seeds (v19), being well-informed about the amount of yeast needed to leaven dough (v20) and being keenly observant of the characteristic manner in which a hen gathers her brood under her wings (v34).

But there is another aspect to his teachings. While all the sayings and parables show a mind that was very familiar with and respectful of the *Torah* and all the *nabiim* had taught, there is not a single instance in which Jesus is represented as calling directly upon these written scriptures as his authority. Instead, the authority with which he spoke – and the gospels attest to the fact that he did speak with authority and that it was specially remarked upon by his contemporaries – was one coming from *within* him. It derived not from any written text, nor from inspiration gained from standing in front of the Yahwistic Ark, as in the case of the earlier *nabiim*, but instead from what we can only term, if we wish to avoid using the faith-word 'God', 'heart'.

And this utterly distinctive heart stamp is upon everything. In parables such as the 'Prodigal Son' and the 'Workers in the Vineyard', all our normal rules of fair play and justice are turned upside down in favour of heart or love transcending all. Earlier *nabiim*, when they were not in their all-too-frequent wrath mode for their Yahweh utterances, undeniably had their moments of sublimity. But Jesus was different from these. If it was

A fishing boat (top) from Jesus's time, discovered in the mud of the Sea of Galilee and (above) a reconstruction of the same vessel. Both are displayed at the Yigal Allon Centre near Migdal, Galilee.

not he who was behind the sayings and sentiments attributed to him, we should have to look for someone equally remarkable who was.

What was his justification for speaking with such authority? It is quite clear (the alleged circumstances of his birth notwithstanding) that he perceived himself as having a very special relationship with the universal God, one that was quite different from the relationship enjoyed by his *nabi* predecessors. 'My teaching is not from myself: it comes from the one who sent me', he is quoted as saying (John 7:16). Superseding all the normal protocols concerning use of the divine name, Jesus reputedly used the Aramaic word *Abba*, or 'Daddy'. No parable more clearly or poignantly evokes this special relationship than that of the 'Tenants in the Vineyard', the only parable in which he cast himself as one of the characters:

> There was a . . . landowner, who planted a vineyard . . . then he leased it to tenants and went abroad. When vintage time drew near he sent his servants to the tenants to collect his produce. But the tenants seized his servants, thrashed one, killed another and stoned a third. Next he sent some more servants, this time a larger number, and they dealt with them the same sway. Finally, he sent his son to them thinking: 'They will respect my son.' But when the tenants saw the son they said to each other: 'This is the heir. Come let us kill him and take over his inheritance.' So they seized him and threw him out of the vineyard and killed him.
> (Matthew 21:3-39)

It does not take a genius in theology to recognise what this parable was all about. The vineyard owner was God, the vineyard God's earth and the tenants mankind. The servants were the Old Testament *nabiim*, some of whom were certainly badly treated for speaking the vineyard owner's mind. But suffering by far the worst fate was the son, whose lot it was to be killed.

Nothing is clearer from the gospels than Jesus's sense of this role. Being killed as the vineyard owner's son was what Jesus perceived that he, a descendant of King David, had come to suffer. Three times in as many chapters of the Mark gospel, he is represented as warning his disciples of this, specifically using the *nabi* Daniel's messianic phrase, 'Son of Man', to describe himself in this context:

> Then he began to teach them that the Son of Man was destined to suffer grievously, and to be rejected by the elders and the chief priests and the scribes, and to be put to death . . .
> (Mark 8:31)

> The Son of Man will be delivered into the power of men; they will put him to death . . .
> (Mark 9:31-2)

> Now we are going up to Jerusalem, and the Son of Man is about to be handed over to the chief priests and the scribes. They will condemn him to death and will hand him over to the Gentiles, who will mock him and spit at him and scourge him and put him to death . . . (Mark 10:33-34)

It is the third prophecy that names the place, Jerusalem. Among the gospels' more convincing features is the way they refer authoritatively to topographical features in Jerusalem that have been corroborated archaeologically. The previously-maligned John gospel is the very best in this regard. It is this gospel that mentions an edifice called Bethesda, or Bethzatha, with twin pools and five porticoes, where Jesus reportedly cured a paralytic (John 5:1-9). Exhaustive excavations by Israeli archaeologist Professor Joachim Jeremias have brought to light precisely such a building, still including two huge, deep-cut cisterns, in the environs of Jerusalem's Crusader Church of St Anne. Likewise, the John gospel specifically refers to the Pool of Siloam (John 9:7), now well-known to us as the water supply from the Gihon spring which King Hezekiah's engineers had so cleverly diverted to within Jerusalem's walls.

However, the Jerusalem landmark that all the gospels refer to most frequently – the key backdrop against which the events of Jesus's death would take place – was, of course, the Temple. Herod the Great had begun its aggrandisement two generations earlier, but work on it continued in Jesus's time. By way of prologue to the final drama, the gospels repeatedly describe the disciples and Jesus in the context of the Temple. The disciples are seen admiring its enormous stonework: 'Master, look at the size of those stones!' (Mark 13:1). Together with Jesus, they watch the rich and the poor bringing their offerings to its Treasury (Luke 21:1-4). As was Jesus's right as a rabbi, or recognised and respected teacher, he is described teaching within its vast precincts (Luke 19:47; 21:37, etc). But there seems always to have been a cold shudder in his attitude towards this extraordinary mini-metropolis. This is nowhere more clear than when he grimly predicted that the time would come when 'not a single stone will be left on another; everything will be destroyed' (Luke 21:6).

It was within these same Temple portals, so the gospels tell us, that this seemingly so gentle man committed the most violent act anywhere recorded of him. Seeing traders 'selling cattle and sheep and doves, and the money-changers sitting there', Jesus reportedly made 'a whip out of cord [and] drove them all out . . . sheep and cattle as well'. He 'scattered the money-changers' coins, knocked their tables over, and said to the dove sellers "Take all this out of here and stop using my Father's house as a market" ' (John 2:15-16).

It matters very little that the author of the John gospel differs from his three fellow-gospel writers by relating this incident as if it happened at an earlier phase of Jesus's life than they suggest. The crucial element is that every gospel writer records it. It seems to have been *the* action, more than any other, that brought Jesus into open conflict with the Temple's Sadducee high priest proprietors, and thereby precipitated the decisions they took to bring about his death.

With regard to the Sadducee proprietors, the archaeology of recent years has revealed a great deal about them. In the course of excavations of Old City Jerusalem, veteran Israeli archaeologist Nahman Avigad brought to light the princely houses they had built for themselves just to the south-east of the Temple Mount. The remains of these can still be viewed in the basement of the Arches House in Jerusalem's Tifferet Israel Street. It would have been to one of these houses that Jesus was brought following his arrest. According to the John gospel, Jesus's disciple Peter and 'another disciple' 'known to the high priest' (probably the John gospel author himself)[12], gained entry to an inner courtyard. This was the famous occasion when Peter was reportedly so frightened that he three times denied any association with Jesus. It is apparent from the John gospel that the priestly house had a porter-controlled gate, behind which lay an open-air courtyard for guards and servants, complete with a fireplace where they could warm themselves when nights were cold. Beyond this lay the mansion's inner sanctum, where the Sadducee high priest and his aides would have conducted their interrogation of their prisoner. From Avigad and his helpers' findings, this layout is not only broadly confirmed, we also know that the floors of this inner part would have been of fine mosaics, that fine frescoes decorated its walls, and that the interrogators would have had their refreshments served in the very finest crafted glassware.

According to the Matthew and John gospels, Jerusalem's high priest during Jesus's last days was Caiaphas (Matthew 26:3; John 11:49). This is confirmed by Josephus in his *Antiquities*, where we learn that Caiaphas held this office between the years AD 18 and 37

An ossuary bearing the name 'Joseph Bar Caiaphas', generally recognised as the full name of the high priest who sentenced Jesus to death.

(by our present-day reckoning). Additionally, as recently as 1990, Israeli archaeologists found what may well be Caiaphas's skeleton. During construction of a water park in south Jerusalem, an old cave was discovered containing several limestone ossuaries, or bone boxes, from around the 1st century AD. One of them had particularly beautiful ornamentation, and bore the inscription 'Yehosef bar Qayafa', i.e. Joseph, son of Caiaphas. According to Josephus, this was the correct full name of the very Caiaphas who was high priest in Jesus's time. Inside the ossuary were the bones of four children, one adult woman and one elderly man, the last evidently the Joseph, son of Caiaphas of its inscription.

Many features of the interrogation and its associated sequence of events are intriguing and often still unsatisfactorily explained. Among them is the exact nature of the charges that Caiaphas and his aides bought against Jesus. According to the Mark author, 'the chief priests and the whole Sanhedrin were looking for evidence against Jesus in order to have him executed but could not find any' (Mark :14:55). What purportedly sealed Jesus's death sentence was his answer to Caiaphas's question: 'Are you the Messiah, the Son of the Blessed One?' This prompted the reply: 'I am, and you will see the Son of Man seated at the right hand of the Power and coming with the clouds of heaven' (Mark 14:62). Crying 'blasphemy!', Caiaphas reportedly called for his colleagues' unanimous endorsement as he sentenced Jesus to death for this outrage, and immediately received it (Mark 14:64).

As several modern scholars have commented, the puzzle here is that there was no great blasphemy in being a Messiah. As anointed monarchs, King David and Israel's other monarchs had all been Messiahs. Also in AD 132 when the Jewish guerrilla leader, Simon bar-Kokhba, rebelled against Rome, he would be acclaimed with the words, 'This is the king Messiah', by none other than the highly revered Jewish rabbi Akiba.

Whatever the answer, the chief priests reportedly handed Jesus over for execution to the Roman Pontius Pilate. Since Pilate is independently known to have been Judaea's prefect between AD 27 and 36, and as already noted Caiaphas was high priest between AD 18 and 37, these events must have occurred some time within these years. Further corroborating Pilate's historicity is a fragmentary, but still explicit, dedicatory inscription: '[Pon]tius Pilatus [Praef]ectus Iuda[ea]e', Pontius Pilate, prefect of Judaea. It was discovered in 1961 in the ruins of a Roman temple at Caesarea Maritima, the seaport that Herod the Great had chosen for Judaea's capital.

As represented in the gospels, Pilate was most unwilling to have Jesus executed. He agreed only when goaded with the suggestion that if he let Jesus go he would be no friend of the Roman emperor Tiberius. Even then, he reportedly washed his hands publicly, as if to absolve himself. Some historians see this as transparent make-believe by the gospel writers, who wanted to represent the Romans in a favourable light at a time when they needed to win friends among them. Another view is that Pilate may genuinely have been in some kind of superstitious awe of Jesus. This was the same Pilate who once, according to Josephus, abandoned the setting up of his legions' 'idolatrous' standards in Jerusalem, in the face of an impressive five-day Jewish passive resistance demonstration.[13]

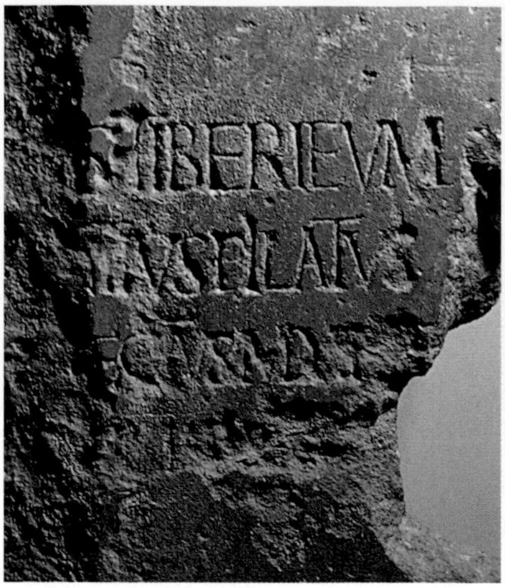

An inscription bearing the name of the Roman prefect, Pontius Pilate, found at the capital of the Roman province of Judaea, Caesarea.

Whatever the answer, there is general agreement that Jesus was scourged, i.e. whipped with a metal or bone-tipped whip. He was then forced to carry what was probably the cross-beam of his cross through Jerusalem's streets to the Golgotha, or Place of the Skull, just outside the walls. This seems to have been the city's well-established execution area. He was stripped naked, fastened to a combination of cross-beam and upright, i.e. the cross, and left to hang. It was essentially the same mode of punishment that 'King Jonathan' had so horrifyingly inflicted upon the eight hundred Pharisees just over a century before.

Today, we can all too easily fall into certain assumptions about Jesus's crucifixion, deriving from traditional church crucifixes which show him with his back to the cross, a nail through each palm and a third nail through both feet, neatly placed one on top of the other. It is rarely realised that the only textual indication that Jesus was nailed at all derives from a reported remark by the disciple Thomas, who, when told of Jesus's post-crucifixion appearance, reportedly said: 'Unless I can see the holes that the nails made in his hands, I refuse to believe' (John 20:25). There is little help to be had from two hard-to-interpret graffiti. They are virtually our only pictorial representations of crucifixion, dating from before the punishment was abolished throughout the Roman Empire in the early 4th century AD.

Nonetheless, valuable fresh light was thrown on the matter when an ossuary unearthed in Jerusalem was found to contain the bones of a young man from the 1st century AD called Jehohanan.[14] Scratches to the end of his forearm bones indicated that he had been suspended by nails in the wrists.

Contemporary graffito of a Roman crucifixion.

A large nail was still lodged tranversely through one of his ankles, suggesting that his feet had been nailed sideways against the upright of a cross. And a strip of wood beneath the nail head seems to have been intended to prevent him from pulling the nail head through his ankle in his desperate attempts to alleviate his agony. Medically, deductions of a similar crucifixion arrangement have been made from the controversial Turin Shroud.

One element that all the gospels agree on was a placard fixed on Jesus's cross, apparently written by Pilate himself: 'Jesus the Nazarene, king of the Jews' (John 19:19). Ostensibly, this was the ultimate epitaph for anyone foolish enough to make such a claim for himself.

As for Jesus's burial, we have the puzzle of how and why it should have fallen to a rich secret follower, Joseph of Arimathea, an individual not hitherto mentioned in the gospels, to step forward. While Jesus's corps of disciples seem to have been in total disarray, he sought a special urgent audience with Pilate, and obtained the appropriate permission to give Jesus's crucified body a decent burial in his own tomb. Of this tomb, reportedly rock-cut, just outside the city walls, and with a rolling-stone at its entrance (Matthew 27:60; Mark 15:46; 16:3-4), the gospels give us a totally convincing picture.

Admittedly, what is claimed as *the* location, long incorporated within Jerusalem's Church of the Holy Sepulchre, is completely unrecognisable as such. This is partly a result of seventeen centuries of well-meaning Christian embellishments combined with repeated Moslem destructions of the same embellishments. Even though its totally inappropriate 19th-century covering *edicule*, or 'kiosk', is in a state of near-collapse, its Greek Orthodox, Roman Catholic and Armenian Orthodox joint controllers have been endemically incapable of agreeing how it should be conserved. Nonetheless, archaeology has confirmed that this location would genuinely have been just outside Jerusalem's walls as they existed in Jesus's time. And a ten-year survey, the first since 1849, recently conducted by Oxford University's Martin Biddle, seems to enhance, rather than detract from, the case for this site's authenticity.[15] Furthermore, all around Jerusalem, tombs from the 1st century AD can be seen that readily convey what Jesus's would have looked like, whether he was buried at the Holy Sepulchre site or elsewhere. These even make sense of the gospel phrase 'in which no one had yet been buried' (John 19:41), because as they make clear the contemporary custom was for several generations of a family to be laid in a single tomb. Normally, bodies would first be laid out to decompose, then the bones would be gathered up into an ossuary, sometimes three of four skeletons to one bone box. Then, as further members of a family died, extension chambers, or *loculi*, would be cut into the rock, so that any one tomb might ultimately be the resting place of some seventy people.

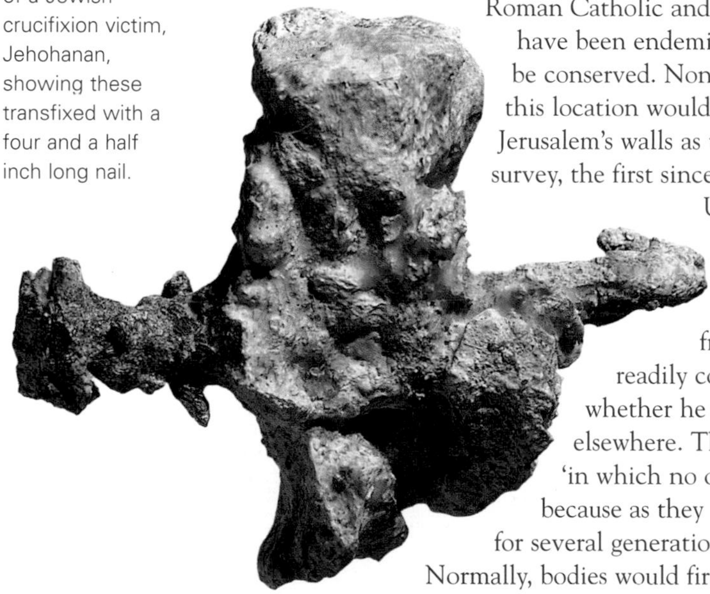

The ankle bones of a Jewish crucifixion victim, Jehohanan, showing these transfixed with a four and a half inch long nail.

Despite the various uncertainties, all of this might make it perfectly reasonable for the world to accept that, yes, Jesus was an inspired 1st-century AD Galilean teacher. He really did exist and caused a stir with his teaching, only to be crucified by the Romans at the instigation of Jerusalem's Sadducee high priests because of his stance against their Temple.

Except that, as is well-known, this was very far from what all his followers would subsequently claim for him.

19

'A VERY MINOR GALILEAN EXORCIST'?

ACCORDING TO THE John gospel, Jesus's crucifixion and that of the two robbers executed with him happened on the eve of the Passover Sabbath. It would have offended Jewish religious sensibilities for their dead bodies to be left hanging in public overnight on any night of the year, let alone at such a specially holy time. So Jerusalem's leaders reportedly asked the Romans to break the legs of all three. This apparently routine procedure was to hasten the deaths of anyone still alive towards the day's end. Once the crucified people's legs were broken, they could no longer push themselves up on the nails through their feet. As a result, they quickly died of asphyxiation.

Reportedly, Jesus, unlike the other two men, seemed to be 'already dead' (John 19:33). However, the men of the Roman execution squad were evidently trained to take no chances. We learn, again exclusively from the author of the John gospel, that one of the soldiers thrust his lance through Jesus's side, clearly in order to double-check that he was dead. Only then was Jesus's body handed over for a decent burial.

The first night that Jesus's corpse lay in the tomb would have been the Friday. So far as we can understand, this passed without incident, as did the Saturday. The indications are that, throughout this period, those who had been Jesus's followers assumed that their association with him had been in vain. After all, even if they had not been present, they would have heard how Jerusalem's Sadducee leaders had publicly taunted him, calling on him to get down from the cross if he was truly all that he had claimed to be (Luke 23:15). With Jesus's equally public death, without any such demonstration of divine power, it seemed as if all the hopes his followers had pinned upon him died too.

Then, suddenly, on the Sunday morning, all began to change. Although no one can deny that the gospel accounts have confusions and inconsistencies one with another, nonetheless these are not like the birth-story confusions. They are the sort of discrepancies that can occur among any group of witnesses present at a happening they are unable fully to comprehend. Thus, was it just Mary Magdalen who first found the tomb empty, as reported by the John gospel author? Or was she

'They had been saying one to another: "Who will roll away the stone for us from the entrance to the tomb?" ' (Mark 16:3). Here is a typical rolling stone tomb of Jesus's time, from near Jerusalem.

accompanied by 'Mary the mother of James and Joseph', as the Matthew author would have us believe? Or was there even a third woman, Salome, if we choose Mark, or Joanna if we prefer Luke?

Whatever the truth may have been, such differences are trifling. The essential point, upon which all the witnesses were agreed, was that the tomb was found to be empty, with according to the John author, the burial linens left lying *in situ* in an astonishing way. So astonishing, indeed, that when John (for it is pretty obvious that here the gospel writer was speaking of his own experience) arrived at the scene together with Peter and looked inside, both men immediately 'saw and believed' (John 20:8). The John author even explains precisely what he meant by this 'belief': 'till this moment they had not understood the scripture that he must rise from the dead' (John 20:9).

There survives, of course, in Turin Cathedral, a 14-foot length of linen supposed to have been the very winding sheet that Peter and John came upon at that moment. The Shroud is certainly compatible with Jewish custom and with the sweat-cloth which, according to John, had been 'over' Jesus's head, but had now, in the empty tomb, been 'rolled up in a place by itself' (John 20:7). Its most astonishing feature is a shadowy imprint. When viewed in negative, this reveals the 'photograph' of a naked, bearded man so convincingly covered in scourge and crucifixion wounds that fakery claims have yet to be satisfactorily sustained.

The arguments surrounding the Shroud, and the claim for it as some kind of snapshot of Jesus's 'rising from the dead', have been so intense that it is impossible to cover them adequately here.[1] Nonetheless, the utterly sober and clear-headed attestation of the gospels is that the Jesus who had been so publicly killed was now reported as being seen alive. And not just via enigmatic glimpses or as some still half-dead quirk of resuscitation. Instead, really alive. Walking and talking with a couple of disciples journeying to Emmaus. Appearing as if by magic through closed doors in a room full of his disciples. Yet he was no ghost. As if to prove this, he reportedly ate and drank in his disciples' presence. He also allowed the most sceptical, Thomas, to scrutinise the holes in his hands and probe the wound in his side.

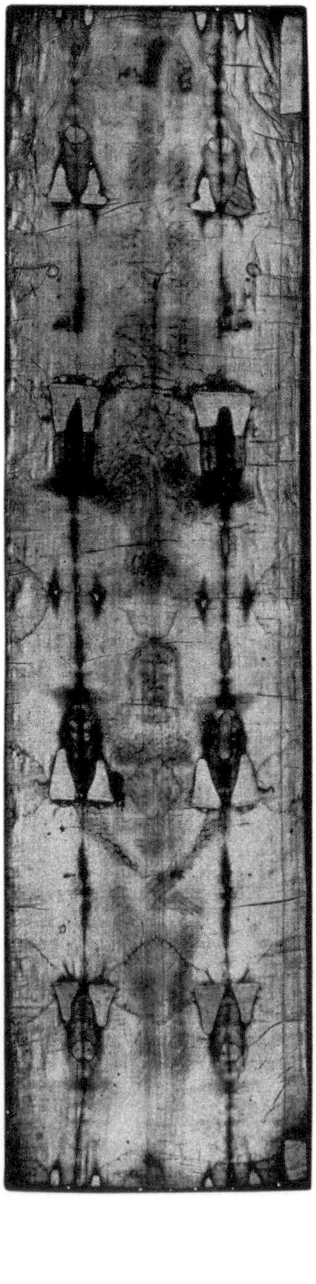

The controversial Shroud of Jesus, preserved in Turin (far left), bears a double imprint seemingly created by the body having been laid on one half of the cloth, and the other brought over the head and down to the feet. When viewed in negative (see page 241), this imprint takes on an extraordinary photographic quality.

Yes, of course, it's unbelievable. Reportedly, Jesus's own disciples, when they first heard what the women told them, thought that they were talking 'pure nonsense' (Luke 24:10). And if even Thomas, who had directly known the pre-crucifixion Jesus, was permitted some honest scepticism, should not we, two thousand years later, be allowed the same? Before taking up any dismissive stance, however, it is important to consider some of the other aspects of Jesus's life that belong to this same 'beyond normal explanation' category. It is important to assess the extent to which these, too, should or should not be taken seriously.

Jesus is reported to have carried out dozens of miracles of healing and exorcism. They are well known and common to all four of the gospels. Under the influence of philosophers

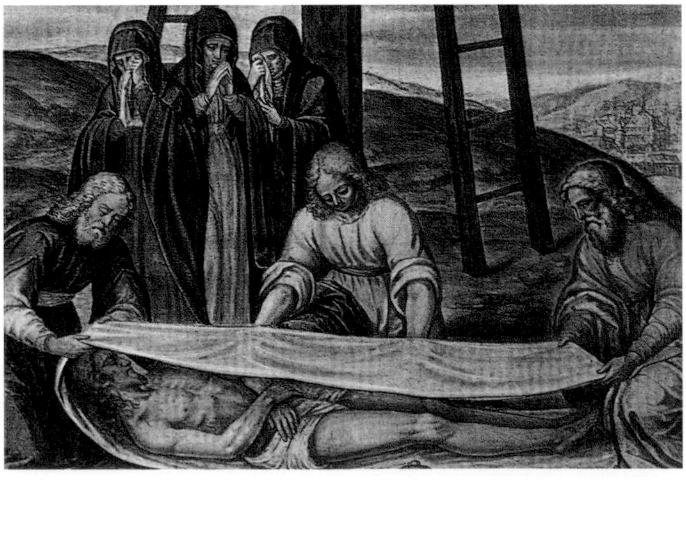

Jewish custom prescribed the use of such a cloth in the case of a corpse covered in bloody wounds. A 16th-century painting reconstructs (left) the wrapping of Jesus's body.

'Jesus said "Be cleansed!" And at once the skin disease left him and he was cleansed.' (Mark 1:40-42). Jesus heals a man with a virulent skin condition, from a 5th-century ivory from Palermo, Sicily.

such as Kant and Hegel, Christian rationalists, including the highly-influential German theologian Rudolf Bultmann, have tended to dismiss such gospel claims. These were added in, they assert, to make Jesus appear superhuman. Yet for anyone with a knowledge of some of the more obviously invented stories of history – for instance, some elements of Marco Polo's travels – there is a striking matter-of-factness in the way Jesus is described performing such deeds. And this demands at least a cautious respect.

Thus, the healing stories are among the rare instances where the gospels' original Greek texts sometimes recorded Jesus's words in their original Aramaic. This happens, for example, in the account of how he restored the hearing of a deaf man: '*Ephphatha*' – 'Be opened!' (Mark 7:34). It also occurs in the case of his bringing back to life a synagogue official's daughter: '*Talitha kum*' – 'Little girl, get up!' (Mark 5:41). It is as if the gospel writers were trying particularly hard to record these baffling circumstances as accurately as possible. There is also a strikingly consistent 'short, sharp command' authority in the way that Jesus speaks on these occasions, as if this really was how it happened. Moreover, even non-believing outsiders, such as the near-contemporary Josephus, seem to have attested positively that Jesus did perform these kinds of wonders. Josephus, called them 'paradoxical deeds', his own distinctive way of referring to miracles.[2] Some of the Talmudic references, despite being otherwise hostile to Jesus, likewise acknowledge his wonder-working abilities.[3]

Furthermore, if we suspect at least a hint of a strange-but-true, mind-over-matter approach to such healings, the same was also apparent in an incident recorded in the first chapter of the John gospel. Here, the newly-recruited disciple Philip, from Bethsaida, brought a friend called Nathanael to meet Jesus. When Jesus immediately praised Nathanael for his lack of any deceitfulness, Nathanael not surprisingly asked how Jesus could possibly have known such a thing about him. Jesus replied, 'Before Philip came to call you, I saw you under the fig tree' (John 1:47-49).

To this day, we have no idea what Nathanael was doing under the fig tree. But one thing is clear. To Nathanael, the fact that Jesus 'saw' him under the tree was apparently a mind-blowing demonstration of some paranormal ability. And it was just one of several examples. A Samaritan woman whom Jesus met at a well reportedly rushed back to tell her neighbours: 'Come and see a man who has told me everything I have done' (John 4:29). Elsewhere, the John gospel remarks: 'He [Jesus] never needed evidence about anyone, he could tell what someone had within' (John 2:25). The inference is that, 1800 years before the term 'telepathic' was coined, Jesus had a telepathic faculty. Arguably, this was none other than the same 'spirit of insight' that the *nabi* Isaiah had predicted of him.

Yet, if this was all that Jesus was about, if he was simply a teacher, healer, exorcist with some telepathic abilities, he might have merited A.N. Wilson's dismissive summation of him as just 'a very minor Galilean exorcist, no more significant than dozens of other similar prophets and preachers'.[4] After all, even Rasputin, in our own century, *seemed* to exhibit much the same collection of powers[5], whatever truth may have lain behind these.

Whoever Jesus was, however, the claim he made for himself was much more serious – and more unbelievable – than this. In the face of the 'telepathic' demonstration, Nathanael thought he was being bold enough when he acclaimed Jesus with the words: 'Rabbi: you are the Son of God, you are the king of Israel' (John 1:49). Others reacted in much the same way. After Jesus's purported feeding of the five thousand, for instance, the whole crowd were convinced that he was 'the *nabi* who is to come in the world'. Reportedly, they were 'about to come and take him by force and make him king', obliging him to flee 'back to the hills alone' (John 6:15). But, as Jesus insisted to the bemused Nathanael, he had seen nothing yet:

> You believe just because I said I saw you under the fig tree. You are going to see greater things than that . . . *In truth I tell you, you will see heaven open and the angels of God ascending and descending over the Son of Man*. (John 1:51)

There can be no mistaking Jesus's meaning here. His words were a clear allusion to the *nabi* Daniel's dread vision of the one who was to come 'on the clouds of heaven, one like the Son of Man' (Daniel 7:13). By evoking a heavenly vision and calling himself 'Son of Man' (as we saw in the last chapter, other gospel writers besides John quoted him using this expression), he was unmistakably identifying himself with the same heavenly being described by Daniel. Upon this being would be conferred everlasting 'rule, honour and kingship', with 'all peoples, nations and languages . . . his servants' (Daniel 7:13-14). With an authority and vividness way beyond that ventured by any earlier *nabi*, Jesus was promising Nathanael that he would enjoy the experience of a heavenly realm beyond the earthly order. More than that, he was also saying that he, Jesus, was somehow all-time king of all this.

But, as the Bultmann school of theology would argue, surely this was just a case of a gospel writer trying to 'divinise' Jesus, rather than what the man himself had ever historically claimed? Not a bit of it. Quote after quote from Jesus is indicative of the same line of thought, particularly in the John gospel, which appears to have been intended more for initiates than the other three were. And nowhere is this more clear than in the John gospel's chapter 8. In this, Jesus responded to the doubts expressed by critics that he could be greater than their revered patriarch Abraham. He claimed not only to know Abraham – prompting the incredulous sneer 'You are not fifty yet, and you have seen Abraham?' – but he also pronounced:

> In all truth I tell you,
> Before Abraham ever was,
> I AM . . . (John 8:57, 58)

In the face of these words, even claims that Jesus rose from the dead are almost as nothing. Either Jesus was stark, staring mad, madder by far than any of the earlier *nabiim*, with their wild dances and habit of wandering around naked. Or he was telling the truth, just as he most soberly insisted. Along with the A.N. Wilsons of the world, we are, of course, fully entitled to prefer the former. Jesus's detractors in his own lifetime told him to his face: 'Now we *know* you are possessed' (John 8:52).

But as we also know, the events that followed Jesus's death had a most extraordinary effect in persuading his previously so-dispirited followers that he had, indeed, been telling the sober truth. He really was the 'one who was to come', the one the *nabiim* had foretold. And they, his followers, were his witnesses.

Already, before the crucifixion, something of this should have become impressed upon at least a select few. This would have happened during the so-called Transfiguration experience while Peter, James and John were with Jesus on a mountain. Reportedly, he suddenly became transformed before them into an other-worldly Being of Light, accompanied by two other beings they somehow 'knew' to be the long-dead Moses and Elijah (Matthew 17:1-8; Mark 9:2-8; Luke 9:28-36). During this same incredible experience, the trio also apparently heard a disembodied voice telling them: 'This is my Son, the Beloved . . . Listen to him.'

However, after the crucifixion, there were some rather more down-to-earth happenings that transformed much wider groups of Jesus's followers. A particularly telling example is the Luke gospel's account of how two followers, one called Cleopas, the other unnamed, were walking the 7 miles from Jerusalem to Emmaus. They had just heard about the tomb being found empty, but at this point it still seemed to be completely unbelievable to them. As they told a stranger who joined them:

> Jesus of Nazareth, . . . showed himself a *nabi* powerful in action and speech before God and the whole people, . . . [yet] our chief priests and leaders handed him over to be sentenced to death, and had him crucified. Our own hope had been that he would be the one to set Israel free. And this is not all; two whole days have now gone by since it all happened, and some women from our group have astounded us. They went to the tomb in the early morning, and when they could not find the body, they came back to tell us they had seen a vision of angels who declared he was alive. Some of our friends went to the tomb and found everything exactly as the women had reported, but of him they saw nothing. (Luke 24:19-24)

The stranger to whom they confided all this was, of course, Jesus himself. But before he revealed his identity, he reportedly admonished them:

> You foolish men! So slow to believe all that the *nabiim* have said. Was it not necessary that the Messiah should suffer before entering his glory? Then starting with Moses and going through all the *nabiim*, he explained to them the passages throughout the scriptures that were about himself. (Luke 24:25-27)

The more this story is considered, the more it has the ring of a real-life event. Arguably, it was told direct to the Luke author either by Cleopas (thought to have been an uncle of Jesus) or by his unnamed companion. It is equally intriguing that in both this and his subsequent post-crucifixion appearances, Jesus clearly had every semblance of solidity. Thus, in the case of his appearance to the whole assemblage of his disciples in Jerusalem (Luke 24:36ff), he reportedly perceived intuitively their astonished thoughts that 'we must be seeing a ghost'. He specifically invited them to:

> See by my hands and my feet that it is I myself. Touch me and see for yourselves; a ghost has no flesh and bones as you can see I have. (Luke 24:39)

Even when the disciples were allowed to do this, they were still very understandably 'dumbfounded'. They could not believe their own senses. Their disbelief was scarcely eased when Jesus asked for some food and they offered him a piece of grilled fish: 'he took [this] and ate [it] before their eyes' (Luke 24:41-43).

As the Luke author goes on:

> Then he told them: 'This is what I meant when I said, while I was still with you, that everything written about me in the *Torah* of Moses, in the writings of the *nabiim* and in the Psalms, was destined to be fulfilled.' He then opened their minds to understand the scriptures.

And he said to them: 'So it is written that the Messiah would suffer and on the third day rise from the dead, and that in his name, repentance for the forgiveness of sins would be preached to all nations, beginning in Jerusalem. *You are witnesses to this*.'

To reinforce all this Jesus promised the disciples a 'power from high' that would help them go out and tell the world this incredible story. That power reportedly descended on the fiftieth day after the crucifixion. The descent took the form of an extraordinary psychical event, during which members of a huge crowd of visitors to Jerusalem all seemed to hear the disciples speaking in their own languages.

In this regard, nothing can be more telling than the extraordinary transformation that now became evident in the fisherman disciple Simon Peter, the disciples' deputed leader following the crucifixion. Only fifty days earlier, Peter had sat with John in the courtyard of the high priest's residence, while Jesus was being interrogated. He was so frightened for his own skin that he was prepared repeatedly to lie and to deny everything. Now, however, although fully aware of his leader's recent and appalling execution, he fearlessly and eloquently delivered the first fully public testimony of Christian belief in all history:

Men of Israel, listen to what I am going to say. Jesus the Nazarene was a man commended to you by God by the miracles and portents and signs that God worked through him when he was among you, as you know. This man, who was put into your power by the deliberate intention and foreknowledge of God, you took and had crucified and killed by men outside the *Torah*. But God raised him to life . . . and of that we are all witnesses. Now raised to the heights by God's right hand, he has received from the Father the Holy Spirit, who was promised, and what you see and hear is the outpouring of that Spirit . . . For this reason the whole House of Israel can be certain that the Lord and Messiah whom God has made is this Jesus whom you crucified. (Acts 2:22-36)

Whatever anyone's rationalist instincts may make of this 'outpouring of the Spirit' on Peter and the others, it is an incontrovertible historical fact that the belief that Jesus had indeed come back from the dead, that he genuinely had been the prophesied Messiah, began spreading like wildfire. In a way that had never before been even contemplated, it was recognised that Jesus's unspeakably agonising and degrading ordeal of crucifixion represented no stumbling block in the way of a belief that he had been the Messiah. Rather, it had become its very raison d'être.

According to the Lukan book of Acts, the disciple Philip found himself explaining this very point to the Queen of Ethiopia's treasurer. While journeying towards Gaza, he came across the treasurer, parked in his chariot by the roadside, reading the harrowing Suffering Servant passages in the book of Isaiah. These spoke of the Suffering Servant being 'like a lamb led to the slaughterhouse' (Isaiah 53:7). When the Ethiopian asked Philip: 'Is the *nabi* referring to himself or someone else?', Philip 'with the text of the scriptures' told him 'the good news of Jesus' (Acts 8:35). Philip then personally baptised the treasurer at the next watering place they came across.

Part of this new understanding was the belief that, whatever the sufferings a follower of Jesus might have to undergo for the sake of Jesus's 'good news' in this life, these would be as nothing compared to the rewards in the next life. Up to this point, Jewish understanding of an afterlife had generally been only of the very vaguest kind. The Sadducees of Jesus's time reportedly disbelieved in any kind of 'angelic' entities (Acts 23:8), also in any kind of resurrection (Matthew 22:23). And although some Jews, martyred during the Antiochus Epiphanes persecutions, died insisting that the 'King of this world' would raise them up 'to live again forever' (2 Maccabees 7:9), throughout most of the Old Covenant period the general concept seems to have been of a vague and gloomy Sheol. Only very exceptional beings such as an Elijah went to any kind of heaven.

What Jesus had taught, however, changed all this. Frustratingly, Jesus had never been altogether explicit about the nature of any heaven, or a hell. All the same, his 'Rich Man and Lazarus' parable – in which poor Lazarus goes to heaven after starving at an uncaring rich man's gate, while the rich man's fate is the exact reverse (Luke 16:19-31) – was plain enough. Herein lay an unequivocal promise that, however lowly your station in this earthly life, and whatever pain and suffering you might have to undergo, something infinitely more wonderful lay beyond. And not just for those who were punctilious (and self-satisfied) in the way they observed the *Torah*. It was overwhelmingly more important that you genuinely cared and had *heart*. There was a burgeoning flame of enthusiasm for this message. Reinforced by eyewitness reports that Jesus really had risen from the ghastliest of deaths, it could only be fanned, rather than quenched, by all attempts to repress it.

The case of Stephen was typical. He was a Jew who expressed rather too much enthusiasm for Jesus's 'good news' and was arrested by the Sanhedrin – the Jerusalem Jews' own 'high court'. The book of Acts describes Stephen rounding on his accusers. Their scriptures, he pointed out, were full of stories of their ancestors unjustly persecuting the *nabiim* for telling them what they did not want to hear. Their recent murder of Jesus had been in much the same vein:

> They killed those who foretold the coming of the Upright One [i.e. Jesus] and now you have become his betrayers, his murderers. (Acts 7:52)

Echoing Jesus's condemnation of the venality and corruption of the Temple's Sadducee proprietors, Stephen quoted Isaiah's words:

> 'With heaven my throne, and earth my footstool
> what house can you build for me?' says the Lord. (Acts 7:49)

Well aware that he had most likely thereby signed his own death warrant, Stephen reportedly cast his eyes heavenwards, exclaiming as he did so: 'Look! I can see heaven thrown open and the Son of Man standing at the right hand of God' (Acts: 7:56). Without further ado, his enraged hearers seized him and stoned him to death. Stephen's last words, like Jesus's, were ones of forgiveness for them.

In this regard, the extraordinary paradox for any cynic is the seminal effect of Stephen's execution, so swiftly following that of Jesus himself. For as the author of Acts tells us, with considerable authority, one witness to the deed, and one who temporarily approved of it, was a young Jew from Tarsus called Saul. It was at his feet that the stoning party laid their outer garments so that they could throw with the least encumbrance. That very day, Saul reportedly started his own campaign of 'bitter persecution' against those of Jesus's followers who remained in Jerusalem. The effect of this was to scatter Jesus's followers and so spread the 'good news' in rather more directions than might have happened otherwise.

Then something remarkable occurred. It was while Saul was on a mission to bring back to Jerusalem one such group of Jesus's followers who had taken refuge in Damascus, some 150 miles north of Jerusalem. According to the Lukan author of Acts:

> It happened that while he [Saul] was travelling to Damascus and approaching the city, suddenly a great light from heaven shone all round him. He fell to the ground, and then he heard a voice saying 'Saul, Saul, why are you persecuting me? 'Who are you, Lord?' he asked, and the answer

came 'I am Jesus, whom you are persecuting. Get up and go into the city, and you will be told what you are to do.' (Acts 9:3-6)

Blinded, Saul was reportedly led into Damascus by the hand. He spent the next three days in a house in the city's Straight Street without eating or drinking, until a disciple called Ananias arrived at his door. Ananias, we are told, had in his turn received a message from Jesus to call upon Saul. In view of Saul's reputation, he needed considerable reassurance that this was the man who would be Jesus's 'chosen instrument to bring my name before non-Jews and kings and before the people of Israel' (Acts 9:15).

As is now part of Christian Bible folklore, Ananias healed Saul of his blindness, and Saul received baptism shortly afterwards. Under the new name Paul, he became, in New Testament terms at least, the most vociferous and fearless proponent of the new cult of Jesus, after Jesus himself.

Just as in the case of Jesus, the Saul who became Paul was anything but folklore. Even G.A. Wells, the chief proponent of the 'Jesus never existed' school, has readily acknowledged Paul's historicity. The Lukan account of Paul's missionary activities in the book of Acts, combined with the survival and incorporation into the New Testament of fourteen of Paul's letters to people and communities he helped evangelise[6], are all of a piece in attesting to this.

For instance, even though we do not have any original manuscripts of Paul's letters, their whole phraseology as quoted in Acts and as attributed to him evokes that of early originals found archaeologically. Furthermore, however early or late we date the writing of the gospels, there can be no doubt of Paul's close proximity to Jesus's lifetime. The Acts account of his second great missionary journey describes the occasion, at Philippi, when he and his companion Silas preached what may well have been the first-ever Christian sermon on European soil. It also mentions his arrival in Corinth, when he was brought before the Achaean proconsul Gallio (Acts 18:12). Thanks to an inscription discovered in Delphi, Gallio's proconsulship can be precisely dated to AD 51-2.[7] From a simple back-calculation based on the known events of Paul's life, he must have begun believing in Jesus at least as early as AD 40, and according to some authorities even four years before that.

Nor is this the only element of Paul's life that is archaeologically checkable. In his letter to the Romans, written most likely from Corinth, he passed on messages from those he was with to the community of Jesus's followers in Rome. Among those sending messages was 'Erastus, the city treasurer, [who] sends greetings to you' (Romans 16:23). In 1929 archaeologists of the American School of Classical Studies in Rome were excavating in Corinth in a paved square just east of the city's Roman theatre. Here, they found a broken inscription datable to the second half of the 1st century AD, the surviving portions of which read: '*ERASTVS PRO AEDILIT[AT]E S P STRAVIT*' ('Erastus, in return for his aedileship, laid [this pavement] at his own expense').[8] Even though an aedile was not actually a city treasurer, but more like a city engineer or chief of public works, there is a general recognition that this may well have been an earlier stage in Erastus the treasurer's career in local government. At very least, there is a reasonable case for Paul's Erastus and the Erastus of the Corinth inscription being one and the same.[9]

Paul's third missionary journey reportedly took him to Ephesus, on the western coast of what is today Turkey. The vast theatre still exists where, according to Acts, the city's silversmiths gathered to protest at the threat Paul's new cult of Jesus posed to their trade in cult statues of the goddess Artemis. Artemis was, of course, none other than the old enemy Astarte/Asherah in her Greek guise.

Among the Roman remains at Corinth (above), the inscription (right) reads: 'Erastus in return for his aedileship laid [this pavement] at his own expense.' There is a strong likelihood that this was the same Erastus referred to in Paul's letter to the Romans, thought to have been written from Corinth.

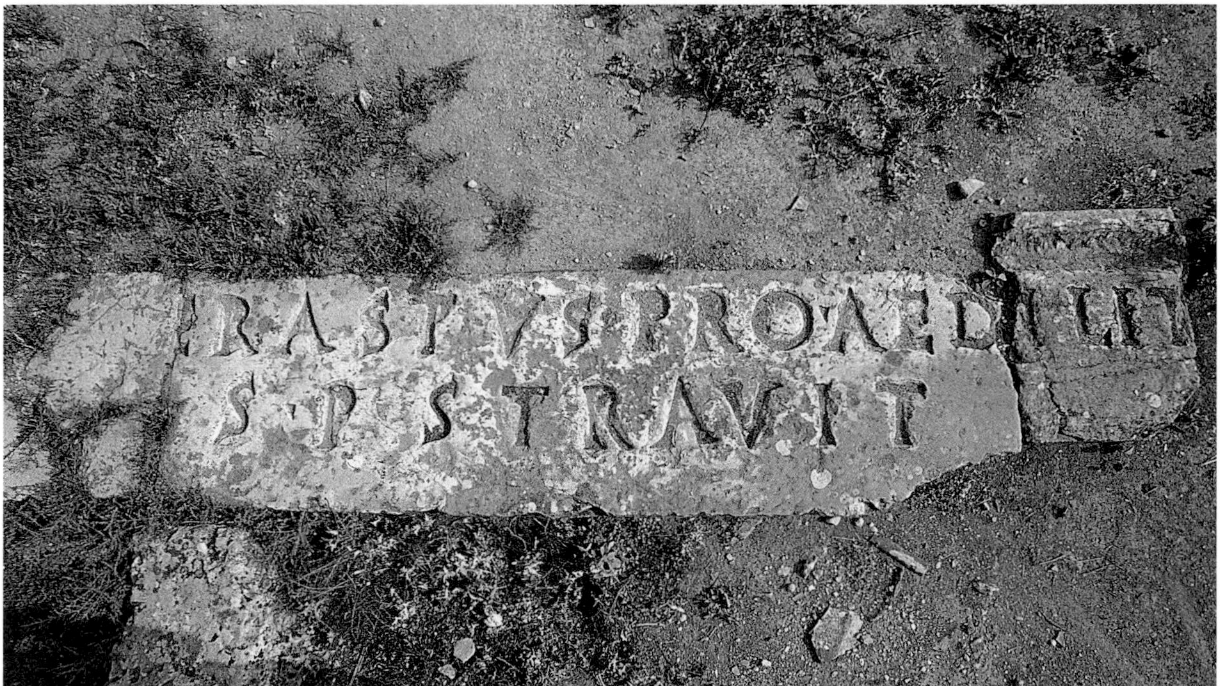
RASTVS PRO AED
S P STRAVIT

After a return to Corinth, Paul went to Jerusalem with donations from communities in Greece and Asia to help Jesus's original followers who were still in Jerusalem. These, however, were angry with him for evangelising non-Jews. On top of that, he had to face the outright hostility of those still implacable enemies of the Jesus cult – the Sadducee priesthood. The latter brought him before the Roman procurator, Felix, on charges that the message he was preaching encouraged people to flout the *Torah* and brought non-Jews into the Temple. At his headquarters in Judaea's capital Caesarea, Felix reportedly appeased the Sadducees by keeping Paul a prisoner, though apparently only in light captivity because he personally saw no harm in him (Acts 24:22). Thanks to very recent excavations at Caesarea, directed by Israeli archaeologist Yosef Porat, a palatial 15,000-square-foot complex has come to light, which may well have been the very building where all this took place. One 'office wing' sector, with a mosaic floor inscribed '*adviorib(us) offici custodiar*', 'I came to this office – I shall be secure', is thought by Porat to include Felix's audience hall. Elsewhere, there may have been Paul's cell.

Two years later Felix died. His successor Festus was at a similar loss to know what to do with his prisoner, and acceded to Paul's request, as a Roman citizen, to have his case heard in Rome. As described in Acts, Paul and other prisoners, still only lightly guarded, were escorted aboard a vessel some time around AD 61. This ship would take them at least part of the journey to Rome, only to be shipwrecked off Malta, which meant that Paul had to remain on the island over winter.

The next year, he was able to head onward. According to the Acts author: 'on the second day we made Puteoli [near present-day Naples], where we found some brothers and had the great encouragement of staying a week with them' (Acts 28:13-14). Since 'brothers' for the Acts author meant fellow Christians, there can be no doubt that the area of what is now Naples, some 1300 miles from Jerusalem, had already received

Present-day Caesarea, where Paul was kept prisoner for two years. Recent excavations have brought to light what may be the very building in which he was held.

evangelists for Jesus, even before Paul reached it. The book of Acts concludes by recording that Paul spent two years in rented lodgings in Rome, awaiting trial, still under a kind of house arrest. This suggests (though many scholars would beg to differ) that the book of Acts' author may well have completed his work before Paul's ultimate fate had become known.

Meanwhile, another individual seems to have had similarly colourful adventures – Jesus's direct disciple, Simon Peter. The book of Acts recounts some of these, though not as fully as Paul's. Reportedly, Peter was a particularly proficient exponent of the talent for healing that Jesus had taught all the disciples. With Paul, he also aligned himself in favour of non-Jews, as well as Jews being accepted as followers of Jesus. Acts 10 describes him visiting Caesarea, like Paul, and making a memorable speech in the house of a Roman centurion called Cornelius. In the speech, he insisted yet again that he and his fellow disciples had 'eaten and drunk' with Jesus 'after his resurrection from the dead'. Reportedly, Cornelius and his family were so moved that they received Christian baptism, and were among the very first non-Jews to do so. They insisted on Peter staying on with them 'for some days'. Peter, like Paul, would be last heard of in Rome – in keeping with this same evangelisation of so-called gentiles.

As in the case of Paul, the book of Acts tells us nothing about how or when Peter died. The early 4th-century Church historian Eusebius, however, had access to sources lost to us, and reported authoritatively that Peter had been crucified during the Emperor Nero's famous anti-Christian Rome pogrom of AD 64. Paul was also beheaded during the same atrocity. Those who survived seem to have given them both decent burials. Eusebius quoted this account by a late 2nd-century Rome Christian called Gaius:

> I can point out the monuments of the victorious apostles. If you will go as far as the Vatican Hill or the Ostian Way, you will find the *tropaia* (funerary monuments) of those who founded this church.[10]

Eusebius was writing in the time of the Roman emperor Constantine the Great. As he was well aware, these funerary monuments were rediscovered in his time and incorporated into basilicas that are today, respectively, Rome's St Peter's on Vatican Hill and St Paul-outside-the-Walls on the old Roman Via Ostia. By way of confirmation, archaeological excavations were carried out below the altar of the present-day St Peter's during and shortly after the Second World War. They revealed not only Constantine the Great's altar for the St Peter's of his time, but also, directly below this, the remains of a red-walled building incorporating a 2nd-century AD funerary monument, seemingly the same Vatican Hill *tropaion* of Peter that Gaius had referred to.

Reconstruction (above) of a 2nd-century tropaion, or funerary monument, built over what is now thought to have been Peter's grave. Right: A piece of plaster found adjacently, seemingly inscribed in Greek: 'Peter is within'.

If this, indeed, marks the spot where Peter was buried, what of his actual remains? There was a marble box which the excavators expected to contain them. When this was found to be empty, it was initially assumed that the remains must have disappeared long ago. Then, on a piece of plaster from the red wall below the high altar of St Peter's, someone discerned the faint Greek letters: '*PETR[OS] ENI*', 'Peter is within'. This led Italian archaeologist and epigraphist Margherita

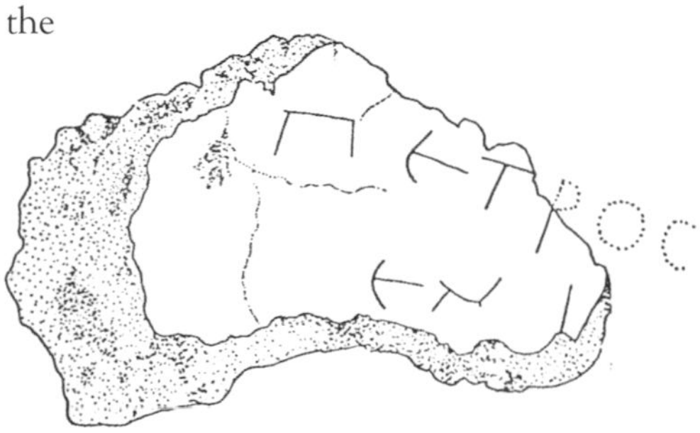

Guarducci to a set of bones that the excavators had originally stored away as of no consequence. According to her deductions, they had been buried exactly where she would expect Peter's body to have been laid. When forensically examined, the bones were found to be those of a man who in life had been around 5 feet 5 inches tall, robustly built and aged between 60 and 70. This is readily consistent with the age Simon Peter is likely to have been around AD 64. Earth particles still adhering to them matched the Guarducci location. Similarly, clinging particles of a purple cloth with interwoven gold threads corresponded to a cloth of purple recorded as being wrapped around Peter's bones for their reburial in Constantine the Great's time. There is, then, a very reasonable case for saying that the bones at St Peter's genuinely are those of the sturdy Galilean fisherman whom the earthly Jesus dubbed the '*Petros*', or rock, upon which his Church would be founded.

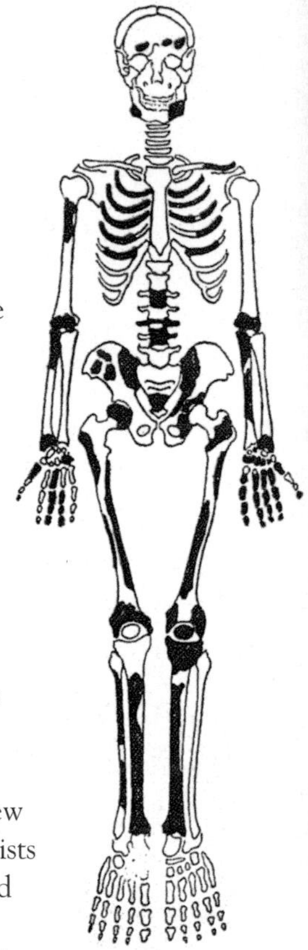

A set of bones (from which the skeleton above has been reconstructed) was discovered below the High Altar of St Peter's, Rome (right). The bones may have come from the body of Jesus's original disciple, Peter.

Certainly, what Jesus, Peter, Paul and others most successfully built among them, despite the intense opposition of the establishments of their time, was the institution we know today as the Christian Church. If they are evidence of nothing else, Paul's letters, as well as those attributed to Peter, John, Jude and James in the canon of the New Covenant, attest to the extraordinary vitality of the Church's earliest members. They also bear witness to these people's willingness to undergo the most agonising martyrdoms for the belief that somehow or another the one-time Galilean called Jesus had truly broken the bounds of death.

Equally, it is a straight fact of history that Herod's seemingly so-permanent Temple, which Jesus had predicted would be destroyed within a generation of his time (Matthew 24:1-3; Mark 13:1-4; Luke 21:5-7), did indeed suffer this very fate. When Jewish nationalists revolted in AD 66, putting up such strong resistance that it took the Romans four hard years to bring them all to heel, the Roman reprisal was to destroy the Temple (see picture, page 241). This task was carried out so completely that by the end of a second and final revolt in AD 130-5, not a stone of it was left standing above its platform base. From this disaster the populist Pharisees, with their scattered synagogues, emerged to form a new Temple-less, and therefore sacrifice-less and priest-less, Judaism. The priestly Sadducees, meanwhile, who had sent Jesus and his associates to their deaths, and for whom the Temple had been so lucrative a livelihood, were finished forever.

Inevitably, scholars will squabble till doomsday about whether Jesus really made the prophecy concerning the destruction of the Temple, or whether it was simply written in after the event had happened. In favour of the former is the fact that not a single writer tries to capitalise upon so dramatic a fulfilment of the prophecy. Whatever the truth, argument over this represents but a trifle compared with the huge enigma raised by Jesus in relation to our central subject: the book that all the world, Christian and Jewish alike, can call the Bible.

For can we accept that Jesus *truly* was the one whose coming was foretold by the Old Covenant *nabiim*? Can we believe that he *really* did come back from the dead to physically eat and drink with his disciples, as some seemingly sensible, down-to-earth individuals of his time certainly went to their deaths insisting. Is it totally inconceivable that he was *not* just 'some minor Galilean exorcist', but instead a supranormal being who existed and still exists beyond the bounds of time and space, and who will actually confront each one of us upon our deaths?

No issues can be more central as we marshal the ultimate evidence for and against the significance of the book we call the Bible. Yet no age more than our own, standing at the brink of the 3rd millennium AD, has been so full of individuals eager publicly to deny, twist and deride all such possibilities as outdated . . . So what, in truth, *are* the answers?

FIDES
MVNDO

20

BEHIND THE 'BONES AND FLESH'

AS HAS BEEN sagely remarked by the veteran Israeli archaeologist Avraham Biran, discoverer of the King David inscription at Tel Dan:

> . . . archaeology is not here to prove or disprove the Bible. What archaeology does is make the references in the Bible a reality. Archaeology gives these references some bones and flesh.[1]

Hopefully, throughout this book, we have managed to convey something of the 'bones and flesh', thanks particularly to the fruits of the many archaeological endeavours such as Biran's. In this way, we have shown that the references have a strong underlying element of historical truth.

Inevitably, it has been difficult to provide this evidence for some of the very earliest Biblical events. In the case of the Adam and Eve story, for instance, no rationalist would seriously argue that it is historical in the literal sense, though there must have been some point in human development when our undeniably natural nakedness became publicly offensive and shameful. In the case of a Flood, whatever event it was that lay behind the Biblical story, happened far too long ago to be considered history. All the same, Pitman and Ryan's evidence of a huge inundation in the Black Sea region, *c.*5600 BC, is undeniably compelling. With regard to the Biblical Abraham, even though he appears in no contemporary record, it at least makes sense that the age-old Jewish circumcision custom originated with some such itinerant Middle Bronze Age sheep-herder who substituted it for the horrifying Canaanitic child-sacrifice rite.

Coming onto firmer historical ground, the fact that kindred of this Semitic sheep-herder settled in large numbers in northern Egypt, may now be considered essentially established, thanks to Dr Manfred Bietak's Nile Delta excavations. Likewise, that centuries later descendants of these former settlers departed Egypt in some kind of major exodus cannot seriously be denied. The main difficulties here are exactly when this occurred, and whether it was genuinely associated with the eastern Mediterranean's spectacular Thera eruption. Certainly, in the light of Dr Bietak's recent findings of caches of Thera pumice in the Nile Delta, there are

Evidence that Jesus really did rise from the dead? The haunting 'photographic' likeness that is seen when the Turin Shroud facial imprint is viewed in negative.

fresh grounds for considering the Biblical Exodus story as fundamentally true. With regard to the Biblical Joshua, quite possibly there was rather more time and less continuity between the Moses group's departure from Egypt and the Joshua mercenaries' conquests in Canaan than the Bible account conveys. Nonetheless, the similarities between the Biblical book of Joshua's account of Jericho's fall and the demise of the Canaanitic city that archaeologists call Jericho IV are surely too close for coincidence.

Likewise, that a people called Israel, the name Biblically given to descendants of Abraham via Jacob, were occupying parts of Canaan at least as early as the late 13th century BC, may be regarded as firm, thanks to the clear testimony of the so-called Merneptah Stele. Again, as evident from Egyptian records, supplemented by archaeology, it is certain that Canaan was shortly after invaded by fearsome

Aegean peoples called *P-l-s-t*, and there is no doubt that these were the same as the Bible's Philistines.

Nor can there be any reasonable doubt that around the late 11th century BC, *someone* pushed these Aegean warriors back to the Mediterranean coast. The Bible attributes this to the mercenary war-lord David. This claim, although unprovable, accords with the Tel Dan inscription which confirms that there was a royal house bearing the name of David. In the case of David's son Solomon, while documentary evidence for him remains elusive, someone can be seen to have initiated major construction projects during what would have been his time. There is also evidence that he set up a Red Sea base for trading expeditions. Clear Egyptian documentation, again supplemented by archaeology, shows that shortly afterwards the new kingdom suffered a setback when the Egyptian Pharaoh Shoshenq attacked it in force and relieved it of much of Solomon's recently-won wealth.

From this point on, Biblically-named kings such as Jehu, Ahab and others begin to appear also in the records of other neighbouring nations, readily corroborating the supposition that the Biblical books of Kings and Chronicles embody true history. The same pertains to subsequent Biblically-described events such as Sennacherib's attack on King Hezekiah's Jerusalem around 700 BC, and Hezekiah's ingenious foiling of this. All the indications are that court scribes conscientiously chronicled the main events of these times. Their annals, now lost, were taken over by the compilers of the surviving Biblical books, whose penchant for national self-criticism, most unusual among the ancient world's surviving records, further corroborates their strong concern for truth. Nor can there be any doubt that this same reliable reporting tradition continued in the time of Nehemiah and Ezra, as well as later during the Hasmonean struggle to combat Antiochus Epiphanes' Hellenism.

Admittedly, during certain phases when earlier lost texts were drawn together to form the books of our present-day Bibles, some theologically-influenced interpolations and anachronisms crept in. Although these *are* Bible mistakes, as we should unflinchingly recognise, none of them are sufficiently serious to negate the strong underlying truth. Furthermore, by the 2nd century BC, the Dead Sea Scrolls provide surviving copies of Biblical texts that correspond essentially word-for-word with our present-day Bibles. This very fact shows that a tradition of excellence in copying and record-keeping had already been established, and arguably stretched back significantly further in time.

Once we depart from the Hebrew Bible, however, and venture into the New Covenant and all that is claimed of the Galilean called Jesus, difficulties proliferate once more. As we have seen, there is essentially no difficulty with regard to Jesus's historicity. We may not know the exact dates of his birth or death, but that he was a Galilean crucified on the orders of the Roman prefect Pontius Pilate some time between the years AD 27 and 36[2] may be considered as near firm history as makes no difference. We can also be sure that some surviving early gospel texts that recount his life and death genuinely are from very close to his lifetime. Although fragmentary, these again bear a close, word-for-word relationship to those appearing in present-day Christian Bibles.

Altogether more problematic, however, is the Christian claim that only very shortly after Jesus's crucifixion, even though his death had been carefully verified by the Romans, he reappeared alive and well. Thereafter, he was reportedly seen on a variety of occasions, and on one of these, according to the apostle Paul, by 'more than five hundred [people] . . . at the same time' (1 Corinthians 15:5-8). A variety of explanations have been offered, among them that the women witnesses went to the wrong tomb, that someone unknown removed his body and that the disciples hallucinated his resurrection appearances. However, by far the most popular 'explanation' has been that his resurrection was some

In a detail from Rome's Arch of Titus, Romans return from razing the Jerusalem Temple to the ground in AD 70, as Jesus had predicted just one generation before. They carry trophies, among these a great *menorah*, or candelabrum.

kind of cheating of death, much in the manner of those who are today clinically resuscitated.

Thus, for D.H. Lawrence seventy years ago in his short story, 'The Man Who Died'[3], Jesus merely fainted, then recovered to make his way to a Lebanese temple where his wounds and manhood were tended by a priestess of Isis. Hugh J. Schonfield likewise argued for resuscitation in *The Passover Plot*, a bestseller of the 1960s. In 1980 Baigent, Leigh and Lincoln revived this idea with huge success in their *Holy Blood, Holy Grail*, spicing it up with a South of France tryst with Mary Magdalen. In 1992 Australian academic Barbara Thiering took up much the same resuscitation stance in her *Jesus the Man.*

Also popular among sceptics has been the notion that the story of Jesus's resurrection was invented to divinise him after the failure of a militaristic uprising he led. As has been noted by several Jewish scholars, Jesus's disciples included at least one Zealot, Simon (Luke 6:15; Acts 1:13; Mark 3:19). Zealots were the early Jewish equivalent of today's terrorists. This, according to some, would explain why Jesus was so pointedly executed as 'King of the Jews' between two 'brigands', as some translations have it.[4] Joel Carmichael's *The Death of Jesus* adopted this theme in the 1960s, and Hyam Maccoby took it up with his *Revolution in Judaea* in the 1970s. A current torchbearer is Californian professor Robert Eisenman, by no means the first to argue that Paul divinised Jesus out of all recognition. In Eisenman's view, Paul was the 'Man of Lies' of the Dead Sea Scrolls.

Of course, it can be argued that such 'knockers' of the Christian story have simply chosen what they *want* to believe about Jesus, and then set out to find evidence to fit this. And who is to say that they are wrong? After all, those who claim gospel truth for the Biblical account of Jesus's rising from the dead can be accused just as easily of wanting to believe their version, a version that is altogether more incredible.

In this regard, although Jews for the last two thousand years have most strenuously denied the possibility, a reasonable enough case can be made that Jesus truly was *the* 'one who was to come', the Messiah of the Hebrew Bible/Old Covenant. According to all available evidence he genuinely was a descendant of King David, as predicted by Jeremiah 23:5. He genuinely was from Galilee as required by Isaiah's prophecy that the Messiah would honour 'Galilee of the nations' (Isaiah 8:23; 9:1). When he made his triumphant last entry into Jerusalem he did so, quite deliberately it would seem, riding 'a donkey' and 'a colt, the foal of a donkey', exactly as foretold of the Messiah in Zechariah 9:9. When the Roman soldiers prepared him for execution they 'took his clothing and divided it', then threw dice for one garment (John 19:24), precisely in accord with Psalm 22's 'They divide my garments among them and cast lots for my clothing'. Just as Psalm 34 prophesied: 'Not one bone of his will be broken', so Jesus was spared the leg-breaking meted out to his two companions (John 19:31-36). And just as Isaiah 53:9 predicted that the 'Upright One' would be given 'a grave with the wicked and his tomb . . . with the rich', so Jesus was executed between two 'bandits' (Matthew 27:38), then interred in the tomb of the wealthy Joseph of Arimathea (Matthew 27:57).

But as we saw in the last chapter, the Jesus of the New Covenant was far more unbelievable than this. If we accept what the gospel writers wanted us to accept, he passed through locked doors, yet he was able to be touched as if solid. He appeared and disappeared in a trice, yet he was physical enough to eat a piece of fish. If this really is what actually happened, then all attempts at rationalisation are useless. This man was either genuinely outside the earthly order, or you might as well tear the gospels up as pure fiction. You either accept his unearthliness, or dismiss it out of hand.

But if you have been educated to evaluate evidence – and evidence is, after all, this book's keynote – in order to accept it do you *have* to cast all your training in cautious scepticism aside and leap helplessly into the clouds of faith? The answer is that it does not have to be totally helpless. Even so, it *is* ultimately a matter of whether you can or cannot open your mind to the possibility that we really are something more than just 'bones and flesh'.

For, although as evidence-seekers, our concern throughout this book has been to check out the historicity of the people and places appearing in the Bible's pages, what has made the Bible special for so many people is precisely its harking to a something more behind our 'bones and flesh'. In particular, it is special for its characters' claimed interactions with a deity.

A qualification is needed here, for as we have seen the early Biblical writers, in common with most ancients, envisaged a deity behind even natural disasters and defeats, as in the case of the Flood, the destruction of Sodom and Gomorrah, the parting of the Red Sea and the collapse of the walls of Jericho. Yet atheists, agnostics and minimalists aside, even most thinking modern-day Jews and Christians will usually prefer a natural, rather than a 'divine', explanation for such events, just as we have adopted throughout this book.

Rather my interest concerns the many instances where the Bible deity instructs the Bible's characters, not so much how they should escape a Flood or conquer the Canaanites, but how they should *live*.

King David is a case in point. Although the 'bones and flesh' account of his reign mostly heroised him, the Bible also unhesitatingly recounted how he sent off one of his best soldiers, Uriah, to the front line of battle quite deliberately to get him killed. This was so that he, David, could then take over Uriah's wife. Ostensibly (i.e. at 'bones and flesh' level), David's crime might not seem so dreadful. After all, he did not personally, physically murder Uriah, and if Uriah just happened to have died on some distant battlefield, then what was so wrong in David marrying his lovely widow? For many, going about their daily jobs in the cut-and-thrust of the world's big cities, variants of such David-and-Uriah deeds are committed *almost* thoughtlessly every day. It is what the world does. It is what the TV 'soaps' are all about.

Only at the level of the mind, the heart, *or the Bible*, could David be perceived as having quite deliberately manipulated matters to his own selfish ends. This made him as much responsible for Uriah's murder as if it was he himself who had driven in the blade. Hence, the *nabi* Nathan's parable which so penetratingly appealed to David's sense of justice in 'doing for your neighbour as you would wish to have done for yourself'. This led David to recognise the injustice he had committed and his sincere repentance.

The amazing part is that when Jesus arrived a thousand years later with his quiverful of parables and his Sermon on the Mount, that sense of justice was set out so simply and perfectly for all minds to recognise and follow that, at a stroke, there was no need ever again for another *nabi*. And there never has been one. Thus, in the case of his 'Prodigal

Son' parable, in normal, 'bones and flesh', 'eye for an eye' values, all fairness had to be on the side of the 'goody-goody' son who stayed faithfully at home, while the 'prodigal' blew his chances. But this was not Jesus's justice. His justice, subject to sincere repentance, was for forgiving . . . and forgiving . . . and forgiving. And this is why, although so difficult for each one of us to follow in our daily lives, it was, is, and always will be, *truly* perfect.

By the same token, this is why the unearthliness of Jesus's teaching, the unearthliness of the circumstances surrounding his death and return to life, as well as of his 'I AM' utterances, are also all of a piece. They are absolutely intrinsic to the Bible as a book that is made whole only by their inclusion. You either recognise and accept these elements as belonging to the same fundamental truth as all its 'bones and flesh' material. Or you harden your heart, and go on again in the world much as you did before.

If the Bible were our only word for it all, perhaps we might still very justifiably plead that the times of the *nabiim* and of Jesus were far too long ago, and so why should we take any notice? What possible relevance can such ideas have for us in the 3rd millennium AD? However, it is worth noting that, only comparatively recently, we have seen an intriguing new twist upon Jesus's seemingly unique 'returning from the dead' and the message that accompanies this.

As is well known, some perfectly sane and ordinary non-religious people who have temporarily 'died', and been resuscitated from cardiac arrest and similar crises, can and

Just as, even in his lifetime, Jesus reportedly became 'transfigured' before his disciples, so some who clinically 'die' return to report their encounter with a 'Being of Light'.

do come back from this 'death', with strange stories of having glimpsed an unearthly dimension.[5] They describe meeting a 'Being of Light', strikingly reminiscent of the earthly Jesus's self-description: 'I am the light of the world' (John 8:12), and of his extraordinary Transfiguration. They describe how this Being read their thoughts, just like the earthly Jesus read Nathanael's in John 1:47-49, and how the Being exuded an ineffable love, as the love of the earthly and unearthly Jesus is described in 1 John 4:7-10.

There is an even more remarkable aspect of these testimonies. People who experience 'near-death', whether they were previously religious or not, return to life almost as if they have become 'down-loaded' with values that are *indistinguishable from those of Jesus's parables and the Sermon on the Mount.* They will often have a greater appreciation of nature, altogether less concern for their worldly possessions and personal appearance, and a markedly lesser fear of dying. Not least, they claim that the Being guided them through a series of 'out of time' flashbacks from their life, and by means of these allowed them to judge themselves. One Australian housewife, Laurel Lloyd-Jones, who was agnostic at the time, has described her 'life review': 'I can remember looking at it and assessing it and really judging it myself. I felt no one else judged me. I judged myself.'[6] Although hardly conforming to the conventional Last Judgment as envisaged by a Michelangelo, this is surely uncannily in accord with Jesus's Sermon on the Mount: 'The judgments you

give are the ones you will get, and the standard you use will be the standard used for you' (Matthew 7:12). It also recalls his 'Rich Man and Lazarus' parable, which concludes with the words: 'If they will not listen either to Moses or to the *nabiim*, they will not be convinced even if someone should come back from the dead' (Luke 16:31).

Ultimately, this can lead to only one conclusion. Either the whole 'shebang' – the Bible, Jesus's long-foretold Messiahship, his unearthly return from death, 'near-death experiences' and our sense of *something* death-transcending behind our 'bones and flesh' – either all these are just moonshine, in which case both the Bible and this book have been a waste of time and effort, or they are mutually corroborative evidence that there is some unearthly dimension behind our 'bones and flesh'. Either the whole thing is bunk, or there really is *some* Being – named 'Yahweh', 'Jesus', 'I AM', 'God' or whatever – who longs for *you* to turn *your* mind to some greater attention to Him/Her. And most particularly, as Jesus instructed, this Being longs for us to turn our minds to Him/Her in earthly form, as the individuals we may be most inclined to despise and reject.

For today's trend-setters, the 'Bible is bunk' argument holds sway. Under their 'progressive thinking', church attendances have been declining, Bible education is being replaced in our schools by ever-more liberal sex education, and BC and AD are likely anytime to disappear from our calendars in favour of BCE (Before the Common Era) and CE (Common Era). With triumphant self-justification, they point to all the many faults that have plagued Christianity durings its two thousand years – to its killings and persecutions of Jews, Moslems, Aztecs and Incas, schismatic fellow Christians, Galileos and others. And they say, with no little glee, that it has obviously failed, just as the Sadducees mocked Jesus on the cross for having obviously failed, and as the Canaanitic rulers tormented the Hebrew Bible's *nabiim* during the centuries preceding Jesus's coming.

Yet, Jesus never promised that his followers would lead perfect earthly lives as Christians. Less than twenty-four hours before his death, he coolly predicted that his own number-one disciple, Simon Peter, would shamefully disown him, as indeed took place. Well within a generation of his death, deep divisions broke out (I Corinthians 1:12-13). The present successor to Peter, Pope John Paul II, has recently gone out of his way to acknowledge and apologise for Christianity's historical failings throughout the twenty centuries since.

Likewise, Jesus never promised his followers that their lives would be blessed with earthly success. Very much the reverse. He warned them that they would have to suffer much, and told them that their role-models, those he deemed truly blessed, should be, not the rich, the famous or the trend-setters, but the poor, the widowed, the persecuted, and those ever-willing to give up their earthly place for others (Matthew 5:1-10).

It is undeniably true, of course, that the majority of people today continue to live out their lives oblivious to that message. They relentlessly devote themselves to the treadmill pursuit of the gods of money, fame, power, security and/or sex according to their particular inclination. To witness the TV soap glamorisations of lying and cheating, violence, extra-marital sex, occultism and much else, is to realise that in a very real sense the Canaanites are still among us, still upholding and abiding by the very values most abhorred by the Old and the New Covenants.

Ultimately, however, even if the earthly Canaan remains unconquered, and may forever stay that way, nothing of this can diminish the Bible, which embodies real history, and for all prepared to listen to it, enshrines what are still the truest, the most important and the most influential life-guidance messages ever written. As G.K. Chesterton remarked three generations ago: 'The Christian ideal has not been tried and found wanting. It has been found difficult and left untried.'[7]

Being of Light? Valiantly attempting to picture the unpicturable, Los Angeles artist Isabel Piczek's 'Risen Christ'. A detail from her 1300-square-foot mural of the Resurrection in the Holy Cross Mausoleum, Los Angeles.

NOTES AND REFERENCES

Introduction, pp 10 to 15
1 In the present-day state of Israel, vehicles owned by Palestinians are distinguished by blue number-plates.
2 *Tanakh The Holy Scriptures: The New JPS Translation According to the Traditional Hebrew Text* (Philadelphia, New York, Jerusalem, The Jewish Publication Society, 1988).
3 Professor Harold Bloom of Yale University has been quoted in the *New York Times Magazine* (William Safire 'BC/AD or BCE/CE?', 17 Aug 1997), as stating, 'Every scholar I know uses BCE and shuns AD.'
4 In the same article referred to in the previous note, another correspondent, Michael McGonnigal, is quoted as stating: 'It is one thing to deny the divinity of Christ. It is quite another to deny his historical existence, which is what is implied by the superfluous switch from the traditional BC to the PC [i.e. politically-correct] BCE.'
5 As but one example, the period 2200-200 BC has been labelled 'Intermediate Early Bronze Age-Middle Bronze Age' by the British archaeologist Kathleen Kenyon; Early Bronze Age IV by most American archaeologists; Middle Bronze Age I by the American archaeologist William F. Albright; and Early Bronze Age IV-Middle Bronze Age I by the Israeli archaeologist Amihai Mazar.
6 See James K. Hoffmeier, Professor of Archaeology and Old Testament at Wheaton College, Wheaton, Illinois, writing in *BAR*, Nov/Dec 1993, p. 8.
7 In actuality, Wyatt is understood to be a hospital anaesthetist.
8 David Rohl, *A Test of Time: The Bible from Myth to History* (London, Century, 1995).
9 Cemal Pulak, '1994 Excavation at Uluburun: The Final Campaign', *The INA* [Institute of Nautical Archaeology] *Quarterly*, 21.4, Winter 1994, pp. 8-16.
10 'Shipwreck gives up secrets of luxury in Homeric world', report by Andrew Finkel and Quentin Letts in *The Times*, 28 Oct 1996.

Chapter 1, pp 16 to 23
1 From an interview with William Dever, 'Is this Man a Biblical Archaeologist?', *BAR*, July/Aug 1996, p.62.
2 Like ancient Egyptian, also some other Semitic languages, Hebrew was originally written in essentially consonantal form only, without letters representing vowels.
3 N.K. Sanders (trans.), *The Epic of Gilgamesh* (Harmondsworth, Penguin, 1960).
4 Leonard Woolley, *Ur of the Chaldees* (London, 1929).
5 For instance, excavations even at neighbouring sites, such as Abu Shahrain, the Biblical Eridu, failed to reveal this same silt layer.
6 William Ryan and Walter Pitman, *Noah's Flood: The New Scientific Discoveries About the Event that Changed History* (New York, Simon & Schuster, 1998).
7 From the high proportion of tree pollen found in bore-holes, the Israeli pollen specialist Aharon Horowitz and others argue that the period between 7500 and 3500 BC was exceptionally wet.
8 See Patrick E. McGovern, Stuart J. Fleming and Solomon H. Katz, eds., *The Origins and Ancient History of Wine* (Philadelphia, University of Pennsylvania Museum/Gordon & Breach, 1996).
9 See *The Oldest Gold in the World – Varna, Bulgaria* (Jerusalem, Israel Museum, 1994).
10 I am indebted to geologist Professor Ian Plimer of Melbourne Unversity for helpful correspondence on this particular point.
11 Abraham is first called Abram in the Biblical texts, then this name is changed, but for simplicity this distinction is omitted here.
12 Leonard Woolley, *Ur 'Of the Chaldees': The final account, Excavations at Ur*, revised and updated by P.R.S. Moorey (London, Herbert Press, 1982).
13 J.B. Segal, *Edessa: 'The Blessed City'* (Oxford, Clarendon, 1970).
14 A prime Urfa tourist spot is the Birket Ibrahim, or Pool of Abraham, teeming with 'sacred' carp known as the 'fish of Abraham', and adjoined by a mosque, the Halil Camii, dedicated to Abraham. Another mosque, the Makam Ibrahim, marks a cave in which Abraham was purportedly hidden as a child, and includes a well which is the Turkish equivalent of Lourdes.

Chapter 2, pp 24 to 33
1 This tale exists in a number of copies, indicating that for the ancient Egyptians it was a prose classic, much like Homer's *Iliad* and *Odyssey* for the ancient Greeks.
2 A.M. Blackman, *Middle Egyptian Stories* (Brussels, Édition de la Fondation Egyptologique, 1932), pp. 23:32, 24:5.
3 These are the dimensions of an Early Bronze Age example excavated at Megiddo.
4 See examples in J.B. Pritchard, *Ancient Near Eastern Texts Relating to the Old Testament* (Princeton University Press, 1955), pp. 130, 131, 137.
5 As on the famous alabaster vase found at Uruk, Biblical Erech, the present-day Warka. See Henri Frankfort, *Art and Architecture of the Ancient Orient* (Harmondsworth, Penguin Books, 1954), pl.3a & b.
6 For examples and persuasive discussion of the prevalence of this in antiquity, see Julian Jaynes, *The Origin of Consciousness in the Breakdown of the Bicameral Mind* (Boston, Houghton Mifflin, 1976).
7 Sarah is initially called Sarai in the Biblical texts but for clarity this distinction is omitted here.
8 Yannis Sakellarakis and Efi Sapouna-Sakellaraki, 'Drama of Death in a Minoan Temple', *National Geographic*, February 1981, p. 205ff.
9 See Robert Graves, *The White Goddess* (London, Faber & Faber, 1961), p. 263.
10 Kenneth Kitchen, 'The Patriarchal Age: Myth or History', *BAR*, March/April 1995, p. 56.
11 Hence Sarah's words: 'Perhaps I shall found a family through her' (Genesis 16:2).
12 Kitchen, *op. cit.*, p. 56.
13 Paul W. Lapp, 'Bab edh'Dhra tomb A76 and Early Bronze I in Palestine', *Bulletin of the American Schools of Oriental Research*, 189, 1968, pp. 12-41.
14 See Walter E. Rast 'Bronze Age Cities along the Dead Sea', *Archaeology*, Jan/Feb 1987, pp. 42ff.
15 Graham M. Harris and A.P. Beardow, article in the *Quarterly Journal of Engineering Geology*, Nov 1995.
16 Nancy Miller, 'Patriarchal Burial Site Explored for the First Time in 700 Years: Twelve-Year-Old Girl Lowered into Cave of Machpelah', *BAR*, May/Jun 1985, pp. 26-43.
17 Rivka Gonen, 'Was the Site of the Jerusalem Temple Originally a Cemetery?', *BAR*, May/Jun 85, p. 53.

Chapter 3, pp 34 to 41
1 J. Elgavish, entry 'Shiqmona' in *Encyclopaedia of Archaeological Excavations in the Holy Land* (Jerusalem, Israel Exploration Society and Masada Press, 1975), vol II, p. 110.
2 Donald B. Redford, *Egypt, Canaan and Israel in Ancient Times* (Princeton, Princeton University Press, 1992), p. 424.
3 Barbara Bell, 'Climate and the History of Egypt', *American Journal of Archaeology*, 79, 1975, p. 258.
4 See W.C. Hayes, 'The Middle Kingdom in Egypt', *Revised Cambridge Ancient History*, fascicle 3 (1961), pp. 44-5.
5 This papyrus is the *Papyrus Brooklyn* 35:1446, so called because it is preserved in the Brooklyn Museum, New York.
6 This has been strongly argued by David Rohl, *A Test of Time, op. cit.*, p. 364ff.
7 Manetho's history, although lost as anything like an intact manuscript, has been fragmentarily preserved in extracts quoted by later writers of the Graeco-Roman era, chiefly Josephus (in *Against Apion*), also Eusebius and Julius Africanus.
8 Manetho, *Aegyptiaca*, frag. 42, 1.75-79.2.
9 A.M. Blackman, *Middle Egyptian Stories, op. cit.*, p. 15:3.
10 Donald B. Redford, *Egypt, Canaan, op. cit.*, p. 68.
11 Good News Bible.
12 Jerusalem Bible.
13 *Tanakh*, Jewish Publication Society.
14 New Jerusalem Bible.
15 The Septuagint's Genesis 46:34 specifically refers to Goshen as 'Gesem Arabias', *Gesem/gsm* being the ancient Egyptian equivalent of the Hebrew 'Goshen', and 'Arabias' linking it with Faqus, ancient Phakusa, capital of the Nile Delta's 'Arabia' district in ancient times.
16 Manetho, *Aegyptica*, frag. 42, *op. cit.*
17 Such looking out of the window appears to have been characteristic of the Canaanite female aristocracy, as will become evident from further texts and images later in this book.
18 Quoted in Donald Redford, *Egypt, Canaan, op. cit.*, p. 122.
19 This derives from the Carnarvon Tablet I, found in western Thebes, and appears to be a schoolboy's copy from a contemporary inscription. For the full text, see J.B. Pritchard, *Ancient Near Eastern Texts, op. cit.*, p. 232.

Chapter 4, pp 42 to 53
1 This particular translation is from the New Jerusalem Bible (London, Darton, Longman & Todd and Doubleday, 1985).
2 Edwin Yamauchi on what, in his opinion, has been Biblical archaeology's greatest failure, in *BAR*, May 1995, p. 35.
3 Martin Noth, *The History of Israel* (New York, Harper & Row, 1960).
4 The title 'admiral' is used very loosely here, largely to distinguish him from the pharaoh of the same name.
5 J.B. Pritchard, *Ancient Near Eastern Texts, op. cit.*, p. 233. It was ancient Egyptian army custom for soldiers to cut off the hands of enemy killed in battle as the proof of the deed so that they could claim reward.
6 Joshua 19:6.
7 D. Ninkovich and B.C. Heezen, 'Santorini tephra', *Submarine Geology and Geophysics*, Colston Papers, vol 17 (Bristol, 1965), pp. 413-52.
8 For an excellent account of the effects of the Krakatau eruption, see Tom Simkin and Richard S. Fiske, *Krakatau 1883: The Volcanic Eruption and its Effects* (Washington DC, Smithsonian Institution Press, 1983).
9 A. Herdner, 'Nouveaux Textes Alphabetiques de Ras Shamra', *Ugaritica*, VII, Paris, 1978, pp. 31-33.
10 Translation from Karen Polinger Foster and Yale University's Robert K. Ritner in 'Texts, Storms and the Thera Eruption', *Journal of Near Eastern Studies*, 55, 1, 1996, p. 11.
11 C. Vandersleyen, 'Une tempête sous le regne d'Amosis', *Revue d'Egyptologie*, 19, pp. 123-159.
12 Donald Redford, *Egypt, Canaan, op. cit.*, p. 420.
13 Manfred Bietak in Malcolm H.Wiener (ed.), *'Discussions' in Trade, Power and Cultural Exchange: Hyksos Egypt and the Eastern Mediterranean World 1800-1500 BC: An International Symposium*, The Metropolitan Museum of Art, 3 Nov, 1993. *Ægypten und Levante*, 5, 1995, pp. 123-4.
14 Manfred Bietak in *'Discussions' Ægypten und Levante*, 5, 1995, pp. 123-4.
15 Manfred Bietak, *Avaris: The Capital of the Hyksos Recent Excavations at Tell el-Dab'a* (London, British Museum, 1996), p. 68.
16 Vronwy Hankey, 'A Theban "Battle-Axe": Queen Aahotpe and the Minoans', *Minerva*, May/June 1993, p. 13. One theory is that the family bond prompted the Minoans, with sea power, to help dislodge the Hyksos/Canaanites from Avaris.
17 As in the JPS translation, used for most Old Testament passages quoted in this book.
18 From the *Bombay Catholic Examiner* reprinted in the *Times of Ceylon*, 18 Sept 1883, quoted with other examples in T. Simkin and R.S. Fiske, *Krakatau 1883, op. cit.*, p. 147.
19 According to relatively recent calculations made from Greenland ice core samples, the Thera eruption took place in the year 1628 BC. But in the light of the pumice found by Bietak in such a firmly datable context at Tell el-Dab'a, the ice core samples are now thought to relate to a different event. See forthcoming article by Peter M. Warren 'The Aegean and the Limits of Radiocarbon Dating' in K. Randsborg, ed., *Acta Archaeologica*.

Chapter 5, pp 54 to 63
1 See 'The Legend of Sargon' in J.B. Pritchard, *Ancient Near Eastern Texts, op. cit.*, p. 119.
2 Itzhaq Beit-Arieh, 'The Route through Sinai: Why the Israelites Fleeing Egypt went South', *BAR*, May/June 1988, p. 28ff.
3 See Donald Redford, *Egypt, Canaan and Israel, op. cit.*, p. 272. Also, R. Giveon, *Les bédouins Shôsou des documents Égyptiens* (Leiden, 1971), p. 26ff, doc 6a; 74ff, doc 16a.
4 See T.C. Mitchell, *The Bible in the British Museum* (London, British Museum Press, 1994), p. 31.
5 A cylinder seal of the mid-2nd millennium BC from Acemhöyük in modern-day Turkey, depicts a 'calf' poking its head out from a similar shrine.

Chapter 6, pp 64 to 77
1 C.M. Bennett, 'Excavations at Buseirah, Southern Jordan, Preliminary Reports', *Levant*, V, VI, VII, IX.
2 Gösta Ahlström, *The History of Ancient Palestine* (Sheffield, Sheffield University Press, 1993).
3 J.B. Pritchard, *Ancient Near Eastern Texts, op. cit.*, p. 259. This appears to have been a school copybook text, but based on a genuine frontier official's report of the period.
4 Charles R. Krahmalkov, 'Exodus Itinerary Confirmed by Egyptian Evidence', *BAR*, Sept/Oct 1994, p. 58.
5 For helpful discussion, see Duane Christensen, 'The Lost Books of the Bible', *The Bible Review*, Oct 1998.
6 Julius Wellhausen, *Prolagomena* (Berlin, 1901), p. 452.
7 See also Norman K. Gottwald, *The Tribes of Yahweh* (New York, Maryknoll, 1979).
8 The references repeatedly tell us that these were 'chariots of iron'. The iron is

another anachronism that crept in with later story-telling, since the metal did not come into general use until centuries later.
9 The notable exception to this is the Bristol-based Old Testament scholar John Bimson to whose *Redating the Exodus and Conquest*, originally written as a doctoral thesis, I am deeply indebted.
10 Bryant T. Wood, 'Did the Israelites Conquer Jericho? A New Look at the Archaeological Evidence', *BAR*, March/April 1990, p. 44ff.
11 Kathleen Kenyon, *Digging Up Jericho* (London, 1957), p. 230.
12 See Kathleen Kenyon, *Excavations at Jericho, Vol. 3: The Architecture and Stratigraphy of the Tell (Jericho 3)*, ed. Thomas A. Holland (London, BSA, 1981), p. 110.
13 Amos Nur and Hagai Ron, 'Earthquake!', *BAR*, July/August 1997, p. 54.
14 For a comprehensive catalogue of all seismic incidents recorded since 64 BC, see D.H. Kallner-Amiran, 'A Revised Earthquake Catalogue of Palestine', *Israel Exploration Journal*, 1, 4 (1950), pp. 223-46.
15 Kathleen Kenyon, *Archaeology in the Holy Land* (London, Ernest Benn, 4th ed., 1970), p. 181.
16 Kathleen Kenyon, *Jericho 3*, *op. cit.*, p. 370.
17 Kathleen Kenyon, *Excavations at Jericho, Volume 5: The Pottery Phases of the Tell and Other Finds (Jericho 5)* (London, BSA, 1983), p. 763, sample BM-1790.
18 Recorded events include 1927, 1906, 1834, 1546, 1267 and 1160.
19 This is in the form of the so-called Amarna Tablets, to be discussed later in this chapter.
20 Quoted in Donald Redford, *Imperial Egypt*, *op. cit.*, p. 26.
21 Amarna letter RA, xix. p. 106. The translation is from J.B. Pritchard, *Ancient Near Eastern Texts*, *op. cit.*, p. 487.
22 Amarna letter EA no. 288. The translation is from Pritchard, *Ancient Near Eastern Texts*, *op. cit.*, pp. 488-9.
23 See Donald Redford, *Egypt, Canaan and Israel*, *op. cit.*, p. 274.

Chapter 7, pp 78 to 87
1 See Lawrence E. Stager, 'The Song of Deborah', *BAR*, January/February 1989, p. 53, footnote.
2 See Michael D. Coogan, 'A Structural and Literary Analysis of the Song of Deborah', *Catholic Biblical Quarterly*, 40 (1978), pp. 143-166. According to Coogan, the Song's latest possible date is the 11th century BC.
3 Charles R. Krahmalkov, 'Exodus Itinerary Confirmed by Egyptian Evidence', *op. cit.*, p. 62.
4 This would again seem to have been adulterated by a 'd'/'r' interchange.
5 Wayne Horowitz and Aaron Shaffer, 'A Fragment of a Letter from Hazor', *Israel Exploration Journal*, vol 42, nos 3-4 (Jerusalem, 1992), pp. 165-7.
6 Adam Zertal, 'Israel Enters Canaan', *BAR*, Sep/Oct 1991, p. 32.
7 Lawrence E. Stager, 'When Canaanites and Philistines Ruled Ashkelon', *BAR*, Mar/Apr 1991, p. 31.
8 See Israel Finkelstein, *Shiloh: The Archaeology of a Biblical Site* (Tel Aviv Institute of Archaeology, 1993).
9 In ancient Egyptian, hash marks denote that the subject matter they refer to is plural.
10 J.B. Pritchard, *Ancient Near Eastern Texts*, *op. cit.*, p. 477b.
11 See Benjamin Mazar, 'The Early Israelite Settlement in the Hill Country', *Bulletin of the American Schools of Oriental Research*, Winter 1981, p. 75.
12 Such a fashion is further indicated by Exodus 20:6 which proscribes the use of steps to ascend altars to Yahweh 'for fear you expose your nakedness', an injunction that would surely have been unnecessary had their garments been anything like Canaanite-style ankle length.

Chapter 8, pp 88 to 101
1 Avraham Negev, 'Understanding the Nabateans', *BAR*, Nov/Dec 1988, p. 39.
2 *Bible Encyclopaedia*, Vol 4, p. 773 [Hebrew].
3 Adam Zertal, 'Has Joshua's Altar Been Found on Mt Ebal?', *BAR*, Jan/Feb 1985, p. 35.
4 Aharon Kempinski, 'Joshua's Altar – An Iron Age I Watchtower', *BAR*, Jan 1986, p. 42ff.
5 Leviticus 1:10.
6 200-600°C.
7 See illustration in *BAR*, Jan/Feb 1985, p. 42.
8 Israel Finkelstein, 'Shiloh Yields Some, But Not All, of Its Secrets', *BAR*, Jan/Feb 1986, pp. 22-41.
9 For this dating Finkelstein principally relied on a sherd of 'chocolate-on-white' pottery, archaeologically dateable only from this time onwards.
10 Finkelstein, 'Shiloh Yields Some, But Not All, of Its Secrets', *op. cit.*, p. 39.
11 Asher S. Kaufman, 'Fixing the Site of the Tabernacle at Shiloh', *BAR*, Nov/Dec 1988, pp. 46-52.
12 Exodus chapters 25-31.
13 Charles W. Wilson, 'Jerusalem', *Palestine Exploration Fund Quarterly Statement* (London, 1873), p. 38.
14 One certainty, from the tablets found at Ugarit, is that at the time the king of Ugarit was sending grain to southern Turkey 'to alleviate the famine there'. From tree rings, pollen deposits and related evidence, there is also much to suggest some climatic crisis around 1200 BC, which caused peoples formerly on the Hungarian plain to move into Greece and then out into the Aegean.
15 Quoted in Michael Wood, *In Search of the Trojan War* (London, BBC, 1995), p. 221.
16 Avner Raven and Robert R. Stieglitz, 'The Sea Peoples and their contributions to Civilization', *BAR*, Nov 1991, pp. 37-8.
17 The Jerusalem Bible translation has been used here as it is clearer than its JPS equivalent.
18 Pronounced MEEK-neh
19 For instance, the late Benjamin Mazar's excavations at the similarly Philistine Tel Qasile, just outside Tel Aviv.
20 George L. Kelm and Amihai Mazar, 'Excavating in Samson Country', *BAR*, Jan/Feb 1989, p. 41.
21 That is, cows not normally used as draught animals.
22 It was the redoubtable Edward Robinson who was again the first to make this identification, in this instance thanks to the nearby Arab village of Ain Shems, or 'Well of the Sun' having preserved Beth-Shemesh's name.
23 See Shlomo Bunimovitz and Zvi Lederman, 'Beth-Shemesh, Culture Conflict on Judah's Frontier', *BAR*, Jan/Feb 1997, p. 42ff.
24 Kelm and Mazar, *op. cit.*, p. 41.
25 David Ussishkin, 'Lachish: Key to the Israelite Conquest of Canaan', *BAR*, Jan 1987, p. 31.

Chapter 9, pp 102 to 117
1 The Egyptian 'Tale of Wen-Amon' mentions the *s-k-l* or Sikils as rulers of Dor at this time.
2 See Ephraim Stern, 'How Bad was Ahab?', *BAR*, March /April 1993, p. 22.
3 Confirmed as such by the finding of a 2nd-century BC inscription, reading 'the god who is in Dan'.
4 See Joseph Patrich, 'Hideouts in the Judaean Wilderness', *BAR*, Sept/Oct 1989, p. 35.
5 Some three dozen ancient slingstones have recently been found in an archaeological dig at Khirbet el-Maqatir, 10 miles north of Jerusalem.
6 According to Judges 20:17, the Benjaminite tribe included an elite corps of left-handed slingers: 'Every one of them could sling a stone at a hair and not miss.'
7 Volkmar Fritz, 'Where is David's Ziklag?', *BAR*, May/June 1993, pp. 58ff.
8 For a full account of this discovery, see ' "David" Found at Dan', *BAR*, March/April 1994, p. 26ff.
9 From a transcript of the heated discussion, see *BAR* July/Aug 1997, p. 37.
10 Philip R. Davies, ' "House of David" Built on Sand', *BAR*, July 1994, p. 54.
11 For detailed evidence, see Nadav Na'aman, 'Canaanite Jerusalem and its Central Hill Country Neighbours in the Second Millennium BC', Ugarit-Forschungen 24, 1992, pp. 275-291. Also, the same author's 'Cow Town or Royal Capital? Evidence for Iron Age Jerusalem', *BAR*, July 1997, p. 43 ff.
12 The JPS translation has been followed here up to 'get up the *tsinnor*', a phrase which is the subject of innumerable translation variants.
13 For a full list of the different translations of *tsinnor*, see Terence Kleven, 'Up the Waterspout: How David's General Joab got inside Jerusalem', *BAR*, Jul/Aug 1994, p. 35.
14 Charles Wilson and Charles Warren, *The Recovery of Jerusalem* (New York, D. Appleton, 1871).
15 Dan Gill, 'Geology Solves Long-standing Mystery of Hezekiah's tunnels', *BAR*, Jul/Aug 1994, p. 20ff.
16 Ronny Reich and Eli Shukron, 'Light at the End of the Tunnel', *BAR*, Jan/Feb 1999, p.22 ff.
17 2 Samuel 5:11 and 1 Chronicles 14:1.
18 From this vantage point, for instance, he was able to view army officer Uriah the Hittite's wife Bathsheba taking her bath (2 Samuel 11:2).
19 E.g. the late Yigal Shiloh. See also Eilat Mazar, 'Excavate King David's Palace!', *BAR*, Jan/Feb 1997, p. 52ff.
20 See 'Readers Speak Out', *BAR*, March 1995, p. 43.
21 Moshe Kochavi, Timothy Renner, Ira Spar and Esther Yadin, 'Rediscovered! The Land of Geshur', *BAR*, July/Aug 1992, p. 30ff.
22 See interview with Hershel Shanks, 'Avraham Biran – Twenty Years of Digging at Tel Dan', *BAR*, July/Aug 1987, p. 14.
23 Nehemiah 3:16.
24 Kathleen Kenyon, *Digging up Jerusalem* (New York, Praeger, 1974), p. 156.
25 Quoted by Hershel Shanks in 'Archaeological Encyclopedia for the '90s', *BAR*, Nov/Dec 1993, p. 60.
26 David Ussishkin, *The Village of Silwan* (Jerusalem, Israel Exploration Society and Yad Izhak Ben-Zvi, 1993), pp. 298-9.

Chapter 10, pp 118 to 133
1 1 Kings 3:1; 7:8; 9:16; 24.
2 See Hershel Shanks, 'Magnificent Obsession: the Private World of an Antiquities Collector', *BAR*, May/Jun 1996, p. 34.
3 As assembled in 1 Kings chapters 3-11.
4 1 Kings 11:41.
5 See *BAR*, Jan 1990, p. 44.
6 See *BAR*, May/Jun, 5, p. 67.
7 Nehemiah 2:8. The original Hebrew is often mistranslated as 'palace', or as in the New Jerusalem Bible 'citadel'. For discussion, see Leen Ritmeyer, 'Locating the Original Temple Mount', *BAR*, March/April 1992, p. 29.
8 Middot 2.1.
9 1 Kings 6:3.
10 1 Kings 6:17.
11 Leen Ritmeyer, 'The Ark of the Covenant: Where it Stood in Solomon's Temple', *BAR*, Jan/Feb 1996, p. 48.
12 Ritmeyer, 'The Ark of the Covenant', *op. cit.*, p. 71.
13 *Ibid.*
14 *Ibid.*
15 1 Kings 8:8.
16 See, for instance, T.C. Mitchell, *The Bible in the British Museum*, *op. cit.*, p. 42.
17 Trude Dothan, 'Ekron of the Philistines . . .', *BAR*, Jan/Feb 1990, p. 32.
18 1 Kings 6:30, 21, 22, 30; also the parallel passage in 2 Chronicles 3:4-7.
19 James H. Breasted, *Ancient Records of Egypt* (Chicago, University of Chicago Press, 1907), vol II, para. 883.
20 See Alan R. Millard, 'Does the Bible Exaggerate King Solomon's Golden Wealth?', *BAR*, May/Jun 1989, pp. 27-8, after Pierre Lacau, 'L'or dans l'architecture egyptienne', *Annales du Service des Antiquités de l'Egypte*, 53, 1956, pp. 221-250.
21 For background on Frank and Glueck's roles as wartime spies, see Floyd S. Fierman, 'Rabbi Nelson Glueck: An Archaeologist's Secret Life in the Service of the OSS', *BAR*, Sept/Oct 1986, p. 22.
22 From Glueck's official report on his excavations as quoted in Werner Keller, *The Bible as History*, p. 197.
23 Alexander Flinder, 'Is this Solomon's Seaport?', *BAR*, Jul/Aug 1989, p. 39.
24 As found by Flinder's expedition, and a few years later by a further visit by Rothenberg.
25 See Gary D. Practico, 'Where is Ezion-Geber? A Re-Appraisal . . .', *BAR*, Sept/Oct 1986, p. 24ff.

Chapter 11, pp 134 to 145
1 Ze'ev Herzog, Miriam Aharoni, Anson F. Rainey, 'Arad, An Ancient Israelite Fortress with a Temple to Yahweh', *BAR*, Mar/Apr 1987, p. 20.
2 Israel Finkelstein and David Ussishkin, 'Back to Megiddo: A New Expedition Will Explore the Jewel in the Crown of Canaan/Israel', *BAR*, Jan/Feb 1994, p. 41-3.
3 Kenneth A Kitchen, 'Where Did Solomon's Gold Go?', *BAR*, May 1989, p. 30.
4 *Ibid.*
5 John Baines & Jaromir Malek, *Atlas of Ancient Egypt* (Oxford, Phaidon, 1980), p. 48.
6 The possibility should be noted that the Jeroboam referred to was the second of that name, who reigned 793-753 BC.
7 This low platform may have been for a king's throne (which would thereby make sense of 'The king got up and took his seat at the gate' in 2 Samuel 19:8), or it may have been the base for a cultic statue.
8 G.A. Reisner, C.S. Fisher, D.G. Lyon, *Harvard Excavations at Samaria* (Cambridge, Mass, 1924); J.W. and G.M. Crowfoot, *Samaria-Sebaste II: Early Ivories from Samaria* (Palestine Exploration Fund, 1938).
9 Ephraim Stern, 'How Bad was Ahab?', *BAR*, March/April 1993, p. 26.
10 The scholars Yigael Yadin, John Holladay, Gabriel Barkay and David Ussishkin have all defended the identification of these buildings as stables. James Pritchard, Yohanan Aharoni, Ze'ev Herzog, Anson Rainey, Larry Her, Volkmar Fritz and John Currid have all disagreed, preferring to identify them as storehouses, markets or even barracks for troops.
11 T.C. Mitchell, *The Bible in the British Museum*, *op. cit.*, p. 44-5.
12 For full text, see Siegfried H. Horn, 'Why the Moabite Stone was Blown to Pieces', *BAR*, May/Jun 1986, p. 59.
13 Ze'ev Herzog and others, 'Arad, An Ancient Israelite Fortress with a Temple to Yahweh', *BAR*, March/April 1987, p. 34.

Chapter 12, pp 146 to 157
1 A slightly different translation to the JPS one has been used here, for its vigour.
2 D.D. Luckenbill, *Ancient Records of Assyria and Babylonia I* (Chicago, 1926-27), para 590.
3 The fact that the obelisk inscription describes Jehu as 'son of Omri', when Biblically all the indications are that he tried to obliterate Omri's descendants, may indicate that like Ahab, Jehu was descended from Omri, but via a different mother. Polygamy was rife among both Judah's and Israel's kings at this time.
4 1 Kings 18:46.
5 2 Kings 9:1.
6 2 Chronicles 21:16-17.

7 See Ze'ev Herzog, Miriam Aharoni and Anson Rainey, 'Arad, An Ancient Israelite Fortress with a Temple to Yahweh', *BAR*, Mar 87, p. 22.
8 Translation by André Lemaire in 'Fragments from the Book of Balaam found at Deir Alla', *BAR*, Sept/Oct 1985, p. 34.
9 See Ephraim Stern, 'What Happened to the Cult Figurines? – Israelite Religion Purified after the Exile', *BAR*, July/Aug 1989, p. 54.
10 See Nahman Avigad and Benjamin Sass, *Corpus of West Semitic Stamp Seals* (Jerusalem, Israel Exploration Society, 1997), p. 51; also Robert Deutsch, *BAR*, May/June 1998, p. 54.
11 See Zvi Gal, 'Israel in Exile Deserted Galilee Testifies to Assyrian Conquest of the Northern Kingdom', *BAR*, May/June 1998, p. 48ff.
12 J.B. Pritchard, *Ancient Near Eastern Texts*, *op. cit.*, p. 284.
13 The last two lines of this have been modified from the 'harlotry' of the JPS translation.
14 J.B. Pritchard, *Ancient Near Eastern Texts*, *op. cit.*.

Chapter 13, pp 158 to 165
1 Level VIII.
2 This is another matter of controversy among archaeologists. Yigael Yadin favoured the view that this particular altar's dismantling was due to later, further reforms by Josiah.
3 T.C. Mitchell, *The Bible in the British Museum*, *op. cit.*, pp. 66-7.
4 Magen Broshi, 'Estimating the Population of Ancient Jerusalem', *BAR*, June, 1978.
5 See Nitza Rosovsky, 'A Thousand Years of History in Jerusalem's Jewish Quarter', *BAR*, May 1992, p. 26.
6 The Jerusalem Bible translation has been used in this and some other instances in this chapter.
7 2 Kings 20:20.
8 Translation quoted by Jo Ann Hackett, *BAR*, March/April 1997, p. 42.
9 This is supported by the fact that Hezekiah described himself, in the reported words of his prayer on this occasion, as 'in the presence of Yahweh . . . enthroned on the winged sphinxes'.
10 Although caution is always needed with Biblical numbers, for Sennacherib to withdraw so abjectly necessitates that his losses were catastrophically high.
11 See Ronny Reich and Eli Shukron, 'Light at the End of the Tunnel', *BAR*, Jan/Feb 1999, p. 31.

Chapter 14, pp 166 to 177
1 From the prism in the British Museum.
2 Menahem Haran, *Temples and Temple Service in Ancient Israel* (Oxford, Clarendon Press, 1978), pp. 277-81.
3 Among the evidence that this colony was founded during the reign of Psammetichus I is the 2nd-century BC 'Letter of Aristeas'. See R.H.Charles (ed.) *The Letter of Aristeas* (Oxford, Clarendon Press, 1913).
4 Bezalel Porten and Ada Yardeni, *Textbook of Aramaic Documents from Ancient Egypt Newly Copied, Edited and Translated into Hebrew and English* (Jerusalem, Academon, 1986-1993), vol. II, B3.13:2.
5 See Bezalel Porten, *Archives from Elephantine* (Berkeley, University of California, 1968); also by the same author, 'Did the Ark Stop at Elephantine?', *BAR*, May/June 1995, p. 54ff.
6 Graham Hancock, *The Sign and the Seal: A Quest for the Lost Ark of the Covenant* (London, Heinemann, 1992).
7 Richard Elliott Friedman, *Who Wrote the Bible?* (London, Jonathan Cape, 1988).
8 *Ibid.*, p. 127.
9 See Tsvi Schneider, 'Six Biblical Signatures: Seals and Seal Impressions of Biblical Personages Recovered', *BAR*, Jul/Aug 1991, pp. 29-30.
10 The Jerusalem translation's 'fathered' has been preferred here in place of the JPS translator's archaic 'begot'.
11 British Museum 21946, 18-20. Translation in Lawrence E. Stager, 'The Fury of Babylon: Ashkelon and the Archaeology of Destruction', *BAR*, Jan/Feb 1996, p. 58. For scholarly discussion on the identification of this passage as referring to Ashkelon, see Stager's note 3.
12 Donald J. Wiseman, *Chronicles of Chaldaean Kings (626-556 BC) in the British Museum* (London, British Museum, 1956).
13 British Museum catalogue number WA 21946. See T.C. Mitchell, *The Bible in the British Museum*, *op. cit.*, p. 82. Photo is on p. 83.
14 This is now in the State Museum, Berlin.
15 That Ezekiel was among this first wave of exiles is evident from the fact that he foresees the final fall of Jerusalem from this perspective.
16 Quoted without source in Magnus Magnusson, *BC: The Archaeology of the Bible Lands* (London, Bodley Head and BBC, 1977), p. 205.
17 Jane Cahill, Karl Reinhard, David Tarler and Peter Warnock, 'It Had to Happen: Scientists Examine Remains of an Ancient Bathroom', *BAR*, May 1991, p. 64ff.
18 The New Jerusalem Bible translation has been used here as the more vivid, and will become the standard Biblical translation used throughout the rest of this book.

Chapter 15, pp 178 to 189
1 Paper given at the Second International Congress on Biblical Archaeology, Jerusalem, June 24-July 4, 1990, reported in *BAR*, Nov/Dec 1990, p. 51.
2 See Zechariah chapters 7 and 8.
3 In the light of this same passage, anyone who thinks that these Judahite exiles might at last be free of any Canaanite influence is misguided, for the words 'If I forget you, O Jerusalem, let my right hand wither' have an almost exact parallel in Canaanitic texts found at Ugarit.
4 Translation abbreviated and modernised by the author, after J.B. Pritchard, *Ancient Near Eastern Texts*, *op. cit.*, pp. 315-6.
5 The Talmud specifically states: 'In five things the First Sanctuary differed from the Second: in the Ark, the Ark-cover, the Cherubim, the Fire and the Urim-and-Thummim.' From Hebrew-English Edition of the Babylonian Talmud (London, Jerusalem, New York, Soncino Press, 1974), Tractate Yoma 21b.
6 See Lawrence E. Stager, 'Why were Hundreds of Dogs buried at Ashkelon?', *BAR*, May/Jun 91, p. 29.
7 *Ibid.*
8 Eilat Mazar, 'Royal Gateway to Ancient Jerusalem Uncovered', *BAR*, May/Jun 1989, pp. 38-51.
9 Ephraim Stern, 'What Happened to the Cult Figurines? – Israelite Religion Purified after the Exile', *BAR*, Jul/Aug 1989, pp. 22-29 and 54.

Chapter 16, pp 190 to 199
1 Lawrence E. Stager, 'Why Were Hundreds of Dogs Buried at Ashkelon?', *BAR*, May/Jun 1991, pp. 29-30.
2 Ecclesiasticus 50:27.
3 Ecclesiasticus Prologue 7-10.
4 Ecclesiasticus Prologue 27.
5 For the story behind this, see Molly Dewsnap, 'The Twins and the Scholar – How Two Victorian Sisters and a Rabbi Discovered the Hebrew Text of Ben Sira', *BAR*, Sept/Oct 1996, p. 54ff.
6 The dating is by the Seleucid era, which began with the accession of Alexander the Great's general Seleucus I in 312 BC. Seleucus's successors continued to date their years by his reign, even long after his death.

Chapter 17, pp 200 to 211
1 Michael Baigent and Richard Leigh, *The Dead Sea Scroll Deception* (London, Jonathan Cape, 1991)
2 Credit for this goes in no small measure to *Biblical Archaeology Review* editor Hershel Shanks.
3 Although we do not know when the first synagogue appeared, a famous inscription to a 1st-century BC synagogue in Jerusalem mentions one Theodotus as grandson of an archisynagogue, indicating that there must have been a synagogue in Jerusalem as early as the 2nd or 1st century BC.
4 Josephus, *The Jewish War*, Book 1, 110-112, trans. G.A. Williamson (Harmondsworth, Penguin, 1981), p. 41.
5 Esther Eshel, Hanan Eshel and Ada Yardeni, 'Rare Dead Sea Scroll Text Mentions King Jonathan', *BAR*, Jan 1994, pp. 75-78.
6 See Josephus, *The Jewish War*, Book 1, 110-112, trans. G.A. Williamson (Harmondsworth, Penguin, 1981), p. 42.
7 For some of the argument over the exact nature of the Qumran settlement, see 'What was Qumran?', *BAR* Nov/Dec 1996, p. 37ff; Jodi Magness, 'Not a Country Villa'; and Edward E.Cook 'A Ritual Purification Center'.
8 See Al Wolters, *The Copper Scroll: Overview, Text and Translation* (Sheffield, Sheffield Academic Press), 1996. See also Manfred R. Lehmann 'The Key to Understanding the Copper Scroll', *BAR*, Nov/Dec 1993, p. 39.
9 Despite popular supposition, calendrically the year 0, whether BC or AD, does not exist. Theoretically (based on calculations made in the 6th century AD), Jesus was born 25 Dec AD 1.

Chapter 18, pp 212 to 225
1 Acts 26:5
2 G.A. Wells, *The Jesus of the Early Christians* (London, Pemberton, 1971); Did Jesus Exist? (London, Elek/Pemberton, 1975); *The Historical Evidence for Jesus* (New York, Prometheus, 1982).
3 C.H. Roberts, *An Unpublished Fragment of the Fourth Gospel* (Manchester, Manchester University Press, 1935).
4 The supplements in question are the Baraitha and Tosefta. For the Baraitha passage, see the Babylonian Talmud, Sanhedrin 43a; for the Tosefta one, see Hullin (Profane things) II, 22, 23 & 24. A useful authority on these is Rabbi M. Goldstein, *Jesus in the Jewish Tradition* (New York, Macmillan 1950).
5 See my discussion of this, with sources and a proposed text free of tampering, in *Jesus: The Evidence* (London, Weidenfeld, 1984), pp. 60-62.
6 John Robinson, *The Priority of John*, ed. J.F. Coakley (London, SCM Press, 1985).
7 Isaiah 11:1: 'A shoot will spring from the stock of Jesse [father of David]'; Jeremiah 23:5: 'I shall raise an upright Branch for David; he will reign as king . . .'
8 Josephus, *Antiquities of the Jews*, 18.
9 See Stanislao Loffreda, *A Visit to Capharnaum* (Jerusalem, Franciscan Printing Press, 1980); also *Recovering Capharnaum* (Jerusalem, Edizioni Custodua Terra Santa, 1985).
10 John Wilkinson (ed. and trans.), *Egeria's Travels to the Holy Land* (London, SPCK, 1972).
11 Galilee's Yigal Allon Museum.
12 Even Jewish writer Hugh J. Schonfield argued convincingly for this in his *The Passover Plot*.
13 See Josephus, *The Jewish War*, trans. G.A. Williamson (Harmondsworth, Penguin, 1981), pp 38-9.
14 See Nicu Haas, 'Anthropological Observations on the Skeletal Remains from Giv'at ha-Mivtar', *Israel Exploration Journal*, vol 20, nos. 1-2, 1970.
15 See Martin Biddle, *The Tomb of Christ* (London, Sutton, 1999).

Chapter 19, pp 226 to 239
1 For an appraisal of the arguments, see my own *The Blood and the Shroud* (London, Weidenfeld, 1998).
2 Josephus, *Antiquities*, XX, 3, 3 (63-4).
3 According to one Talmudic reference: 'On the eve of the Passover they hanged Yeshu . . . because he practised sorcery and enticed and led Israel astray.' According to another, 'Jacob, a man of Kefar Soma, came to heal him in the name of Yeshu Ben Pantera'.
4 A.N. Wilson, 'Paul: The Inconvenient Christian', article in *The Times*, 23 Feb 1997.
5 See Alex de Jonge, *The Life and Times of Grigorii Rasputin* (London, Collins, 1982).
6 There is some legitimate scholarly doubt about Paul's authorship of the two letters to Timothy and one to Titus. Computer tests have served to corroborate what theological scholars have long suspected from linguistic and stylistic analysis, that whoever wrote these 'pastoral' letters was not the same person (indisputably Paul) who wrote the letters to the Galatians, the Romans and the Corinthians.
7 For a full discussion of this inscription, see A. Deissmann, *St Paul, A Study in Social and Religious History*, trans. L.R.M. Strachan (London, Hodder & Stoughton, 1912), Appendix I, p. 244ff.
8 John Harvey Kent, *Corinth: Results of Excavations Conducted by the American School of Classical Studies at Athens, 8/3: The Inscriptions 1926-1950* (Princeton, New Jersey, The American School of Classical Studies at Athens, 1966), pp. 99-100
9 It is worth noting that Timothy and Erastus are quoted as associates of Paul in Acts 19:22. Also, in the second letter of 'Paul' to Timothy, although this is thought to be by a later hand than Paul's, occurs the mention 'Erastus stayed behind at Corinth' (2 Timothy 4:20).
10 Eusebius, *History of the Church*, trans. G.A. Williamson (Harmondworth, Penguin, 1965), p. 105.

Chapter 20, pp 240 to 247
1 Avraham Biran interviewed by Hershel Shanks in *BAR*, Jul 1987, p. 22.
2 Most likely in either 30 or 33 AD.
3 D.H. Lawrence, 'The Man Who Died', short story first published in 1929, and republished by Penguin Books 1960 as part of the collection *Love Among the Haystacks and other Stories*.
4 Among the principal Jewish exponents of this idea have been Joel Carmichael in his book *The Death of Jesus*; also Hyam Maccoby, who in his *Revolution in Judaea* argued that Paul completely invented the idea of Jesus having risen from the dead as 'sacrificial victim' and thereby brought a fake 'Christianity' into being.
5 The pioneering book on these experiences was of course Dr Raymond Moody's famous *Life after Life*. But see also Kenneth Ring's Lessons from the *Light: What We can Learn from the Near-Death Experience* (New York, Plenum, 1998), and my own *Life after Death: The Evidence*.
6 Cherie Sutherland, *Within the Light* (London, Bantam, 1993), p. 200. In this, Laurel Lloyd-Jones is given the pseudonym 'Janet'. Laurel's story is told in detail in my own *Life After Death: The Evidence*, chapter 10.
7 From G.K. Chesterton, *What's Wrong with the World* (London, Cassell, 1910), p.36. I am indebted to Fr Bill O'Shea for first alerting me to this quote, and to Tony Evans of the G.K. Chesterton Society of Western Australia for kindly locating it for me.

GLOSSARY

Adonai (Hebrew) 'Lord'. In readings from the scriptures Jews to this day automatically substitute this rather than utter the Tetragrammaton YHWH, the four Hebrew letters that denote the name of God.
Asherah (Hebrew) Name associated with the Canaanite/Phoenician fertility goddess Astarte, the consort of Baal. There are some forty references to Asherah in the Hebrew Bible, mostly thought to denote some symbol of the goddess in the form of a figurine, tree or pole (ancestor of the May pole).
Astarte The Canaanitic fertility goddess represented via Asherah, and worshipped at high places and open altars. She went under a variety of names, another being Ashtaroth. In Ugarit she was Athirat-Elat. In Byblos she was called Baalat Gebal, and was depicted as the Egyptian goddess Isis. In Carthage she was known as Tanit Pane Baal, and in Sidonian Sarepta as Tanit-Ashoteret. In Mesopotamia she was Ishtar.
Baal (Hebrew) 'The Lord'. Canaanite/Phoenician god who went under many local names, and in imagery took the form of a young bull. Some Baals were connected with sacred mountains, such as Baal Saphon, and perhaps Baal Carmel. Others were connected with regions such as Baal Lebanon. Mainly they were connected with different cities where Baal had different names, e.g. Baal Ashmun in Sidon, Melqart in Tyre, Baal Gebal in Byblos, Baal Haman in Carthage.
Bamah (Hebrew) 'High Place.' Denoted a large platform as Biblically used for cultic rituals such as offerings or sacrifices.
Bayit l'Yahweh (Hebrew) The 'House of the Lord', often used to refer to the Jerusalem Temple.
Bet, beit, beth (Hebrew) House.
Bere sit (Hebrew) 'In the beginning.' The name by which Jews know the Biblical book of Genesis.
Bulla (Latin) Lump of clay used in antiquity to seal a papyrus document with the sender's seal, in much the same way that sealing wax continues to be used by some present-day law firms.
Canaan/ites (Hebrew) In the Hebrew Bible the land of Caanan is the *'eres-kena'an*, i.e. land of Canaan. In Hebrew the word *caana'ani* denotes 'merchant', and the Canaanites were certainly proficient traders. But another possible etymology derives from the Akkadian word *kinanhu*, referring to the red-coloured wool that was a major export. The Canaanites' later name Phoenicians derived from the Greek *phoinikis*, similarly denoting red- or purple-coloured cloth.
Cubit (Latin) Unit of measure, broadly based on the length of the arm from the elbow (in Latin, *cubitum*) to the tip of the middle finger. Biblically, various measures were used as standard. The most common seems to have been the royal cubit of 20.67 inches, or 0.525 metres. The original square platform of the Jerusalem Temple, as traceable from the length of the northern wall between the step and the eastern wall, has been measured as 861 feet, an exact 500 of these royal cubits. Many of Jerusalem's ancient tombs have been cut into the rock using this same cubit as their unit of measurement. The royal cubit originated in Egypt, and is referred to in 2 Chronicles 3:3 as the 'cubit of the first measure'.
Debir (Hebrew) The section of the Jerusalem Temple containing the Holy of Holies. It is sometimes translated 'shrine', sometimes 'oracle', sometimes 'inner sanctuary'.
Deir (Arabic) Monastery.
Ein, En (Hebrew) Spring of water.
El (Hebrew) 'God'. In Canaanitic mythology, chief of the gods (or Elohim), and associated with the bull. But the term is also used to refer to the Hebrew god in the 'E' strand of the Five Books of Moses.
Ephod (Hebrew) This could mean a linen, kilt-like cloth, as worn by King David when he danced and whirled before the Ark. Later it became a kind of breast-plate as worn by the Temple high priest.
Genizah (Hebrew) Repository for worn-out, discarded religious texts, which it was forbidden to destroy or discard, because they bore the name of God. According to Jewish law, books and ritual objects bearing the divine name were never to be destroyed, and should be buried in consecrated ground.
Habiru/Hapiru (Various) Also rendered 'Apiru. Denoted stateless peoples of no common language or ethnicity. They were apparently widely scattered across the Near East during the 2nd millennium BC, since they are referred to as living along the Tigris and in Anatolia, northern Syria, Canaan and Egypt. They are not specifically associated with a pastoral way of life, and in 18th-century BC documents from Mari they were mercenaries. An important recent find from the mid-2nd millennium BC is a cuneiform prism of King Tunip-Tessup of Tikunani, an obscure kingdom near the present Syrian-Turkish border, on which 438 masculine names, many Hurrian, many Semitic, are each identified as Habiru. According to Prof. Mirjo Salvini, this shows it was not an ethnic identification. Once thought to denote the Biblical 'Ibri, or Hebrews, current thinking is that the Hebrews were simply one small sub-group of the larger Hapiru class, and that while early Hebrews were broadly part of the Hapiru, by no means all Hapiru were necessarily Hebrews.
Hekal (Hebrew) 'Great Hall', or 'Great Chamber'. This denoted the inner part of the Jerusalem Temple, preceding the *debir*, or Holy of Holies. Some Biblical translations variously and misleadingly give it as 'temple', 'nave' or sanctuary' (see *BAR*, July 1987, p. 49).
'ibri (Hebrew) In Exodus 1, *'ibri* appear as slaves of Israelites; in 1 Samuel 14:21, they are mercenary soldiers serving the Philistines. Biblically, the word is most commonly used of so-called Israelites by non-Israelites. It is also used by Israelites to refer to themselves when speaking to non-Israelites.
Jebel (Arabic) Mountain.
Kodesh Ha-Kodashim (Hebrew) 'Holy of Holies', or 'Most Holy Place', depending upon the preferred Biblical translation.
L'mlk (Hebrew) 'Belonging to the king.' Inscription typically found on the handles of storage jars from around the time of Hezekiah.
Massebot (Hebrew) Sacred pillars.
Mechona, pl. **mechonot** (Hebrew) Translated 'base' in the King James Authorised Version when describing the furnishings of the Jerusalem Temple (1 Kings 7: 27-37). Now thought to have denoted wheeled laver stands of a kind that have been found in Cyprus, also at Philistine Ekron.
Mishkan (Hebrew) Usually translated into English as 'tabernacle'.
Mishnah (Hebrew) The collection of laws, regulations and customs governing Jewish religious practices as assembled during the latter part of the Second Temple period and subsequently after the destruction of the Temple of Jerusalem in AD 70.
Nabi (Hebrew) Usually rather unsatisfactorily translated in English-language Bibles as 'prophet'. Whereas the modern understanding of prophet is one who foretells the future, the principal attribute of the biblical *nabiim* (plural form) was as a voice or oracle for the Israelite deity Yahweh. Although some *nabiim* did utter prophecies, this was not regarded as their prime function
Palimpsest (From Greek) A manuscript on which the original text has been deliberately effaced so that its material, e.g. vellum, can be reused for another text.
Pharaoh (Egyptian) As *pr-o*, literally meant 'great house'. Egyptian rulers did not become so described until the 18th Dynasty.
Pym (Hebrew) Originally translated 'file'. Now understood to denote a balance weight made to an exact weight of two-thirds of a shekel to measure out silver. Biblically used just once, in 1 Samuel 13:21. The use of pyms died out after the 7th century BC, with the introduction of what we now term 'money'.
Se'ir (Egyptian) Place-name understood to denote the territory Biblically known as Edom.
Shasu, Shosu (Egyptian) Used in Egyptian inscriptions throughout the 18th and 19th Dynasties to refer generally to itinerant, pastoralist peoples, irrespective of their ethnicity. In Coptic, the successor language to ancient Egyptian, the word became *'shôs'*, or 'shepherd'.
Shekel (Hebrew) Unit of metal weight. Biblically, the most famous example occurs in Genesis 23:16, in which Abraham weighs out '400 shekels of silver according to the weights current among the merchants'. The Israelite shekel is thought to have weighed 11.4 grams, or 0.4 ounces. The *beqa* mentioned in Exodus 38:26 and Genesis 24:22 represented half a shekel
Sheol (Hebrew) Used to refer to the realm where the dead were believed to live on in darkness and helplessness, unable to know or praise God, until divinely rescued. Referred to in Psalms 16:10, 30:3 and elsewhere. That arrival in this post-death realm included a 'life review' (as subsequently taught by Jesus), is indicated in Isaiah 14:16.
Shittim (Hebrew) Acacia.
Stela, stele (Greek/Latin) Upright stone slab bearing an inscription and possibly accompanying imagery.
Succoth (Hebrew) 'Shelters' or 'Tabernacles'. Particularly denotes the temporary dwellings used by the Israelites during their wilderness years, the major feast of this name apparently having been introduced by Ezra.
Tanakh (Hebrew) Acronym for the three divisions of the Hebrew Bible: the Torah or Law (also called the Pentateuch or Five Books of Moses); the Nevi'im or Nabi'im (i.e. Prophets), and the Ketuvim or Writings.
Tel, tell (Hebrew/Arabic) An artificial mound created by accumulated human habitation over hundreds and sometimes thousands of years.
Terebinth (Greek) Turpentine tree.
Tophet (Hebrew) Location immediately south-west of Jerusalem where Canaanite-style human sacrifice was carried out up to the time of the reforms of King Josiah (see 2 Kings 23:10; Jeremiah 7:31).
Tsinnor (Hebrew – rare) Conduit for rushing water.
Ulam (Hebrew) The portico, or porch, of the Jerusalem Temple.
Yahweh (Hebrew) As YHWH in consonantless written Hebrew, the name of the Hebrew God used in the 'J' strand of the Five Books of Moses and later. Some Biblical translations inaccurately render this Jehovah. Jewish tradition forbade utterance of the Sacred Name, and the synagogue reader always substituting *Adonai*, or lord. Yet the name was sometimes added to personal names, e.g. in Israel's northern kingdom *Yo-* (YW) was generally used at the beginning of a name and *-yo* (YW) or *-yah* (YH) at the end of a name. In the southern kingdom of Judah it was *Yeho-* (YHW) at the beginning of a name and *-yahu* (YHW) at the end.
Yahweh Sabaoth (Hebrew) Yahweh of 'hosts', or 'armies'. The deity the Hebrew peoples traditionally invoked to help them against a great power, as in the case of Egypt in Exodus 7:4, and Assyria in 2 Kings 19:15.

INDEX

Page numbers in *italics* denote illustrations

ACKNOWLEDGMENTS

Abbreviations:
T=Top; M=Middle;
B=Bottom;
R=Right; L=Left

BAR= *Biblical Archaeology Review*

1 Sonia Halliday Photographs/ Laura Lushington. 6-7, 8 Colin Woodman. 11 Radovan. 13 Courtesy of the Leon Levy Expedition to Ashkelon/ photography, Carl Andrews. 14, 15 Courtesy of the Institute of Nautical Archaeology. 17 Robert Harding Picture Library. 18 Courtesy of the British Museum, London/ Western Asiatic (K3375). 20, 21 Colin Woodman. 21 Antonia Benedek, BL. 22 Colin Woodman. 22-23 Robert Harding Picture Library. 25 Science Photo Library/NASA. 26 Zev Radovan, TR, BR. 27 Louvre Museum, Paris. 28 Ian Wilson, TR, B. 29 Scala. 30 Science Photo Library/Earth Satellite Corporation. 31 Colin Woodman. 32 Sonia Halliday Photographs. 33 Courtesy of Theodore Rosen/BAR May/June 1985. 34 Haifa Museum. 35 Science Photo Library/Earth Satellite Corporation. 36 Michael Holford, T; AKG/Eric Lessing, B. 37 Courtesy of Dr Manfred Bietak, redrawn from *Avaris: The Capital of the Hyksos*, by Manfred Bietak, British Museum, London, 1996/Roger Hutchins. 38 Courtesy Dr Manfred Bietak. 40 AKG/Eric Lessing. 41 Peter Clayton. 43 David Harris. 44 Peter Clayton. 45 Colin Woodman. 46 Roger Hutchins, TL; G. Goakimedes, B. 46-47 Jürgen Liepe. 47 Colin Woodman, ML. 49 BAR January 1990. 50-51 Roger Hutchins. 52 AKG/Eric Lessing. 55 Science Photo Library /Earth Satellite Corporation. 56 Colin Woodman. 57, 58-59 David Harris. 59 Courtesy of the British Museum, London/Egyptian Department (41748). 60 Ian Wilson. 61 Zev Radovan. 62 The Griffith Institute/ Howard Carter Archive. 63 Roger Hutchins, T; David Harris, B. 65 Zev Radovan. 67 AKG/Eric Lessing. 68 Colin Woodman. 69 Roger Hutchins. 70 Zev Radovan. 71 Kathleen Kenyon/BAR March 1990. 72 Roger Hutchins. 73 Christine Osborne, TL; Jericho Excavation Fund/BAR March 1990, MR; T. Sagin, Israel Department of Antiquities/BAR March 1990, BR. 74 Werner Braun. 76 Jürgen Liepe. 79 David Harris. 81 Zev Radovan. 82 Werner Braun. 84 Colin Woodman. 85 Werner Braun. 86 Jürgen Liepe. 87 Garo Nalbandian/BAR July/August 1997, T; BAR July/August 1997, B. 89 Adapted from drawing made under the direction of Professor Lawrence E. Stager/BAR January 1989/ Roger Hutchins. 90 Zev Radovan. 92 Zev Radovan, T; Judith Dekel/BAR January 1985, B. 93 Paul F. Kiene copyright 197 The Zondervan Corporation/BAR November 1988. 94 Zev Radovan. 95 AKG/Eric Lessing. 96 AKG/ Eric Lessing, TL; Colin Woodman, BR. 97 Zev Radovan, TL; Ilan Sztulman/ BAR September 1993, BR. 98 Israel Antiquities Authority/ Roger Hutchins, T; Zev Radovan, B. 100-1 Zev Radovan. 103 Sonia Halliday Photographs/Laura Lushington. 104 Gabi Laron/BAR September 1989, T; C.M. Dixon, B. 105 Gary Byers, *To Sling or Not To Sling – That Was Never The Question*, (http://christiananswers.net/abr/ scoop.html) As downloaded in July 1999/Israel Department of Antiquities. 106, 108 Zev Radovan. 110 Werner Braun. 112, 114 Zev Radovan. 115 Scala. 116 Werner Braun. 117 Roger Hutchins. 119, 121 Zev Radovan. 120, 122 David Harris. 123 BAR March 1987. 124 Leen Ritmeyer, TR. 124-125 Roger Hutchins. 126 David Harris. 127 Leen Ritmeyer. 128 Michael Holford. 129 AKG/Egyptian Museum, Cairo, TL; Zev Radovan, BR. 130 Colin Woodman. 132-133 Werner Braun. 135, 136 Peter Clayton. 137 Zev Radovan. 138 Ian Wilson. 140 David Harris, T; Zev Radovan, B. 141 Zev Radovan. 142 Courtesy of the British Museum, London/Western Asiatic (118884). 143 AKG/ Louvre Museum, Paris/Eric Lessing. 144 Sonia Halliday Photographs/Jane Tatlor. 145 Zev Radovan. 147 Zev Radovan, L; Avraham Hai/ BAR November/December 1984, TR, MR. 149 Courtesy of the British Museum, London/ Western Asiatic (118159). 150 AKG/British Museum, London/Eric Lessing. 152 City of David Archaeological Expedition/Drawing by Sarah Halbreich/BAR March 1988. 153 André Lemaire, adapted from a drawing by G. Van der Kooij/BAR September 1985. 154-161 Zev Radovan. 162 David Harris. 163 Zev Radovan. 164 Werner Braun. 165 Sonia Halliday Photographs. 167 Zev Radovan. 168 Bruce & Kenneth Zuckerman, West Semitic Research, State Museum, Berlin/Egyptian Department/ BAR May/June 1995. 172, 173 Zev Radovan. 175 Courtesy of the Leon Levy Expedition to Ashkelon/ photography, Carl Andrews. 176 Courtesy of the British Museum, London/Western Asiatic (125702), T; Ancient Art & Architecture/Ronald Sheridan, B. 177 City of David Society/BAR May 1991. 179 AKG/Archaeological Museum, Istanbul/Eric Lessing. 180 AKG/State Museum, Berlin/Eric Lessing. 182 Courtesy of the British Museum, London/Western Asiatic (90920). 184 AKG/ Louvre Museum, Paris/Eric Lessing. 186 Sonia Halliday Photographs, TL; Roger Hutchins/Plan redrawn from map by J.J. Bimson & J.P. Kane from *New Bible Atlas*, Lion Publishing/BAR January 1997 TR. 188 Zev Radovan. 191, 192-193 AKG/National Museum of Archaeology, Naples/Eric Lessing. 194 *The Great Sea*, 1870, painting by W. Simpson/Palestine Exploration Fund. 196 Zev Radovan, T; Leen Ritmeyer, MR. 197 AKG/Israel Museum, Jerusalem (IDAM)/Eric Lessing, TL; Reliefs from base of statue in Athens/Athens National Museum, from *Hella And Rome, The Classical World in Pictures*, by W. Zschietzschmann, A. Zwemmer Ltd, London, 1959, BL. 201 David Harris. 203 Israel Antiquities Authority. 204 Zev Radovan, T; The John M. Allegro Archive, BR. 205 The Shrine of the Book, the D. Samuel and Jean H. Gottesman Centre for Biblical Manuscripts/The Israel Museum, Jerusalem. 207 Sonia Halliday Photographs/Laura Lushington. 208-209 Leen Ritmeyer. 210 Leen Ritmeyer. 213 Peter Clayton. 214 Courtesy of the Director and University Librarian, the John Rylands University Library of Manchester. 218 Sonia Halliday Photographs. 219 Werner Braun. 220 Zev Radovan, TR; Ian Wilson, MR. 223 Biblical Archaeology Society. 224 Zev Radovan, TR; Ian Wilson, BL. 225 Zev Radovan. 227 Zev Radovan. 228 Bridgeman Art Library, L; Ian Wilson, R. 229 Victoria & Albert Museum, London. 235, 236 Zev Radovan. 237, 238 from *The Bones of St Peter*, by John Walsh, Victor Gollancz Ltd, 1983. 239 Scala. 241 AKG. 243 AKG/Eric Lessing. 245 Sonia Halliday Photographs. 246 *Risen Christ*, detail, mural by Isabel Piczek.